The Town House in Georgian London

The Town House in Georgian London

Rachel Stewart

Published for the Paul Mellon Centre for Studies in British Art

By Yale University Press ∼ New Haven and London

Designed by Sarah Faulks

Printed in China

Library of Congress Cataloging-in-Publication Data

Stewart, Rachel, 1959–
  The town house in Georgian London / Rachel Stewart.
    p. cm.
  Includes bibliographical references and index.
  ISBN 978-0-300-15277-7 (cl : alk. paper)
  1. Row houses–Social aspects–England–London. 2. Home
ownership–England–London–History–18th century. 3. Architecture and
society–England–London–History–18th century. 4. London
(England)--Buildings, structures, etc. I. Title.
  NA7332.S74 2009
  728'.31209421–dc22
                                            2009003005

A catalogue record for this book is available from The British Library

Frontispiece: *Frederick Elegantly Furnishing a Large House*, detail, c.1782, etching
and engraving with hand colouring. Courtesy of The Lewis Walpole Library, Yale
University.

For Laura and Joe

Acknowledgements

The doctoral research that was the starting point for this book was funded by the (then) Arts and Humanities Research Board, and was thoroughly supervised by Christine Stevenson, to whom I am very grateful. I received additional funding from the University of Reading, as well as support and encouragement from other students and staff in the Department of History of Art there. Further work to turn the text from thesis to book was funded by the Paul Mellon Centre for Studies in British Art. In his inimitable style, Steven Parissien generously shared his time and knowledge to help me in this task. Along the way, I was also helped by many staff at county record offices, libraries and museums across the country, as reflected in my bibliography. The Duke of Beaufort and the late Marquess of Tavistock kindly allowed access to and use of the estate records in their care, while the late 12th Earl of Scarborough volunteered useful information about his eighteenth-century ancestor, the fourth earl, as well as documents from the archives at Sandbeck. In the final stages, Steven Astley and Susan Palmer at the Sir John Soane Museum were especially helpful with illustrations, as were staff at the British Museum and British Library, London. Sarah Faulks at Yale University Press was amazingly patient and forgiving.

I was only able to undertake this research and write this book because my elder two children – Laura and Joe – misspent their youth minding and entertaining their younger siblings for my benefit. I am pleased to dedicate this book to them, with much love, pride and belated thanks.

Contents

Illustrations

29   John Crunden, plans and elevation for a five-bay town house, from *Convenient and Ornamental Architecture*, 1767, plate 13. © British Library Board. All Rights Reserved (Shelfmark Cup 504e35)

30   John Crunden, plan and elevation for a seven-bay town house, from *Convenient and Ornamental Architecture*, 1767, plate 14. © British Library Board. All Rights Reserved (Shelfmark Cup 504e35).

31   John Crunden, plans and elevation for a town or country house, from *Convenient and Ornamental Architecture*, 1767, plate 19. © British Library Board. All Rights Reserved (Shelfmark Cup 504e35).

32   John Crunden, plan and elevation for a mansion for either town or country, from *Convenient and Ornamental Architecture*, 1767, plate 53. © British Library Board. All Rights Reserved (Shelfmark Cup 504e35).

Plates 33–63 (between p. 100 and p. 101)

33   John Crunden, plan and elevation for a town mansion, from *Convenient and Ornamental Architecture*, 1767, plate 46. © British Library Board. All Rights Reserved (Shelfmark Cup 504e35).

34   John Crunden, plan and elevation for a town mansion, from *Convenient and Ornamental Architecture*, 1767, plate 67. © British Library Board. All Rights Reserved (Shelfmark Cup 504e35).

35   Robert Morris, design for a row of three houses, from William and John Halfpenny, Robert Morris and T. Lightoler, *The Modern Builder's Assistant*, 1757, plate 44.

36   Robert Morris, design for a town house, from William and John Halfpenny, Robert Morris and T. Lightoler, *The Modern Builder's Assistant*, 1757, plate 46.

37   John Crunden, design for a row of three houses, from *Convenient and Ornamental Architecture*, 1767, plate 29. © British Library Board. All Rights Reserved (Shelfmark Cup 504e35).

38   John Carter, design for a town house, from *The Builder's Magazine*, c.1775, plate 20. © British Library Board. All Rights Reserved (Shelfmark 61e14).

39   John Carter, section of an elaborate staircase for the town house in plate 38, above, from *The Builder's Magazine*, 1775, plate 60. © British Library Board. All Rights Reserved (Shelfmark 61e14).

40   John Carter, design for a town house, from *The Builder's Magazine*, 1777, plate 117. © British Library Board. All Rights Reserved (Shelfmark 61e14).

41   John Carter, plans for the house in plate 40, above, from *The Builder's Magazine*, 1777, plate 129. © British Library Board. All Rights Reserved (Shelfmark 61e14).

42   Pierre Le Muet, design for a town house, from *Maniere de bien bastir pour toutes sortes de personnes*, 1647, plate 1. By courtesy of The Trustees of Sir John Soane's Museum.

43   Pierre Le Muet, design for a town house, from *Maniere de bien bastir pour toutes sortes de personnes*, 1647, plate 3. By courtesy of The Trustees of Sir John Soane's Museum.

44 Home House, 20 Portman Square, James Wyatt and Robert Adam, begun 1772, street façade, with later attic storey.

45 1 Bedford Square, doorcase, attributed to Thomas Leverton, c.1778. Photo © Stephen Whitehorne.

46 1 Bedford Square, ground and first-floor plans.

47 Robert Adam, Derby House, 26 Grosvenor Square, 1773–4, ground and first-floor plans, from Robert and James Adam, *The Works in Architecture*, vol. 2, 1779, part 1, plate 1. By courtesy of The Trustees of Sir John Soane's Museum.

48 Derby House, 26 Grosvenor Square, 1773–4, view of the great drawing room, engraving by B. Pastorini from Robert and James Adam, *The Works in Architecture*, vol. 2, 1779, part 1, plate 5, detail. By courtesy of The Trustees of Sir John Soane's Museum.

49 Robert Adam, designs for the furnishings and fittings at Derby House, Grosvenor Square, from Robert and James Adam, *The Works in Architecture*, vol. 2, 1779, part 1, plate 8. By courtesy of The Trustees of Sir John Soane's Museum.

50 Robert Adam, Home House, 20 Portman Square, design for the south wall of the Etruscan Room, c.1777. By courtesy of The Trustees of Sir John Soane's Museum.

51 Robert Adam, Wynn House, 20 St James's Square, ground and first-floor plans, 1771–4, illustrated in Robert and James Adam, *The Works in Architecture*, vol. 2, 1779, part 2, plate 1. By courtesy of The Trustees of Sir John Soane's Museum.

52 Robert Adam, Wynn House, 20 St James's Square, elevation, 1771–4, illustrated in Robert and James Adam, *The Works in Architecture*, vol. 2, 1779, part 2, plate 2. By courtesy of The Trustees of Sir John Soane's Museum.

53 James Paine, plans of Dr Heberden's house in Pall Mall, 1769–71, from *Plans, Elevations and Sections*, part 2, 1783, plates 76–7. © British Library Board. All Rights Reserved (Shelfmark 3 Tab 30).

54 James Paine, elevation of Dr Heberden's house in Pall Mall, 1769–71, from *Plans, Elevations and Sections*, part 2, 1783, plate 78. © British Library Board. All Rights Reserved (Shelfmark 3 Tab 30).

55 James Paine, plans of Thomas Fitzmaurice's house in Pall Mall, 1779–80, from *Plans, Elevations and Sections*, part 2, 1783, plate 78. © British Library Board. All Rights Reserved (Shelfmark 3 Tab 30).

56 James Paine, elevation of Thomas Fitzmaurice's house in Pall Mall, 1779–80, from *Plans, Elevations and Sections*, part 2, 1783, plate 81. © British Library Board. All Rights Reserved (Shelfmark 3 Tab 30).

57 Robert and James Adam, Chandos House, Chandos Street, 1770–1, ground and first-floor plans. Cumbria Record Office, Carlisle. By kind permission of The Trustees of the Lowther Estate.

58 View of the staircase hall at Wynn House, 20 St James's Square, Robert and James Adam, 1771–4. Photo: © Martin Charles.

59 Robert Adam, Wynn House, 20 St James's Square, design for the ceiling of

the second drawing room, *c.*1772. By courtesy of The Trustees of Sir John Soane's Museum.

60 38 Grosvenor Square, remodelled by John Johnson, *c.*1776, ground and first-floor plans (reproduced from *Survey of London,* vol. 39, 1977).

61 Home House, 20 Portman Square, James Wyatt and Robert Adam, begun 1772, ground and first-floor plans.

62 Robert Adam, Home House, 20 Portman Square, design for the staircase, *c.*1775. By courtesy of The Trustees of Sir John Soane's Museum.

63 [James Paine?], plan for the ground floor of a house for the Earl of Scarborough in Chesterfield Street, n.d., unexecuted. By courtesy of the late Earl of Scarborough.

Plates 64–77 (between p. 148 and p. 149)

64 44 Berkeley Square, William Kent, 1742–4, view of the staircase, drawn for Sir John Soane's Royal Academy lectures, *c.*1809–36. By courtesy of The Trustees of Sir John Soane's Museum.

65 Houses in St James's Square as they looked in 1821 (reproduced from *Survey of London,* vols 29 and 30).

66 37 King Street, Covent Garden, attributed to James Paine, 1777. Photo © the author.

67 31 and 32 Old Burlington Street, Colen Campbell, 1718–23. Photo © Stephen Whitehorne.

68 Ely House, 37 Dover Street, Robert Taylor, 1772–6, front elevation in an anonymous aquatint, *c.*1780. By courtesy of the Guildhall Library, City of London.

69 7 Soho Square, Robert Taylor, 1745–8, in a watercolour by J. P. Emslie, 1883. Courtesy of City of London, London Metropolitan Archives.

70 View of Soho Square from *The Repository of Arts, Literature, Commerce, Manufactures, Fashions, and Politics*, printed for R. Ackermann, vol. 8, 1812, plate 22. © British Library Board. All Rights Reserved (Shelfmark C119f1).

71 George Dance the Younger, design for the elevation of 6 St James's Square, n.d., unexecuted. By courtesy of The Trustees of Sir John Soane's Museum.

72 15 St James's Square, James Stuart, 1764–6, view of the front, drawn for Sir John Soane's Royal Academy lectures, *c.*1809–36. By courtesy of The Trustees of Sir John Soane's Museum.

73 Robert Adam, design for new elevation for Sir William James's house in Gerrard Street, 1781, unexecuted. By courtesy of The Trustees of Sir John Soane's Museum.

74 Adam House, Adam Street, Adelphi, Robert and James Adam, *c.*1770. Photo © Stephen Whitehorne.

75 R. Rushworth, *The Supplemental Magazine*, published by S. W. Fores, 1786, hand-coloured etching. © The Trustees of the British Museum.

76 Robert Adam, Home House, Portman Square, design for a section of the music room, 1775. Courtesy of The Trustees of Sir John Soane's Museum.

77 Philip Dawe, *Pantheon Macaroni, c.*1773, mezzotint. © The Trustees of the British Museum.

Introduction

Questioning the Town House

John Summerson argues in *Georgian London* (first published in 1945)
that 'members of the aristocracy were not interested in their town
houses to anything like the same extent that they were in their country
dwellings' and that 'for the most part [they] were content with the standard product of the time, the terrace-house'.[1] In support of this asser-   1
tion, Summerson refers to John Stewart's *Critical Observations on the
Buildings and Improvements of London* (1771), in which the author
states that 'many a nobleman whose proud seat in the country is adorned
with all the riches of architecture, porticos and columns . . . is here
content with a simple dwelling, convenient within, and unornamented
without'.[2] Damie Stillman uses the same authority to back up a similar
argument in another important work in this field, *English Neo-classical
Architecture* (1988). He writes of the 'natural tendency of peers and
gentry to view their country houses as their principal places of residence
and to use their homes in the metropolis only for Parliamentary sessions
and the winter social season', adding that 'the result was the willingness, much deplored by the author of . . . *Critical Observations*, of
people in this position in society to make their London abode a narrow
three-, four-, or five-bay . . . terrace house'.[3]

These and similar statements present the landowner's house in
London as an insignificant adjunct to the country house, in other words,
as the relatively standardised, functional, unprepossessing product it
appears to be. But there is a whole other story to be told, of which the
physical evidence says little or nothing at all. Contemporary, published

reception is important to any reconstruction of the past, but it is never the whole picture, either of the reception or of life in general. Looking elsewhere for evidence, with a more open mind, we find that the town house unsettled many eighteenth-century observers, and we might wonder why. For example, the year 1771 also saw the publication of Tobias Smollett's novel *The Expedition of Humphry Clinker*. Smollett's main character, Squire Bramble, sees the town house as a symptom of the 'tide of luxury' which 'has swept all the inhabitants from the open country'. 'The poorest squire, as well as the richest peer, must have his house in town, and make a figure with an extraordinary number of domestics', he reports at the start of his London visit.[4] Using examples from amongst his friends, which I will discuss later, Bramble expostulates at length about the financial and emotional distress caused by ownership of the supposedly standard, humdrum and unpretentious property that John Stewart bemoans and John Summerson and others play down. Now, Tobias Smollett may have been a biased source, given his well-known and undisguised prejudice against England's capital city, but it is nevertheless notable that he identifies the town house (and not just the city within which it sits) with a particular set of ills. Nor was Smollett alone in his antipathy to the town house: his insinuations about the town house's damaging financial impact are matched by an abundance of evidence from public and private papers, as I will show. Yet this story of the town house as an unaffordable and injurious luxury – being virtually unreadable from the built evidence – has remained well hidden, as, too, has its uncomfortable relation to assumptions about the 'plain' town house not meaning much to its occupiers.

Both Smollett and Stewart were writing at a time of unprecedented activity in the design, construction and refurbishment of houses in the West End, where most landowners chose to have their base in town. The years *c*.1765–*c*.1785 in particular, saw, firstly, an exceptional level of building demand and supply; secondly, a wave of rebuildings, refurbishments and redecorations of existing building stock; thirdly, new styles of interior and exterior decoration and some exceptional developments in house planning; and, fourthly, public and private, descriptive and prescriptive comment on all of the above. All four features of the period are potentially indicative of new attitudes to the town house, or to town-house ownership. The proliferation of public comment in particular suggests that something new (and discomfiting) was afoot in this period.

Many eighteenth-century critics focus on the town house's physical qualities as mostly shoddy. This criticism is strongly echoed in modern-day writings. While the Georgian terrace house is currently fêted as an exceptionally desirable property in terms of aesthetic appeal, accommodation and general cachet, writings by some of its latter-day scholars (including its advocates) retain a hint or more of disapproval about its true nature that can be traced back to public responses in the time of its creation. See, for example, how Dan Cruickshank and Peter Wyld criticise what they call the 'facadism' which allowed the terrace house to appear to be something that it wasn't, as discussed further in my Conclusion.[5] Such criticism, past and present, is somewhat justified by the physical evidence, but it is notable that it has an extra dimension that is harder to account for by that means. Despite its popularity then and now, writers have conflated the terrace house's notorious physical instability and insubstantiality with a kind of ideological unsoundness.

So while 'traditional' stories of the town house as a utilitarian and hastily constructed London base for the landed classes sit well together and are comfortably corroborated by the built evidence and familiar eighteenth-century written sources, there are hints of other stories waiting to be told. The familiar stories sometimes play down the terrace house's great popularity in this period and look neither to the house itself nor to its occupant's relationship with it for an explanation of this popularity. Although well-known eighteenth-century sources seem to hold sway with modern writers, there is one type of contemporary evidence that is not matched in the modern-day historiography: what owners and occupants of town houses thought about their property, why and how they chose or built it, paid for it, used it, decorated it, sold it, and so on, and what uses it had for them beyond just accommodation. The existing literature on or relating to the town house, while thorough and thoughtful in other respects, stops short of any serious analysis of clients' wants and needs. The purpose of this book is to move a significant step further to recreating the 'whole picture'. It is not possible in the present, let alone with regard to the past, to provide a total picture of reality, but we can go some way towards representing things as they are or were by changing our viewpoint, particularly where a given perspective has dominated research and publication to date. To this end, I take the houseowner, occupant or architect's client as my starting point, in contrast to the bulk of the architectural-historical literature on this topic. By this means I open up a wealth of unforeseen values, uses and connections relating to the London West End house which must contribute significantly to the 'whole picture'.

Focusing mainly on members of the landed classes, who created such demand for houses in the West End in particular, the book is principally concerned with houseowners' attitudes towards, and treatment of their property, the options available to them and the foundation on which they made their decisions. In writing this book, I have therefore asked and attempted to answer the questions that should inform existing and future research and writing on the town house, and tried in particular to clarify the prevailing cultural and socio-historical conditions in which architectural and construction practice took place. Rather than challenging or replacing the existing types of analysis (discussed further below) the book creates a context for them, by investigating the circumstances in which individuals made decisions about living in London, and about their house there, so that conventional interpretations can be re-examined and new narratives created.

At the same time as looking at private expectations and perceptions of the town house in the later eighteenth century, I look at those 'disinterested' opinions expressed through such public vehicles as newspapers and magazines, architectural treatises and pattern-books and writings on London and its architecture. I do this partly to reveal and explain a conflict of interests – an important facet of any picture – and to demonstrate the dangers of relying on public, prescriptive writings to gauge private attitudes; and partly to unearth the roots of present-day pre-judgements about town houses, as expressed in the architectural historiography quoted above and elsewhere.

Missing pieces

There is already a good deal of writing about the town house, but while few people would deny that the built environment is a social and cultural product, the existing literature on the town house generally either fails to examine seriously 'the inter-relations between architectural, cultural and societal dimensions of housing history',[6] or does so on the basis of assumptions about the house's insignificance to its owners, at least in comparison to the country house. Yet, as Matthew Johnson points out, there is value in attempting to 'move away from *a priori* assumptions about what the past was like and towards an empirical exploration of whether in fact our assumptions are correct'.[7] There appear to be three main explanations for the especially inadequate consideration of clients' or occupants' wants and needs in literature surrounding the town house. Firstly, the house often features in surveys, which necessarily make generalisations about it over broad sweeps of time: the age of neo-classical architecture, the Georgian period, or even the eighteenth and nineteenth centuries.[8] There is no place within such surveys for close studies of the house's use or attitudes towards it, and sometimes there is no place for the town house at all, as in the case of

Giles Worsley's *Classical Architecture in Britain: The Heroic Age* (1995).[9] As with other areas of research, 'schematic and generalised' economic and social backgrounds 'often make it difficult to distinguish the ideological wood from the historical tree'.[10] Secondly, authors implicitly equate the absence of individuality of houses within rows with an absence of significance, within both owners' lives and architectural history. Damie Stillman and John Summerson seem to make this equation with help from their eighteenth-century source John Stewart. Lastly, the town house is too often presented only as part of people's lives in town, rather than as a part of their lives in general. Yet the house's use comprised much more than how life was lived in it on a day-to-day basis, or even how it served special occasions, and included how it functioned in the context of family relations, financial, legal and property transactions and the market, as well as in the construction of personal identity, as I will show. Nonetheless, writers often ascribe to it a single role and, as a result of their focus on high-profile projects, the town house is often simultaneously admired and dismissed as being purely for show or entertainment. In this way, in an article on Home House in Portman Square, built and lavishly decorated from 1772 for the Dowager Countess of Home by James Wyatt and then Robert Adam, A. A. Tait distinguishes between the country house, which 'dealt in family, continuity and territorial power' and the town house, which was 'essentially a place of show, often temporary but always dazzling'.[11] While this characterisation of the London house may be true for Home House, it is not true for all or even most of the others.

A focus on building use, in this limited sense, is one approach used by writers on the town house. Others use a framework defined by technical building practice. Some authors look at the house in its group identity, as a component of urban design and planning; others as a subsection of a particular architect's works. Lastly, some writings are devoted to exceptional individual town houses – such as Home House – and these also receive special attention in monographs on architects and in broader surveys of architectural history.

Authors in the first category, building use, include Mark Girouard, whose chapter 'The Social House 1720–1770' in *Life in the English Country House* (1978) describes the social functions of larger (atypical) town houses in that period. Authors in the second category of technical building practice include Dan Cruickshank and Peter Wyld in *London: The Art of Georgian Building* (1975, revised edition 1990), who provide a thorough description of terrace-house construction, as well as a detailed guide to changes in the house's appearance in the Georgian period in response to the demands of fashion and legislation. Dan

Cruickshank and Neil Burton's excellent *Life in the Georgian City* (1990) straddles the first three categories, describing day-to-day life in the house, the house's design and construction and the process of speculative development that produced it, all over a broad sweep of time.

Donald Olsen defines and illustrates the processes of estate development and speculative building more fully in his *Town Planning in London: The Eighteenth and Nineteenth Centuries* (1964). Landowners, developers, the impact of parliamentary legislation and the pattern of development and its legacy in present-day London are the chief concerns of this and similar works in my third category. Such coverage is concerned less with the individual house than with its collective place in the history of London. The house has no individual identity; it is just one of many near-identical components of a much wider urban geographic and economic picture. In Jules Lubbock's story, for example, West End houses are little more than signs of efforts to keep visual control of London or seats of purchasing power.[12] There is no place for the individual actor in such an analysis, no acknowledgement of choice and action at the individual level. Both house and occupant are subsumed within the bigger story of economic and legislative imperatives.

Some authors give particular consideration to the impact of planned speculative development on the appearance of terraces of houses in the form of the so-called 'palace front', such as that given to Robert and James Adam's Royal Terrace, Adelphi (begun 1768), which, in giving a terrace the appearance of one grand building, further subsumed the identities of individual houses. For example, Damie Stillman, who includes comprehensive chapters on town residences and urban design in his *English Neo-classical Architecture*, highlights architectural (as opposed to construction) practice, describing and illustrating significant projects by well-known architects, both for individual houses and for whole terraces.[13]

Monographs on such architects comprise the fourth of my categories and bring together the diverse approaches outlined above in discussions of a single designer's grand London houses, speculative developments and minor town-house projects. Unsurprisingly, this type of presentation tells us little about the nature of the town house itself, although much about how such architects as Robert Adam, Robert Taylor, James Paine and William Chambers operated in this field, and what of note each contributed to it. The town-house projects, like all others, are firmly set within the context of the designer's *oeuvre* – and the writing is often essentially about the subject, not the object.[14]

Where town-house projects contribute little or nothing to an understanding either of the architect or of the history of architecture conceived

3

as a story of innovation and development, the author of a monograph may omit them altogether. John Martin Robinson's doctoral thesis on Samuel Wyatt is an interesting case in point, and his reasons for denying Wyatt's town-house projects a chapter of their own also explain further why other writers often neglect the town house. Robinson argues that 'although [Wyatt] executed much work in London, most of it was not exceptional by contemporary standards [and] consisted of alterations to existing buildings and expensive redecoration'. He made 'no novel contribution to town-house plans'. While it is no fault of the thesis to find the town house omitted, the omission shows how the town house can be pushed to one side when it does not reflect an architect's most characteristic, important or best work, in terms of innovation or originality, when his town work was limited either in number or scope of projects, or when little of it was recorded, another problem with Samuel Wyatt's London work.[15] What is true for Wyatt's houses is also true for town houses more generally. One problem with the architectural history of the town house is that it does not lead anywhere. While the country house fits into a more satisfying and longer-term developmental history, both of the building type and of classicism, the Georgian terrace house was essentially a developmental dead end. Even unusual projects were not a step 'forward', just an exception to the norm.

The fifth, and final, context in which the town house appears is the repeated and extensive coverage given in the literature, particularly journal articles, to a handful of individual houses, focusing on their ingenious remodelling, lavish decoration or distinctive façades.[16] Examples include William Kent's achievements at 44 Berkeley Square (1742–4), James Stuart's performance at 15 St James's Square (1764–6) and especially Robert Adam's feats at Home House, Wynn House, St James's Square (1771–4), and, the apogee of the whole sequence, Derby House, Grosvenor Square (1773–4). Close studies of such exceptional projects always rest on the justified assumption that the work itself is significant in the history of architecture, design, or interior decoration. The approach relies on setting the architect or innovation within the appropriate history. The exceptional town house takes its individual place within the history of architecture and design in a way generally reserved for the country house or villa, and, unsurprisingly, denied to the unexceptional house.

The town house is not alone in suffering at the hands of the traditions of architectural historiography. In the preface and introduction to *Articulating British Classicism* (2004), Barbara Arciszewska and Elizabeth McKellar note the general biases and deficiencies of the literature, and particularly the dominant and often obstructive use of 'classicism' as a methodology, as 'a seemingly indispensable tool for expressing our views on architecture, and a critical component of our understanding of how architecture changed over time'. Viewing eighteenth-century architectural history through the lens of classicism (more or less synonymous in this period with 'high' architecture) gets in the way of alternative ways of looking at (and therefore ascribing value to) buildings. And it leaves some groups, such as vernacular buildings, out of the frame altogether.[17] Certainly in this analysis the town house is a half-baked and contingent second to the classically potent, fulfilled and fulfilling country house. I show in Part Two how this attitude was evident at the time and remains so in some aspects of the architectural historiography. Although Arciszewska and McKellar claim that 'the Georgian townhouse has become accepted as architecturally significant',[18] it has yet to be given the full treatment that usually comes with that acceptance, as I discuss below.

Looking beyond the strictly architectural literature, Arciszewska and McKellar also note that 'despite the emphasis on towns as generators of modern society and culture – exemplified by Peter Borsay's *The English Urban Renaissance* [1989] – architecture has remained strangely absent from the discussion'.[19] The town house, as the eighteenth-century town's most prevalent component, is the most notable absentee. Where mentioned at all, it remains the unexceptional, uninteresting background against which newly observed actions take place. It is never the main protagonist, partly because of the assumptions that are made about it (as outlined above), including the belief that its story has already been well covered.

The West End house has fared less well in some respects than its near neighbours. In his recent and welcome study of the artisan house in eighteenth-century London, Peter Guillery suggests that the smaller house had previously been neglected because the balance of surviving built evidence is strongly in favour of the West End town house.[20] That is true (and fortunate for the larger house), but the built evidence is nonetheless misleading. To bolster his argument, Guillery quotes Raphael Samuel's observation that 'despite, or perhaps because of its apparently solid location, the built environment, as historical evidence, conceals far more than it reveals'.[21] This is also true, but in more ways than Guillery interprets it (or even, perhaps, than Samuel intended it): it is what the built evidence (or records of it) cannot tell us about the London town house that is in fact most pertinent to this book.

Guillery also argues that the smaller London house has lost out to the tendency 'to rely on aesthetic valuations of artefacts as stylistically progressive or otherwise, on Whiggish top-down models that stress the spread of the polite. Classic ideals of urban space have been pervasive and their deep influence has steered the gaze away from diversity and tradition in eighteenth-century London'.[22] Again, there is no disputing with Guillery on this point, but those same ideals have also got in the way of a proper understanding of the West End house. What is more, we find this both in the writings of the time and in the modern-day histories, including the assumption that the middling classes wanted what their 'superiors' had: a well-turned-out West End house. But we could usefully turn that argument on its head and ask why the upper classes were content to have houses so much like those of the middling classes. That is the material point, and it can only be made when 'Whiggish top-down models' are abandoned as a useful means of structuring our understanding of eighteenth-century London and its domestic architecture, or the social history of the later eighteenth century generally.

As the literature stands, for the town house to be discussed in its own right, or in connection with an architect, it must be distinguished by some feature or treatment, particularly one characteristic of its designer. But if, instead, we view the house from the client's perspective, it might be distinguished by the expense or duration of a refurbishment project, or the attention paid to it by the client and disinterested observers. William Weddell's house in Upper Brook Street, remodelled by Samuel Wyatt from 1787, was clearly important to Weddell, who was prepared to invest several years and untold expense in its interior transformation. The project also attracted attention among his friends, and in the press,[23] even if it is denied special notice in Robinson's doctoral thesis.

Another result of the (perfectly understandable) bias towards choosing projects for discussion on the basis of architectural distinction is that other, non-architectural but often pertinent aspects of those projects are overlooked. For example, the financial distress that Sir Watkin Williams Wynn suffered as a result of his ambitious remodelling of 20 St James's Square, and creditors' invasions of Lord Derby's splendid Grosvenor Square house, are facts rarely, if ever, mentioned in connection with these famous and much-examined projects by Robert Adam. I discuss both cases in later chapters and consider what reasoning may have been behind the ambitiousness of the projects and the willingness to incur such debts. However, I will argue here that a less circumscribed outlook can set the importance of Wynn House, for example, in a broader context, and thereby suggest what the excess and exquisiteness of its decoration, its carefully contrived planning, and the means of funding both, reveal about the owner and his ambitions; that is, why Sir Watkin chose to spend a staggering £40,000 on a three-bay terrace in St James's Square.[24] More importantly (for the study of the town house as much as the study of Wynn House), examining general behaviour regarding town-house purchases and commissions, including aspects of house occupancy or ownership that are not obviously readable from the architectural evidence, we can see more clearly what was exceptional about Wynn House (such as its planning and decoration) and, at the same time and equally as important, what was unexceptional; that is, what the house or its owner had in common with other, lower-profile homes and residents (such as the project's damaging financial impact).

The rich and varied town-house literature does not disregard clients and occupants, but it says little or nothing about the house's function or impact in the broader context of people's ongoing lives, concerns and aspirations. Writers will sometimes discuss an architect's relationship, or at least correspondence, with his client in connection with a given project, but no wider investigations are undertaken nor inferences drawn. *Country Life* articles on individual buildings often have a strong client focus, but information about occupants generally focuses on genealogy and social connections: the various authors stop short of investigating, analysing or even discussing the attitudes to the house held by the successive, well-placed owners named. Likewise, the *Survey of London* volumes, an invaluable resource for building descriptions, detailed construction and refurbishment histories, and lists of 'principal' residents,[25] have no room for speculation about the links between these disparate components, either in respect of individual houses or London homes generally.

The conspicuous absence of any real analysis of clients' and occupants' wants and needs is by no means a deficiency of individual writings, which rarely pretend to have such aims, but of the literature as a whole. Despite my observations on the weaknesses of the existing literature, I warmly recommend the publications referred to above as essential and often excellent contributions to the 'whole picture' in their own rights. Although I have small disputes with some of them during the course of this book, I mean to supplement rather than replace them. In particular, I have no intention of repeating here or later in any great detail what is far better explained in the existing literature, as outlined above and referenced below: the typical town house's form, appearance and physical nature;[26] building legislation and its impact; the processes of speculative development through which most terrace houses were constructed; daily life in the house and the use of space, gendered or otherwise; or the full building histories and architectural and decorative details as well as the merits of such 'special' projects as Home, Wynn, or Derby houses. I cover some of these matters along the way to provide a context necessary to understanding the remainder of the book rather than as a comprehensive and definitive account of those topics.

A move towards the 'whole picture'

The client perspective is a vital aspect of the social context that Adrian Forty complains much architectural history pays only lip service to, if it bothers at all. Forty compares 'cursory references to the social context' to 'the weeds and gravel around a stuffed fish in a glass case: however realistic these may be, they are only furnishings, and taking them away would have little effect on our perception of the fish'.[27] If design is 'the result of the conditions of [its] making', of the relationship between the people who design and make and the society in which their products will be sold, as Forty suggests,[28] then we need to know far more about purchasers and clients than the town-house literature currently offers – if we want to assess adequately the products produced for them outside of the architect-based, aesthetic, or developmental frameworks which dominate the architectural history of this building type.

This book is not architectural history with a nod to social history; it is a re-creation of the social and familial context in which this particular architectural story took place. I use social history as a basis for exploring architectural history. In investigating aspects of house occupancy or ownership that are not obviously readable from the architectural evidence, this book necessarily departs from some of the practices that often govern the discussion of architecture generally, and the town house in particular. I rely principally on documentary and anecdotal evidence to frame my analyses of the built or visual evidence, rather than on the 'evaluative, aesthetic criteria' often used to select buildings for study,[29] or the economic framework within which much writing about the terrace house is firmly placed. Although the houses discussed tend to be large to medium sized, merely because they housed the class of occupants who left documentation about themselves and their homes, neither size nor exceptionalness of planning or finish is a criterion for inclusion. I look at the work of well-known architects in this field, such as Robert Adam and James Paine, but such architects' specific contributions to some aspects of town-house design and clients' needs are arrived at in the book's natural course; they are not a point of departure.

The archaeologist Martin Locock argues for such a shift of emphasis in his introduction to a collection of essays on *Meaningful Architecture: Social Interpretations of Buildings*. He proposes that architectural history's heavy reliance on materialist and functional explanations for the form of past buildings should be tempered by 'the analysis of buildings primarily in terms of their role in the constructing society, as a mode of creating and transmitting social statements'. Likewise, Johnson upholds the view that 'material things are not merely constraints upon human action . . . but that they themselves carry (at the level of the implicit and taken for granted) the values and messages being fought over at the level of the overt'.[30] For Locock, 'meaning' resides in the choices made prior to or during design and construction, and beyond into sequential occupation, in things not always physically evident in a building's form.[31] I am therefore concerned throughout this study not simply with 'materialist and functional explanations' for the town house's form and appearance, but also with notions of 'use' and 'value' (components of Locock's 'meaning'), which include, as I have suggested, functions beyond practical use, including financial uses, and such abstract, yet specific functions as self-presentation. Such uses and values are not always evident in the built form; they do not sit on the surface, ready to be observed. They may reside not just in a house's look or form, but also in its location and size, in its contents, and in non-physical properties such as expense and pattern of ownership.

In outlining new and revisionist approaches to the history of houses and housing, Alice T. Friedman articulates the benefits of the more imaginative, flexible, embracing approach that architectural history now offers, including a broader notion of value. 'Under the influence of post-structuralism', she suggests, 'three notions have become commonplace',

> first, that the boundaries of the field are fluid and permeable, and that interdisciplinary research and analysis provide the fullest access to complex questions; second, that the critique of social relations and of ideology is inherent to the study of built form; and third, that a focus on narrowly defined sites of research – case studies, local cultures, and specific historical moments – interpreted within a framework of overlapping typological structure (patterns of everyday use, the forms of language, and conventions of all kinds, including building types and architectural styles), in fact produces the broadest and richest interpretations of built form.

'Nowhere is this more apparent', she suggests, 'than in the field of domestic architecture.' Within that field, the prominent 'methodological tendencies and analytical strategies' include 'a focus on individual buildings or groups of buildings within specific cultural or historical contexts; studied in this way, buildings can be documented, analyzed, and discussed as the products of overlapping but identifiable systems of values, typological and cultural conventions, institutional forces, and individual actions', and 'an increased emphasis on vernacular architecture and on material culture (research that not only enhances our understanding of the spectrum of types but also sets aside traditional values in favor of a broader view of architectural value)'.[32]

Clients' or purchasers' needs, uses and values are hard to identify and pin down. They are not only transient but also seen differently by different people, both then and now.[33] If the town house, like any other object, acquires meaning in the act of possession[34] – that is, if the house-owner does not find meaning lying dormant in the empty house, but *gives* it meaning – then needs, uses and values potentially vary from person to person, even for the same house. As Stana Nenadic suggests, the biography of any object contains 'the possibility that at various points in its history of ownership . . . it held different kinds of value, simultaneously and successively'.[35] Sir Watkin Williams Wynn recognised and effectively realised, with the help of Robert Adam, the potential of 20 St James's Square to serve his self-promotion as a man of wealth, taste and fashion, potential presumably of no interest to his predecessor in the house, the 1st Earl Bathurst. Likewise, the 12th Earl of Derby's ambitions for Derby House and for himself were a world apart from those of his father (from whom he inherited the house), who had 'devoted himself chiefly to politics and the turf rather than to entertaining'.[36]

Secondly, any one owner or occupant makes a house serve his own multiple uses, and he and others imbue it with assorted values. As Roderick Lawrence points out, 'housing units are commonly attributed an economic value, an exchange value, . . . and a use value', as well as an aesthetic one. A home, moreover, 'is usually attributed a sentimental and symbolic value'.[37] Even from the occupant's perspective, we have a multiplicity of values within the time span for each individual – and not just for those commissioning architectural projects, but also those simply living in, buying and selling their homes.

It is no surprise, therefore, that in the absence of any obvious or easy methodological approach to such an examination, the literature on the town house either disregards or shies away from reconstructing or analysing this complex array of uses and values, and its effects on client and purchaser behaviour. Instead, it makes general assumptions about the status of town houses in people's lives, based either on notions of sameness (rows of terrace houses, supposedly expressive only of occupants' indifference to their homes) or splendour (Home House).

Although this book could not have been conceived or taken shape without the context of the abundant literature on eighteenth-century property, and on consumption in particular, that same literature also makes little direct contribution to the picture I am trying to recreate. Despite the wide range of its interests in terms of the goods and sites of eighteenth-century consumerism, the consumption literature is concerned with the acquisition, and sometimes just the buying, of things, in other words, moveable possessions. Houses in general feature 'only as contexts for property acquisition and ownership rather than as property in their own right',[38] while in the property literature the only house to receive serious consideration is the country house. But despite disregarding the town house, the property and consumption literature does offer methodological tactics little tried in architectural history, as do such writers as Roderick Lawrence, who are concerned specifically with expanding architectural history's methodological approaches.

Since the publication in 1982 of Neil McKendrick, John Brewer and J. H. Plumb's *Birth of a Consumer Society: The Commercialization of Eighteenth-century England*, works of social, economic and cultural history have increasingly turned their attention to the consumer rather than the producer.[39] Within art history, audiences are now given the attention formerly due only to makers, or powerful patrons.[40] The literature of eighteenth-century consumption is therefore the communal centre at which diverse disciplines now meet. The present attempt to introduce a firm and informed consumer perspective to the study of the eighteenth-century London town house is as much a response to the opportunities and stimuli presented by the consumption literature as a reaction to the deficiencies in the architectural-historical literature.[41]

Within the consumption literature, Colin Campbell argues that 'actual subjective meanings that prompt and guide action remain an indispensable ingredient in any successful theory of conduct and that the only proper place in which to search for such meanings is in the conscious minds of acting individuals'.[42] In the absence of any specific articulation of motives, Campbell suggests the use of diaries, letters, autobiographies, histories, dictionaries and novels to plot the range of potential meanings.[43] What individuals thought they were doing, they constructed out of the available vocabulary, he argues. We can begin to reconstruct those motives by studying the material from which meanings were constructed. This study therefore makes extensive use of anecdotal evidence, from many of the source types Campbell recommends, which, while not always directly pertaining to architecture or a given house, nevertheless contribute to a picture of the context in which houses and their ownership and occupancy functioned.

Anecdotal evidence,[44] especially from private papers such as letters and diaries, can offer realistically varied answers to the types of question posed by my readings of Smollett, Stewart and others. What did people want from their houses? What roles did town houses play for their owners and how were they perceived by others? What did people look for when they purchased a house, or commissioned a rebuilding or refurbishment? What factors governed their decisions? Importantly, anecdotal evidence also draws attention to the diversity of players interested in the house: not just occupants but also visitors and other observers. Its use brings its own problems, however. It is difficult to draw specific conclusions from individual cases – that is, motives for purchasing, selling, building, or refurbishing – even those as well documented as Sir Watkin's, and dangerous to generalise from such examples. There is also the general problem of defining and articulating the link between anecdote and architecture. Having stepped away from the built or visual evidence and created a context for it, it is often difficult to return and point to any direct correspondence between text and object. The anecdotal evidence is often unrelated to an identified house, or to one whose form and finish has been recorded. With the exception, therefore, of a few cases where building, client, and circumstances are all well documented, anecdotal evidence serves best in reconstructing the range of motives recommended by Campbell.[45]

I also make extensive use of the personal and family papers from which such anecdotal evidence often derives. Private papers, including family, legal and estate correspondence, bank accounts, stewards' accounts, bills and vouchers, wills, settlements and deeds, can reveal what individuals or families thought of their London residence, how they used it (in the broader sense defined above) and how they treated it, again in the widest sense and not just architecturally or decoratively. They allow us to view houses not just as entities in themselves, with their own histories, in which successive occupants were actors, but as functional objects in the histories of those occupants. The two approaches are not mutually exclusive, but complementary. The personal and estate papers consulted in this instance are principally from landowning families resident in the West End's better streets and squares, not just because they are generally easy to locate, archived and catalogued, or published, but also because I am most concerned with those people who may have had some choice as to whether or not to take a town house – rather than the London-based middling classes whose town home was their principal and most often sole residence.[46]

In addition to manuscript material and published private papers, I also (as recommended by both Campbell and Lawrence) draw on many descriptive and prescriptive texts published in the period,[47] including professional publications, such as architectural treatises, building manuals, pattern-books and architects' own published designs; newspapers and magazines; and writings on London's development and houses, such as John Stewart's *Critical Observations*, mentioned earlier, and John Gwynn's *London and Westminster Improved* (1766). I also use such novels as Smollett's *The Expedition of Humphry Clinker*, and

Frances Burney's *Evelina* (1778) and *Cecilia* (1782). Although contemporary critics praised the veracity of the two authors' works, I do not take these novels as evidence in themselves. Rather, some of their inferences prompted further investigations, as in the case of *Humphry Clinker*, or illustrate findings derived from other sources.[48] In combination, these sources are both descriptive and prescriptive and make clear that perceptions of a house's fitness and value were not the province of its owner or occupant alone.

The use of these various sources stretches the mind to admit the possibility that the town house may have had not simply 'use' (particularly in the limited sense expressed in the existing literature) but 'meaning', in Locock's terms, as discussed above. Neither the architectural-historical accounts nor the literature of eighteenth-century consumption or property reveals much if any effort at all to understand the town house's peculiar status as symbol, property, home, commodity or personal possession, even if it happily and widely considers the country house in some or all of those terms. For example, Dana Arnold's preface to her edited collection of essays on *The Georgian Country House: Architecture, Landscape and Society* (1998) takes as a given that the country house has and had 'meaning' (and that the reader will agree and also know, intuitively, what this 'meaning' might comprise), and advocates the reading of the country house as text. Arnold, like many others, describes the 'metaphorical function' of the country house as 'its status as a symbol of the power and wealth of the landowner and more broadly the social, cultural and political hegemony of the ruling classes', a role which reinforced the building's physical function. The country house has importance and significance well beyond the personal or familial interests of its owners: its meaning extends 'beyond a set of architectural forms or styles to something more intrinsic to the national consciousness' and it 'helped to define and promote a cohesive national identity'.[49] The town house can make no such claims, and perhaps that is one reason why architectural historians have been reluctant to credit it with any 'metaphorical function'. It is also hard to imagine any reciprocal relationship between such a function and the town house's physical function, and certainly its typical appearance.

But just because the town house so often looks as if it would make pretty dull reading as 'text', we should not assume it has nothing interesting to say. The town house must be allowed to have 'meaning', even if it is of personal rather than national (or even simply familial) significance. So, I take as my starting point that while the town house's relegation to second place in the literature is not necessarily unfair, the consequences of that relegation are. (I do not seriously intend to argue here, against Summerson, that an aristocrat's town house was more important to him than his country house – at least not in such simple terms.) The country house may continue to dominate the literature, but it should not be allowed to stand alone. A study of the town house is, in fact, as critical to a full understanding of the country house as it is to the town house itself, and certainly critical to understanding the lives and values of the people who lived in both.

Comparisons with the country house are, in any case, unhelpful. Like any other object, houses are designed to perform certain functions, not to be ill-equipped to perform others. We need to distinguish between these functions in order to understand why the town house was the way it was, and how successful or otherwise it was at performing its various tasks, which were both distinctly different from those performed by the country house and yet, like the latter, not limited to straightforward, practical uses. We need to understand more about how their own and other town houses functioned in owners' and occupants' lives in order to put architectural projects (commissioned and speculative) into context. The remainder of this book is concerned with those two objectives and falls into two parts: the first looks at the West End house in its social context, while the second carries forward the findings from the first part to inform a more explicitly architectural approach. Chapter One looks at why people came to London, and rented or bought houses there, in increasing numbers during this period. It considers the roles performed by residence in the West End, and by the house itself, particularly for women, who appear to have had an especially strong association with both. I note in this and subsequent chapters how such associations – real, imagined and implicit – gave (and give) the town house a gendered shading. Chapter Two discusses the town house as property type, and the uses to which it was put in that capacity, such as raising or guaranteeing money. I look, too, at property transferral outside of the market – that is, at the house's disposal within the family, and particularly at the strong legal associations of town houses and widows. Chapter Three concludes Part One with an exploration of the house as a commodity and an expense, noting the active house market and the often-damaging personal financial impact of London life, and particularly of the house itself. I discuss what people looked for in a house, how they afforded it, and what they were prepared to risk, financially and socially, to own one.

Part Two looks at the house as a design task, in theory and practice, and in public and private. Chapter Four explains how the town house's character and its owner's needs are reflected in its form and appearance, the demands that disinterested observers made on the house, and why, generally, these were not met. Chapter Five explores the negative attitudes of eighteenth-century architectural theorists towards the town house, the terrace house in particular, and takes a close look at how its treatment in pattern-books was generally at odds with the house's true nature and the exigencies of London circumstances and town life. Chapter Six then demonstrates how some architects, principally Robert Adam, acknowledged the town house's real character and thereby allowed it to come into its own, architecturally, in the 1770s.

The book concludes with a review of my findings, particularly in respect of what they can tell us about the real significance of town houses in this period. Using evidence garnered in the intervening chapters, I also consider further the reluctance that is evident in the writings of both the time itself and the present day to accept that people were very often happy with the standard offer – the three-bay terrace house – and that there was nothing especially wrong with them if that was the case. I look further, too, at eighteenth-century criticisms of London's domestic architecture, which fall into two contradictory categories: disappointment with the tendency to sameness (the inevitable corollary of standardisation, whether it comes by design or chance) and disapproval of expressions of difference. Critics of sameness blame a lack of ambition (among landlords, developers, builders and houseowners); critics of difference are rather dismayed by the form in which ambition was sometimes expressed, such as 'over elaborate' interiors and house fronts. Yet the two branches of criticism share a common language which focuses on weakness, insipidity, flimsiness, superficiality and other qualities which closely map eighteenth-century female stereotypes. That is, the language of architectural criticism in connection with these houses is essentially misogynistic – as are (bizarrely) some elements of modern-day accounts of the same buildings. In the eighteenth century itself this negative perception of the town house is bolstered by its association with luxury and excess. On the basis of a variety of evidence unearthed in the intervening chapters, I suggest in my conclusion how and why the town house was associated with notions of transience, changeability, imperfection, luxury and selfishness, which resulted in its characterisation in the eighteenth century, and sometimes more recently, as inconsequential, inconstant, insubstantial, intemperate and ultimately emasculate.

A 'rage of building'

The domestic architecture of the West End in the later eighteenth century was in many respects retrograde. It was resistant to 'progress'. The standardisation of the London house, as well as being overstated,[50] is some-times portrayed as a 'modern' concept. Yet standardisation reflected more than anything a disinclination to depart significantly from the existing model which, we must presume, served most purposes. Stand-ardisation suggests that one size fits all, or most. Innovation is found in the exceptions, the variations on a theme, and while the standardised model remains prevalent (while it fits all), individual innovations will not shift it 'forwards'.

This study is concerned with understanding both the ordinary (resis-tant) and extraordinary (ambitious) elements of the London town house in this period. It focuses on the West End house in the period *c.*1760–*c.*1790, the first four decades of George III's reign for reasons given above. I would not wish this book's arguments relating to the later eigh-teenth century to be generalised to the preceding or ensuing periods nor is it my intention to offer comparisons between periods (or between classes of house or occupant). The circumstances in which people came to occupy houses in London and the numbers in which they did so varied greatly throughout the eighteenth century alone, even if the type of house available for them to occupy remained much the same during that time. Many assumptions that architectural historians and other writers have made about the town house derive from studying the house over a broad sweep of time and generalising time-specific anecdotal evidence to the whole century; yet good rather than general understanding requires a more determined focus. In *Spaces of Modernity: London's Geographies 1680–1780*, Miles Ogborn is intent on achieving a balance between 'totalisations' on the one hand and, on the other, specifics which tell us nothing beyond themselves. To this end, he interrogates 'quite particular spaces and contexts', and 'allows these detailed cases to read-dress "grand" theoretical issues'.[51] Thus while Ogborn does not dismiss 'modernity' as a useful lens for viewing the eighteenth century, he is keen to militate against any tendency to allow it to filter out difference and disjunction. Similarly, I do not say that all prior lenses for viewing the domestic architecture of eighteenth-century London are worthless – far from it – but I am keen that they should not obscure the evidence of activity at the individual level or even the need to study it in its own right. It is important, I feel, to create a space for that evidence to tell a new story.

I want to convey how things were for these people at this time, and I generally introduce comparisons only where they derive from con-temporary comment. However, this new, clearer picture of the London town house in the eighteenth century will ultimately allow more useful comparisons with town houses in other areas or periods, or between town houses and country houses or villas. To cover all these possibilities here would be to dilute the impact of the new thinking and material presented.

The period following the Peace of Paris (1763) was the first and most significant phase of building activity and expansion in London's West End after an earlier wave of development in the 1720s and 1730s.[52] The building boom lasted through the 1760s and 1770s, with occasional, temporary downturns.[53] Contemporary commentators corroborate evidence found in the Middlesex deeds registry about the 'rage of building', particularly in the mid- to late 1760s.[54] In 1771, Smollett's Matthew Bramble reported that

> London is literally new to me; new in its streets, houses, and even in its situations . . . What I left open fields . . . I now find covered with streets and squares . . . I am credibly informed, that in the space of seven years, eleven thousand new houses have been built in one quarter of Westminster, exclusive of what is daily added to other parts of this unwieldy metropolis.[55]

Here Bramble presents as a recent phenomenon the fashion for town-house ownership or occupancy that he finds so abhorrent. The 'rage' was still worthy of comment by the late 1770s, when Horace Walpole remarked that 'rows of houses shoot out every way like a polypus'.[56] The press paid particular attention to the 'new buildings' in and about Marylebone – 'a soil in which esquires spring up as plentifully now as mushrooms did formerly', according to *Town and Country Magazine* in 1772.[57]

The shift of the fashionable population and its service providers westwards, away from the City, as well as the influx of new permanent and temporary residents from outside the metropolis, made the period a particularly propitious time for West End landlords to undertake building to satisfy housing demand and generate income.[58] This land was largely in the hands of a few aristocratic families, and often entailed, so that it could not be sold outright. Other estates were in the hands of corporate landowners, for whom they provided a steady revenue. But restrictions on the sale of freeholds did not preclude development. On the Cavendish-Harley Estate, new blocks began to spring up to the west of Cavendish Square (begun in 1717), previously an isolated representative in Marylebone of the wave of building activity in the first decades of the century. The new blocks gradually filled up the space defined by the New Road,[59] including the lands of the Portman Estate, on which Portman Square (begun in 1764) was now developed as well as other streets and supporting service areas, tied to the neighbouring layouts by main streets extending existing ones to the south and east.[60] Developments beyond the bounds of Marylebone included the Adelphi, south of the Strand, overlooking the Thames.

The mid-1770s marked the beginning of a phase of more rapid estate development, including Stratford Place, Oxford Street (1774), Portland Place (1776–90), Manchester Square (1776) and Finsbury Square (1777–92).[61] Developments which had begun on the Bedford Estate in Bloomsbury a century earlier were also resumed in the 1770s and these included Bedford Square (begun *c*.1775), although the area's fashionable prestige had been ceded to the prominent developments further west.[62]

In addition to new building, this period also saw the remodelling and refitting of many earlier houses.[63] Late seventeenth- and early eighteenth-century developments were redeveloped on a plot-by-plot basis as leases expired. A purchaser might take the existing house, 'negotiate for a new or extended lease, and commission an architect to build a new structure or dramatically remodel the existing one in the latest style'.[64] At the upper end of the market, therefore, redevelopments of building stock within established built-up areas, and extensive remodelling and refitting of existing properties, accompanied the westward expansion of the city into fresh territory.

The wave of building, rebuilding, refurbishment and decoration also coincided with a striking change in fashions in interior decoration, known retrospectively as the 'Adam style', which, in its genuine and imitated forms, inspired many comments, not all favourable. Within new and existing building stock the Adam brothers, and others, also made radical changes to the planning of some terrace homes, as I discuss further in Chapter Six.

Lastly, the boom period coincided with developments that affected the town house's external appearance, in particular the more successful attempts by developers to achieve uniformity in street façades,[65] and the introduction of legislation partly to that effect. Speculating developers had been erecting rows of regular town houses in London since at least the first half of the seventeenth century (for example Great Queen Street, 1637), but the 'palace front', in which architects and other designers brought together the façades of a row of houses in one grand design reminiscent of a larger, more noble building, came into its own in this later period. Colen Campbell had proposed a palace front for Grosvenor Square in 1725, and it was materialised there on a limited scale by Edward Shepherd a few years later, around 1728. But the earlier part of the period covered here saw the palace front take off in London, or at least more coordinated attempts at articulating a row of fronts to good visual effect.[66] In 1768, the Adams began the Adelphi development, which largely depended on terraces styled to suggest a Roman seaside palace for its modishness. In the previous year, William Franks had begun Percy Street, which was more uniform than palatial. Bedford Square followed shortly afterwards in the 1770s, and 'thereafter it seemed almost inevitable that a major square would be designed with balanced, symmetrical façades'.[67]

By 1785 the rage of building had subsided. In 1784, Robert Grews, one of the builders of Bedford Square, wrote to the estate surveyor, Robert Palmer, of 'the great scarcity of Money, occasioned by the unhappy American War' which had greatly slowed the Square's development over the previous few years, and resulted in financial losses for those selling and letting the finished houses.[68] In August of the same year, the architect Robert Brettingham wrote to his aunt of his difficulty in finding a place in London for his relation Matthew, 'there being much less Business than there used to be'.[69] The proliferation of comment that the 'rage' had induced also subsided. The rage was no longer topical, and neither was the new decorative style that had often come with it, although Adam's work was still used for unfavourable comparisons with newer decorative styles, such as Henry Holland's work at Carlton House (begun 1783), of which Horace Walpole wrote in 1785 'how sick one shall be, after this chaste palace, of Mr Adam's gingerbread and sippets of embroidery'.[70]

Like the Adams at the Adelphi, many architects undertook the design of houses in speculative developments on their own initiative and at their own risk, as well as being involved in individually commissioned projects for new houses, or for the rebuilding, interior remodelling, refurbishment or redecoration of older ones. The Danish architect Steen Eiler Rasmussen writes that the Adelphi was

> not only a dream of antique architecture, it was just as much a finance-fantasia over risk and profit; the financier was an artist and the artist a financier. This creative speculation is something very English, and it is no less typical that when it turns out to be a failure the enterprise is saved by a lottery – an appeal to people's gambling instinct – business adventure and excitement in another form.[71]

The client's or occupier's perspective, which is this book's main concern, cannot be separated from the other forces that operated in the period and this balance of aesthetic, practical, economic and financial interests among diverse parties is the background against which town-house development and redevelopment was undertaken and clients' choices made.

Part One

~

A Place in Town

One

Occupying the West End

The London house's significance to its occupier can be defined as comprising the mesh of practical and abstract roles that the house performed. This chapter begins the exploration of those roles in respect of the house as a whole. I am not concerned here with what people looked for in a house, but rather with what prompted them to take a house in town in the first place.

The thousands of homes built during the major waves of development in the eighteenth century, identified and characterised by Summerson,[1] bear witness to a greatly increased demand for permanent and temporary accommodation in the West End, particularly in the 1760s and 1770s. John Gwynn, proposing improvements to London in 1766, was unsure of the reasons for the 'prodigious encrease of building [which had] been encouraged in this metropolis', but he was prepared to venture explanations for further investigation:

Whether it proceeds from the migration of foreigners or from so many convenient roads being made from all parts of the kingdom, whether it be owing to our own people's deserting their native homes and quitting their innocent country retreats for the sake of tasting the pleasures of this great city, whether the profits of a successful war has enabled some to keep houses who were formerly contented with lodgings; whether it is owing to the arrival of others, who, having acquired fortunes in the plantations, come to spend them here; or to the monopolizing of farms, that is, making a large farm out of three or four small ones, and thereby compelling the farmers who are turned out of them to seek their bread in this metropolis, are all considerations well worth enquiring into.[2]

No doubt the availability of suitable housing, eagerly provided by estate owners and speculative builders, in turn enhanced the attraction of longer periods of London residence. This chapter looks at why people came to London during this period and why they took houses in the West End. What did ownership or tenancy of such a house mean to them? What was a 'good' house and what practical and other purposes did it serve? (Eighteenth-century sources often make reference to a 'good' house or location, without defining the term. To the individual, the notion of good was no doubt relative: good for what or whom, and compared with what? Nevertheless, for the purposes of this book I assume that three-bay houses in the main (principally residential) streets and squares of Marylebone and Bloomsbury, such as Harley Street, Berners Street, Portland Place and Arlington Street, and other locations mentioned in the Introduction, set a minimum standard for a 'good' house, and there was plenty of scope for bigger houses and better locations, such as Grosvenor and St James's Squares. Sequential pieces of building legislation established what was a first- or second-rate house, but ultimately it was individual perceptions that determined what was 'good'.[3])

Two problems with judging solely from the built evidence are central to this chapter's concerns. Firstly, the West End was home to both landowners and non-landowners, great and small.[4] Evidence from the ratebooks shows that members of several classes were intermixed in any major street or square,[5] and although West End houses can be divided into categories or classes, according to both the prevailing eighteenth-century building regulations and other criteria, such as size and location, it is difficult to categorise who lived where and in what type of house. That is, it was not only aristocrats but also wealthy members of other groups who occupied exceptionally large, or detached, properties. Aristocrats are known to have occupied less grand houses too.[6] Not all members of the landed classes sought to keep a step ahead of the 'monied' classes that followed swiftly on their heels in the westward move. Some aristocrats were content with a less fashionable area: members of the highest society continued to inhabit apartments in Covent Garden throughout the once-fashionable piazza's decline in this period. Commissioned work by fashionable architects in unfashionable locations, such as designs by the Adams for houses in Soho Square and Gerrard Street in the 1770s, also demonstrates 'the continuing viability of these older West End neighbourhoods for elegant housing, even if they were no longer the height of fashion'.[7] Other aristocrats resolutely maintained family links with now outmoded locations, and not necessarily because their visits to town were only few and brief: Michael Port notes the 5th Duke of Argyll's determination to stay in unfashionable Argyll Street, despite spending long periods in London. He also notes the impossibility of fully accounting for why aristocratic housing habits varied so widely.[8] Likewise, Peter Guillery argues that 'it should not be assumed that people always lived in the largest house that they might have done. Without other information house size can only be a general guide to status.' (I do, however, have some dispute with Guillery's statement that 'clearly people lived only in houses they could afford', and I will show below how untrue this proves to be for occupants of many 'good' houses in the West End.)[9]

Secondly, the homogeneity of houses and developments is too easily mistaken for uniformity of attitudes and circumstances among their occupants, reflected in the reluctance of Georgian London's historiographers to investigate the diverse motives behind seemingly uniform residential habits and proclivities. Not only were members of various classes living side by side in similar houses, but, as Port has pointed out, even the nobility was not a single category of landowners, but a fragmented one, including brothers, younger sons and widows of noblemen, with different reasons for being in town and country, and varying degrees of attachment to family properties in both locations. So, we cannot ascribe even to members of the landowning classes a unitary pattern of behaviour with respect to town residence, and I show later in this chapter and in the next the particularly strong connection between women of this class and London houses.

We can, therefore, make no simple judgements about the importance either of residence in London, or ownership of a house there, purely on the basis of the built evidence, surviving or recorded. Neither can we assume that terrace houses meant little to their occupants on the strength of their typical appearance. With the help of anecdotal evidence from letters and diaries, we can identify a range of reasons why members of the landowning classes were drawn to London. We can also gauge the uses to which a good West End house might be put; not just practical functions such as accommodation and entertainment, but also its more abstract uses as a marker of new status, or an essential part of making a proper figure for oneself, for example. Indeed the house sometimes surpassed notions of 'use' and became the very reason for being in town.

'Tired of worsted' – reasons for coming to London

The typical landowner had several roles to perform, or aspire to – estate owner, business man, financial investor, political representative and social magnate, to name but a few – many of which relied on, or were served by, residence in London. In this first section I explore some general and personal incentives for heading to town, before looking at the uses to which landowners put their London town house; that is, at the supporting roles it was asked to perform in the landowner's life. By 'landowner', I generally mean any member of the landowning classes, and it will be apparent from the context where I am talking specifically about patriarchs.

Landowners came to town for private business purposes, overseeing commercial and industrial interests, as well as seeking the professional services of lawyers, brokers, conveyancers and architects in connection with their country property and increasingly their town property too. Both outright sales and mortgage arrangements (sometimes necessitated by the expense of town residence itself, as I show in Chapter Three) required the collective services of some or all of those professionals. For example, the Fox-Strangways family's solicitor was kept busy not only with matters relating to the late 1st Earl of Ilchester's heavily encumbered estate but also with the 2nd Earl's move to Grosvenor Square in 1777, the year after his father's death. By 1779 Ilchester had mortgaged the Grosvenor Square house and soon after sold it on to Earl Percy, to whom the mortgage was transferred.[10] Some owners sought the services of architects in assessing houses for mortgage purposes: Robert Mylne's diary records many occasions on which he surveyed London houses to determine whether or not they were sufficient security for the sums to be raised on them.[11] Others employed them to adjudicate in property-related disputes. Maria Stavordale, later Lady Ilchester, reported that her husband's cousin 'Mr Fox came up to Town about a Law suit he has with a Builder that undertook his House, both partys have refered [sic] it to a Taylor [presumably the architect Sir Robert Taylor], and it is to be finally determined by him before the next term'.[12] Presence in London therefore enabled property owners to draw on the best of the diverse but sometimes interrelated professional services.

Landowners had, perhaps, more need than ever to borrow against their real assets, as they bore the brunt of increased fiscal burdens resulting from the heavy financial cost of successive wars. On a brighter note, the conversion of government debt into stock at the conclusion of such conflicts as the Seven Years' War allowed them to diversify their sources of income, and there was good money to be made in the closely related fields of public and private borrowing.[13] In any case, London was both the place to get credit, and to put one's money to work by lending it to other people.

Residence in London was not only necessary for attendance at increasingly lengthy parliamentary sessions, and at court – and for maintaining close ties with social and political factions generally – but it was also a means to further advancement in the military and other careers, in which members of the landed classes were increasingly likely to be involved. John Brewer explains how army commissions were bought and sold, their traffic 'determined by a mixture of market forces and political clientage', and while 'commerce in naval commissions was forbidden . . ., at higher levels the choice commands and stations were likely to go, especially in peacetime, to those in political favour'. In the 1770s, the future major-general James Mure Campbell was advised, 'If your inclinations are to push forward in the army, undoubtedly being in parliament is the only way.' Established officers 'needed to develop "an interest" both with the crown and with powerful political patrons if they were to achieve promotion'. Likewise, posts in government administration, which proliferated in response to the heavy administrative demands of maintaining the army and especially the navy, were by now a respectable and reasonably rewarding employment for members of landowning families, which could be secured by the right political or family connections. As Brewer observes, 'the frequent changes in office-holding made administration highly permeable', and no doubt the eager and well-connected candidate, on the spot in London, was well placed in all respects to seize any such opportunities.[14]

It was not only Parliament's extended sessions that drew people to town in greater numbers and for longer periods, but also the social and cultural attractions that had developed alongside them. Balls, assemblies, parties both large and small, plays and operas kept London residents entertained through the winter and spring months and constituted the 'season', which became part of an established calendar of events followed by all those with the requisite money and leisure time: October to April in town, May in Bath and the summer months at home in the country or visiting friends. As the century progressed, therefore, 'the lone MP in lodgings, still a familiar figure in the 1750s, was increasingly replaced by the political family living on a fashionable street in the West End by the last quarter of the century', as wives had their own reasons for coming to town.[15] As Paul Langford notes, 'the sheer regularity of parliamentary sessions had doubtless helped stimulate the development of the London season [but] it was hardly necessary to sustain it', and 'even the lesser gentry, those accustomed to live on their estates during the London season, frequently found the temptation of a trip to the capital too much for them'.[16] Smollett's Matthew Bramble, himself a temporary visitor to the city, criticises those other gentry who allow themselves to be lured there and describes at length the differences between his 'town grievances' and his 'country comforts'.[17] The extreme tone of Bramble's tirades reflects Smollett's great antipathy to the English capital, but he was not alone in perpetuating this 'common rhetorical pastime', dating back to classical times, 'to deplore the iniquities of the city and speak affectionately of the virtues of the country life; and (alternatively) to deplore the uncouthness and boredom of the country life, and speak affectionately of the civilizing excitement of the city'.[18] Town certainly had much to offer those who found rural residence tiresome and wished to be exposed to higher levels of sophistication than were met with in the country. Sufficient society could be found within members of one's own class; there was no need to mix with those of lesser rank for social or political expediency or simply to make up a party.[19] Despite Mrs Bennet's objections, Jane Austen's Mr Darcy was no doubt largely right in describing country society as 'confined and unvarying' – at least relatively – and closer neighbours and better transport, roads, lighting and pavements allowed women in particular to mix more easily with those of their own sort in town.[20] Even Matthew Bramble admits that 'a companionable man will, undoubtedly put up with many inconveniences for the sake of enjoying agreeable society' in town, although he finds it insufficient temptation to make him 'mortify [his] senses and compound with such uncleanness as [his] soul abhors'.[21] For some visitors social life was London's main attraction: 'the home of politeness was in company, and the place of company was in the institutions that lay at the heart of urban culture'.[22] Town etiquette – the set of habits and manners shared by people in the West End in contrast to those of the country or the City – was an attraction in itself.[23]

London's particular advantage was the choice of society it offered, unlike what Mrs Elizabeth Montagu called in 1778 the 'higgledy-piggledy of the watering places', where everyone was thrown together indiscriminately.[24] Fanny Burney, too, ranked London's merits in this respect above those of country towns, where she found herself obliged to make and receive visits. In London, she wrote in 1769, 'restraint of this kind is much much less practiced or necessary . . . excuses there are no sooner made than admitted – acquaintances as easily drop'd as courted – & company chose or rejected at pleasure'.[25] Likewise, in 1787, Mary Noel found it easy enough to avoid the encumbrance of numerous visitors – described by her as the 'usual embarras' at her door – by taking no measures to announce her arrival in London.[26] On the other hand, Anna Barbauld saw the value of getting 'into the visiting way' when in town and did not consider it 'quite as idle employment, because it leads to connexions'.[27]

For those who wanted it, the capital facilitated variety and choice in companions and lifestyle, not only by comparison with the country, but even from day to day. The Duke of Norfolk, it was said, would on one day 'be the high-bred nobleman at the magnificent table of his prince; the next he would take a chop tête-à-tête at the Shakspear with any respectable professional man . . . when his manner was as free from ostentation, as it were possible to conceive any great lord's could be'.[28] As the epitome of the pluralist society, London offered the greatest scope for social role-playing, particularly by people 'not instantly known by their birth, parentage, and background'.[29] It also offered plenty of opportunities for giving the game away, as shown by the attention contemporary literature pays to social gaffes. For example, in Frances Burney's *Evelina* (1778), Madame Duval reveals the baseness of her English origins, as well as an unseemly assimilation of Parisian with London manners, when she openly declares her shock 'to see ladies come to so genteel a place as Ranelagh with hats on'. The vulgarity of which she accuses these ladies is too evidently an attribute of her own.[30] London was the place where class stratifications were most acute and ruthless, the ultimate testing ground. In contrast to country life, where estate ownership was sufficient for ranking purposes, London residence was perhaps a choice to be judged by those more exacting standards, a conscious display of property and manners to make an immediate impression on comparative strangers. John Brewer therefore writes of how 'cultural sites', which abounded in London, 'were places of self-presentation in which audiences made publicly visible their wealth, status, social and sexual charms . . . access to culture and self-presentation in the cultural arena was a vital means of maintaining or attaining social status and of establishing social distinctions'.[31]

Anna Barbauld may have complained in January 1784 that 'constant visiting' left little opportunity for seeing the sights, but then, as now, there was much for the provincial visitor to marvel at and even Mrs Barbauld had time to see such spectacles as the hot-air balloon 'now exhibiting at the Pantheon', the object of great public curiosity. Five years later she counted 'the trial, the parliamentary business' (in particular the 'noble effort making for the abolition of the slave-trade'), 'fêtes and illuminations, and the Shakespear Gallery' among the attractions that had 'contributed to fill the great hive', neatly summing up the diversity of interests that London catered for, deliberately and incidentally.[32]

London was not only the place to get credit; it was the place to spend it too. As Gwynn suggests, the more solid 'profits of a successful war' or of plantation ownership, among other sources of income, were often turned into material form there. Shopping trips in the newly paved and better-lit streets were an important attraction for many visitors from outside the city. Judith Baker regularly travelled all the way from Durham to shop in town, demonstrating through her surviving records a preference for buying such goods as expensive foods, fabrics and clothing. She also shopped and settled bills for her Durham acquaintances, and had a reciprocal arrangement in that respect with her close friend Lady Windsor, among others. Helen Berry suggests that such distance from London provided goods purchased there with something of the exotic appeal of imported rarities,[33] a view compounded by Anna Barbauld's spoof letter under the pseudonym 'Henry Homelove', which also confirms the practice of buying goods on behalf of friends and neighbours. Homelove declares he only comes to town 'as a proper compliance with the gayer disposition of [his] wife, and the natural curiosity of the younger part of [his] family', but allows that the visits have material benefits, in which he finds some satisfaction:

9, 10

> Our journey gave me an opportunity of furnishing my study with some new books and prints; and my wife of gratifying her neighbours with some ornamental trifles, before their value was sunk by becoming common, or of producing at her table or in her furniture some new-invented refinement of fashionable elegance. Our hall was the first that was lighted by an Argand lamp; and I still remember how we were gratified by the astonishment of our guests, when my wife with an audible voice called to the footman for the tongs to help to the asparagus with.[34]

One gentleman's carnal desires drove him to the capital, but even the terms in which he expressed *these* reflect the general hankering for material sophistication which brought many others to town. 'My Dear Duke', wrote General Mostyn to the Duke of Newcastle in 1776, 'Tired of worsted . . . I took a run to London last Saturday to fuck somebody in silk'.[35] London was not only the marketplace for fashion and every luxury, home-grown and imported, but also the site of their display, in public places and private homes, on walls, floors, tables, sideboards and bodies. But of all the things one could acquire and take away from the metropolis, an air of sophistication and urbanity was perhaps the most valuable to most. On returning to the country Homelove could not only show off his stylish purchases, but also 'talk of capital artists and favourite actors' and make a 'better figure' in political debates 'having heard the most popular speakers in the House'.[36]

Stage of life, marital status and gender all affected choices or obligations to reside in London. Newlywed couples might wish to enjoy

London life before having a family. The fictional Mr and Mrs Heartless 'resolved to see the shows, and feel the joys of London, before the increase of our family should confine us to domestic cares',[37] while in real life Judith Milbanke and her husband took up residence in the London house that he had prepared in Edwards Street, Portman Square, after their wedding in January 1777,[38] and William Weddell bought a 'Large, Noble and Magnificent Mansion with a Stone Front', in Upper Brook Street, Grosvenor Square, soon after his marriage in 1771.[39] Lady Caroline Fox disapproved of the suggestion that her sister and prospective brother-in-law should live only in the country. 'That I objected to of all things,' she wrote in 1762, 'I have no idea of young people burying themselves.'[40] The London experience was therefore not only sought after but also recommended for the young and carefree.

Lawrence and Jeanne Stone suggest that mothers of small children might steer clear of the city,[41] but this tendency was not universally true. For example, the Duchess of Beaufort and her young children spent lengthy periods in Grosvenor Square while the duke was away hunting.[42] Sometimes gender determined which parent, and which children, lived where. Ann Pelham seems to have spent most of her time in town with her daughters, while her sons stayed with their father (Thomas Pelham, later 1st Earl of Chichester) in the country.[43] Stone and Stone also suggest that when children went off to school, parents were more likely to stay in town, or even to go abroad.[44] But education and professional training could be well provided in London and 'town education' was a generic term for the social refinement to be acquired there.[45] Lady Winn was aware of 'the many Advantages [her] Daughter might reap from spending a little time in London . . . both as it would enlarge her Ideas of the World, and further improve her in other Accomplishments'.[46] In 1769, a 'correspondent' to the *Town and Country Magazine* declared that 'the best people in the world, without the polish of a town-education, make a forlorn appearance', although the education in question seems to have comprised socialising with other young ladies and gentlemen, shopping, attending auctions, observing other strollers in Green Park, dinners, 'routs, drums, visits and what not'.[47] Of course, London also constituted a marriage market, where appropriate introductions could more readily be made than in the country and a wider range of alliances was on offer.

A prospective heir might divide his time between the city and the country, being actively involved in local politics in the latter and cultivating contacts on a wider basis in the former. Younger sons with fewer obligations at home might move away from the country residence or from the family's home in town to set up their own establishment.

Gentry sons might move to London in order to seek a fortune and independence in commerce.[48] Other young men sought military commissions or a career in public administration. John Brewer notes the increasing tendency at this time for the gentry and the aristocracy to send more than one younger son into the armed forces.[49]

The elderly, or otherwise infirm, might be tempted or obliged to take up London residence. Any town or city, but particularly London, offered more advanced medical expertise than was found within easy reach of a country residence, as well as support and society for one's carer. Lady Sarah Bunbury reported on her nephew's illness in 1774, and hoped that his wife would get him to town, 'so that her brothers or sister will go to her'.[50] Town was also the preferred location for inoculating children,[51] although Judith Milbanke saw less reason for this in 1786, following the death of the medical expert Baron Dimsdale. She felt that the country air was better for recuperating after the treatment, but she was out of step with the majority on this subject.[52] Many women also thought it wise to move to the capital in time to give birth, especially when a complicated birth was anticipated. The Duchess of Beaufort, like her mother-in-law before her, seems to have gone to her London house to lie in,[53] and in 1781, Sophia Curzon thanked God that she 'did not stay to be confin'd in the Country', suspecting that her baby was already dead inside her.[54] In 1781, the Marquess of Titchfield reported Dr Ford's disapproval of his mother's decision to stay in the country to lie in, while the Duke of Newcastle insisted that the Countess of Lincoln should come to London a month before her confinement in 1783, and offered to put his house at her service.[55] In 1773, Lady Jersey reportedly insisted on lying-in in the country, but as her doctor lived thirty miles away and refused to reside with her for six weeks waiting for the happy event, the Hon. Caroline Howe thought the lady was surely 'running a very foolish risk'.[56] Lady Gower imputed 'her fever and great danger, to have been owing to wrong management in her labour, she had a woman and lay in at Trentham', reported Mrs Howe.[57] The apparent inclination of the aristocracy to give birth to heirs in the 'safety' of London is particularly interesting in view of the intimate associations of the country seat with heritage and lineage. The trend also suggests that the benefits of medical expertise countered any concerns about the proverbial risks of the unhealthy city.

Town was the place for all sorts of communications and the better reliability of postal connections was a possible reason for wives and children to stay in London while the head of the family was away, particularly if a birth was imminent. The Dowager Duchess of Beaufort chose to write to her son at Grosvenor Square rather than his country seat at

Badminton, Gloucestershire, because even if he were in the country, it would be safer, and perhaps quicker, to send letters via London.[58] Lord Nuneham also queried the reliability of the post to the country in comparison to that which went to London, writing to Lord Spencer in 1756, 'I have wrote you twice, & directed both my letters to you in London, as I was not quite certain of the address to Althorpe [sic], which if you think as safe as sending them to London I should be glad to know.'[59] Mrs Howe recognised the combined benefits of regularity, reliability and consistency attached to a London postal address, writing to Lady Spencer, 'I do not know where this will find you so direct to St James's Street [sic]' and asked Lady Spencer to send her replies to Grafton Street, rather than troubling her 'with different directions'.[60]

The extensive variety of information that Caroline Howe sent to Lady Spencer from London is evidence of both the capital's vital function as a communications hub and the central role a well-placed woman could play in other people's lives. Fashion news from town was always welcome in the provinces. For example, Betsy Sheridan reported from London in December 1788 that

> Bonnets I see most generally worn and some with very deep Curtains, The Bonnet itself is small. Hats are also worn, like riding hats. The Hair universally dress'd very loose in small curls – as many in curls down behind as otherwise [. . .] As to gowns all kinds – Chemises – Round gowns with flounce or not. Great coats made very open before to shew the peticoat [sic].[61]

The type of conversational information so readily available in London was also missed by those away from town and was consequently demanded of those still there. In 1781, Miss Herbert was 'dying to know a little more of the *gossipry* of the world in general' and sent a barrage of questions to Lady Louisa Stuart:

> Questions to be answered by return of post:–
> Did Lady Duncannon ever lay in, and of what and when?
> When does Lady Althorp lay in? Who is Nanette to marry?
> What's become of Miss Molesworth?
> What's Lady Betty Compton about? Is Lady Weymouth brought to bed?
> [. . .]
> Is Miss Sackville married yet to Mr Herbert?
> Who else is going to be married, and is anybody dead?[62]

On, arguably, a more serious note, Elaine Chalus has elucidated the function of many well-connected, London-based women in the timely dissemination of critical information to political allies out of town, both male and female, as well as their function as political hostesses and facilitators in the capital itself.[63] Both men and women 'were expected to be sources of "News" ' and some women, such as Lady Anson, relished the role. Living in the Admiralty, she 'benefited from a steady stream of visitors who supplied her with a great deal of information. She put what she learned to good use in what she light-heartedly termed her "Office" as "*News-Writer* to ones freinds [sic]"', chiefly her relations in the country and abroad.[64] Mrs Howe reported not only on town-based gossip and events and parliamentary debates, but also on foreign affairs (while Lady Spencer was abroad), and even acted as go-between in 1772 for the Spencers and their architect Sir Robert Taylor, who was working on the staircase compartment of Spencer House, St James's Place.[65] Likewise, Ann Pelham managed some of her husband's business affairs while she was in town and he in the country. 'I have got you (I believe) £30,000 as mortgage on yᵉ Falmer Estate', she wrote in 1783, 'wᵗʰ which you may therefore pay off Mr Durrant's Heirs, if you chuse to accept the Terms'.[66] By maintaining a presence in town, ambitious or bored wives were able to establish or retain a role in society, politics, or both: Mrs John Crewe was an active participant in canvassing for votes for Charles James Fox in the 1784 Westminster election, as well as a confidante of Edmund Burke, and friend and lover of Richard Sheridan,[67] all activities best pursued out of a good London house.

Residence in town therefore potentially gave wives a role well beyond the domestic management and entertainment assigned to them in the country and women were particularly conspicuous in the townwards move, the country being very much a male preserve.[68] The wife of the hapless Baynard in *Humphry Clinker* reacted badly to her husband's proposal that they withdraw from town: 'So', she objected, '. . . I am to be buried in the country! . . . My fortune, I know, does not exceed twenty thousand pounds – Yet, even with that pittance, I might have had a husband who would not have begrudged me a house in London!'[69] Mrs James in Henry Fielding's *Amelia* (1751) calls her husband 'barbarous' for denying her 'the pleasures of the town', when he resolves to send her into the country as (convenient) punishment for interfering with his own town pleasures.[70] As Joyce Ellis writes of the long eighteenth century, 'women were consistently portrayed in plays and poetry of the period as being ready to adopt any stratagem, however underhand, to escape from the boredom and restrictions of the countryside', with its proverbially dull and limited occupations of needlework, reading, letter-writing and walks, and irresistibly drawn to towns as 'meccas of unbridled consumption and frivolity'.[71] Through his portrayal of Mrs

Baynard, Smollett therefore perpetuates the longstanding literary convention that women's natural tendency to self-indulgence and superficiality made town life particularly attractive to them. In their defence, Ellis has argued that, by this period, part of being a gentlewoman was to possess and display a range of accomplishments ill-suited to country retirement and best set out on an urban stage. In any case, the 'variety of respectable occupations, amusements and companions' was surely sufficient and legitimate justification in itself for coming to town.[72] What is more, some women, and men, no doubt came to town to escape the noise and inconvenience of building works in the country, which was not always the place of retreat it was made out to be.

Colonel James in *Amelia* may have forced his wife 'to content herself with being the mistress of a large house and equipage in the country, ten months of the year by herself' and 'indulged her with the diversions of the town' for only two (during which time 'she had little more of her husband's society, than if they had been one hundred miles a-part'),[73] but some men, perhaps wisely, let their wives decide where to reside. Lord Bracebridge reported in 1796 that 'our determination respecting the house in Stanhope Street [depends] very much upon the Ladies of my Family, for having intention to contract our establishment to one Place, it rests with them to choose if that shall be in the Country or in Town'.[74] Sometimes the loss of a wife removed the need for a London home altogether: Lord Thanet was reported to have given up his house on his wife's death, 'till his daughters are of an age to have it'.[75]

Many women expressed a preference for town life either in words or actions, and it is easy to see why. Caroline Howe, who spent most of her time in London, declared that she was 'never without a party of some sort or other', at least during the season.[76] Mary, Countess of Bute, had constant society in London: 'I have parties at Mrs Blodens, or Lady Mary comes and passes the day with me; I have literaly [sic] not been one evening alone.'[77] London houses were often closely associated with a wife rather than her husband, as both men's and women's diary entries and letters confirm. Sir Gilbert Elliot, in a letter of January 1789, noted how Mrs Legge's control over her Grosvenor Square house was such that Mr Legge 'never sees at his own house any company of his own way of thinking', and Sir Gilbert was not alone in noting dinner and other engagements, political or otherwise, by hostess rather than host.[78] Mrs Montagu's Hill Street house (her residence prior to commissioning, as a widow, the splendid new house in Portman Square, built 1777–82) was considered to be hers rather than her husband's. Lady Fludyer was reportedly kept busy with decisions relating to the building of her Downing Street house in 1764, while her husband, Sir

Samuel, was concerned only with the payments.[79] Mrs Delany's house in Spring Gardens had been purchased 'expressly for herself' around 1754, and was only sold, thirteen years later, to raise a large sum of money to put her ill husband's mind at rest. On his death in 1768, she initially decided against resettling in London, but the Duchess of Portland persuaded her to return, because 'she would then be amongst her friends and relations'.[80] In 1787 Mary Noel was also obliged to retire from London for financial reasons, but hoped by prudent living to return in a few years to 'go off at last in a blaze like a tallow candle wrapt up in brown paper'.[81] Her niece, Judith Milbanke, wrote to her in 1785:

> I only wish Mil [her husband] was as well satisfied with the country as I am . . . certainly men have not half the resources to amuse themselves as we females. I do not carry the Joke so far as to say I prefer the Country, for to own the truth I should like to set out for the gay City tomorrow morning.[82]

Although not all men were wholly content with the attractions of the country, it was less restrictive for them than for women,[83] and it is unsurprising that these women, at least, certainly seem to have preferred the city.

Widows in particular often took up residence in London for longer periods once their late husband's estate had passed to the eldest son or other heir. In the period to 1760, research has shown that 'single women on the Grosvenor estate were predominantly widows, although there were also significant numbers of unmarried daughters of peers, estranged wives and royal mistresses'.[84] The condition of widows was something quite apart from that of other women. In some respects they were honorary men: they were not subject, like unmarried women, to society's protection and restrictions,[85] and they were likely to have some degree of financial independence. As Mr Peachum tells Polly, in John Gay's *Beggar's Opera* (1728), 'the comfortable estate of widow-hood, is the only hope that keeps up a wife's spirits. Where is the woman who would scruple to be a wife, if she had it in her power to be a widow when ever she pleas'd.'[86] 'Easier access to financial services' and spinsters' and widows' freedom in disposing of their wealth, perhaps account further for London's popularity with independent women,[87] and many widows no doubt found the combination of unprecedented freedom and sudden riches the impetus or means to set up a fashionable establishment in town. Christopher Sykes suggests that Mrs Montagu's 'ambitions dramatically increased' along with her wealth on the death of her husband in 1775. Her inheritance enabled her to build 'something more in keeping with her new station'.[88] Not all widows found London irresistible, however. Other widows preferred the retirement of the country, perhaps happily combined with the convenience of a villa. Caroline Howe reported in 1776 that Mrs Vane was going to give up her house in town after the winter, 'fix her establishment entirely in the country, and only come to London occasionally to visit her friends'.[89]

Wealthy widows, especially those with town houses, were an attractive proposition in the marriage market, and magazine tales of the period suggest that residence in Marylebone in particular gave predatory suitors the opportunity to mix with them.[90] Perhaps the prospect of suitors was one reason why widows were drawn to London, if they were inclined to remarry. In any case, a husband's will often made provision for his widow's accommodation there, although this assurance was not always enough to tempt a woman into marriage in the first place. In 1784, Mary Hamilton found a suitor's anticipated offer objectionable, even though he would provide for houses in town and country on his death.[91]

Like widows, spinsters were attracted to town for the society and variety it offered, as well as the relative independence. Following the death of her mother, to whom she had been a constant companion, Isabella Elliot took a tiny house in Chesterfield Street, and reported on its benefits in October 1781:

> Though I shall now be under a roof of my own, I shall continue to find in the society of my brother and Maria my best happiness when they are within reach. My house is the sweetest small place in the world, neat and elegant, and seems made purposely for me; and I have the Edens [her brother-in-law and sister] always close at hand.[92]

Likewise, Louisa Stuart took a house in Gloucester Place, Portman Square when the death of her mother, Mary, Countess of Bute, in November 1794 relieved her of her long-term role of companion and left her financially independent. The house became 'the centre of a circle of devoted friends and relations'.[93] Neat, elegant and convenient accommodation in town was a prerequisite for the combination of society and independence that many single women sought there.

Many new London houses, as John Gwynn suggests, satisfied demand among those who had profited from war or from trade in the West and East Indies, which enabled them to buy homes and much else besides. Essentially, they were there because they could afford to be. But this was not the case with everybody. Stone and Stone may propose that a period in London could be an economy measure for many landed proprietors – a means of avoiding the need to support a country residence's full operation, including the obligations of hospitality[94] – but a closer examination of the financial impact of town-house ownership in this period suggests the opposite, as I explain in Chapter Three. The expense of owning or renting, and running, a town house was burdensome, particularly where it was a second home. Where acknowledged, this simple fact must have deterred some landowners from setting up a town residence. But we should not assume that everyone desired a London house, despite Matthew Bramble's rhetoric. Sir William Bagot, a friend, adviser and supporter of Lord North, bemoaned 'the disagreeable necessity of purchasing a great House in this town',[95] one to which he succumbed in 1776, buying a place in fashionable Upper Brook Street, adjacent to Grosvenor Square. In fact, many of the reasons I have offered for being in London (or the composite effect of them) might just as easily have been reasons for *not* wanting to be there, where there was a choice. Not only was it a drain on finances, but London residence also made a person accessible and susceptible to such impositions as being asked to act as trustee for settlements and wills relating to other people's town and country property. In 1764, Edward Jefreys decided it was high time to retire from town and part with his house there, not just because of the reduction in his income from sugar, but also because, he complained, 'I was continually employ'd in other people's affairs, by which I could not possibly be a gainer, tho' I might run the risque of Involving my Executors in dissentions hereafter.'[96] The very financial and legal deals that drew some people to London therefore repelled others. Equally, not everyone relished being at the centre of the political world, and obliged to function as a reliable vehicle for political and other information: 'Now for News – I am in *London*; for which Reason, I suppose I must not be excused; tho' I hate it, remember very little, and am most likely to blunder in the Recital of that little,' Mr Whistler grumbled to William Shenstone.[97]

Making a 'proper figure' – putting the town house to use

With a lengthy season and so many other reasons for being in town, many landowners spent considerably more time in London than in the country. In fact, contemporary sources suggest that owners of prestigious country seats were never to be found at them. A 'correspondent' to *Town and Country Magazine* (August 1771) reported:

> When I look over *Vitruvius Britannicus* and see the numerous beautiful edifices in this island, I am animated with an unconquerable curiosity to visit every one . . . and am in hopes to find, that an hos-

pitality reigns within the walls proportionable to the beauty of the architecture without; but how greatly I am mortified to find, that scarce one in twenty is inhabited! 'Does my lord reside here constantly?' 'No, sir, he has not been here these four years.' Such is the customary answer.[98]

In 1779, Samuel Rudder found many gentlemen's seats in Gloucestershire 'totally deserted . . . and too many others, in compliance with the taste of the present age . . . left by the owners for the greater part of the year, to partake more largely of the pleasures of the metropolis'. Ten years later, John Byng found hardly a family at home in the great houses of the Midlands in 1789, leading him to conclude 'that noblemen and gentlemen have almost abandon'd the country'.[99] However, both Damie Stillman and Mark Girouard infer that the aristocracy and gentry 'settled' for a terrace house because they were in town '*only* for Parliamentary sessions and the winter social season'.[100] The supposed link between length of residence and size (and magnificence) of house, implied by Stillman, Girouard and others might therefore be too simplistic. House location, size and grandeur did not necessarily reflect time spent in London, and Michael Port has shown how aristocrats resident in London for similar periods, and for comparable reasons, lived in different sizes and standards of house in different areas.[101]

The extent to which members of the landed classes used their homes in town and country varied widely. The Duke of Beaufort's household typically spent a maximum of twenty weeks per year in London in the 1770s,[102] while the Williams Wynn family was there for seven months in each of the years 1770–2, slightly less in subsequent years.[103] Likewise, Sir Edward Littleton implied that a London house was of useful service for seven months per annum, declaring it to be 'of no value between Midsummer & November'.[104] Meanwhile, Lady Grimston travelled between Gorhambury, Hertfordshire, and the family's London house in Grosvenor Square, with or without the family, on a regular basis throughout the whole year,[105] and Sir Gilbert Elliot inhabited his Park Street house much of the year, writing almost daily to his wife in the country of his relentless social life, of entertainments and exhibitions, of parliamentary and other affairs.[106] Residence in London was not, therefore, limited to the season, and entertainments and assemblies continued throughout the summer, with Baron Wentworth reporting 'Ranelagh, Plays, Routs &c innumerable' in July 1789.[107]

There are ways other than studying periods of residence in order to gauge an individual's relationships with his country and town houses, such as the relative money and attention lavished on the two properties.

Some people treated their London home to architectural projects of exceptional scale, magnificence, fashion, quality and expense well in excess of any money spent on remodelling or redecorating their country mansion. Such behaviour suggests that the London house had an equally significant meaning for them, and it is possible to speculate what that was. Two prime examples are Sir Watkin Williams Wynn and Lord Stanley (later Derby), both of whom commissioned the Adam brothers to rebuild or extensively remodel their London houses in the 1770s, at 20 St James's Square and 26 Grosvenor Square respectively. Stanley and his wife were determined leaders of fashionable society, bent on seeking social prominence and pleasure in the capital, and their town house was a means to that end. Sir Watkin, on the other hand, was apparently intent on taking a particularly informed and educated lead in fashionable taste in architecture and design, which could best be expressed in a well-placed house, first in Grosvenor Square (1768–74) and then in St James's Square. While his country seat, Wynnstay, Denbighshire, was an established family property, already suited to its task and very much in the country, the purchase of the Grosvenor Square house was the first stage of Sir Watkin's personal bid for attention, respect and social power in a wider arena. The lengths to which he went to pursue this ambition, especially in St James's Square, are discussed in later chapters, but it is worth noting here, firstly, that plans commissioned for extensive work at Wynnstay were left unexecuted in the 1770s in favour of work on his Grosvenor Square and St James's Square houses,[108] and, secondly, that Wynn twice married into English aristocratic families against the tradition of his ancestors, who had married their equals in Wales.[109]

There were other practical differences between homes in town and country, which both dictated and reflected the ways in which they were used. Although residents in London required many of the same services as they did in the country, these could be bought in or sought away from the house as required. This system of buying, rather than producing, domestic supplies was particularly appropriate, firstly, for the potential pattern of London residence, where a house might not require any sort of service for some months of each year, and, secondly, for some types of resident, as the house might not play host to a family. While some visitors, such as Matthew Bramble, saw this external provision as inconvenient and unhealthy, others might well have relished the pleasures of *not* living off the land. John Byng was surely not alone in recognising that the limitations of a town house were attractions in themselves, when he bemoaned the follies – including dependency on Parliamentary position or favour, gaming and elections – which led many noblemen to forsake their country seats. 'A country residence' he observed, 'at first tiresome, becomes impossible . . . whilst the fine air of Marybone parish is enjoyed to the highest perfection on two closets and a cupboard!'[110] Less was possible, and therefore expected, in town, even of a nobleman, so that town brought a kind of freedom that explains why Byng and others found so many prestigious country seats deserted, even in summer. Living in a terrace house in particular perhaps constituted 'real' city life: it was streamlined for use as a London base, whether permanent or temporary, short or long term. Both the country house and the town house have been described as 'machines',[111] and each facilitated a particular sort of life.

The nature of hospitality was very different in town and country. The town house was the venue for a range of entertainments, sometimes quite independently of its occupant, as a letter of 1785 from Louisa Stuart to her sister demonstrates:

> The French Ambassador was sick indeed, for he had a stroke of the palsy yesterday at the drawing-room, and yet all the town went to his house last night, and played at faro, etc., as if he had not been dying in the next room. We are a curious people.[112]

The town house might cater for large numbers of guests, but they did not require overnight accommodation, or much space in which to move: a mismatch between the number of guests and the available space was sometimes appealing in itself. The rout, whose chief charm seems to have been viewing and experiencing the crush of people, was a phenomenon particularly associated with the town house. As Isaac Ware observed in 1756,

> Our forefathers were pleased with seeing their friends as they chanced to come and with entertaining them when they were there. The present custom is to see them all at once, and to entertain none of them.[113]

In 1787, Louisa Stuart reported on a ball at Lady Hopetown's house in Albemarle Street:

> there assembled the whole town. A thousand pretty dresses on pretty women made it an agreeable spectacle, and though extremely crowded, the house did *hold* us! For my part, I secured a seat in a quiet corner, and there posted myself until supper time, having no mind, and indeed no temptation, to be anything but a spectator.[114]

Sheer size was impressive, and permitted extraordinary entertainment, but it was not absolutely essential to self-promotion through entertainment, which was often an important function of the town house – but not necessarily the sole or even primary one.

The house functioned, too, as a place to conduct business of all sorts, including political affairs, or as a base for exploring London's varied pleasures and opportunities. Much time was spent visiting other people or frequenting public entertainments. Consequently, Mr Harrel in Frances Burney's *Cecilia* (1782)

> seemed to consider his own house merely as an Hôtel, where at any hour of the night he might disturb the family to claim admittance, where letters and messages might be left for him, where he dined when no other dinner was offered him, and where, when he made an appointment, he was to be met with.[115]

Other family members might treat the house as a hotel too, using it as a stopover point when travelling or as temporary lodgings in the city itself. Lady Louisa Conolly put her London house at the service of her sister, even though her husband and his servant were there. 'You remember how well we stuffed in it before', she wrote in 1777, 'and how comfortable we were'.[116] As with routs, the potential crush was no deterrent. Houses could also be lent to friends. Richard Hurd put his Great Russell Street house at Mrs Warburton's service for a planned visit to town in September 1776 as the Warburtons had rented out their Grosvenor Square house and had more or less retired to the country.[117] In 1751, with more obligation than choice, Sir George Savile lent his house in Leicester Square for the use of the Prince of Wales. Gertrude Savile doubted that he would ever get it back. Given the choice of 'any House in Town' in lieu of his own, Sir George removed to the Duke of Bolton's residence in Hanover Square.[118]

Where branches of the same family had their own London residences, 'the reinforcement of family connections appears to have been an important function of the London townhouse'. Certainly on the Grosvenor estate in Mayfair 'members of immediate families often lived within close proximity of one another'. For example, the Dowager Duchess of Rutland 'lived within a five-minute walk of a married daughter, a widowed daughter, a married son and a married grandson'.[119]

House occupancy and location could also be used to demonstrate and reinforce business, political, courtly and parliamentary connections. Wealthy East and West Indians kept each other company in such enclaves as Grafton Street, while the Grosvenor estate was both geographically and socially advantageous for those with affiliations to or courting connections with the Hanoverian court, parliament or both.[120] The house itself could be put to more direct use in this last respect. I have already discussed the important role that a politically minded woman could play as a conduit for 'news' simply by maintaining a presence in London, but the house itself was a vital prop for this as for so many other roles. The West End house was one of the main venues for London's highly politicised entertainments, and for politicking generally. As Elaine Chalus explains, ' "News" entered the home via family members, friends, and visitors (male and female), and was shared as a matter of course during visits, over cards, or with food and drink.' It was then passed on in the same way in other houses, on other social and familial occasions. Some ambitious hostesses, or wives of ambitious or important men, opened their London homes on designated days during the parliamentary season, shaping an arena for the exchange of society and political gossip among select company.[121] Mrs William Eden opened her house so regularly, following her husband's appointment as private secretary to Lord Carlisle, that her contemporaries spoke of her 'constant Supper' and her home became 'a minor political venue much frequented by the members of the *bon ton* and the clientele of Brookes's club'. Other, more glamorous hostesses with even bigger ambitions, such as the Duchess of Devonshire and Lady Melbourne, both of whom were in possession of undeniably 'good' West End houses, were renowned for keeping them ' "perpetually open" and attracting a glittering, if fast, cross-section of elite society'. Having a well-placed house at their disposal allowed leading political hostesses to set up their homes as factional headquarters and as a stage on which to put their own charm, intellect and other fine qualities into action in the name of party politics. The connection between these ladies' carefully orchestrated, home-based entertainments and the benefits that the Foxite whigs, in this instance, gained from them did not go unremarked by contemporaries.[122]

The house did not serve simply as a location for formal and informal events at which 'news' was discussed and spread; it also performed a role in the symbolic, and often politically charged, activities of visiting and not visiting. In 1765, George Grenville noted how Lady Bute had snubbed the Duchess of Bedford, following mob attacks on Bedford House, by being a notable absentee in a stream of sympathetic visitors to her home.[123] Private addresses were also used to locate key family and other events. Even illness had a location: 'the Right Hon. the Earl Temple is again much indisposed with an inflammatory Disorder in his Bowels, at his house in Pall Mall', *The Public Advertiser* reported on 16 May 1775. The papers also noted comings and goings from town houses and, even if individuals identified themselves with their family seats, they were strongly linked with their town houses in the London-based press, as well as elsewhere in the country. Reports from London featured in regional newspapers, so that much of this type of information was repeated for the benefit of those away from town, keen not only to know what was happening where in the capital, but also to keep abreast of critical events within the country's leading families. For example, the *York Courant* reported the death of the Countess of Middlesex 'At her House in Arlington-Street' on 17 May 1763, while the previous week it had included an account of a terrible fire at the house of the Right Hon. Lady Viscountess Dowager Molesworth, in Upper Brook Street, Grosvenor Square, in which Lady Molesworth, two daughters and their governess perished, as did one of the maids who flung herself out of the 'two pair stairs window' and impaled herself on the spikes of the iron rails at the front of the house (a hazard peculiar to town life). On a less gloomy note, the paper reported on 2 August the departure for Chatsworth of 'his Royal Highness the Duke of Cumberland, attended by the Earl of Albemarle and several Persons of Distinction . . . from his House in Grosvenor-Street', while John Wilkes had recently 'set out from his House in Great George-Street for France'. In this way, connections between people and addresses were continually reinforced both within and without the metropolis, and the London house served a critical purpose of locating individuals in geographical, political, commercial and social contexts. The difference in the terminology used to link people with country and town houses is telling in this respect: where as regards to the former the place was put first and the person second – 'Nostell Priory, the seat of Sir Rowland Winn' – for the latter the order was reversed – 'Sir Rowland Winn's house in St James's Square'. The country seat was something to which Sir Rowland was at present attached, but which was not dependent on him, as an individual, for its ongoing status; the town house, on the other hand, was something temporarily attached to Sir Rowland, and had no status without him.

The new, bigger or grander functions and performances a house facilitated might be appropriate to an owner's new status. The acquisition of a town house, or a move within London, often marked a key life or career event for the purchaser. General John Burgoyne looked for a new London residence when elected MP for Preston in 1768,[124] and, like many others no doubt, Thomas Noel, 2nd Viscount Wentworth, looked for a conveniently located and good house on taking up his seat in the House of Lords in 1774. After a rough financial patch during which he gave up his home in Savile Row and lodged with relations, he sought another house, confident in securing from William Pitt the place at court that had not been forthcoming from Lord North.[125] Both the Duke of Beaufort and Sir Watkin Williams Wynn moved to Grosvenor Square on their return from the Grand Tour in 1768, while the less grand Edmund Rolfe, only son of a newcomer to the Norfolk landed gentry, 'persuaded his father to lease and in 1771 buy (for £2500) a house in Wimpole Street where he could entertain the friends he had made on the Grand Tour', and spent a good deal of his time gaming with them there while he waited for his inheritance.[126] Others purchased or acquired houses on coming of age or inheriting an estate and perhaps a title – Lord Stanley moved into the family's Grosvenor Square house on his father's death in 1771 and soon began extensively remodelling it in anticipation of inheriting his grandfather's title of Earl of Derby. Sir Rowland Winn acquired a house in St James's Square in 1766 soon after he succeeded to Nostell Priory,[127] and the 2nd Lord Ilchester bought his house in Grosvenor Square the year after inheriting his title in 1776.[128] Like other heirs, he may have felt obliged to leave the family town house, in this instance in Burlington Street, when it was passed to his mother on his father's death.

A house purchase might also mark the beginning, rupture, or end of a marriage. The 3rd Duke of Grafton marked his separation from his wife with a move to Grosvenor Square, and his divorce with a move away again – and separate residences may have been a respectable or temporary solution to marital rifts. The Graftons' initial move to separate houses within London in 1765 was part of a formal private separation, at the Duke's behest, in response to the Duchess's ill temper and gambling habits.[129] Caroline Howe reported that Lord Craven gave his wife the choice between going into the country for three years or a separate maintenance in town, after the discovery of M. de Guine in her dressing room at an improper time. She chose the country, but Mrs Howe reported a bet 'that she would be in town again before the season is over'.[130] Separate houses were sometimes seen as a defence against, rather than simply a response to marital infelicity, if only in jest. On the occasion of his marriage in 1779, Hugh Elliot was asked: 'do you remember four years ago how you used to abuse all women, and say if ever you married you would live in St James's Street, and your wife in Berkeley Square?'[131] In any case, some women certainly lived apart from their husbands within London, and *Town and Country Magazine* (July 1772) wrote of 'the prevailing taste for separate beds, and separate maintenances at the West End of Town'.[132]

Of course, separate maintenances in town could equally be a contribution to marital infidelity and rupture. The residential split that accompanied the Graftons' separation facilitated the duke's flagrant co-habitation in Grosvenor Square with the high-class courtesan Nancy Parsons, and the duchess's liaison with the Earl of Upper Ossory, conducted in her London house through the winter of 1767–8, which ultimately provided the duke with grounds for a Parliamentary divorce.[133]

Likewise, earlier in the century, the Duchess of Beaufort's lover, Lord Talbot, visited her regularly in the houses she rented in Cavendish Street and New Bond Street in the months following her private separation from the duke in 1740, and before her resultant pregnancy provided the proof of adultery which enabled the duke to divorce her.[134] Court papers and testimonies in respect of separations and divorces therefore provide another, unusual means by which the architectural historian can reveal more about the many uses and values the eighteenth-century West End house had for its owners and tenants.

The Duchess of Grafton's irascibility and infidelity triggered her husband's moves to and from Grosvenor Square respectively, but men often cast women as more actively responsible for moves to and within London. In 1767, Philip Francis supposed Mrs Chandler to be 'at the summit of her wishes', now that her husband had bought a house in Bruton Street,[135] and Frederick Reynolds believed that it was his mother and aunt, 'like the compass, bent on a still farther variation to the westward', who had persuaded his father to take a house in the Adelphi, rather than staying put in Salisbury Square.[136] Just as some eighteenth-century observers saw a widow with a house as a quarry worth hunting in Marylebone, so others presented the West End house as sufficient in itself to make a man attractive to women. Amanda Vickery describes how 'the mercantile Stanhope clan tried to talk their rich heir Watty Spencer Stanhope out of buying a London house as they feared he would surely end up marrying an expensive "woman of quality" '.[137] Women, ambition and the town house seem to have gone together in the popular imagination and sometimes in fact. Richard Hurd resisted pressure from William Warburton's wife to move from Great Russell Street to their vacant Grosvenor Square house following his appointment as Bishop of Worcester, questioning why his current house, which cost him a hundred pounds a year, should not be sufficient. 'Great Bishops, and you Bishopesses, who have great temporal fortunes, may do as you please. But I, who am to be a simple puny Bishop, must be modest and not give myself airs', he wrote in 1774, one of several professions of his aversion to show.[138] Nevertheless, acquiring a town house often indicated a change in an individual's life, and the purchase may often have been intended as a public statement.

Women often saw a house as a means for themselves or other women to pass many leisurely hours, particularly following the death of a husband. In 1759, Lady Hervey referred to her house in town as an 'amusement (for old people must not pretend to pleasures)' and busied herself in 'altering, fitting up, and completing [the] house, which is no small affair'.[139] Twenty years later Sarah Lennox pitied the widowed

Mrs Garrick because not only had her *raison d'être* disappeared with the death of her husband, the actor and theatre manager David Garrick, and the subsequent loss of her role in his social life, but she had already done everything she could to her house: 'the *spirit* of her society is lost, and business she cannot have, for both her Houses in Town and Country are so compleat she has not a chair or table to amuse herself with attiring'.[140] Some widows found a London house, or the work that needed to be done on it, therapeutic. The Duchess of Ancaster was said to have made many alterations to her house in Berkeley Square, 'to take off from the melancholy Idea's it must naturally bring to her mind'.[141] In 1782, Mrs Montagu thought her new house had taken years off her, 'from its chearfulness, and from its admirable conveniences and comforts', which made her less afraid of growing old. 'A good House', she wrote, 'is a great comfort in old age and among the few real facilities that money will procure.'[142] For Mrs Montagu, the pleasure was in the finished house, or the anticipation of it, not in its construction.[143] Her new townhouse project enabled her to satisfy her desire to be surrounded by pleasing, tasteful things at this late point of her life. 'In so little while', she told her sister-in-law, 'I shall never see any thing belonging to me that is not pretty, except when I behold myself in the looking glass.'[144] Despite her friend Anna Barbauld's remark in 1778 that 'Mrs Montague, not content with being the queen of literature and elegant society, sets up for the queen of fashion and splendour. She is building a very fine house, has a very fine service of plate, dresses and visits more than ever',[145] the new house was not simply a machine for entertaining, and the evidence afforded by Mrs Montagu's letters warns against viewing any town house as solely, or perhaps even primarily, fulfilling one role.

The importance to women of the practice and the results of doing up a house is evident from the remarks of Mrs Montagu and others. For some women, the town house was effectively the project of a lifetime, and was guarded jealously. The unmarried Lady Isabella Finch, living in the small but splendid house built for her in Berkeley Square by William Kent in 1742–4, took measures to ensure that whoever lived in it after her death would 'make no Alteration in the building or disposition of the Rooms on the first and second Floors of the said house or in the Furniture of the said Rooms'. Lady Isabella also guaranteed that the house would be kept in good condition: her beneficiary was obliged to spend on its upkeep the £30 per annum allowed for by her will.[146]

The town house not only facilitated being in London but also became, for some, a reason for being there, or an inducement to spend time in town. Mrs Montagu was emphatic about the importance of a good house not just 'in the Winter of life' but also in the winter of the year:

'a good Winter habitation', she wrote in 1781, 'like a good friend is a comfort in all seasons and circumstances, and most particularly felt in bad seasons, bad health, bad spirits'.[147] Lady Holland hoped that the Duke of Leinster's 'pretty house in Arlington Street would tempt him to come to London' in 1768.[148] Roy Porter has suggested that the style of the town house in this period had to 'woo the eye and mind away from the country estate. Crucial in this 'were the more intimate designs and decorations created after 1760 by the Adam brothers.'[149] Not everyone shared Mrs Montagu's enthusiasm for decorating and furnishing a house – Richard Hurd predicted, in 1773, that fitting up his new town house in Great Russell Street would bring 'a new scene of trouble to go thro'[150] – but a tastefully and comfortably furnished house, primed for city life, perhaps superseded those other inducements that persuaded or obliged people to take it in the first place. In such cases, the house did not just serve a purpose, but became the purpose.

While I am principally concerned here with the landed classes, no doubt city-based men also found a good house essential to cutting an appropriate figure in town. It might be an essential element of the professional persona created by a doctor or lawyer, instilling trust, confidence and respect in his clients. As architects, the Adam brothers were well aware of the role of houses in creating impressions and recognised the particular importance of image to their own professional ambitions. Robert foresaw in 1756 that the brothers would need to 'blind the world by dazzling their eyesight with vain pomp'. He took a house in St James's Place, well located for making connections and displaying his talents, and had six servants to help him appear the gentleman while he entertained prospective patrons. As he said himself, there is 'no way so good or proper to get a good price as to take all methods to show you despise a bad one'. Practical use, personal fancy and public perception therefore combine to create a wider sense of the usage and usefulness of the town house.[151]

For both the professional and leisured classes, appearances counted for much and a 'good' house had an immeasurably important part to play in this respect, as further anecdotal evidence of aristocratic lives nicely illustrates. The young Lord and Lady Ilchester moved into Grosvenor Square in 1777, intending a longer stay but selling up only two years later, most likely for financial reasons. Lady Ilchester was from an Irish family and unfamiliar with the London social world. She made very few acquaintances in the little time that she had spent in town and her relation Sarah Lennox thought this a pity, writing that 'so charming as she is, she need only try to make herself known to be sure of being liked and *recherchée*.'[152] Perhaps the Grosvenor Square purchase was a move to remedy this situation by spending more time in town and on the right footing because Lady Ilchester was in danger of becoming known for the wrong reasons, as Sarah Lennox again reported at the end of the year of the move:

> I thought she had too much sense not to make a proper figure if she undertook to make any at all; . . . [W]hat I heard was a little circumstance that made me see more than ever the absurdity of prejudice among *fine* people and on the other hand the necessity of attending a *little* to it if one lives among them; I hear she appeared at the Opera without powder dressed in a poking, queer way . . . and caused great speculation to know *who that queer but pretty little vulgar woman could be that L^{dy} Sefton brought with her.* [N]ow to be sure it requires nothing but a short examination to find out that the Genteel L^{dy} Sefton is *in nature* a most compleat Vulgar[;] to my certain knowledge her gentility never went further than her dress and the pretty Vulgar little Woman has more true real gentility about her than most people I know . . . but such is the World that a little Powder and Gauze properly disposed secures a proper respect and the neglect of it gives a mauvais ton which is sometimes a little troublesome to overcome but I fancy a good House and good suppers will soon recover the faux pas of going to the Opera sans powder.[153]

Sarah Lennox explains the need to attend to appearances in order to stand still in society's rankings, let alone climb them, and the West End resident's obligation to be governed by the judgements and standards of the circle in which she moved or aspired to move. A good house could play a role in both respects, if one had the requisite money or credit, and could compensate for worse behaviour than going to the opera 'sans powder'. Unlike Lady Ilchester, Lady Derby reportedly made a good figure early in her first London season as a married woman in November 1774.[154] At her peak she was a formidable and powerful hostess, 'one of the most principal' of 'the several *Belligerent* powers in London', wielding her authority through the force of entertainment. 'There is every night a Commerce or Quinze party at her house and of course a supper', reported Mrs Howe in 1776.[155] The location, planning, accommodation and finish of her husband's Grosvenor Square house, and the ruthless and relentless programme of entertainment they facilitated, all contributed to the Derbys' fashionable image in London, and apparently acted as an antidote to less polite behaviour. In 1778, the Duchess of Devonshire was wary that people might think she shunned Lady Derby not because of the exposure of her affair with the Duke of Dorset, but simply because she no longer had the use of the magnificent

12

Derby House at her disposal. 'I have the greatest horror of her crime', the duchess wrote to her mother,

> but her conduct has long been imprudent, and yet, I have sup'd at her house . . . and now it does seem shocking to me . . . that at the time all her grandeur is crush'd around her, I should entirely abandon her, as if I said, I know you was imprudent formerly, but then you had a great house and great suppers and so I came to you but now that you have nothing of all this, I will avoid you.[156]

The Duchess of Devonshire may not have wanted to condone an outlook that perceived a good West End house, and the entertainment that it facilitated, as an antidote to other forms of behaviour, but the attitude was nevertheless prevalent in a society preoccupied with appearances. Sarah Lennox's articulation of the basis on which London society operated in this period is central to the concerns of this book, which considers both the function of the town house in making a 'proper figure' and the need to make a proper figure of one's town house.

It is not sensible to look for a single governing principle for choosing to come to London or to occupy a West End house, for the choice of house, or for its use, in respect of a given group or class, particularly in the absence of any apparent general correlation between rank of person and house. Nevertheless, it is clear that the London house had a particular attraction and meaning for women and that associations of the house with women stemmed from a variety of real and imagined links. On the other hand, men also had more reason than ever to be in town, for politics, patronage, business, pleasure and society. The male landowner's relationship with his town house was set in the context of his estate ownership. The differences in attitude to the two houses, town and country, and the use that was made of them can be telling. Certainly, assumptions about the length of time spent in town prove to be an insufficient explanation for why members of the nobility and the upper gentry 'settled' for a terrace house. In fact some uses might suggest that they would have preferred a much bigger, freestanding house. I therefore explore in the remainder of this book, particularly Chapters Three and Four, other reasons why a house in a row or square served their purposes.

A good West End house was fundamental to making a proper figure, or cultivating an image generally – for men and women alike. But the ultimate objectives of such common uses varied from group to group, and person to person. Entertainment, whether on an ambitious or a modest scale, was often an important function of the town house, but it was neither the house's sole purpose nor the root of everyone's satis-

1 (left) 'First Rate' house, classified according to floor area and cost, as prescribed in the Building Act of 1774, Baker Street.

2 (below) Robert Adam, Home House, 20 Portman Square, laid-out wall elevations for back parlour, c.1776.

3 Royal Terrace, Adelphi, Robert and James Adam, begun 1768, view of the south front from Robert and James Adam, *The Works in Architecture*, vol. 3, 1822, plate 1.

4 Thomas Rowlandson, *Vauxhall Gardens*, undated, watercolour. All sorts contributed to the collective fashionable spectacle at popular venues.

5 (left) Anonymous, *What is this my Son Tom*, published by Sayer & Bennett, 1774, mezzotint. Urban over-refinement and insubstantiality is contrasted unfavourably with the robustness of the country gent.

6 (below) Thomas Rowlandson after Humphry Repton, *1784 or The Fashions of the Day*, published by E. Bull, 1784, etching. Inappropriate gazes and unfashionable inelegance betray some of the promenaders in St James's Park.

What is this my Son Tom.

1784, OR THE FASHIONS OF THE DAY.

The BUTCHERS WIFE dressing for the PANTHEON

7 (left) Philip Dawe, *The Butcher's Wife Dressing for the Pantheon*, published by W. Humphrey, 1772, mezzotint. No amount of fashionable trim can help the tradesman's wife who tries to get above her proper station.

8 (below) Anonymous, *The City Rout*, published by M. Darly, 1776, etching. Satirists denied the existence of refinement in the City, no matter how hard its inhabitants tried to look sophisticated.

THE CITY ROUT.

9 (left) After H. Gravelot, *Exeter Exchange*, 1762. A wide range of goods was available for perusal in fashionable shopping locations.

10 (right) R. Dighton, *A Morning Ramble; or The Milliner's Shop, c.*1782, pen and ink and wash. Boxes labelled 'love' and 'coxcomb' reveal the dual purpose of these gentlemen's shopping excursion.

The FARMER'S DAUGHTER'S return from LONDON.

Published 14 June 1777 by W. Humphrey Gerrard Street Soho.

11 Anonymous, *The Farmer's Daughter's Return from London*, published by W. Humphrey, 1777, etching. Even the farmer's daughter has her head turned by London, but there is no room for metropolitan fashions in the honest country home.

12 Derby House, 26 Grosvenor Square, Robert Adam, 1773–4, view of the great drawing room, engraving by B. Pastorini from Robert and James Adam, *The Works in Architecture*, vol. 2, 1779, part 1, plate 5.

13 Portland Place, Robert and James Adam, *c*.1777–80, view from Thomas Malton, *A Picturesque Tour*, vol. 1, 1792, plate 88.

14 Robert Adam, 20 Soho Square, London, design for the new elevation, 1771–2.

à la Zodiaque

15 (left) *A la Zodiaque*, 1777, from the *Lady's Magazine*. Any theme could inspire a fashionable hairdo.

16 (below) Richard Newton, *September in London – all our Friends out of Town!!!*, published by W. Holland, 1791, hand-coloured etching. An absence of patrons out of season left some ladies with nothing to do but pawn their fashionable garments.

September in London — all our Friends out of Town!!!

THE EXTRAVAGANZA .
OR THE MOUNTAIN HEAD DRESS OF 1776.

17 (left) Anonymous, *The Extravaganza* or *The Mountain Head Dress of 1776*, published by M. Darly, 1776, etching.

A Side Box at the Opera.

18 (right) H. Kingsbury, *A Side Box at the Opera*, 1792. Architecture and fashion make a coordinated display at the opera.

19 *Frederick Elegantly Furnishing a Large House*, c.1782, etching and engraving with hand colouring.

20 James Lewis, elevation of three houses built in Great Ormond Street, from *Original Designs in Architecture*, 1780, plate 7.

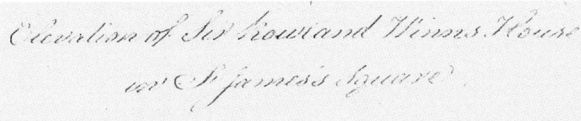

21 (left) Robert Adam,
11 St James's Square,
design for the elevation,
c.1774.

22 (below) James Adam,
Portland Place, design for
the main block, west side,
1776.

23 Robert and James Adam, Wynn House, 20 St James's Square, south elevation of the wall in the back court, 1771–4, illustrated in Robert and James Adam, *The Works in Architecture*, vol. 2, 1779, part 2, plate 3.

24 George Dance the younger (and James Peacock?), Finsbury Square, begun 1777, west side, in an early nineteenth-century watercolour.

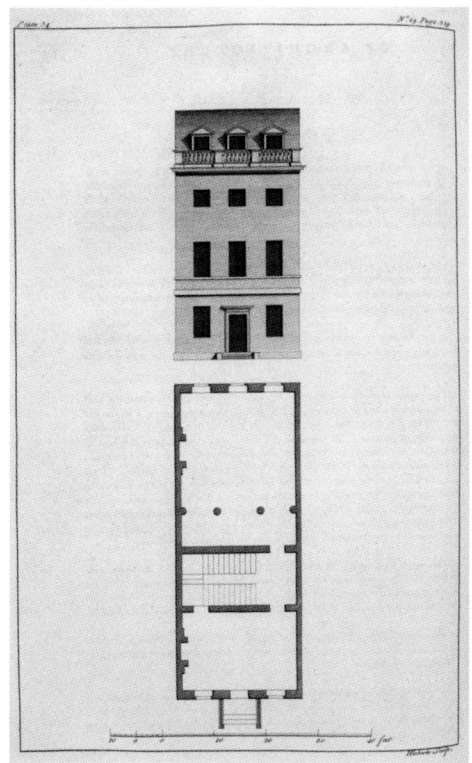

25 (left) Isaac Ware, design for a basic town house, from *Complete Body of Architecture*, 1756, plate 34.

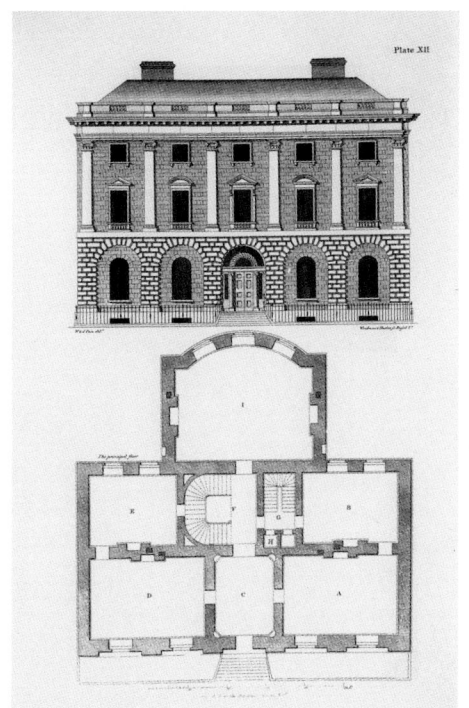

26 (right) William and James Pain, design for a town house, from *Pain's British Palladio*, 1786, plate 12.

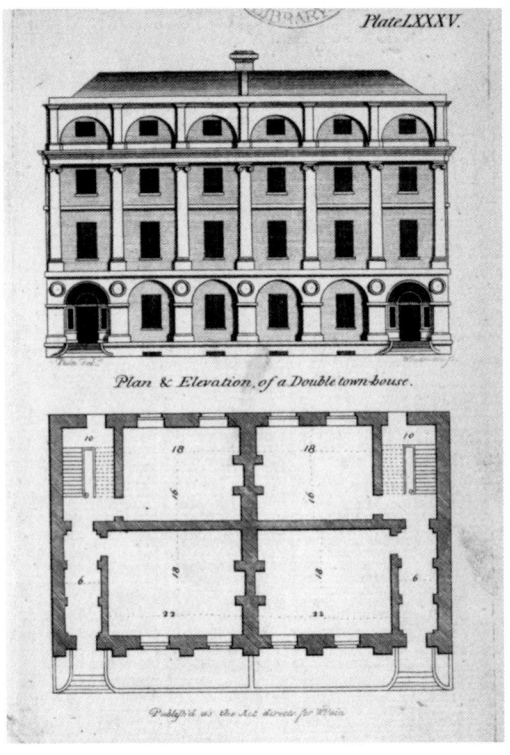

27 (left) William Pain, plan and elevation of a double town house, from *The Builder's Golden Rule*, 1781, plate 85.

28 (below) William Pain, plans, elevation and section of a house, from *The Practical House Carpenter*, 1794, plate 116.

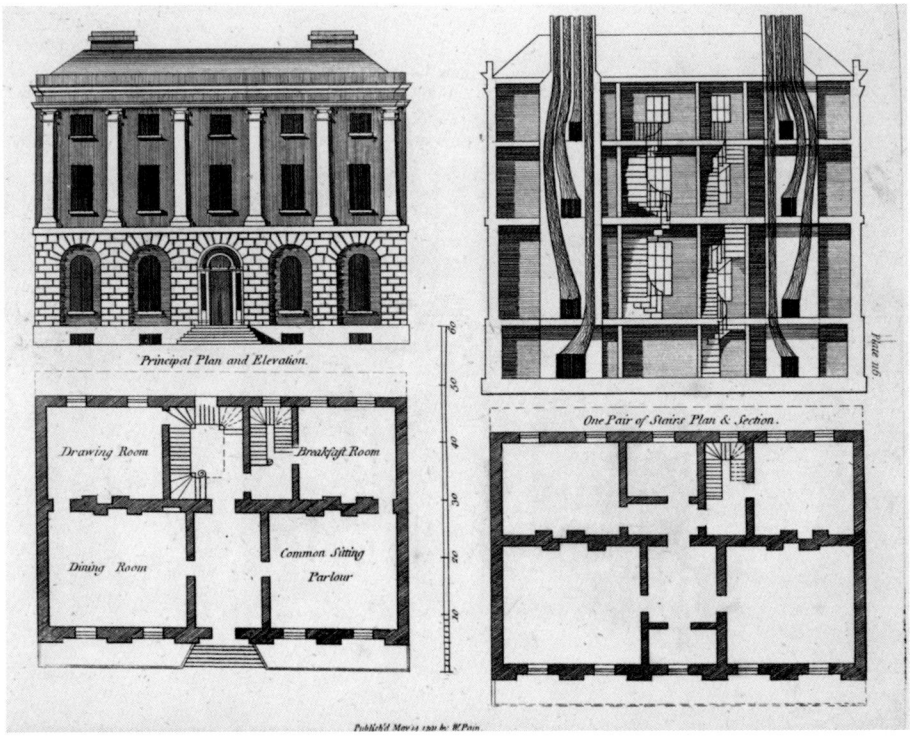

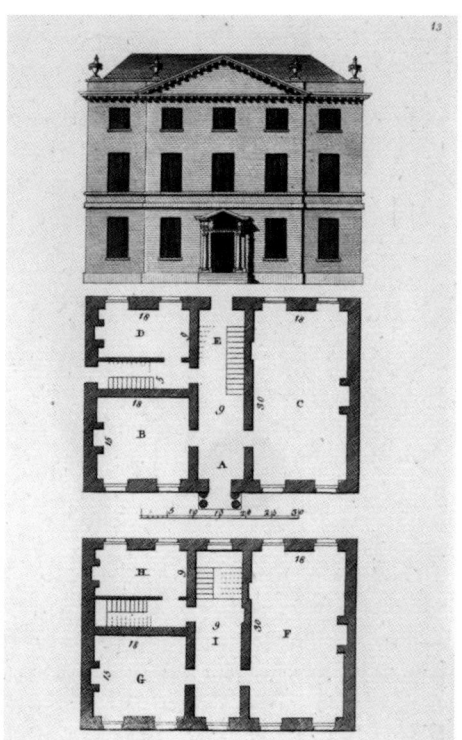

29 (left) John Crunden, plans and elevation for a five-bay town house, from *Convenient and Ornamental Architecture*, 1767, plate 13.

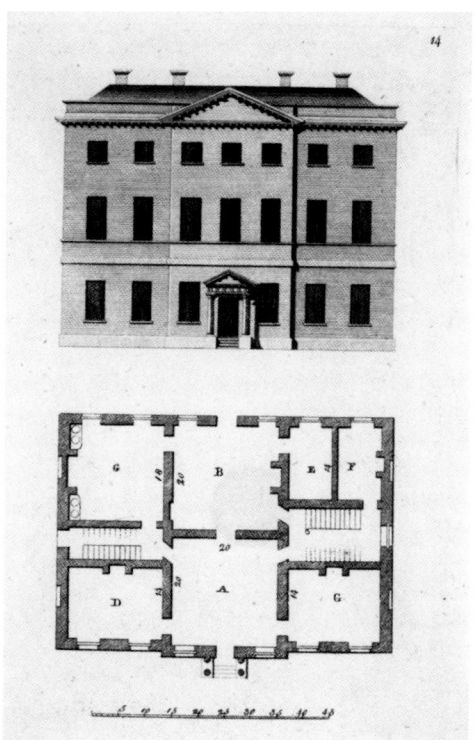

30 (right) John Crunden, plan and elevation for a seven-bay town house, from *Convenient and Ornamental Architecture*, 1767, plate 14.

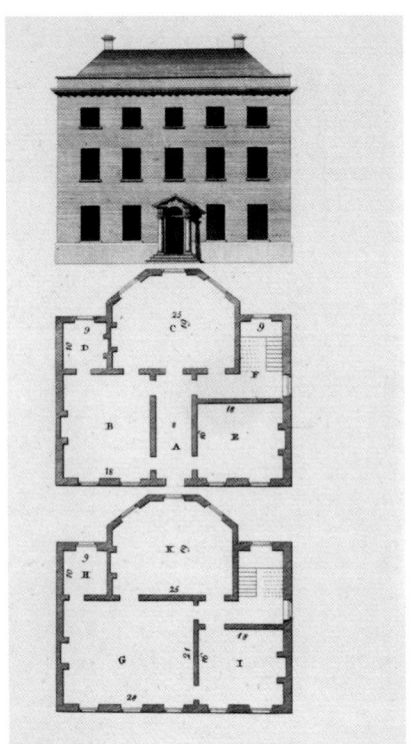

31 (left) John Crunden,
plans and elevation for a
town or country house, from
*Convenient and Ornamental
Architecture*, 1767, plate 19.

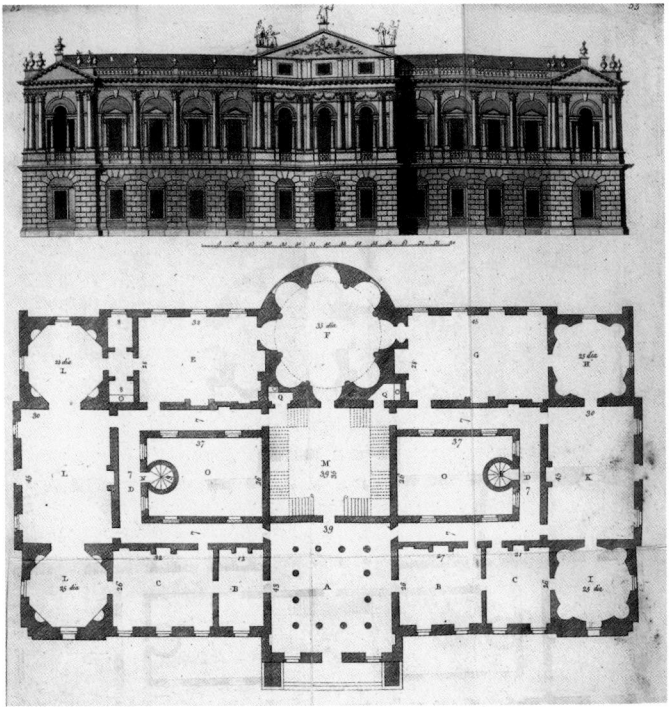

32 (right) John Crunden,
plan and elevation for a
mansion for either town or
country, from *Convenient
and Ornamental
Architecture*, 1767, plate 53.

faction in it. In fact, sometimes the attraction was the house itself. A broader understanding of the uses, values and appeal of the town house is the essential context for studying its form and finish.

There is necessarily some overlap between what the resident intended by his or her town-house occupancy and the house itself and what others read into them, but subjective and objective expectations and perceptions of the house were not always wholly in agreement. In 1765, for example, General Robert Clerk described the role of the town house as a place

> where a man of property can act a part in publick affairs in opposition to the Court or with the Court against popular violences . . . [T]ranquillity, quietness, retirement when one pleases, with real dignity are the proper qualities in a house for [a man of property].[157]

The particular qualities sought and embodied in town houses were not always those Clerk recommended, but his implication that the town house did much more than simply allow someone to maintain a presence in town was more broadly relevant. Clerk's model was Burlington House, a seventeenth-century mansion on Piccadilly, remodelled after 1717, and few town houses were ever on that scale. Nevertheless, it is significant that Clerk saw the house itself, and not just the owner's presence in London, as integral to acting one's part. Some roles were facilitated by town-house occupancy, but the most important 'prop' was the house itself.

Two

Owning, Using, Passing On

The ins and outs of property ownership and transmission may seem a little anticlimactic at this point after so many tales of elegance and intrigue in the West End, but they are an essential part of the fuller picture of the London town house. The world of wills and settlements offers an easily overlooked insight into how houses were both valued and used for a variety of less obvious purposes which were in no way revealed by their form and finish.

The leasehold house occupied an ambiguous place between real estate and chattels, falling into the legal category of chattels-real, midway between real property and personal or moveable property. Like realty, it had a fixed location – but then again it was not inalienable; like personalty, it was alienable – but it was not moveable. Its ambiguous status means that it has subsequently fallen between two stools in the abundant literature on eighteenth-century property ownership, acquisition and transmission, which tends to focus on realty, with a central role for the country house and estate, or on moveable possessions and chattels. In the former category, many writers have considered the country house as a form of property, its function in this respect within the immediate family unit and the means of its acquisition, legal protection and disposal.[1] Yet such issues have never been formally raised in respect of the West End house in this period, which is left shuffling its feet outside the discourse of the literature of property and consumption.

The town house's status as a distinct property type, quite different from the freehold country house, impinged on various aspects of its treatment: its acquisition, use, disposal and, not least, its architectural form and finish. Yet the literature on the architecture and planning of eighteenth-century London considers the leasehold status of the town house, the main form of property ownership in London at that time, more as part of the tale of speculative development, and less as a characteristic of the individual house and the leaseholder's relation to it. This chapter explores the specific nature of the London house as a type of property and shows how the house was often central to personal or familial financial and legal transactions among the landed classes. The chapter also accounts further for the strong links between women and town houses, created in this instance particularly through inheritance strategies benefiting widows. But it discovers, too, efforts to devise the house as if it were freehold property, in a pattern imitative of male primogeniture more usually associated with the country house and estate.

The leasehold town house can be compared and contrasted not only to the freehold country house, but also to other forms of property, particularly the intangible forms gaining prominence and influence by this time, such as stocks and bonds, in practical as well as philosophical terms. I consider the place of leasehold property, and the town house in particular, in the web of new property types that was spun more elaborately during this period, and explore the connotations and the obligations attached both in theory and practice to the ownership of a West End house.

One of the town house's property attributes was that it was commonly a market commodity, freely bought and sold; a characteristic less typical of the family country house, which was generally (although not universally) retained within the family and transmitted to other family members outside of the market framework. Nonetheless, the town house could play its own role within family concerns, as restrictions were sometimes placed on the disposal of town houses, which featured prominently in wills and other familial legal transactions. In their study of property and inheritance in eighteenth- and nineteenth-century British towns, Alastair Owens and Jon Stobart argue that research into inheritance, and other property transmission outside the market, can offer fresh insights into the significance of property. The study of inheritance, they suggest, not only 'provides a glimpse of the material goods that people possessed', but also discloses 'something of the significance of these possessions to their owners and kin'. By its very nature, inheritance emphasises the social aspects of ownership: 'it exposes the social networks within which property as a "thing" took on meaning and significance'.[2] When balanced by other approaches, the study of inheritance strategies and patterns in respect of the West End house can therefore be revealing of the house's meaning to individuals and families.

Property, personality and obligation

The leasehold town house did not come with land, and the consequent political, financial and social power; nor was it in itself, as the country house was, an emblem of land ownership, although it could be a marker of wealth or success in various spheres, of which land ownership might be one. The security afforded by the country house and estate was grounded, firstly, in the unequivocal and immutable nature of the freehold property, enhanced by the legal restrictions placed on its disposal and, secondly (and related), in the property's close association with family, in which context each successive owner's identity was firmly set. Even a freehold London house in an aristocratic enclave could not offer such certainty and invulnerability, and in *Cecilia* (1782) Frances Burney explains why the 'imperious' Mr Delvile, younger brother of a peer, was more secure and therefore more supportable at his rural castle than in his house in St James's Square. In the former

> he looked around him with a pride of power and possession which softened while it swelled him. His superiority was undisputed, his will without controul [sic]. He was not, as in the great capital of the kingdom, surrounded by competitors; no rivalry disturbed his peace, no equality mortified his greatness.[3]

The country house and estate were cause, effect and symbol of financial security, national political authority, local superiority and power, long-standing family connections with the land, and the prospect of the continuance of all of these for the future. The family seat and estate ideally, and perhaps most usually, passed in its entirety from generation to generation, largely untouched by the fluctuating values of the market – although we cannot say for certain, in the absence of extensive research into inheritance and other property transmission patterns in respect of country estates, the extent to which the ideal was adhered to in practice.

The town house, on the other hand, was more likely to be the home of an individual member, or one subset, of a family. The wider family group associated with the country seat was often splintered in town, with younger brothers, younger sons, and sometimes wives, going their own way into separate properties, even if they remained close neighbours. As such, the town house was generally personal rather than family property, more akin to chattels than to real estate, and could therefore often be retained or disposed of according to its owner's fancy or their practical and financial needs.

The house's leasehold status also gave it links with intangible property forms. While there were simple and incontrovertible differences between types of property, there was no simple divide between the spheres in which they operated, and West End houses were implicated in the kind of web of real and intangible property that characterised the whole century. The realms of old and new property and attitudes to money increasingly overlapped and the town house fell into this area of overlap in several respects. Firstly, most of the larger London estates on which the town house stood were entailed or held in trust, a traditional pattern of ownership and inheritance that facilitated the way of living that fell outside it by largely preventing London householders from being freeholders. Secondly, the process of developing these estates relied on investment and speculation, and the growing importance of leasehold ownership, particularly prevalent in London, represented a way of making land and property more alienable and commercially viable.[4] Thirdly, the demand for houses, which led to such development, arose not only because dealings in both real property and intangibles brought landowners to town, but also because the lavish West End house was a means of making visible the riches acquired by financiers and others through a range of speculations.

The fourth and final way in which the spheres of old and new property types overlapped was in the mortgaging or sale of land in the country to finance a house in town. According to both contemporary witnesses and modern consensus, most land-owning dynasties prized their country property, particularly the principal family estate, over their individual town houses, but the value of different property types at any given time was often a matter of individual perspective. Sir Watkin Williams Wynn sold off some of his land assets in 1775 to help fund the purchase and rebuilding of 20 St James's Square. At the same time, his agent suggested that he should buy some available lands in Montgomeryshire, for the sake of political power, or at least security, but the baronet was willing to relinquish the certain power associated with extensive land-ownership in favour of the social power promised by a distinguished town residence.[5]

The leasehold house's property status and character were therefore as ambiguous as the country house's were clear. The town house, deeply embedded in the market economy, had more correspondence and affiliation with mobile than with real property. It was not burdened (or credited) with the connotations and obligations of land ownership. It did not contribute to the nation's wealth, standing and security, nor did it foster coincidence of its owner's outlook and the national interest, as the country estate was understood to.[6] But, by virtue of its location in the West End, it did bring obligations of its own.

The West End house sat in the most public of arenas and drew its occupants into the particular community of Westminster dwellers. Membership of that public was sometimes formalised by the payment of rates and duties, including Riot Duty.[7] In this respect, the town house held its occupiers accountable to the public good. But the need to express civic virtue was also evoked in less formal, if no less mandatory ways. For example, the practice of illuminating houses as a demonstration of national interest and pleasure in major events, such as naval victories, made it impossible for the householder to shy away from involvement in public displays. Sir William Bagot wrote from Upper Brook Street in February 1779, 'I have had the honour of illuminating my house for three nights already, for Adl Keppel's Victory: & suppose I shall be obliged to do so again tonight to save my windows.'[8] In the same month, Philip Francis's wife recorded in the journal she kept for her absent husband,

> Just as we were going to bed before eleven comes a great mob in the street and calls for Lights in every House. We accordingly did as our neighbours did – lighted up Flambeaux and tied them to the Rails outside the House; all this rejoicing was for Admiral Keppel and those who were against him and would not illuminate had all their windows broke to pieces.[9]

March 1789 saw a particularly patriotic display on the occasion of George III's 'recovery' from a severe bout of the illness that periodically troubled both him and the state. Sir Gilbert Elliot reported to his wife that

> The town was illuminated yesterday with a good deal of magnificence. Many houses had devices of different sorts executed in coloured lamps and transparent paintings . . . The prevailing devices were prodigiously ingenious – namely G. R with a crown in the middle, God save the King, etc. We agreed in Park Street to light up only to the street, but the mob chose it also to the Park, and John not being expeditious enough, I had a pane of plate-glass broke in the library window . . . The Queen certainly drove about London to see the illuminations.[10]

The town house allowed the display of support or allegiance, although a householder's choice in this respect was limited by the threat of violent punishment to the house itself.

The town house of a public figure was an accessible face in which the disgruntled populace readily spat. During the Gordon Riots of 1780 the mob burned Lord Mansfield's house in Bloomsbury Square 'quite to the Ground, not a single Paper or one bitt of Furniture saved'.[11] In 1763, Lady Bute reportedly laughed 'as if she enjoyed the joke when stones came hurtling through the window of her bedroom in South Audley Street', one of many public responses to her husband's unpopularity as prime minister.[12] Glass was often targeted by the mob not just for the inherent satisfaction of hearing it shatter, but also because good glass was a status symbol and object of envy.[13] This particularly destructive way of registering disapproval provided employment not just for glaziers but for architects and other members of the building trade. For example, John Johnson reconstructed Sir Hugh Palliser's house in Pall Mall, after the mob gutted it in 1778 in celebration of the popular hero Admiral Keppel's acquittal at a court-martial instigated by Palliser.[14]

The West End house therefore had an extraordinary mix of property characteristics. Although immoveable, it was closer to moveable, intangible property and chattels than to the freehold country house. It generally served personal rather than national or family interests. Yet not only did its position in the West End draw public attention to, and make demands on this non-territorial, private property, but a house could also be drawn into a web of family interests.

Putting property ownership to use

The town house could serve abstract financial functions, in addition to practical ones, including its use as a means to fund or guarantee payments, which will be discussed in this section. Land was the best security for loans and was readily mortgaged in this period. By means of the equity of redemption, the landed were able to borrow against their real estate without really risking its loss to the family.[15] Newspaper advertisements for money-lending services were aimed at those with a secure grip on landed property, such as 'the Nobility, Gentry and other persons in possession of estates or yearly incomes for life, having occasion to raise a temporary sum of money'.[16]

In practice, however, the town house was often used as security for raising money in the present or guaranteeing its availability in the future, and it was easier for a creditor to take possession of, should things come to that. In 1769, the Duke of Buccleuch borrowed £10,000 plus interest at 5 per cent from the Earl of Westmoreland, and a further £3,000 in 1772, on freehold and leasehold properties in Orange Court, Orange Street and Grosvenor Square.[17] In 1774, the Duke of Leeds mortgaged his St James's Square house and appurtenances to secure £5,000 and interest.[18] The sale or mortgage of a town house may also have been a way of protecting the main freehold estate from being encumbered with debts. In the late 1770s, the 2nd Earl of Ilchester's solicitor was handling the mortgage and sale of the earl's Grosvenor Square house, as well as arrangements for the portions to be provided for the earl's brothers and sisters, presumably in accordance to his father's will.[19] Ilchester certainly did not anticipate relinquishing his house so soon after buying it, as will be shown below. Possibly he had not only bitten off more than he could chew with its purchase, but was also obliged to sell the house to raise the money required to fulfil the legal demands placed on him as his father's heir. As Leonore Davidoff and Catherine Hall explain, mortgaging a country estate meant striking a balance between the 'desire to hand on an unbroken patrimony and to support a variety of dependants'. There were constant pressures to break entail to this end.[20] The town house offered an alternative, additional, or simpler means of raising money and thus became involved in wider family interests than its ownership by an independent family member might suggest.

Ilchester's mortgage is one of several instances in which Grosvenor Square houses were used in this period to raise or guarantee money for legally binding commitments. Edward Walter MP gave his house to his daughter (and heiress) and son-in-law, the 3rd Viscount Grimston, on their marriage in 1774, constituting £8,000 of a £20,000 settlement, as a means of guaranteeing portions for all the younger children of that marriage. The marriage settlement required the trustees to sell the house to realise the requisite funds if Grimston failed to secure the stipulated £5,000 for settling on his children. If he found the means elsewhere, the house would become his, to be left according to his will. To protect the house in its role as security, the settlement required him to do his best to renew the lease at his own expense in the names of the trustees and to keep the property insured against fire. References to the Grosvenor Square house take up the bulk of the thirty-one page marriage settlement, far more than any other property or property type.

At the same time, Grimston was struggling to find money to pay portions due to his siblings and his mother on his father's death, not helped by the latter's debts, including some related to his house in Upper Grosvenor Street. This house and its contents were sold and the proceeds divided between the seven brothers and sisters. The country estate could not always offer such flexibility, and its division among joint heirs was a measure only reluctantly and injuriously adopted. Northbourn Court, near Deal, Kent, for example, was left jointly to the descendants of four daughters, who were so numerous that the property had to be split among them, to the point of destroying the old family seat and selling the materials, the subject of stern criticism from Mrs Elizabeth Carter in 1782: 'They who enjoy the estates of their ancestors, should at least show that respect to the place of their abode, as to let it sink with dignity into a venerable ruin. The heirs of this estate seem to have been singularly careless of every thing prior to their individual selves.'[21] It is unlikely that there was equivalent disapproval when Grimston divided the proceeds of the sale of his father's town house so that all siblings could benefit from the estate. The town house often offered not only practical ease of disposability and therefore divisibility, but also legal and ethical freedom in contrast to the notions of integrity and continuity attached to the country house.

Passing on – the town house in wills and settlements

The country estate was a 'true vehicle of family purpose',[22] providing a sense of identity between generations. The status of the country house as a family property, in both the present and the long term, stems from and is reflected in the legal restrictions typically governing its disposal. Land could be protected from disintegration by hereditary arrangements, such as strict settlements, used to keep estates whole and to sustain family interests over the decades and centuries, and by other means, such as the equity of redemption. The estate was 'not to be squandered on personal pleasure' but held in trust for future generations as the family inheritance.[23] Male primogeniture, by which the principal freehold estate went to the eldest son, or the next male in line, was the predominant bequeathal pattern.

The landed classes generally bequeathed as part of the main estate those things that could be expected to last, or of which the ownership was secure and permanent, such as the country house itself, other real property and plate. Things with a limited life span, either in real terms or in terms of ownership, which were transient, temporary or otherwise susceptible to loss or destruction, such as china, linen, horses, stock or the leasehold town house, were left with or away from the main estate as the testator wished.

The town house was often the most significant item of non-entailed property left in a will. Its ambiguous place in the middle ground between real estate and chattels, or land and mobile property, left it open to disposal according to the whim and needs of its owner, in theory at least. Even though members of the landed classes were likely to have made wills according to the strict rules governing the testamentary disposition (transmission of property by will) of realty, the fact remains that the rules for making wills of personal property, in which category the lease-hold house fell for testamentary purposes, were far less formal,[24] and awareness of the testamentary flexibility of personalty may have encouraged buyers and owners to consider the leasehold house in that category when it suited them. The house may have been attractive for that reason, although to some owners it was a disadvantage that it could not easily be protected from squander or sale, or kept in the family, as discussed below. As already shown, this lack of restriction and protection could be turned to the benefit of the landed estate and help to protect its integrity, particularly when a testator had to make financial provision for a range of close relatives.

Wives, daughters and sisters often received chattels or personal property, which compensated them for their lack of real property.[25] Among the landed classes, at least, the town house was generally the most significant item of personal property left to widows in wills of this period, which very often deal with it first, or nearly first, before any consideration of country houses and estates or other personal property. It appears that a widow of that class inherited her husband's town house almost by right. For example, an ecclesiastical court ruled that Henry Harpur's widow was entitled to his house in Upper Grosvenor Street when he died intestate in 1761.[26] Widows were also often bequeathed the contents of a town house, and sometimes of other houses although they might only be allowed the use and not the property of some durable goods, such as plate, which formed part of the hereditary estate. In 1789, in a manner typical of the time, William Weddell bequeathed his wife the use of his furniture at Newby, Yorkshire, his plate, jewels, pictures, books and carriages, as well as his house in Upper Brook Street, while his eldest son and heirs male inherited his real estate.[27] The bequest of town houses and chattels to wives and daughters is further evidence of the comparability of the two property types, as well as the particular links between widows and London homes.

The bequest of a town house to a widow was ideal for satisfying her lifetime needs, and providing an element of continuity and security, while not affecting the wider interests of the male inheritance pattern. Rights of dower, entitling widows to a third of a late husband's real property owned at any time in the marriage, were increasingly unpopular because they interfered with the integrity of the estate.[28] Their progressive disappearance prior to this period may explain why widows were so often left town houses by this time, often as part of a marriage settlement, although any connection between declining rights of dower and bequests of town houses to widows would be difficult to verify, for two reasons. Firstly, it would be necessary to determine the pattern of disposal prior to the decline and disappearance of rights of dower, and, secondly, town-house ownership was less prevalent in earlier periods thereby making any comparison difficult. Research relating to Grosvenor Square and its principal neighbouring streets in the immediately preceding period (the reign of George II, 1727–60) shows not only a very high proportion of widows among the ratepayers on the estate, but also confirms that most of them had acquired their house on the death of their husband.[29] Sometimes, a widow received instead a specified sum with which to rent or buy a house of her choice. For example, in 1772 Lord Albemarle was reported to have left £400 a year to his wife for that purpose as his house in Berkeley Square, as well as its furniture, was to be sold.[30]

Testators often placed their town house in trust for their widow, giving her the right to 'enjoy' the property in her lifetime, but not always, without difficulty, to sell it and buy an alternative house. 'Enjoyment' usually implied, however, profiting from rental income, if the widow preferred country life or a different town house.[31] The instructions for Richard Benyon's will of 1781 include a marginal note that says, 'It is Mr Benyon's intention that in case Mrs Benyon shall not chuse to Reside and Make Use of the Town House [in Grosvenor Square] that it shall be Let . . . for her benefit.'[32] In 1786, the Dowager Duchess of Ilchester took legal advice from several quarters on whether she was bound to keep the house in Old Burlington Street left to her by her late husband, the 1st Earl.[33] A house left in trust would usually revert to the normal male inheritance pattern if the widow died, and sometimes if she remarried. Sir Richard Lyttleton left his house in Piccadilly and its contents to his wife for life, after which both were to be sold and the proceeds divided between his brother and his nephew.[34] A house could therefore be successively a home for a widow and a financial legacy. Sir Henry Harpur's son, also Sir Henry, left his town house and other chattels for his widow's use unless she remarried, in which case the house would go directly to his son and heirs.[35] A second husband who survived the widow might have no claim on her town house where she had only held it for life: the bequest of a house to a widow was sometimes only a temporary step out of the normal male inheritance path.

A house might pass on to a son and heir, either as a condition of a husband's original bequest, or by a widow's own will, although women sometimes passed houses to daughters or other female relatives. For example, the unmarried Lady Isabella Finch originally left the lease of her house in Berkeley Square in trust for her nieces until they were 'of an age to enjoy it'.[36] David Green suggests that the significance of women's bequests to daughters and nieces 'can be interpreted partly as a way of providing a portion sufficient to secure unmarried women an advantageous match, and partly as an attempt to provide for their independence'.[37] A London house, or financial provision for one, perhaps fostered both the independence and the match.

Marriage settlements, which replaced rights of dower, often, like Lord Grimston's, included provision of or for a town house, either at the time of marriage or in the event of the bride's widowhood. In 1762, Charles Bunbury's father reportedly promised that he would give him, on marriage, houses in town and country in addition to an estate of £2,000 a year,[38] while the trustees of the 2nd Earl of Dartmouth's marriage settlement were empowered to spend £5,000 on the purchase of a house in Westminster or within the Bills of Mortality, and contracted the builders of the newly rebuilt No. 1 St James's Square for that sum in June 1757.[39] When Viscount Beauchamp, later 2nd Marquess of Hertford, married for the second time in 1776, the settlement included 'A house in Stanhope Street, leased from the Dean and Chapter of Westminster . . . assigned to them for their lives',[40] while his sister's marriage settlement, drawn up the previous year, included a house in Arlington Street.[41]

My evidence that houses were very often left to widows is drawn principally from wills of members of established land-owning dynasties who were resident in Grosvenor Square, St James's Square and the main streets around them, which were the traditional haunts of such families. There is other, conflicting evidence that must be mentioned here, however. The wills of some newcomers to the landed classes, resident in the same aristocratic enclaves, suggest that such men left town houses to their eldest sons, rather than to widows, in a more direct method of what I shall call 'dynastic' disposal; that is, the bequest of a house to another family member, and particularly its direct or indirect passing from generation to generation. The two Richard Benyons, father and son, successive owners of a Grosvenor Square house, belonged to this group, as did Thomas Brand of The Hoo, Hertfordshire, who left his house in St James's Square to his son of the same name.[42] Sir John Boyd, who owned a country villa as well as a town house, left his Grafton Street house to his son in 1784.[43] On the other hand, evidence from lists of residents in some of the main streets of Marylebone in this period – that is, in newer areas less dominated by the presence of the landed classes – suggests that few owners of any class passed houses to either wives or sons, as apparently unrelated occupiers succeed them in the ratebooks.[44] The sources studied therefore indicate but do not necessarily confirm a correlation between residents' class origins, or their places of residence in London, and their approaches to property transferral and disposal.

It is worth mentioning, too, that the practice of bequeathing a house to a widow for life is neither unusual nor specific to either London or this class. Research into bequests among other classes in other times and places confirm this as a familiar inheritance strategy, even if the rationale behind it may have varied. Similarly, eighteenth-century London was not the only place where leasehold houses were used as a means of generating a form of provision for women and dependents.[45] Nevertheless, knowledge of these practices in this period adds to our understanding of the meaning and uses of the West End house, particularly among those classes whose principal residence was in the country, and who had some element of choice in acquiring a London house or not. The purchase of a house in town was a positive decision, and in some cases it was made specifically to make this sort of provision for a widow, or against other anticipated financial needs. In this respect, the practices of the landed classes in this period and place are distinctive.

Whether widows or elder sons were the initial beneficiaries, a freehold house offered the greatest potential for a dynastic approach to property bequests. It could be left to later generations without restriction and tied into strict settlements. Unsurprisingly, many of the freehold houses in St James's Square remained in families for decades or even centuries. The earls of Dartmouth owned No. 1 St James's Square for 87 years and occupied it for most of that time. The Boscawen family owned and largely occupied No. 2 from 1752 to 1923; while in 1720 the Duke of Cleveland bought No. 19 as a new house, which stayed in the family until 1894.[46] Otherwise, the freehold house displayed the same flexibility for disposal and division as the leasehold house, although its guarantees were potentially perpetual. In his will of 1781, Sir Peircy Brett left his freehold house in Great Marlborough Street to his wife for the rest of her life; then in trust for the use of his daughter for her life, then in trust to secure income for a succession of heirs in the normal pattern of male primogeniture, from his eldest grandson downwards. The trustees had the option to sell the house and other freehold property and invest instead in public funds or government securities for the same purpose: even the freehold town house could offer financial versatility.

It is difficult to say what advantages a freehold house had other than the potential to be retained indefinitely in a family's ownership. Perhaps such security sometimes encouraged high levels of investment in the fabric and finish of a house. When he spent around £40,000[47] on his new home in St James's Square between 1771 and 1775 – an exceptionally large amount for a three-bay terrace house – Sir Watkin knew that only the financial means to support it were necessary to keep the property in his family for ever. But whether this awareness loosened his purse strings is impossible to say. Certainly, a century earlier, Lord St Albans had made his petition to the king regarding the original scheme for grand palaces in St James's Square on the basis that 'men will not build Palaces upon any term but that of inheritance',[48] but few people were interested in building 'grand palaces' in the second half of the eighteenth century. Neither did contemporary newspaper advertisements place any special emphasis on a property's freehold status, and the active market in renting, buying and selling town houses, discussed in Chapter Three, suggests that many people had no great interest in the long-term outlook that freehold property could offer them.

Inheritance of a freehold house was not always welcome, in any case. The 3rd Duke of Grafton inherited from his grandfather a house in Bond Street, where much of the Grafton town property was situated. The bequest came with the proviso that the house must pass along the male line in strict settlement to be linked with the title 'Duke of Grafton', and placed the onus on the 3rd duke to do his utmost to uphold his grandfather's wishes. But although the house itself was freehold, the stables were leasehold, and the lease that expired in 1766 could not be renewed. The duke's representatives argued that the house would 'thereby be rendered very incommodious and unfit for the said [duke] to reside in' and he could not, therefore, fulfil the intentions of the will. An Act of Parliament was necessary to allow Grafton to sell the freehold property, on the understanding that the Bank of England would mind and pay interest on the proceeds until a property suitable to answer the purposes of the will could be purchased.[49]

Permanency and the leasehold house were not mutually exclusive. Many such houses, whether initially left to a widow or not, were kept within the family at least for the duration of the existing lease and sometimes for much longer. Lord Clive's house at 45 Berkeley Square stayed in his family from his purchase of the property in 1760 until the 1930s, while the neighbouring house, No. 46, was the London home of the earls of Darnley from 1745 to 1835.[50] Some testators went to great lengths to try to keep a house in the family even into the unforeseeable future, though leasehold property did not lend itself to long-term planning because it could not be protected or bequeathed with the same assurance as freehold property. For example, Lady Isabella Finch requested her trustees, when there was the money and the opportunity, to purchase the 'Inheritance forever of the Ground whereon my said House . . . and Appurtenances now stand.' If it could not be purchased then the trustees were to renew the lease 'for a further term of Years on the same terms that other Tenants do that hold Leases under the said Lord Berkeley of

Stratton for their House in Berkeley Square'.[51] Some owners tried their hardest to put their house on a par with their country estate, in hereditary terms, by protecting it from sale and ensuring its transference to male heirs. The two Richard Benyons made successive changes to their wills, in which their Grosvenor Square house played a key part. Richard junior changed his will between 1781 and 1789, with the result that the house was not simply left to his widow for her life, but was afterwards to be held in trust for his son and heir in the same manner as his country estate was devised or as near as the law would allow, given that it was a leasehold property. Benyon gave his trustees the power to renew the lease; that is, to take money out of his estate to ensure that this property remained within it.[52] Through Benyon's will, the leasehold property thereby attained, as near as possible, parity with the country seat.

A bequest could only take effect, of course, if the testator had kept hold of the house. The 2nd Lord Ilchester's widow would have received his town house (in trust) by his will of 1778, if he had not sold it soon after the will was drawn up.[53] No doubt other houses, too, fell prey to the immediate need to realise assets, before any long-term dynastic ambitions could be served, but this was the very essence and advantage of the town house's duality.

Treating the house in the manner of a freehold estate, or as an heirloom passing from generation to generation to male heirs via widows, was the more formal of two basic ways in which a family interest in a property was maintained. The alternative was a pattern of occupancy or ownership that reflected a broader notion of family, in which the house passed to mothers-in-law, sons-in-law, cousins, nieces, nephews and so on, or was owned and occasionally occupied by the family but used to generate rent rather than to promote more abstract family interests. In 1763, the Dowager Duchess of Beaufort succeeded her son-in-law, the 7th Earl of Northampton at 33 Grosvenor Square, and then moved to Grosvenor Street in 1768, taking the house formerly occupied by his brother, the 8th Earl.[54] From 1744, 43 Grosvenor Square passed from the 5th Baron Maynard to his brother, the 6th Baron, later 1st Viscount Maynard, and then to the latter's third cousin, Sir William Maynard, 4th baronet, and then to *his* son, the 2nd Viscount Maynard. After being let to other parties, the property came back into the occupancy of the 2nd Viscount, who in turn left it to his nephew.[55] A house was sometimes passed on to another family member by sale, or even by simply letting them know that the lease or tenancy was available. In 1784, Lady Louisa Stuart reported that 'Miss Herbert . . . has sold the lease of her house to her cousin Neville, and has his leave to live in it till Christmas into the bargain, so is no longer upon the *pavé*.'[56] The disposal of a house could sometimes frustrate a relative who had hopes of the option of buying or renting, if not inheriting it. In 1772, a disappointed young man teased his aunt for not looking far enough into his bright future, writing from Calcutta: 'Julia has mentioned in one of her L^{rs} that you have left your house in Great Russell Street. I thought it was intended to have been kept for me against I come home a Rich Nabob'.[57] Much of the impetus for retaining a house within the broader family did not derive from dynastic ambitions for it, but from a general preference for good and familiar accommodation.

The diverse legal and financial functions of the town house and the ways in which it could contribute to broader family interests are nicely summarised in the history of one individual in this period, Lewis Watson, 1st Baron Sondes, heir to the Rockingham estates. In 1736, the 2nd Earl of Rockingham bought a house in Grosvenor Square in compliance with a marriage agreement,[58] which gave the house to his wife for life, if she survived him, and then to his heirs male. On his death in 1745 the house passed to his childless widow, who remarried in 1751 to become Lady Guilford. On her death in 1766 the house passed to Sondes, Rockingham's cousin. The parties to Rockingham's marriage settlement had ensured that, after the practical matter of his widow's accommodation was taken care of, the house was retained in his family and with the main estates, no matter how tenuous the link with the next male heir, and regardless of the fact that Lady Guilford's second husband survived her. Sondes's own marriage settlement, drawn up in 1752, had assigned to his wife, on trust, his reversionary interest in the Grosvenor Square house, in the event of his death, even though he would only own the property when Lady Guilford's interest in it expired with her.

The Grosvenor Square house is the focus of many legal documents among Sondes's extant papers. In his will of 1781, after the death of his wife, he bequeathed it to his son. However, it was taken away from him prematurely through his son's marriage settlement of 1785, in which the bride's father offered a portion of £10,000 for his daughter on Sondes's undertaking 'to give up the house in Grosvenor Square with the Plate Jewells and Furniture there' and assign the same to his son. Sondes required the permission of the trustees of his own marriage settlement in order to reassign the property to his son and heir. The new settlement also required Sondes to 'procure a Renewal of the Lease if in his Power at his own Expense'. His son's interest in the house was thereby assured at least for his lifetime, although in practice he preferred the house's financial to its domestic or symbolic attributes, leasing it out to a series of well-placed tenants. The case of the Rockingham/Sondes house in Grosvenor Square shows how, through restrictions imposed by trusts, the interests of two (and subsequently more) generations of widows were balanced against the retention of the house in the male line.

Where a house was free from legal restraints, an owner could dispose of it as he chose. After handing the Grosvenor Square house over to his eldest son, Sondes rented and then bought the lease of a property in Berkeley Square, which he left to his two younger sons, together with other personal property, including the furniture and effects in it and 'all his ready Money Securities for Monies in the Public Stocks and Funds'.[59] Clearly, the house previously untouched by wills and settlements had more in common with chattels than with real property, and close links with the financial, speculative nature of intangible property. Like the former, it was personal and disposable; like the latter, it was dissolvable and divisible.

The London town house was a peculiar property type, whose legal and social characteristics, though not well addressed in the literature, are essential to a full understanding of its treatment by and meaning to its occupants, and other, disinterested parties. The evidence emphasises the very public nature of the West End residence and shows how town houses and their owners were sometimes unwittingly caught up in demands for civic responsibility of a type usually associated with the ownership of freehold land. Because the town house lacked the symbolic and legal characteristics of the country house, however, it had the potential to be treated in a variety of ways by its owners and occupants. It was often free from real and ideological restrictions regarding its treatment and disposal, offering its owners a choice as to how they viewed and used it. A good house in a good area had, for example, financial and prestigious values which were relatively more important to different people at different times. Certainly owners did not always take advantage of the town house's disposability, preferring instead to shape it into a familial or patrimonial property. Others kept the house in the broader family because it was convenient to do so – people liked a house they knew.

Many owners attached immense importance to the town house. The built evidence sometimes reveals little or nothing of that importance, but it comes to the fore in an exploration of the house as property type. The town house's extraordinary prominence in legal documents, especially marriage settlements and wills; its role as a guardian, sometimes in a roundabout manner, of various financial and other family interests; and the lengths to which people went to determine patterns of ownership and disposal, all bear witness to a significance among the landed classes far greater than Summerson and others have allowed.

Three

Buying and Affording the
West End House

Despite measures taken by some families to pass it down from generation to generation, it remains a fact that the town house was commonly considered to be a market commodity. The period discussed here accordingly saw an active market in the buying and selling of houses in the West End of London. Documentary and anecdotal evidence about the purchase and sale of houses provides a further insight into the nature of the town house as well as its uses and values to its owners and occupants. In particular, the financial and ultimately social impact of expenditure, and especially over-expenditure in this area, reveals a dangerous but alluring game of risk and reward, gamble and forfeit.

By focusing on individual households and their willingness and ability to engage with the market, we can step back from the global approach, 'which looks at changes in society as a whole and views consumption and property ownership in terms of broadly conceived social and cultural transformations'. Instead, we should focus on 'the scale at which decisions about property acquisition, ownership and disposal were actually made', while also reintroducing 'an important economic dimension to the discussion'.[1] That is, we need to strike a balance between the broader scene and the individual actor within it. Certainly, in order to explain why both exceptional and unexceptional town houses were the way they were, we need to move away from narratives of speculative estate development and modern preconceptions based on the physical evidence of rows of uniform houses, and investigate exactly what it was that people wanted from a London house and how they went about getting it – and to choose our sources accordingly.

Newspaper advertisements and anecdotal sources reveal what people looked for in a town house, making clear the importance of location as well as the practical convenience of good offices and stabling, and how purchasers discriminated between what, to modern eyes, seem to have been basically similar houses. Advertisements support evidence that prospective buyers paid little attention to decorative qualities of houses, both internal and external, at the point of purchase. They show, too, that neither unusual size nor planning contrivances were necessarily an attraction in the regular market; rather they were markers of extraordinary provision in excess of what most people required or could afford.

The many properties advertised for sale by auction suggest a need to dispose of houses quickly, which is surely indicative of sudden changes of mind and fortune. The first four decades of George III's reign saw a sequence of financial crises, both public and private, most notably those of 1772, 1778, 1788, 1793 and 1797.[2] Robert Brettingham ascribed both sorts to the same causes, writing of the banking crisis in 1772 that 'such is the effect of Betting in the Stocks, and the Luxury of the Times – Families living at a Rate beyond their Income to vie with each other in Show and Splendor, when a little more Humility, had sav'd them from the Worst of all distractions Wont and Infamy'.[3] Six years later Mrs Carter was shocked 'to hear almost every day of the explosion of some great fortune'.[4] The decision to reside in London had an inevitable financial impact on the owner, not only buying and owning a house but also the essential and discretionary expense that followed. The West End house functioned as a showroom in that vast marketplace, displaying not just the means but also the taste of its proprietor and his or her suppliers, and remained a spectacle even at the point of its owner's financial failure. Purchasers afforded or alleviated the cost of buying or commissioning a house by various means and often went to considerable lengths to own and finish one to their taste, with concomitant financial risks. The impact of those risks on the person, the house and its designers, builders and finishers was sometimes extreme, and the house became not only the cause but also the target and indicator of debt. Eighteenth-century and modern-day explanations can only partly account for expenditure and over-expenditure on the West End house; the rationale for unaffordable expenditure is to be found in the perceived value of having a 'good house'.

Buying

The increasing numbers of houses expanding the bounds of the West End in the second half of the eighteenth century offered the opportunity for those already in London to move as well as for many newcomers to acquire a West End house. They could choose between a capital outlay on the purchase of a leasehold or freehold house, or taking a house at a set annual rent,[5] with a short-term let or lodgings as an alternative for those intending to be in town only periodically, perhaps for the season. Renting rather than leasing a town house avoided the need to sink personal capital into a property or to raise a lump sum, although it did involve higher annual costs. It also put tenants in a vulnerable position: the shorter the term, the less choice and power they had regarding their accommodation. Renting for the season each year meant taking what one could get each time and a rental agreement might be all but signed when a change in the owner's circumstances led to the house being suddenly unavailable. Mrs Montagu was said to have let her Hill Street house to the Duke of Hamilton in anticipation of leaving for Bath, only to be 'taken with her spasms' and unable to go, 'which will be a distress to ye Duke'.[6] Rental agreements often included an undertaking to vacate the premises before the end of the lease period should the owner require use of the property. The Earl of Hertford, for example, let his Grosvenor Street house to the Duke of Portland for three years from 1763, on the mutual agreement 'that the said Duke of Portland shall quit the said premises in less time than three years if the Earl of Hertford or Lady Hertford should Give Six Months notice for to Occupie the said premises themselves'.[7] Owning a house at least guaranteed accommodation.

If the initial outlay could be afforded and a long-term, if seasonal, London residence was anticipated, buying was also probably the cheaper option. Sir William Bagot, the reluctant Londoner, certainly believed that 'purchasing will in the end be cheapest', although it would make him 'as poor as a Rat for the present'.[8] Bagot, like others, was prepared to suffer in the short term for the long-term benefits and security of house ownership, and spent £1284 13s 8d on doing up his new house,[9] which was a considerable expense for something he claimed not to want. The leasehold of a good house, of the type that features in extant aristocratic and gentry papers, generally cost between £1,500 and £8,000 – comparable at the upper end with the cost of building a modest country house on a smallish estate.[10] Properties at the higher level were likely to be exceptional in size and/or interior finish, in addition to being in a prestigious location. Houses in good squares seem to have attracted a premium, although it is difficult to say whether this was due to location and scarcity or to size, as they tended to be larger. Some valuations included furniture, which, if good and plentiful, could easily double a house's price. The inevitable impact of declining numbers of years on a lease is difficult to quantify.

Rents for good houses in good areas were generally between £100 and £400 per annum, although the range was much wider. A new house in Park Street could be had for seven years at £50 per annum, a smallish house in the Adelphi for £75 and an exceptionally large house in Upper Grosvenor Street for £525.[11] A tenant renting for a shorter period could pay as little as five to six guineas a week, or as much as 300 guineas for four months.[12]

Although it is possible to get a broad picture of property values, as well as the relative merits of buying and renting, it is difficult to compare like with like in terms of location, house size and condition and lease or tenancy length. The length of the lease affected the relative value of paying an annual rent and buying a house, and the calculations involved were as confusing then as they are in retrospect. Mrs Carter admitted as much to Mrs Vesey: 'I am sorry to find the house in Clarges-street is still in suspence', she wrote in 1779, 'yet I think you are perfectly right not to urge the affair. Surely if it lets at ninety pound a year, and is to be sold for eight hundred, the purchase would be much the best bargain. But perhaps I may judge wrong.'[13] Careful calculations were essential to secure a good deal, especially in the face of unscrupulous sellers and landlords.[14]

Having decided to buy or rent, the next task was to find a suitable property. One tactic was to walk out and look for one, or to enlist the help of town-based friends to perform this favour, as William Chambers suggested to Agmondesham Vesey in 1773, when there were plenty of houses available: 'I see bills upon every window & your friend Mr Dunbar who I believe is a Walker might in his Walks perhaps light upon something for you much more eligible.'[15] In 1778, Lady Louisa Stuart hoped that her mother would 'divert herself by looking for a house for Lady Emily, which she desired she might do'.[16] Henry Bridgeman viewed Lady Carpenter's house in Grosvenor Square for Sir William Lee in 1763, knowing what the baronet wanted and recognising how the house in question fell short of it: 'The Rooms are small and bad, and it seems to be very much out of Repair, there are no Stables, and the Offices very bad in general.' He viewed a better prospect in Lower Grosvenor Street belonging to 'Mr Frederick of the Customs' (Sir John Frederick): 'it is to be sold for £5000 and upon my word in my opinion very well worth it. [I]t consists of four rooms on a floor and three staircases; remarkable good offices, and stables for eleven horses.'[17] The combined qualities of good nature and faultless taste meant that Chambers himself was called on by Vesey in 1774 to look out for a rented property for two ladies desiring a house for seven months. The preferred locations were 'Cavendish or Hanover or Berklay [sic] Square or . . . their environs', as the ladies were 'every night of Princess Amelia's party'.[18] Vesey gave Chambers a detailed description of what was required: 'the Sort of house they want must have three bedrooms up two pair of stairs, two rooms on the first floor & room for two Chairs & a good Eating room as the princess often dines with them, the price they propose giving is two hundred and fifty for seven months'. Flattery alone was to induce Chambers to perform this favour: 'the person who builds the most elegant houses, can certainly Chuse the best, & if your taste and politesse have drawn this trouble on you I am not to be call'd to account for this Importunity', wrote Vesey.[19]

Although supply seems generally to have exceeded demand,[20] the more particular a househunter was about accommodation, location and other qualities, and the smaller his budget, the harder it might be to find a house to suit. One very particular advertiser in 1775 sought to rent 'a House unfurnished, of three Rooms, or two Rooms and a Closet on a Floor, in Bolton Row, or the East-side of Clerges [sic] or Half-moon Street, Piccadilly, Rent not to exceed one Hundred Pounds a Year'.[21] In 1779, Robert Mylne spent several days trawling many Westminster streets for a house for Lady St Aubyn, surveying properties in Lower Grosvenor Street and Bond Street, and finally selecting a house in the latter. After a day-long search, Chambers could only find one house 'in the least fit' for the reception and requirements of Vesey's friends.[22] Miss Herbert was prepared to take a house in Edwards Street, Portman Square, despite the evident shortcomings of its accommodation, as described by Louisa Stuart in 1784:

> It would be a very good one . . . only the kitchen is as high as Westminster hall, and fit for any use in the world but that of dress-ing her dinner, and the rooms have all run a race upstairs without any one being able to catch the other, for there are not two exactly upon a floor, and yet no two upon distinct floors. This is her account of it. However, she has it for five and fifty pounds a year. It belongs to an old bachelor with £100,000, and we advised her to take the propri-etor along with the house.

But other factors were less acceptable: Miss Herbert was soon after reported to be 'off her bargain for the house because it is next door to a tallow chandler's'.[23]

Although price was used as a guide to what a person wanted and was prepared to pay, it was not always the final determinant in the choice of a house. Mrs Francis's friends thought that a rent of £200 for a property in Harley Street was more than she could afford, but she believed she could not find a 'tolerable place' to hold her family for anything less. 'I set off again House hunting', she wrote in March 1777, 'but cannot get any thing but at a great Rent, £130 a year is the lowest price and then a very small house, hardly room to put us in'.[24]

The fuss made about finding the right property in a well-stocked market was mocked in the press through fictional accounts of the excess of discrimination applied to the exercise. The newly wed Mrs Heartless, just arrived in town, received plenty of advice from visiting relations:

> One street was recommended for the purity of its air, another for its freedom from noise, another for its nearness to the Park, another because there was but a step from it to all places of diversion and another because its inhabitants enjoyed at once the town and the country.

An even more discriminating friend had 'a fertility of objections' and every day gave 'new testimonies of his taste and circumspection':

> Sometimes the street was too narrow for a double range of coaches; sometimes it was an obscure place, not inhabited by persons of quality. Some places were dirty, and some crowded; in some houses the furniture was ill-suited, and in others the stairs were too narrow.

However, to Peggy Heartless anything was better than the couple's present second-floor lodgings, which were the focus of unwelcome comment from her splendid relatives:

> Lady Stately told us how many years had passed since she climbed so many steps. Miss Airy ran to the window and thought it charming to see the walkers so little in the street; and Miss Gentle went to try the same experiment, and screamed to find herself so far above the ground.[25]

Friends and relations may have helped with finding a house, but they were also the chief critics of the final choice.

Sellers and lessors also needed tactics for finding buyers and tenants. Amongst the upper classes, word of mouth seems to have been the preferred method for getting tenants of the right sort. The advice of Charles Bragge Bathurst to the 5th Duke of Beaufort in 1769 regarding the Beaufort dower house, Stoke, near Bristol, no doubt held true for other property types:

I think it is more likely to fall in[to] good hands if it is only at first mentioned by your Grace to some Friends in Town, for the consequence of applying to the Public in general will be throwing it into the hands of some Wild Creole who are the worst Tenants in the World and will do the Place more damage in one year than seven years rent will repair.[26]

In 1772, William Chambers questioned a client on the character of a prospective tenant for the latter's house:

He says you know him very well. Pray is he a good man according to the mercantile acceptation of the word. Will he pay his rent . . . I shall either let him the House or not according to your Report.[27]

Some landlords were prepared to lose money in the short term for the sake of attracting a quality tenant. It was believed that 'Lord Macartney would have had so much pleasure in having Lord Bruce for his Tenant, that upon such a hope, he would approve of [his representative] deferring for a much longer time to enter upon the engagement for it.'[28] Getting a good tenant was critical, not simply for one's own peace of mind and the protection of one's property, but also to maintain the good profile of the neighbourhood on which the house's marketability depended. The latter also depended on both the owner and the property being known, and liked. Mary Noel doubted her ability to find a tenant for her niece's house:

When I do go out, I see none but old Cats, with whom my dear you know you are no favourite. I have mentioned it in the inquiring way two or three times, & the Constant answer has been *I never saw the inside of it.*[29]

Word of mouth may have been a safe way of letting one's house, but it was not an infallible way of finding a tenant.

William Chambers suggested to Henry Errington that 'if you desire speedily to part with [a house] the Surest way is to Advertise',[30] although in practice advertising was no guarantee of success. In 1778, the substantial town house of Elizabeth Montagu's late brother, Mr Morris Robinson, lay heavy on his widow's hands, despite frequent advertising and a bill posted on the door: 'Some have been to see it but no price has yet been offer'd. People do not care to sell out of the Funds at present as Stock is low, and I fear it may be some time before there is a Purchaser', reported Mrs Montagu.[31] Nevertheless, newspaper advertisements were clearly the most popular option for buyers and sellers, lessees and lessors, and the details given in those advertisements provide much information about the qualities sought, and promoted, in London town houses during this period.[32]

Certain daily journals such as the *Public Advertiser* seem to have been the chief vehicles for advertising houses within the press, each publication offering a wide range of properties and specifying the terms and arrangements on which they could be had. The advertisements usually state whether a property is leasehold or freehold, and, if the former, the number of years remaining on the lease. They specify the rent or purchase price – unless the house was to be sold at auction, which many were – and they describe the property itself, usually briefly. Most of the properties are simply described as a 'house', but some are called 'mansion' or 'mansion-house', although what constituted a mansion is not clear. In the terms of the 1667 Act for Rebuilding the City of London, mansion houses were 'for citizens and other persons of extraordinary quality' and did not stand in streets or lanes.[33] In the later eighteenth century, the label is more ambiguous. Although the descriptions 'noble' and 'magnificent' seem to have been reserved for 'mansions', detachment was not a criterion, nor was excessive size: one property so described was a house on the Royal Terrace, Adelphi, a standard three-bay house of modest frontage (only 22 feet), not even having a share of the terrace's decorated pilasters. On the other hand, a very large house set back from the street beyond a courtyard and containing on the first floor two suites of apartments, the number and dimensions of which were said to be 'almost unequalled in this Capital; there being ten Rooms on a Floor, beside gardrobes', was not styled as a 'mansion'. It is likely that the house, advertised in the *St James's Chronicle* in January 1774, was that built by Robert and James Adam on the corner of Mansfield Street and Queen Anne Street from 1768 – initially for the Countess Dowager of Warwick and then for her husband, General Robert Clerk.[34] Despite going to the extensive practical and financial lengths of building such a big residence, the couple soon let it out, for unknown reasons; from 1775 it was occupied by Sir Thomas Wynn for an initial period of five years at a rent of £350 per annum.[35] This was £100 less than the 'very easy Rate' stated in the advertisement, suggesting that substantial properties were not worth their weight in gold, whether styled 'mansions' or not. The 'mansion' of the Earl of Upper Ossory at the corner of Brook Street and Grosvenor Square – one large residence comprising two properties, with an 80-foot frontage onto Brook Street – had earlier been advertised simply as a 'spacious leasehold house'. Despite later terminological upgrading to a 'mansion', the property was not sold until 1776, and was then subdivided to become two houses again.[36] Whether or not the term 'mansion' was (perhaps misguidedly) used to attract buyers, there was a very limited market for the type of large house that might have deserved the name.

Other big properties went the same way as the Earl of Upper Ossory's Brook Street mansion. The Earl of Bolingbroke's house in the south-west corner of Soho Square had been divided into two properties earlier in the century and was further subdivided between 1768 and 1778.[37] The knowledge that builders were always eager to redevelop large properties in this way may have been some reassurance to those few buyers who were prepared to invest in a large house on a good-sized plot. In 1763, for example, Lady Holland wrote to her sister of her new house in London 'with a court before it and a fine long garden behind . . . The price is immense to be sure. Mr Fox paid £16,000 for it; the builders offer £14,000 tho'.'[38] General Robert Clerk perceived the advantages of such a detached house in its own, secluded ground as having 'all within yourself tranquility, quietness, your mind to yourself and your friends & mankind, without trifling, dissipated, momentary, & in a short while tiresome, pleasures of the eyes. All within yourself.'[39] But what Clerk recommended was the opposite of what other people came to town for, and the limited appeal of the large mansion goes some way to explain why the 'average' West End town house was a comparatively modest affair of three or four good rooms on a floor: the various combinations of accommodation and different emphases available within the fairly standard format were sufficient to answer the needs of most individuals and families, even aristocratic ones. It may be significant that the advertisement for the Mansfield Street house discussed above promoted the house as 'thought particularly eligible for the Accommodation of a foreign Minister'.

Advertisements often suggest, in this way, a property's suitability to a certain class of purchaser, such as nobleman, gentleman, or merchant – or even, more specifically, a 'Dowager Lady' (a prevalent type in London, as already discussed). Where the accommodation was itself exceptional, or at least considered to be so, the advertising was aimed at 'exceptional' families or individuals in terms of rank or status. Quality could therefore be defined in terms of the class of person the house would suit, rather than a description of the physical aspects of the house itself. The standing of the previous or current occupant was also an important component of the house's overall quality, and advertisements sometimes named (or described as 'nobleman', 'gentleman', etc.) the house's seller or tenant, perhaps as a means of differentiating between basically indistinguishable properties.[40]

Location was also a critical contributor to quality. In advertisements, properties for sale or let were located by street name and district, with the best part of the address sometimes emphasised in capitals. The locations of aristocratic households sometimes functioned as markers, and descriptions might refer to prestigious neighbours – 'the fourth Door from Lord Coventry's'[41] – or to notable urban landmarks. Convenient access to sites of business, leisure or entertainment, such as a 'Situation [in] a fine, open airy Street, with a back Door through the Stables that leads thro' Oxford-street into Soho Square and within a Shilling Fare to either of the Theatres',[42] was always a selling point. Lord Bracebridge felt that the desirable situation of his house in Stanhope Street more than compensated for its size, and the offer of a house in 'a situation still nearer St. James's' dissuaded Lord and Lady Lothian from buying Mrs Montagu's Hill Street house.[43] But priorities differed. In 1762, Sir Thomas Robinson advised Lord Bute against building a house close to or on the Portland estate north of Oxford Street, it being 'too far either from publick business or publick pleasure', and Thomas Noel expressed a reluctance to 'put up with one on the wrong side of Oxford road'.[44] On the other hand, General Clerk advised the Earl of Shelburne to go northwards, for the safety of his person and his house:

> You are acting your part well as a Minister. An Alderman Beckford with a Mobb breaks every window of your house in one night. It is confused ideas of such things which prevent many men from going on & acting their part & they become contemptible out of fear of God knows what: Go beyond Portman Square.[45]

The development of Marylebone, immediately prior to and during this period, attests to the popularity of the area when accommodation to the south of Oxford Street could not be found or afforded. Certainly the evidence from Grosvenor Square, where there was the least turnover of residents in the well-situated houses in the east, north and west ranges, and a lower turnover in the square in general in comparison to other squares, suggests that people held on to good, well-located houses when possible.[46]

Very few advertisements mention the gardens of the houses themselves,[47] but views into the gardens of freestanding aristocratic palaces, such as Devonshire House, Piccadilly, were an advantage of some locations. Chandos House, itself a substantial new property, was adjacent to the garden of Foley House and commanded from the back rooms 'a rich and extensive Prospect'.[48] Some advertisements also highlight views of the Thames, across Hyde Park, and, more distantly, up to Hampstead or Highgate, or down to the 'Kent and Surrey Hills'. Rare mentions of a bow window were sometimes made in connection with a view: for example, a house in St James's Place had such a window in front with 'a full View over the Green Park and Surrey Hills', while another, in St

James's Park, had a dining room and drawing room 'with Bow Windows, commanding an uninterrupted View of all the new Improvements, the Canal and the Parade'.[49] Although Mrs Carter denied that a view constituted pleasure – 'am I not prodigiously happy in Clarges Street, where to be sure one's happiness does not depend *absolutely* on a prospect?'[50] – the outlook from a town house was sometimes valued, even if it lacked the associations of proprietorship associated with views from the country house.[51] The banker Mr Coutts took preventative measures, making 'special arrangements with the Adams to preserve the view from his back windows, which overlooked the river', at the time of their Adelphi development on the riverfront.[52] But even adjacent building-in-progress could be a selling point: the situation of a house on the east side of Portland Place, for example, was particularly eligible, as 'Hampstead and Highgate are always in View, which never can be impeded or interrupted, as the capacious new street now erecting, of 160 Feet wide, will form an elegant Visto of Buildings to those rich Scenes'.[53] A building plot that James Paine surveyed for Lord Scarborough had an 'admirable prospect', and while the lane or road was then dirty, Paine was optimistic that it would be 'new built on both sides before any house can be finished on this spot';[54] neighbouring houses were a better prospect than unsophisticated naturalness. Sometimes the streetscape was brought into the house and was considered to add to its charms. A visitor to London in 1775 noted how the mirror panels placed opposite the windows in Lord Chesterfield's music room 'gave a sweet reflected view of Stanhope Street & Hyde Park'.[55] This type of visual exchange between inside and outside, facilitated by deep first-floor windows and reflective interior surfaces, was a desirable and sometimes contrived feature of smart West End homes.

Other advantages of location, where given, are vague, and apparently universal. 'Desirably situate' was the most popular expression, and applicable to anywhere from Savile Row to High Holborn. Other houses were 'agreeably', 'delightfully' or 'eligibly' situated – the last being particularly popular, it seems, for properties in Marylebone, for which the epithet 'airy' also seems to have been reserved. There appears to have been some truth in these claims for Marylebone: Mrs Montagu called Portman Square 'the Montpellier of England', and claimed she had enjoyed the best of health since moving there.[56] She wrote in 1780 that 'when a fog obscures Hill Street there is a blue sky and a clear atmosphere in Portman Square'.[57]

Descriptions of houses themselves generally focused on one or more of three aspects: accommodation, in terms both quantitative and qualitative; the house's physical fabric; and its decoration, almost exclusively interior. The most prominent description was of the accommodation in terms of the number of 'good' rooms per floor, the extent and convenience of offices and sometimes the number of storeys. Human accommodation was usually the first but not the only concern; for example 'Standing for three carriages [and] stabling for five horses' precedes any mention of 'two good rooms and a dressing-room on each floor' in an advertisement for a house to be let or sold in Welbeck Street, Cavendish Square, in 1776.[58] Such facilities were of prime importance to someone maintaining the level of equipage essential to making a 'proper figure' and leading the fullest life in town. A lack of designated stables was sufficient excuse for the Duke of Grafton to persuade Parliament to allow him to sell his entailed house in Bond Street.[59]

Disposition, or planning, is most often discussed with reference to offices, lauded for their convenience and utility. For example, the offices at Chandos House were 'all arched, ample and convenient'.[60] While the apartments of a mansion in Portman Square were simply described as 'noble', the offices were 'numerous, judiciously arranged, and replete with convenience',[61] and the advertisement for the Adams' house at the corner of Mansfield Street praises the offices before outlining, at some length, the exceptional accommodation provided on the first and other floors.[62] A detached kitchen was a bonus, and a combination of attached and detached offices seems to have been the optimum arrangement.

Other planning references are scarce and generally vague. A large, elegant house near Berkeley Square had its principal apartments 'laid out in a masterly stile', while a 'spacious, elegant new-built House, situate on the South Side and most eligible Part of Pall-mall' had a plan 'singular, and well adapted to contain a large Family'.[63] That particular house, furnished by a gentleman for a lady 'who afterwards changed her Mind', was described in far greater detail than any other property advertised in the *Public Advertiser* that year, from the 'Smoak Jack, wind-up Range' and pots and pans in the detached kitchen to the 'India Paper and elegant Gold Border' in the Drawing Room, giving the dimensions of all the major service, family and reception rooms. Presumably the status of the intended occupant, most probably the gentleman's mistress, was no deterrent to prospective purchasers or tenants.

A new, bespoke house, or extensive refurbishment, was the best option where the dimensions and disposition of rooms were particularly important. In 1768, Lady Mary Coke explained that the Dowager Countess Waldegrave had

> changed the House She had in Portman Square for another in the same square, that was not yet built. She found, She said, She cou'd have it

more to her mind; that She was to have one room of forty-two ft long, another of six and thirty, two more good ones, and a Closet upon the Principal floor.[64]

But clients paid for the privilege of choice, as seen by Lady Mary's comments regarding the expense of the dowager's preferences. The new, speculative terraces offered little or no choice regarding the size and arrangement of rooms, although they allowed purchasers some say in the expense and style of the interior finish.

It is difficult to say whether new houses were preferred over old. Some advertisements note that houses were 'modern built' or 'new built', suggesting that newness may have attracted purchasers. A new house built in an established, yet still fashionable area, may have been the optimum choice – expensive by comparison with a speculative property in a new development, but perhaps cheaper and simpler than refurbishing an old house, something which architects often advised against. James Paine reported that modernising a house in King Street, Covent Garden, 'would be a difficult and costly operation' and recommended his client to apply instead for a rebuilding lease', which he understood would be readily granted.[65] Likewise, William Chambers deterred Agmondesham Vesey from buying a property in severe want of repair in Stratton Street, arguing that 'you may buy a new house & in a good part of Town for less money than this Antique & the repairs would cost you'.[66]

Certainly, while the size and convenience of accommodation were top priorities, state of repair and 'completeness' were also important and correspondence confirms that the actual or perceived quality of the house's fabric might be critical. Mrs Howe feared, in 1773, that

Mr Minchin is in a scrape, he has bought the house in Albemarle Street, and had nearly agreed for the selling his present one, but the person about it is off and it has very unjustly been said that it is an ill built one, so that if he cannot set it right again, he will be obliged to live in it himself, and sell again that in Albemarle Street.[67]

'Well built' was one of a stock range of positive terms used to grade or describe advertised houses, some of which related to the house's size, fabric or general condition, and others to its overall appearance or finish. Other adjectives used included spacious, compact, substantial, large, commodious, capital, modern or 'strictly' modern, valuable, elegant, genteel, clean, useful, compleat, convenient, or elegantly or newly furnished. Elegance was the most alluded to quality and was not associated with size. Compactness was highly rated, seemingly something positive in itself rather than second best to roominess. People seem to have accepted the restrictions of a regular West End terrace house and treated them lightly, adapting their entertainments to suit: 'As we cannot pretend to *give Dinners*, we intend giving a *little Music* in return for our numerous invitations', wrote Judith Milbanke in 1778, '. . . the squeeze will consist of about 50 . . . I think the Music will sound well in the Fore Closet, & in the back Cup-board I shall have two Card Tables.'[68] No doubt such amusements also cost less, and the smaller town house may have been an economy in this respect,[69] although a terrace house did not preclude lavish and expensive entertainments.

Popular blanket descriptions of interiors include tasteful decor in the 'latest fashion', the 'present taste' or the 'modern fashion', although what constituted this fashion or taste is never indicated. Occasionally the advertisements mention such good features as marble fireplaces and stone staircases, and, less often, ornamental cornices and ceilings and mahogany sashes. Practicality and functionality were never forgotten: an 'elegantly finished' new-built house in Brompton Row boasted 'Mortis Locks' within a list of decorative embellishments and refinements such as plaster cornices, marble chimney pieces and a handsome bracket staircase with a mahogany rail, as well as 'two good Vaults and a Well sunk for a Pump'.[70] 'Handsome brass locks to all the doors' and an 'Abundance of Closets' were also thought worthy of note, the latter no doubt offering welcome opportunities for storage, privacy, or both.[71] Sometimes practicality and unusual architectural features coincided. David King, in his account of the Adams' house for the Countess Dowager of Warwick and General Clerk, writes that 'a curious feature of the interior was that almost all the rooms seem to have had segmentally-vaulted ceilings'.[72] Assuming that this house was the same one advertised in the *St James's Chronicle* in 1773–4, the explanation for what might be perceived as a decorative feature, at least in the principal rooms, is that the house was 'built on an incombustible Plan, being arched from Top and Bottom'.[73] Such practical innovations in town apparently attracted public attention: in a letter to the Duke of Portland in 1770, Thomas Price recommends a house being built in Queen Anne Street (conceivably the same Adam house) as an example of the method he proposes for fireproofing in architecture, and observes that 'numbers go there purposely to see it for the novelty'.[74]

Exceptional levels of detail about interiors tend to be confined to advertisements for bigger houses. The Adams' Chandos House had

> six noble spacious Rooms on a Floor; a grand Stair case, a back ditto and Escalier derobe all of Stone, with Intervals for Servants, and Water Closets to the different Appartments. The Cielings are highly

finished, with Stucco and painted Ornaments; the Chimney-pieces of Statuary marble, delicately enriched.[75]

The Adams were themselves promoting this grand, but speculative house, so it is no surprise to find the advertisement focusing on the chief merits of their design. The Adams were also responsible for the expensive transformation between 1771 and 1772 of John Grant's house at 20 Soho Square, described in 1775 as an 'elegant, spacious, leasehold mansion, with capacious offices, &c.', and 'interior parts' which were

> an Assemblage of Enrichments, adapted with peculiar Elegance. The First Floor contains a Suite of noble Apartments of four capital Rooms, and two Secondary ones. The Parlour Floor of equal Dimensions, and immediately correspondent. The Second Floor comprehends four elegant bed-chambers, and two Dressing rooms. In the Disposition of the Offices, which are numerous, Utility is singularly conspicuous . . . The above Premises are planned upon a large Scale, and, from their Unique Elegance and abundant Convenience, are very suitable for the residence of a Nobleman, with a large Family, or an Ambassador.[76]

Such houses were sufficiently different from the prevalent three-bay terrace, with its two or three good rooms and a closet per floor, to warrant more extensive description. No doubt purchasers prepared to spend large sums of money on exceptional houses wanted the houses' special qualities spelled out to them. Even so, neither house sold readily. Chandos House took two years to sell despite the great contrivances of interior planning and decoration, and 20 Soho Square remained unsold for ten years.[77]

The advertisements for these two particular properties are also unusual in mentioning the houses' elevations. Even then, they are not described in any detail. Chandos House did not have a particularly ornamented exterior, and was exceptional (externally) principally for the 'beautiful stone front' that the advertisement mentions. 20 Soho Square, on the other hand, had been transformed by Robert Adam with a 'fashionable dress' described in detail by the *Survey of London* as follows. It was

> tailored with his usual skill to disguise its age and the irregular spacing of the windows, which obviously precluded the creation of a central feature . . . He strengthened the ground storey by giving it a rusticated face of twelve courses . . . The eight piers of the two-storeyed upper face were dressed with a giant order of pilasters, their plain shafts rising from plain pedestals and having enriched Ionic capitals, instead of the

Corinthian originally intended. Iron balconies of segmental plan, placed in front of the lengthened first-floor windows, linked the pilaster pedestals, and a guilloche band marking the second floor extended between their shafts. The crowning entablature was composed of a moulded architrave, a frieze enriched with paterae spaced at equal intervals, and a modillioned cornice. A tall balustrade helped to conceal the dormers and reduce the effective height of the original roof.[78]

The advertisement simply notes that 'the Elevation is superb',[79] although the mere fact that it was mentioned, and choice of the adjective employed, were possibly enough to indicate to prospective purchasers that this was something out of the ordinary. Many readers would have been familiar with this exceptional house in any case, and mention of its location on the east side of Soho Square, together with this brief description of its exterior, was sufficient for readers to identify the property for sale. This advertisement is one of only two in the *Public Advertiser* for 1775 in which the front is mentioned at all. And there is a notable absence of remarks on both the exterior condition and decoration of houses. Whereas the condition may have been embraced in general remarks about the 'perfect Repair', the apparent lack of interest in appearance is remarkable. We might assume that other town houses advertised in 1775 had no interesting features and did not even warrant such descriptions as 'neat' or 'elegant'.

Perhaps the sort of house that had an exceptional façade was more likely to have been sold or let by word of mouth among 'persons of quality' – or perhaps the façade's look was simply not a concern to purchasers. But what then of the remarks about saleability made by John Adam to Sir Rowland Winn in 1774 regarding the latter's house in St James's Square? Adam argued that the more elaborate of two proposed façades would make the house easier to sell, if Winn so wished, at a later date: 'in case you should ever incline to dispose of that House, it would sell a good deal better for the Gay Front'. Robert Adam later assured him that his neighbours considered the chosen façade to be a great ornament to the square: 'every creature admires your front & Sir Watkins [sic] told me the square was much obliged to you, as it was a great ornament to the whole inhabitants'.[80] The house does appear to have sold soon after Winn's death in February 1785,[81] but whether because of its 'Gay Front' or its position in St James's Square is unknown. Certainly Baron Grant's 'superb' elevation in Soho Square was not enough to make his house a saleable commodity.[82]

While such general terms as 'elegant' may have been taken to apply to the house as a whole and therefore incorporated the exterior appearance, we could probably conclude that the lack of particular comment on façades arose from the fact that most houses were of unexceptional appearance and the exterior therefore only mattered in terms of its state of repair. Besides the one for Grant's house, the only advertisement in the *Public Advertiser* for 1775 specifically to mention a façade was for a property 'lately modernized and repaired, at a great Expence; the Front entirely new',[83] suggesting that buyers were more concerned with the façade's physical quality and intactness than any embellishments or idiosyncratic features. A good façade might sway the prospective purchaser on viewing the property, but it was unlikely to be a major consideration in advance. Most of the properties for sale were in any case part of a row of houses in a street or square, often little distinguished from their neighbours and sometimes deliberately incorporated in a 'palace front'.

The advertisements sometimes state the number of years remaining on a lease, but, as discussed above, it is hard to say how lease length affected decisions to buy a house, or the impact this had on its price. Michael Port suggests that 'given changes in fashion alone, the attractiveness of long leases may be exaggerated',[84] although there is evidence that security of tenure was important to both the estate landlord and the lessee. When, in the 1740s, the City wished to keep its property in Conduit Mead healthy during a precarious time in the house market, it recognised that the better tenants might desert the area 'for want of renewing their Leases and giving them proper encouragement in due time'. The City therefore took measures to encourage tenants to stay and to maintain their properties, by reassuring them that their leases would be renewable indefinitely, an arrangement that worked to the benefit of both tenants and landlord.[85]

The advertisements identify and promote detachment as a quality, although instances of detached houses were rare. One property was 'quite new, very genteely fitted up, and entirely separate from any other House', while another – the shell of a house in Portman Square – was 'detached from the adjoining Buildings, with a View to provide against Noise and Danger from Fire',[86] making detachment a practical benefit rather than a matter of prestige. The distinction between detached and terraced houses was essentially one between a relatively compact house, forming a community with others in the same street or square, or a large, freestanding house with some surrounding land – although in practice few people could or chose to afford the latter. The advertisements identify corner properties, although chiefly to pinpoint their location. Evidence from the residential patterns in Grosvenor Square suggests that such properties were less popular than those in the main body of the terrace, partly because of their ambiguous location within the square itself, often opening on to an adjoining street, and partly because of the extra liability for Window Tax.[87] They were also structurally weaker, and people preferred to have neighbours, as houses were no doubt both warmer and easier to maintain if adjoined by other properties. The Adams anticipated a rise in the value of their Adelphi houses 'when the whole buildings are finished and inhabited'.[88] Full occupancy of an area was a factor in its perceived and, consequently, actual popularity.

There was also a healthy trade in houses to let. Like the advertisements for houses for sale, those for rented accommodation concentrated on numbers of rooms per floor, completeness of offices and stabling capacity. But they tend to say little of the house's physical quality, or the character of its location. Consequently, details of colour schemes, new and elegant furnishings and staircases and cornices seem more prominent in these than in the 'for sale' advertisements. This relative emphasis on decorative qualities may be partly explained by the activity of upholsterers in the letting market. A well-furnished property could also achieve a substantially better rent than an unfurnished one. For example, the Earl of Rosebery's house in Grosvenor Square was available in 1775 for 400 guineas per annum furnished or for 300 guineas unfurnished.[89] There were some practical advantages, however, to letting one's house unfurnished. Mrs Montagu proposed to let her Hill Street house without furniture until a good purchaser could be found. This step would put her in a position of power: 'should I get a bad Servant', she wrote in 1780, 'I can seize his Goods for Rent, and such security becomes necessary in these extravagant times'.[90]

A comparison of these advertisements for London houses with those for sale or rent in York among the same classes in the same period is instructive, revealing those elements of house buying and selling that were unique to London and those that the capital shared with other metropolitan areas.[91] The advertisements share a common range of general descriptive terms, such as 'neat', 'convenient', 'genteel', 'commodious' and plainly 'good'. Reference is also made in both to present or former residents, as an indication of quality and to identify the house in question. In York, however, there are very few references to the type of person or family a house would suit, unlike in London, perhaps because the building stock was smaller and individual properties were therefore already known to prospective buyers and tenants. Indications of the size of family a house would suit are occasionally given, but there are only a few simple references to house size. The standardised format of the West End house meant that overall size and total number of rooms could pretty well be judged from the number of 'good' rooms per floor, which the advertisements often gave, but the non-standard building stock of

York meant more direct (if few) indications of total numbers of bed and reception rooms in a house. References are also made to offices, stabling and coach-houses, but these are far less prominent within individual advertisements in York than in London – being, perhaps, less critical to prospective residents. On the other hand, and unsurprisingly, more references are made to gardens and views.[92] No rental or sale prices are given in the York advertisements. As in London, the words 'house' or 'dwelling-house' are very often capitalised, but in York the phrase 'sash'd house' also appears regularly (and generally emphasised by capitals), presumably distinguishing a modern or modernised house among a more diverse and potentially ancient building stock than was to be found in London's newly built West End. Unsurprisingly, there were far fewer houses advertised to sell or let in York, reflecting a smaller building stock but also, perhaps, less movement in and out of the city – and fewer abrupt changes of mind.

Auctions were a common means of disposing of a property within a short space of time in both locations, especially in the 1770s,[93] but quick changes of plan were particularly typical of town-house ownership in London, as indicated by advertisements promoting the newness of furniture in houses to sale or let. Descriptions here often emphasise, too, the taste, discrimination and expense vested in the collections of furniture which, like groups of pictures, were often sold with or at the same time as the house. The accoutrements for making a 'proper figure' could be both bought and sold in one transaction. There was apparently no stigma attached to acquiring sale items. Mrs Montagu bought a large glass and some other articles 'pretty cheap' at the French ambassador's sale in April 1778 for her splendid new house in Portman Square.[94] The price achieved at auction depended on the current state of the market and the wider financial climate. In 1773, Therese Parker remarked to her brother that

> Mr Adam's Antiques &ca, sold for nothing – Mr Strange's Pictures if there is any money stirring, ought to bring a good deal, for they are thought very good, but not a Picture this year has sold for half the value . . . all owing to every creature being in want of money . . . tho' in general the bad run that causes such a sale, is what enables another to purchase.[95]

The link between the ill fortune of one party and the good fortune of another held true for the sale and purchase of the houses themselves and, as houses sold by private contract could take some time to shift, it is no surprise that these, too, were most often sold at auction. It was frequently at least, if not more, important to arrange a quick sale as a quick purchase; unlike a bill or private advertisement, a sale by auction set a limit on the time an owner had to wait to realise the capital tied up in a house.[96]

Affording

There were two main financial reasons why an occupant might have to sell or sublet a London house in a hurry: the expense of living in London and the cost of the house itself. Flexibility to change one's mind, to sell off or rent out one's house and contents, was built into the town-house market. Many house advertisements emphasise that owners had intended to use properties for their own purposes, and exercised taste and/or expenditure accordingly. An advertisement in 1775 offered to let, furnished or unfurnished, 'an elegant finished House' on which no expense had been spared by the owner 'who intended to inhabit it himself', but changed his mind for undisclosed reasons.[97] It is quite clear from the documentary evidence that the West End house was seen in two contrasting lights, often simultaneously. First, it was a facility that people wanted and felt that they needed, for the various reasons discussed in Chapter One. At the same time, however, many people recognised, or were forced to recognise, that London life, and particularly the house itself, was a financial burden they could not afford. Edward Jefreys sold his town house because 'sugars do not sell so well as they have done for several years past, which circumstance alone render'd me unable to bare [sic] the expence of two Houses', while Sir Thomas Clavering forsook a seat in Parliament in order to be rid of the expense of his London home.[98] The need to economise reportedly supplied Lord Pembroke with the nerve to ask his wife to join him and Miss Hunter in Utrecht, so that 'the house in town might be let, which would save some money'.[99] And even though many people were in town to make money, Thomas Worsley was surely not alone in finding, on his appointment as Surveyor General of the Works in 1761, 'that the profits of place were partly offset by the increased costs of living in London for long periods'.[100]

In *Humphry Clinker*, Smollett draws on the same two factors that made London life unaffordable. He presents the house as a drain on finances, parasitic and inefficient, and an incitement to, as well as the locus of, frivolous and extravagant consumption. To begin with, his protagonist Matthew Bramble contrasts the spiritual and physical benefits of self-sufficient life on his country estate with the spiritually and physically debilitating effects of city life, a contrast that is seen to have wider implications as the story progresses. Smollett uses examples among Bramble's acquaintances to demonstrate the effects that expenditure on living in town may have on individuals. Firstly, Bramble finds his old friend Baynard in dire straits, with Baynard telling Bramble how his city wife had insisted on having a London house. Their money had run out, and he had proposed selling up and leaving town for the country, but her distress at this thought had been so severe that they had continued 'to be sucked deeper and deeper into the vortex of extravagance and dissipation, leading what is called a fashionable life in town'.[101] A period abroad had failed as an economy measure, so they had moved to the country, where Mrs Baynard had so successfully undermined all the improvements made to her husband's estate that it had become, like a town house, unable to support them or even itself. When Bramble is given the opportunity to help Baynard put his finances right, his first move is to get rid of the London house and to sell off its contents.[102]

Meanwhile, another acquaintance, Charles Dennison, had taken the right path, in opposition to the one trodden so heavily by Baynard. On inheriting a poorly managed estate, Dennison had left his business in town and retired to the country. Instead of spending on a town house, he had made his country house clean and weather-tight, and his estate productive and self-sufficient. He had found that 'he should save sixty pounds a year in the single article of house-rent, and as much more in pocket-money and contingencies' by not living in London. Besides, he would make 'a considerable saving on the side of dress, in being delivered from the oppressive imposition of ridiculous modes, invented by ignorance and adopted by folly'.[103] As I have said, Smollett had an exceptionally strong antipathy to London; moreover, his attitude to luxury was old-fashioned by the standards of his time.[104] Nevertheless, the veracity of these tales in *Humphry Clinker* is borne out by much and varied evidence from the period.

It is clear from account books that people could readily put a price on the time they spent in London. Many people kept separate accounts itemising expenditure on as well as from their London home.[105] In a list of annual domestic expenses for ten years from Michaelmas 1770, Lady Lee noted an 'extraordinary rise of the last three years' and attributed it to expenses in London, where the Lees had just acquired a house after a few years away from the capital to recover their finances.[106] The very fact of residing in town required the occupant to buy in the sorts of provisions and services that were an integral part of a well-managed country household and estate. Smollett had plenty to say on this subject, from the point of view of the negative effects on the health and well-being of the temporary resident in London. Smollett was justified in his implications that living in town also caused resources to leave the estate, in its wider sense, rather than feeding back into the interests of an extended community. For example, while he was in town, Sir Watkin Williams Wynn's kitchen accounts included payments for the butcher, the baker, the poulterer, the fishmonger, the greengrocer, the butterman, the milkman, the charcoalman, the cheesemonger and the pastry cook, whereas at his country seat, Wynnstay, payments were made to the butcher, and the grocer and for salt and tinning coppers.[107]

The London house was also the base for the broader consumption of essential as well as luxury goods, and its role as a centre for consumption, conspicuous or otherwise, was recognised at the time. As the historian Paul Langford reports, 'it was forever being alleged [that] . . . money which might have been spent at home where it would do most good was . . . squandered on urban luxury and vice. Elaborate calculations were made of the sums expended on claret, polite suppers, and Italian musicians, and the quantity of village hospitality they might have financed.'[108] The 5th Duke of Beaufort's list of 'incidental' bills (outside his usual household costs) settled at the end of his period of winter residence in Grosvenor Square in May 1770 comprised twenty-seven creditors, including harness makers, saddlers, bit makers and farriers, brewers and brandy merchants, confectioners and perfumers, purveyors of French robes, lace and millinery, glovers and hosiers and corn and wax chandlers. During the 1770s the Beaufort family typically spent a maximum of only twenty weeks in London annually, but this accounted for nearly 60 per cent of their total expenditure and as much as 70 per cent of a total of £5550 in 1775.[109] Purchases for both town and country use were made in London and accounts usually indicated the destined location of the item or commodity bought.[110]

Householders often could not or did not want to avoid spending on their house's fabric, and accounts itemising London expenditure include work done on the house itself. For example, the expenditure of the Griffin Griffins of Audley End on their Burlington Street house can be tracked through their accounts, which itemise outlay firstly on ground rent, taxes (including rates) and repairs to the London house and stables and, secondly, on furniture for the house. In the five years preceding 1779, when they were billed for work done on the property by the Adam brothers, the average expenditure in the first category was £140 and £14 in the second. These figures jumped to £1741 and £425, respectively, in the year of the refurbishment.[111] Houseowners could put a price on any work done in their London house, from the 1s per year that the Dowager Viscountess Midleton had to pay to her ground landlord, Lord Ashburnham, for opening up a window to light a dingy room in the house that neighboured his in Dover Street,[112] to the total cost of extensive building work, furbishing or furnishing, which was often presented in stitched booklets itemising work done and materials supplied by all involved. The booklet prepared for Jervoise Clarke in 1774 in respect of work at his house in Hanover Square under Charles Cameron, together with assorted loose bills, reveals that extensive refurbishment and redecoration of what was not an exceptionally big house cost over £5000.[113]

Many people laid out considerable sums in refurbishing or decorating a newly acquired house, in addition to the often substantial prices paid for the properties themselves. Sir Gilbert Heathcote purchased his father-in-law's house in Grosvenor Square for £7000 in May 1764, and paid £466 10s in addition for part of the furniture. He then spent over £1800 refurbishing and extending the property.[114] In readiness for his return from India, Lord Clive spent £3718 on his Berkeley Square house between January 1766 and June 1767, more than treble the sum he had paid for the remainder of the lease.[115] However, work done on a house could greatly increase its value despite declining years on the lease. James Shuttleworth MP bought the lease of a corner house in Grosvenor Square for £1700 in 1752 and sold it to John Radcliffe MP for £6300, possibly including the furniture, in 1768. Rating valuations suggest that improvements were made to the property between 1755 and 1768.[116] Such jumps in prices probably reflect substantial improvements to the fabric or size of the house. But increases in value did not always match or exceed the cost of work done on the house. It is unlikely, for example, that Sir Watkin Williams Wynn could have recouped by sale the full cost of rebuilding and decorating his house in St James's Square, which exceeded the £8696 13s 14d for which he had bought the property by more than 300 per cent.[117]

Closer examination of sums spent on town houses often reveals the bulk of the expenditure to have been on practical repairs or on developing the offices and service quarters (which the advertisements suggest were important to housebuyers), with only a fraction on anything involving paterae and fluting. The Drake building accounts are a nice example of expenditure on decorative and practical features. William Drake spent £3022 on embellishing his Grosvenor Square house between 1773 and 1775 under James Wyatt, but work on the exterior and the offices comprised a significant part of the total bill.[118]

Not all such expenditure was made at the owner's behest. A new lease sometimes required the holder to make practical repairs to a house at his or her own expense. Estate records, such as those of Christ's Hospital and the Bedford Estate, include many details of repairing leases granted in this period, stating the number of years for which the lease was granted, the 'fine' or lump sum and the ground rent payable, and the estimated value of repairs to be organised and paid for by the prospective lessee.[119] Mr James Dolling paid the Bedford Estate a fine of £150 for the repairing lease on his house in Great Russell Street for eleven years from Christmas 1767, plus repairs estimated at £146.[120] In the same year the estate required Dr Richard Adams to pay a £630 fine for the renewal of the lease of his house, coach house and stables in Bloomsbury Square, together with repairs estimated at £400.[121] The estate surveyors sometimes grossly underestimated the cost of repairs. In February 1770, a house in Bedford Street, Covent Garden, was said to require repairs to a value of £312, but ultimately needed £1100 spent on it. (The estate generously waived the £100 fine originally proposed.[122]) In other instances of underestimation, the lease length was increased as compensation for the leaseholder's unexpected financial outlay.[123] The Bedford Estate generally required its leaseholders to continue to keep their houses in repair for the duration of the lease.

Long-term rental of a house was sometimes no escape from expenditure on its fabric. Essential repairs were either the responsibility of the leaseholder, or the joint responsibility of leaseholder and tenant. Sir John Frederick laid out considerable money in repairing and fitting up the property he rented in Hanover Square from James Stewart in 1770, settling an account with the builder Charles Evans totalling around £1977 two years later, for which Frederick appears to have received no allowance from his landlord. In 1777, however, he was able to set against his rent half of the amount of sundry workmen's bills for small amounts that had accumulated. Frederick's initial outlay indicates a long-term view on occupation of the property, where he did indeed remain until 1781 at least.[124] Decorative or amenity changes were more likely to fall to the tenant's purse, although he or she might seek some allowance at the end of a tenancy for stylistic and practical alterations that benefited the landlord and incoming tenant. Sir Edward Littleton seems to have met with his landlady, Viscountess Dudley and Ward, or her representative, with a prepared checklist of questions regarding house-related expenses. Lady Dudley was to be responsible for the Ground Rent, Land Tax (typical landlord liabilities), painting and whitewashing of the house in Upper Brook Street, while Littleton was to pay the Water, Paving and Poor Rates and be responsible for future repairs during the seven years of the sublease, after initial repairs made by Lady Dudley.[125] Littleton stayed longer in the house than first agreed, renewing the lease for a further fourteen-year term in June 1779 and having alterations and repairs done to it by Samuel Wyatt in 1779 and the following few years.[126]

In some agreements, the onus for getting the property up to scratch was clearly on the landlord. In December 1778, Sir William Lee rented what must have been a new or nearly new house in Portland Place. The owner, David Williams, agreed to have the house finished to the prior specifications of Samuel Wyatt, who surveyed the property, presumably on Lee's behalf. These specifications had already been satisfied but for a few particulars, including the papering of the first-floor rooms, which Williams undertook to perform 'at such time and with such paper (not exceeding one shilling per yard) as the said Sir William Lee shall direct'. If the works were not completed according to the agreement, Lee would be entitled to employ his own workmen to do the same, with the expenses to be deducted from the rent.[127]

Large, sometimes immense, sums were also spent on furniture and furnishings. In 1771, Sir Watkin settled a bill totalling £2886 with his upholsterer, Bradshaw, largely for furnishing his Grosvenor Square house.[128] The Marquess of Carmarthen bought the house from Wynn in 1774, together with an unspecified amount of the furniture. In addition to building work to the value of £860 in 1774–5, Carmarthen paid about £2570 to John Bradburn, cabinetmaker and upholsterer, for furniture and furnishings for the house, and the account 'appears not to include the important rooms on the first floor'.[129] The most substantial of the bills for the refurbishment of Lord Clive's house was the £1200 paid to the upholsterer Charles Arbuckle.[130] The determination not to spend much money on furnishing a new house was not always enough to avoid the expense. In March 1777, Mrs Francis promised her husband that she would 'lay out as little as possible' in furnishing the house she had recently taken in Harley Street. Yet very shortly afterwards she wrote 'I almost fear I shall be obliged to take too much advantage of your generosity in fitting up this House, but I will be as saving as possible'. By the following year her fears had been realised. 'I asked you for £200 to furnish my house', she wrote to her husband, 'but it was too little and showed my ignorance in asking. I have now paid within a trifle of £500 and yet my best room has no glasses.' The lack of mirrors remained a bugbear for Mrs Francis. 'I can't use my room without them', she moaned in November of that year. In the following June she had hopes of finding some in a sale of furniture at a house in Grafton Street.[131]

It was not only through such sales that town houses functioned as the showrooms of the London marketplace. People gathered ideas about designs and prices for furniture and fittings from houses of others before purchasing or commissioning pieces for their own town and country homes. In March 1770, Lady Louisa Conolly promised her sister that she would 'observe all the furniture' in Lady Egremont's fine London house, 'to inform you of, for your new rooms', and in 1776 she promised her brother-in-law to 'take the very great trouble' of trying to get her sister 'a pretty chimney-piece for the drawing-room to her mind that won't ruin her'. Lady Louisa had clearly been scouting for suitable models in her acquaintances' London homes, and while she did not know the price of Mrs Knox's chimney piece, she could report that two of Lady Roden's 'were about fifty each'.[132]

Furniture was probably the household commodity most susceptible to changes in fashion – especially in London, where there was more choice and more competition. A move to a fashionable location brought attendant responsibilities for furniture and furnishings. Despite exceeding her estimations and budget in furnishing her new house in Harley Street, Mrs Francis reported that her friends still thought some of her furniture 'not good enough'.[133] However, as the advertisements suggest, furniture could also be readily sold off to realise funds once a London house was no longer necessary or affordable. Like the house itself – the largest of chattels – it was easily purchased and redeemed in an active market.

London life's principal concomitant expense was, of course, the cost of the house itself, particularly when building or purchasing rather than renting was involved, and awareness of the precise cost of living in London might have resulted in admitting that the cost was too great. In 1764, James Adair was pleased to tell his son of his move to Soho Square: on the positive side, he reported the house to be 'a most comfortable habitation having every deviseable convenience both for you and us'; but on the negative side he admitted that 'it's true it has fleec'd me pretty well'.[134] Finding the ideal property to buy was fraught enough, but paying for it might have been the biggest difficulty of all. For some lucky purchasers, the life event that prompted the purchase also provided the means to afford it. William Weddell paid £9450 for the house he bought in Upper Brook Street shortly after his marriage in 1771, partly funded by his wife's marriage portion. Even so, he still had to raise £4000 on a mortgage from Hoare's bank.[135] Some house sellers offered to let buyers pay only part of the purchase price, retaining the rest on a mortgage with the premises themselves as security.[136]

Robert Taylor provided a portfolio of services for his network of wealthy clients: not only was he an architect, developer and proto-estate agent, but he also granted mortgages to allow his clients to buy the houses he supplied.[137] As the *Oracle* reported in 1792, 'he would erect you an elegant habitation, he would furnish it as you pleased – deliver in the tradesman's bills more reasonable than you could contract for, and he charged a single *Five* per cent for his trouble', amassing a substantial personal fortune in the process.[138] Architects and builders often allowed for varying degrees of finish in their estimates for new houses, so that clients or purchasers could spend more or less as they wished, or could afford. In 1770, William Chambers broke down his estimate of £4400 for building Henry Errington's house in Cleveland Row into £4000 for the house and about £400 for the three ceilings and chimney pieces and any other 'extraordinary enrichments' that Errington chose to have.[139] Chambers also confirmed to the Rt. Hon. Earl Fitzwilliam that the price of 'Mr Adams's house near Cavendish Square' was £12,000 to £14,000 'according as it is more or less richly finished'.[140] Not everyone took the opportunity to reduce the initial cost of their house. In December 1771, the Adams provided the Countess Dowager of Warwick with a detailed estimate for the cost of rebuilding her house in Mansfield Street. Itemised separately within a total of £8353 18s was the cost of finishing the second-floor rooms, estimated at £438 10s 6d. A note on the document states that this latter sum

> was seperated [sic] on a supposition that the two pair of stair rooms might remain unfinished some time after all the rest of the building was done, but the difference of the Expence not appearing to be sufficiently considerable to [defer] the completion of the whole plan, it was determined to be carried through at once.

The final account anyway exceeded the original estimate by more than £400.[141]

Some new houses never got off the drawing board for lack of money. James Paine's plans for Lord Scarborough's house remained unexecuted as the earl's debts piled up from the mid 1760s.[142] Scarborough moved instead into a plain, three-storey house in Downing Street.[143] But those people who had houses newly built for them often made payments on account.[144] Payments were sometimes infrequent, however, and debts run up at such a rate that they rapidly became beyond the immediate means of the client (as in the case of Sir Watkin Williams Wynn below). Mrs Montagu firmly believed that interim payments were essential for staying within one's means and avoiding a hefty debt on completion of the house, as well as being the only conscionable and respectable way to operate. This was clearly not a popular view, as she recognised: 'I will own my taste is unfashionable, but there is to me a wonderful charm in those words *in full of all demands*.'[145] If others shared her opinion that 'the worst of haunted Houses . . . are those haunted by Duns [creditors demanding payment]', they certainly did not reflect it in their behaviour.[146] For some people, the consequence of not accommodating themselves within their means was ultimately the sacrifice of the house itself.

In March 1772, Baron Grant was still deciding on the position of the front door to his large remodelled house in Soho Square; yet by the following March he had mortgaged the house and had moved within the next twelve months to smaller houses, first in Greek Street and then in Dean Street.[147] The Soho Square house was advertised in the *Public Advertiser* in February 1775 and the 'rich and elegant Household Furniture, Pictures, Plate, fine China, and other valuable Effects', which Grant had taken to his next house, were auctioned by Mr Christie in November 1775.[148]

Debt relating to London life was frequently described as causing 'distress' to both debtor and creditor. Definitions of 'distress' in Samuel Johnson's *Dictionary* (1766) encompass both the emotional experience and the consequences of debt. On the one hand distress is 'calamity; misery; misfortune', and on the other it is 'a compulsion, by which a man is assured to appear in court, or to pay a debt'.[149] Like Baron Grant, Sir Watkin Williams Wynn's tastes and desires clearly surpassed the capabilities of his budget, a situation that came to a head in relation to the rebuilding of his house in St James's Square from 1771. In May 1773, his steward fretted to his agent, Francis Chambre, that 'so many bills are dropping in that it makes me shudder'. Chambre and Sir Watkin discussed raising money through the sale and mortgage of other property, but the sums envisaged were never a match for those in connection with the expense of the house. In September 1774, the agent tried again to present the truth of the situation to his employer, writing:

> Upon looking over my Accounts I find that the Purchase Money for the House with Interest on it to the Time of Payment was £8896:13:4 and that I have already paid on Accot of Building in St James's Square upwards of £15000 besides wch there is near £12000 more now due to the several workmen so that this House will (with what further Charges are yet to come) cost near £40000 and where the Remainder of the money is to be got to pay for it I don't know . . . [N]o greater sum than £2000 can at present be spared to the workmen in St James's Square tho' they really are many of them much Distressed and nearly three Times that Sum ought now to be immediately distributed among them . . . in short Sir unless something or other can be done to prevent any further Effusion of Money at least for some Years to come We shall be much distressed.[150]

Sir Watkin's conscience may have led him to order land to be sold to assuage the financial distress of those working on his house, but not everyone was so sympathetic, and Wynn himself was hardly a model client.[151] The prestigious commission at 20 St James's Square may have been good promotionally for the Adam brothers, but they constantly needed to push for payment.[152] William Chambers's letterbooks are comparably riddled with tactful and reasonable requests, tinged with humour, for payment of significant sums of money:

> I have pleasure to acquaint you that your house is now Covering in, And the sorrow to assure you I never was so poor in my Life; When your house is Covered in there will be two thousand pounds due to me and I must entreat you to let me have the whole or as large a part as you possibly can for I know not how to go on without it.[153]

> By your Lordship's Order I delivered in towards the end of the year 1769 Bills for repairs & Alterations done at the House in Arlington Street under my direction the Summer before . . . which your Lordship said you would pay then, but as I have heard nothing about them since, I apprehend they have been mislaid & forgot.[154]

> I am obliged to your lordship for the 1000£ you were so good to leave a Draught for at Drummonds . . . I wish however it had been 2000 w^h was the sum your Lordship told me I should have; of this thousand the whole must be paid on account of the Extras to Collins and the Carver & Painters who are all very Sharp set, so that no Part of it comes to me on account of the Contract, upon w^h I nevertheless owe money to persons as sharp set as the above mentioned Gentlemen, if your Lordship would therefore be so kind as to double the Dose it would enable me to satisfy all these hungry Gentlemen & all things would go on very smoothly this however I only mean in case it be convenient to you.[155]

Many of Chambers's petitions for payment had a practical bent, emphasising that he needed the money to buy materials, employ extra workmen to speed up the completion of a house, or simply because he was building so much at the time.[156]

The burden of debt and the experience or threat of distress which those involved in construction often had in common with their clients was made public by gossip as well as newspapers, which listed bankrupts great and small. A high proportion of these bankrupts were London based, including many from the building and furnishing trades.[157] But the sale of a house might itself draw unwanted publicity and suspicion. Newspaper advertisements often give the ostensible reason for the sale of a West End property: the owner was typically 'going abroad', 'retiring into the country',[158] 'leaving off housekeeping', 'bankrupt' or 'deceased'. The first three reasons could easily mask financial distress or even be euphemisms for the fourth, or for other embarrassing conditions; for example, a 'correspondent' to *Town and Country Magazine* (1778), having dropped into the King's Bench debtors' prison (in a shower of rain), had met with 'a baronet who was said to have gone upon his travels'.[159] Advertisements were often, therefore, advertising something more than an intention to sell.[160] As the name of the seller was usually indicated, or deducible from the house's location, sales were a very public statement. There is also considerable evidence in private correspondence and periodicals that people knew who was moving in or out of houses and often the sums for which they were bought and sold,[161] and there was no accounting for the conclusions that might be drawn. The Duke of Manchester was rumoured to be retiring into the country and selling his house in town, and therefore supposed to be in financial distress. The duke did not care for such inferences: 'The Duke of Manchester will not now sell his house', reported Caroline Howe, 'they say he has changed his mind on hearing that every body says he is undone'.[162] This conclusion, erroneous or otherwise, drawn from the basis of mere rumours, joins other evidence that the purchase or disposal of a town house was an indicator: on the one hand of wealth, ambition, or good fortune; on the other, of debt, failure, or bad luck.[163]

Unsurprisingly, therefore, people went to some lengths to disguise both sales and the reasons for them. For this reason, no doubt, the Fielding brothers' Universal Register Office, a clearing house established in 1750, which charged a modest fee for selling goods and services, including houses, was promoted as having 'the economic efficiency associated with open marketing without the possibly compromising publicity associated with advertising'.[164] Elsewhere, Sir John Frederick sold his house in Grosvenor Street and rented another in Great George Street, telling prospective purchasers that his sole motive was to be nearer the Custom House. However, as soon as he received the £5000 purchase price he repaid a debt of the same figure to his brother, suggesting that his motives were more pecuniary than practical.[165] The rent for the Great George Street house was £200 per annum; it would, therefore, have been twenty-five years before he laid out in rent the figure for which he sold the Grosvenor Street house.

Sir William Lee, on the other hand, preferred the sorry truth to popular speculation. He was already in debt when he married in 1763, and mortgaged lands to raise money. In August 1765, he wrote to his father-in-law, Earl Harcourt, enlisting his help in letting it be known why he had parted with his London house, because, however embarrassing it might be, it was better than worse speculation and rumour:

I am very much obliged to you for y^r kind Letter just rec^d [. I]t was not my desire to put you upon the trouble of publishing to the World the reason of my parting with my House any more than my own intention to do it myself[. I]f asked my only hope and wish is, that whereas there are several people may ask the reason of it, and the receiving no answer from those that must know the truth, wou'd certainly have a very strange appearance [t]he true reasons may be aprized [sic] and this I trust I may depend upon from y^r justice and humanity.[166]

The 'true reasons' are evident in a note Sir William made of his debts around 1766, in which he mentions the sale of his 'House in Town' for £2300 as a relatively small credit in a statement that totalled his debts at over £22,000.[167]

An owner could dispose of a London town house when it was no longer required, when the money tied up in it had to be realised, or when it was impossible to support financially. But sometimes the decision to realise the capital bound up in the house and its contents was taken out of the owner's hands. In addition to the meanings given above, 'to distress' was also the act of making a legal seizure, 'to prosecute by law to a seizure' and 'to harass; to make miserable'. Whether or not the town house and its contents were the cause of debt, they became its target. Contemporary theatre made clear the link between 'dissipation and extravagance' and 'executions' in town houses – whereby creditors tried to recoup some of their losses by targeting the house and property of the debtor. In Richard Sheridan's *The School for Scandal* (first performed in 1777), for example, Charles Surface suffers successive executions in his house, in which 'not a thing [was] left but some empty bottles that were overlooked, and the family pictures which [were] framed in the wainscot!'[168] The link between gambling debts and executions was frequently made, as when the notorious gambler Stephen Fox suffered an execution in his Upper Brook Street house in 1774.[169] The Marquess of Bath's house in Arlington Street, the renowned location of wild drinking and gaming parties, was often full of bailiffs as a consequence of the damage done to his fortune by extravagant play.[170]

Reports of executions were common in private correspondence and no doubt in town gossip. 'The Foleys have had an execution in their House and all their goods are actually carried off; Lord Foley says, he neither can nor will assist them', reported Mr Stanley in 1778.[171] Bankruptcies as public as that of Sir George Colebrooke, on the failure of his banking house, meant that the public witnessed, through the press and gossip if not in person, the sale of the property for the benefit of creditors.[172] Colebrooke had been in financial difficulties for some years.

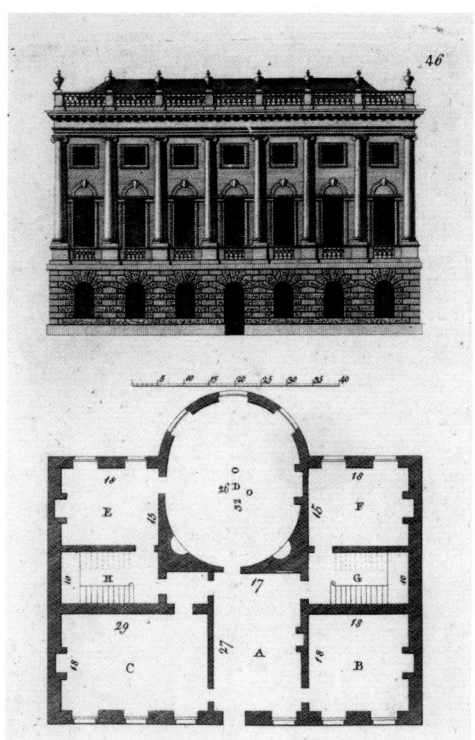

33 (left) John Crunden, plan and elevation for a town mansion, from *Convenient and Ornamental Architecture*, 1767, plate 46.

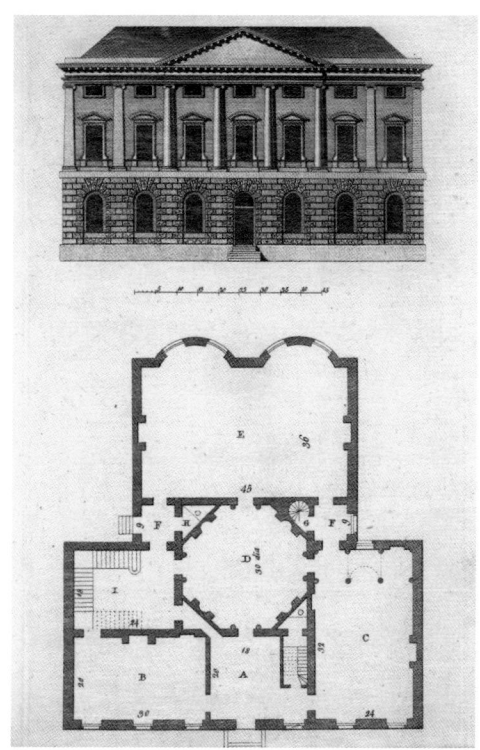

34 (right) John Crunden, plan and elevation for a town mansion, from *Convenient and Ornamental Architecture*, 1767, plate 67.

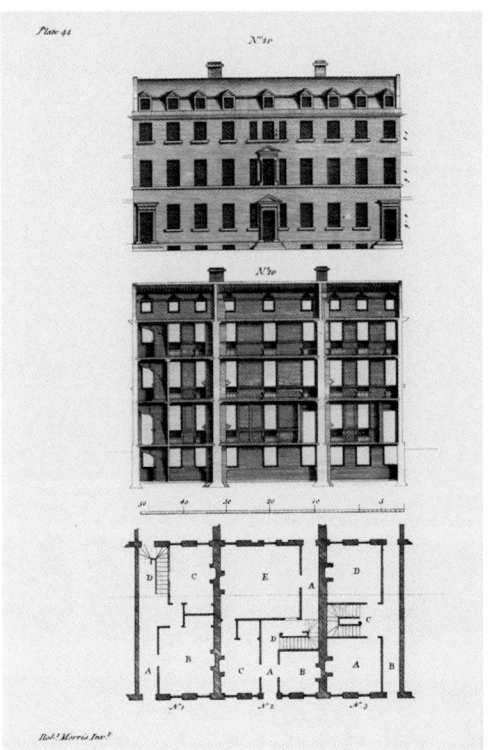

35 (left) Robert Morris, design for a row of three houses, from William and John Halfpenny, Robert Morris and T. Lightoler, *The Modern Builder's Assistant*, 1757, plate 44.

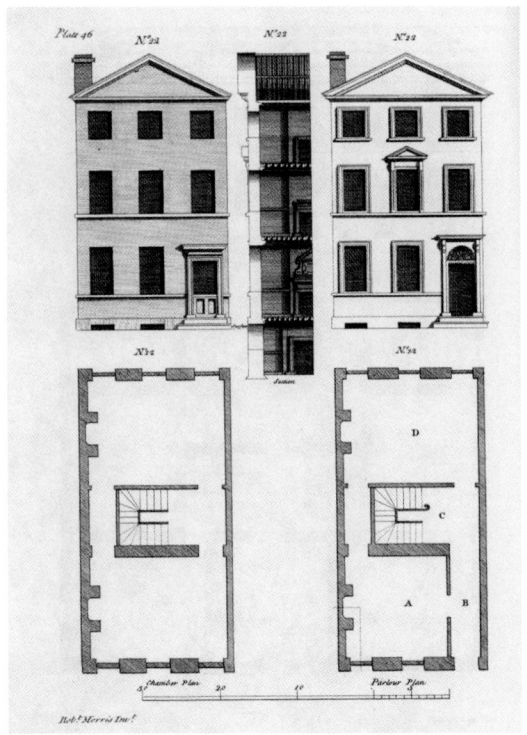

36 (right) Robert Morris, design for a town house, from William and John Halfpenny, Robert Morris and T. Lightoler, *The Modern Builder's Assistant*, 1757, plate 46.

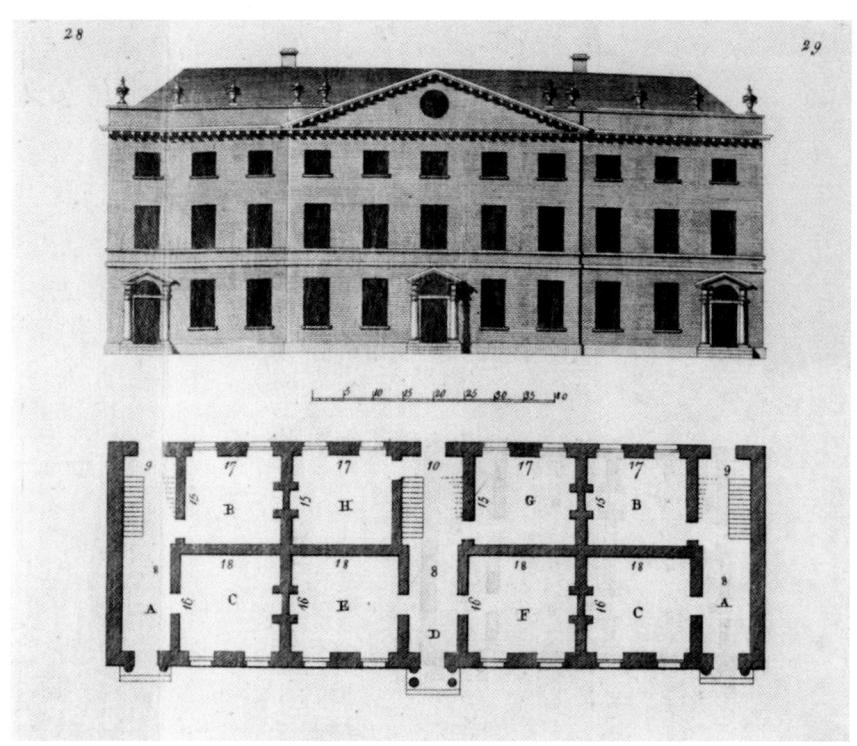

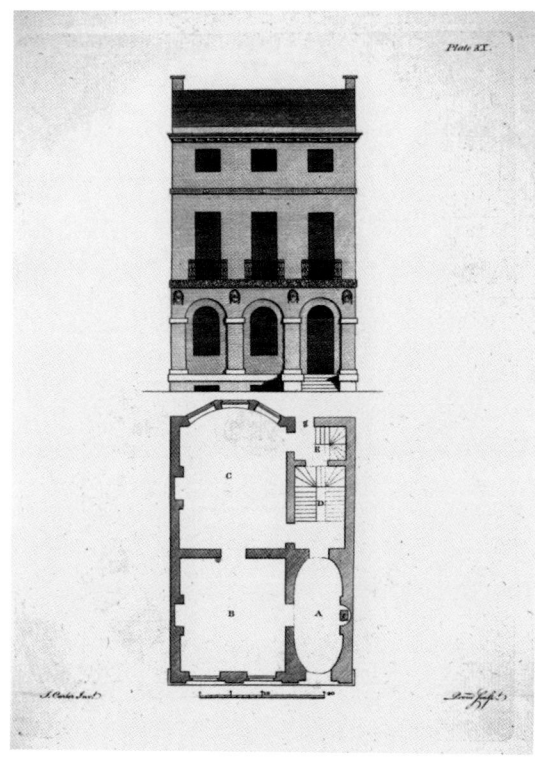

37 (above) John Crunden, design for a row of three houses, from *Convenient and Ornamental Architecture*, 1767, plate 29.

38 (left) John Carter, design for a town house, from *The Builder's Magazine*, c.1775, plate 20.

39 (left) John Carter, section of an elaborate staircase for the town house in plate 38, above, from *The Builder's Magazine*, 1775, plate 60.

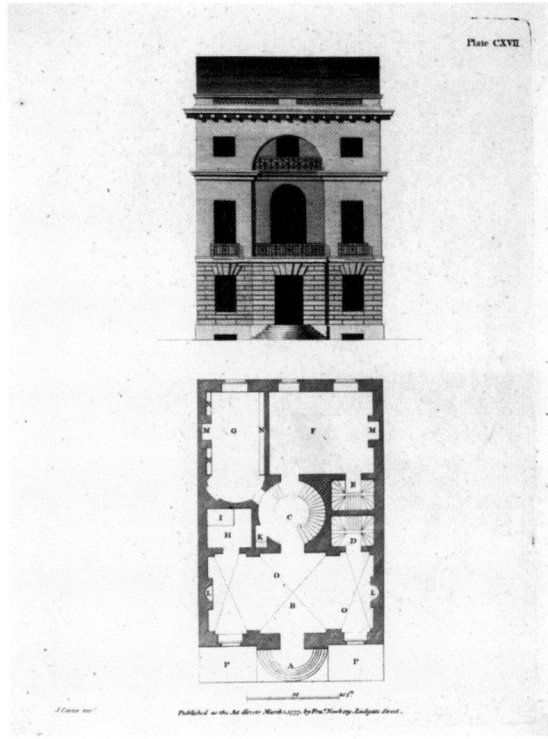

40 (right) John Carter, design for a town house, from *The Builder's Magazine*, 1777, plate 117.

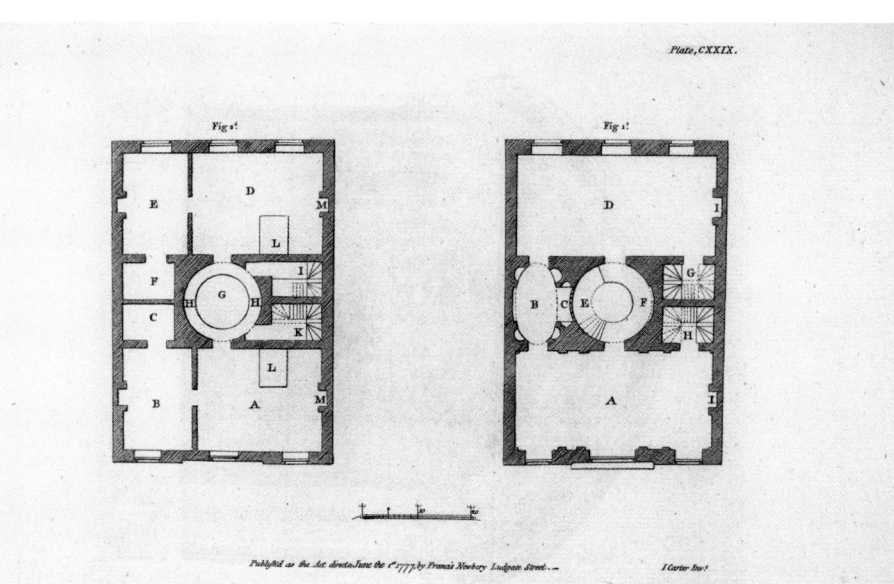

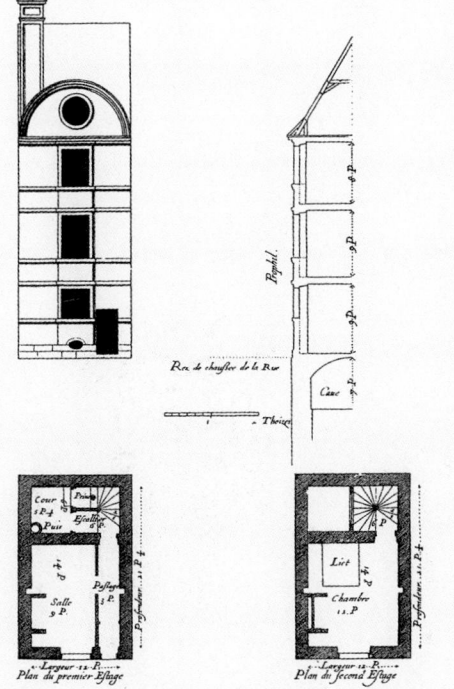

41 (above) John Carter, plans for the house at plate 40, above, from *The Builder's Magazine*, 1777, plate 129.

42 (left) Pierre Le Muet, design for a town house, from *Maniere de bien bastir*, 1647, plate 1.

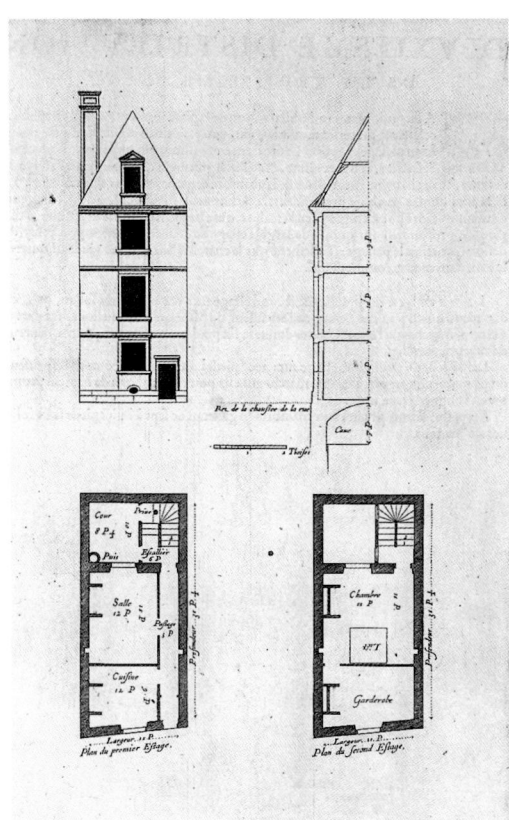

43 (left) Pierre Le Muet, design for a town house, from *Maniere de bien bastir*, 1647, plate 3.

44 (below) Home House, 20 Portman Square, James Wyatt and Robert Adam, begun 1772, street façade, with later attic storey.

45 1 Bedford Square, doorcase, attributed to Thomas Leverton, *c.*1778.

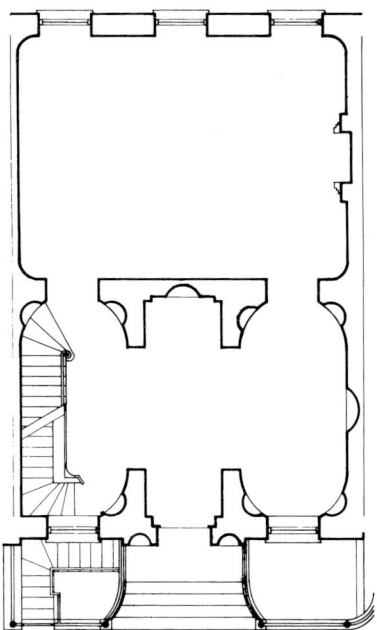
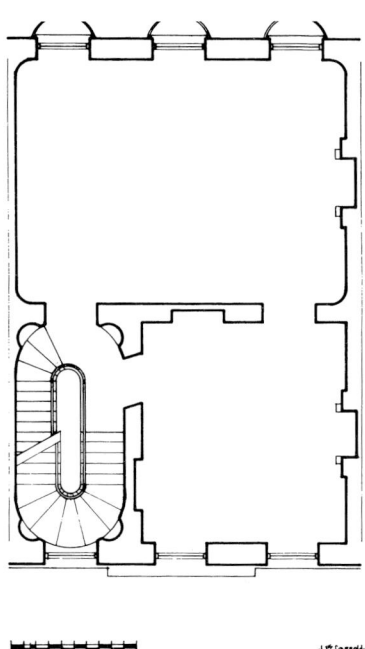

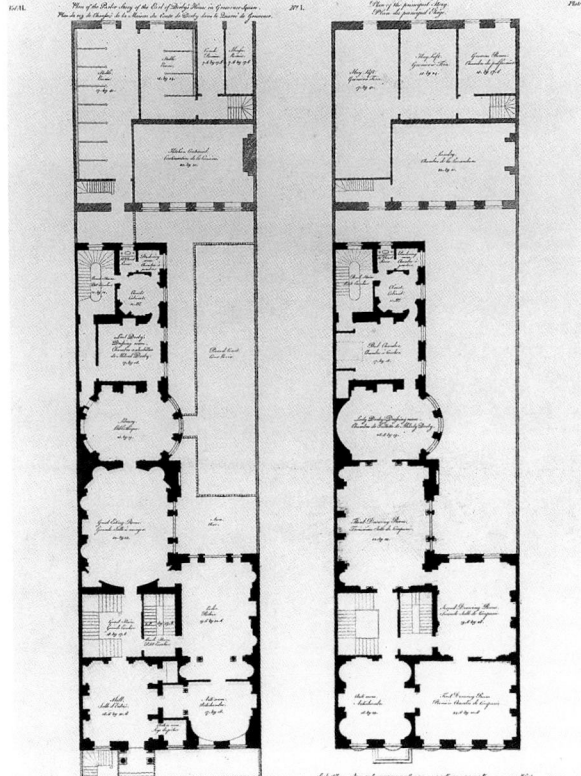

46 (above) 1 Bedford
Square, ground and
first-floor plans.

47 (left) Robert Adam,
Derby House, 26 Grosvenor
Square, 1773–4, ground
and first-floor plans, from
Robert and James Adam,
The Works in Architecture,
vol. 2, 1779, part 1, plate 1.

48 (left) Derby House,
26 Grosvenor Square,
1773–4, view of the great
drawing room, engraving by
B. Pastorini from Robert and
James Adam, *The Works in
Architecture*, vol. 2, 1779,
part 1, plate 5, detail.

49 (right) Robert Adam,
designs for the furnishings and
fittings at Derby House,
Grosvenor Square, from
Robert and James Adam, *The
Works in Architecture*, vol. 2,
1779, part 1, plate 8.

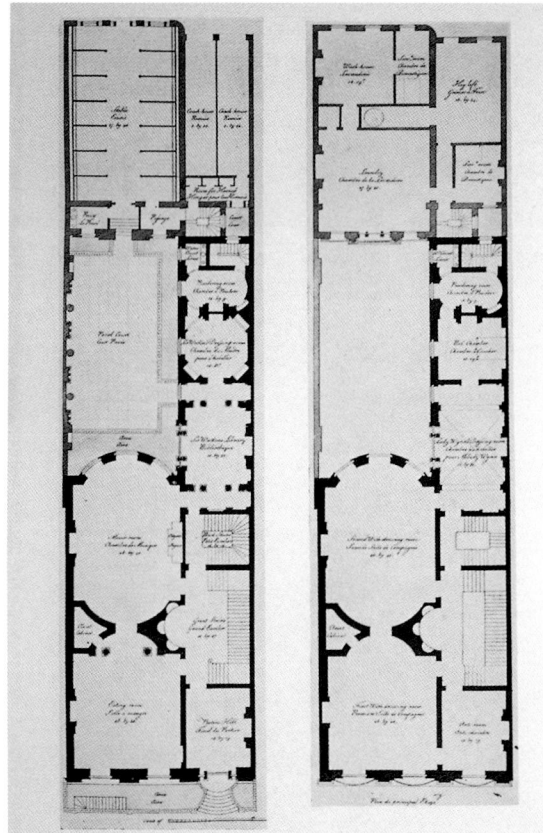

50 (above) Robert Adam, Home House, 20 Portman Square, design for the south wall of the Etruscan Room, c.1777.

51 (left) Robert Adam, Wynn House, 20 St James's Square, ground and first-floor plans, 1771–4, illustrated in Robert and James Adam, *The Works in Architecture*, vol. 2, 1779, part 2, plate 1.

52 (left) Robert Adam, Wynn House, 20 St James's Square, elevation, 1771–4, illustrated in Robert and James Adam, *The Works in Architecture*, vol. 2, 1779, part 2, plate 2.

53 (below) James Paine, plans of Dr Heberden's house in Pall Mall, 1769–71, from *Plans, Elevations and Sections*, part 2, 1783, plates 76–7.

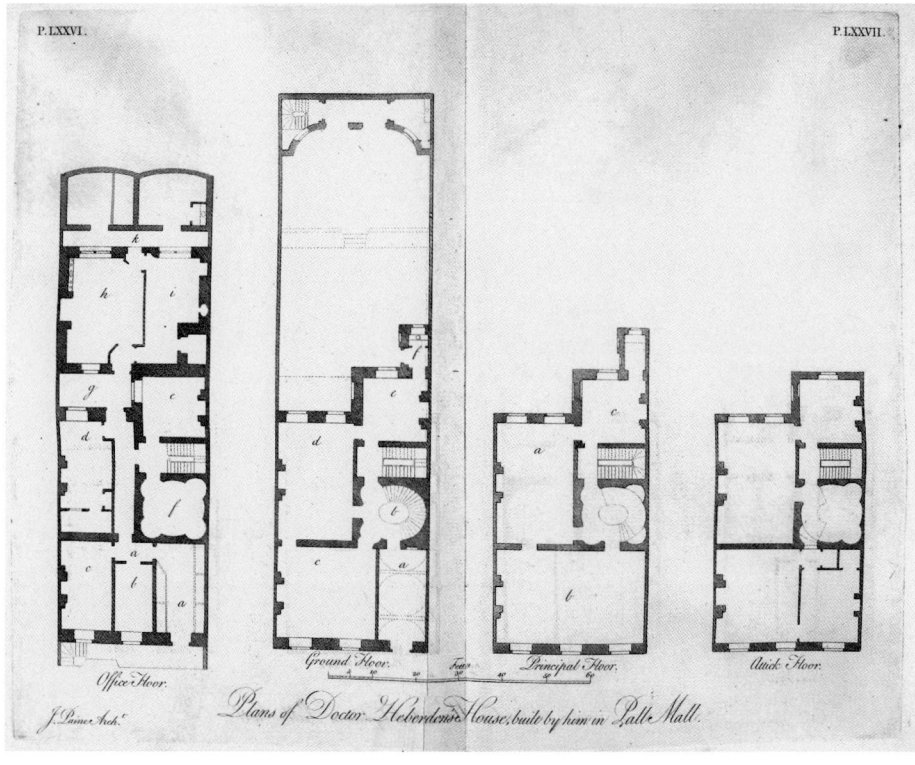

P. LXXVIII.

Front of Doctor Heberden's House, Pall Mall.

J. Paine Arch.

54 (left) James Paine, elevation of Dr Heberden's house in Pall Mall, 1769–71, from *Plans, Elevations and Sections*, part 2, 1783, plate 78.

55 (below) James Paine, plans of Thomas Fitzmaurice's house in Pall Mall, 1779–80, from *Plans, Elevations and Sections*, part 2, 1783, plates 79–80.

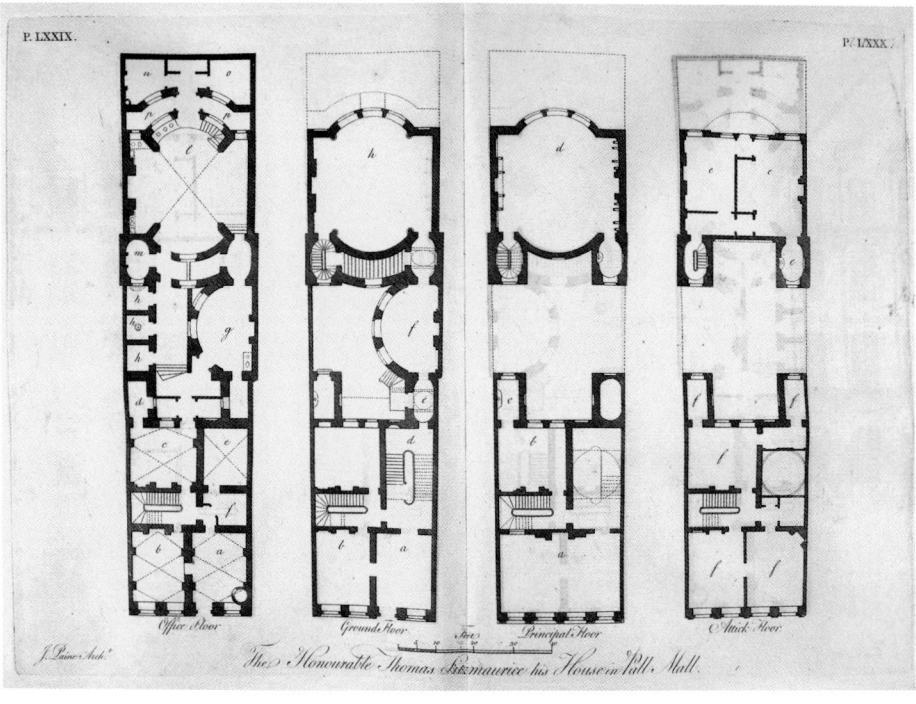

P. LXXIX.

P. LXXX.

Offices Floor

Ground Floor

Principal Floor

Attick Floor

J. Paine Arch.

The Honourable Thomas Fitzmaurice his House in Pall Mall.

P. LXXXI.

Front of the Honble Thos Fitzmaurice's House, Pall. Mall.

J. Paine Arch.^t

56 (left) James Paine,
elevation of Thomas
Fitzmaurice's house in Pall
Mall, 1779–80, from *Plans,
Elevations and Sections*, part
2, 1783, plate 81.

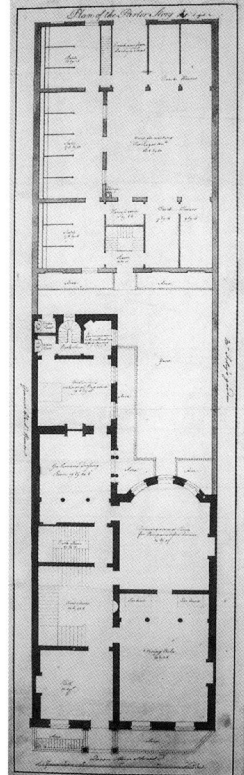

57 (right) Robert and James
Adam, Chandos House,
1770–1, ground and
first-floor plans.

58 (left) View of the staircase
hall at Wynn House,
20 St James's Square, Robert
and James Adam, 1771–4.

59 (below) Robert Adam,
Wynn House, 20 St James's
Square, design for the ceiling
of the second drawing room,
c.1772.

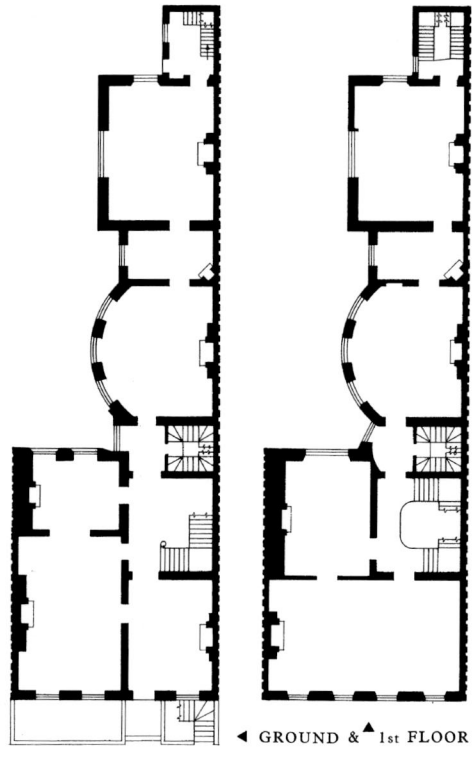

◄ GROUND & ▲ 1st FLOOR

60 (left) 38 Grosvenor
Square, remodelled by John
Johnson, *c.*1776, ground
and first-floor plans.

61 (below) Home House,
20 Portman Square, James
Wyatt and Robert Adam,
begun 1772, ground and
first-floor plans.

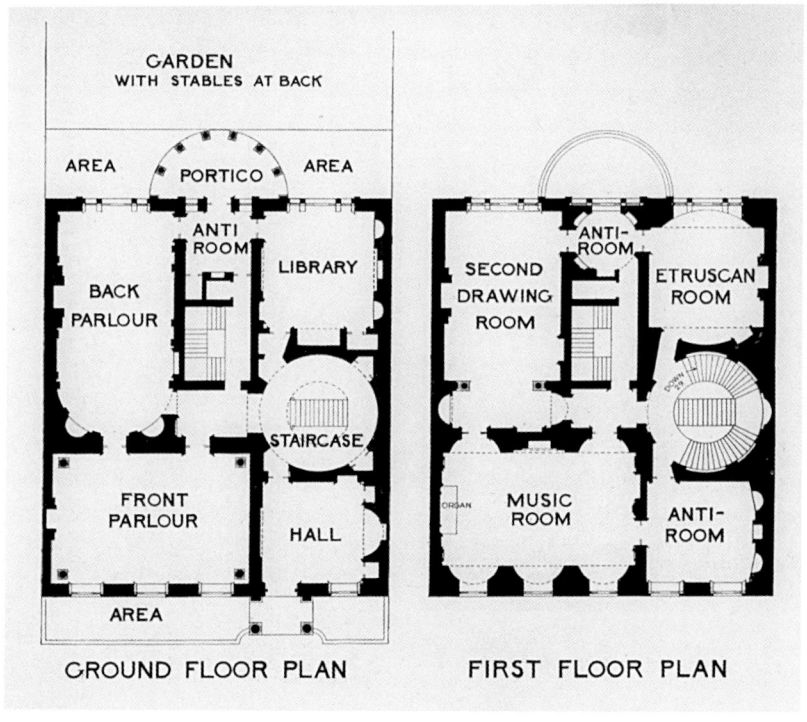

GROUND FLOOR PLAN   FIRST FLOOR PLAN

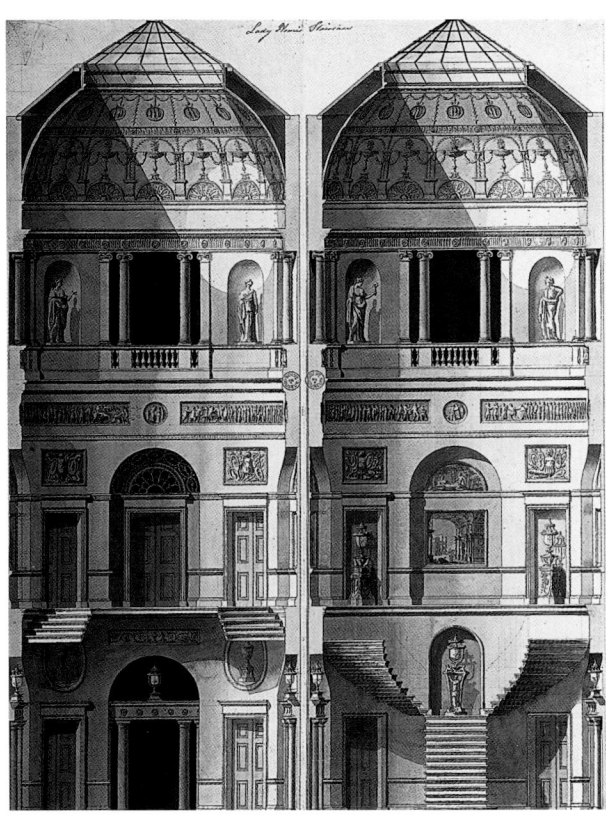

62 (left) Robert Adam,
Home House, 20 Portman
Square, design for the
staircase, *c*.1775.

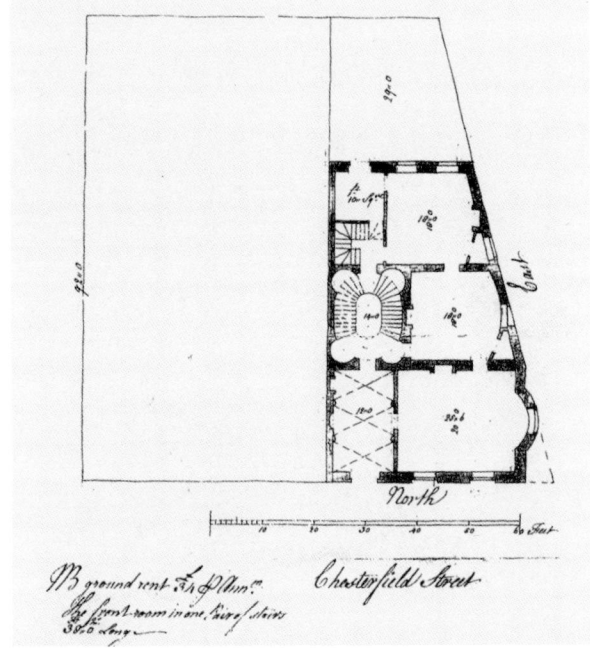

63 (right) [James Paine?],
plan for the ground floor of
a house for the Earl of
Scarborough in Chesterfield
Street, n.d., unexecuted.
NB: west side incorrectly
marked 'east'.

In March 1773, Caroline Howe reported that he would have to sacrifice his grand house in Arlington Street (and possibly even his country property) to satisfy the demands being made on him.[173] The town house was often the first property to be sold, ahead of any threat to the country property, perhaps because it was both easier to get rid of than a country seat (being more saleable and less restricted by entailments) and easier to do without.

The distinction between the source and the target of the debt may not always have been clear, but the evidence suggests that London houses, their contents and running costs, must have contributed to or instigated many a householder's financial problems. The sums involved in executions could be staggeringly high, even allowing for the exaggeration which so often comes with gossip. In February 1778 (a year of financial crisis), Judith Milbanke reported from London to her aunt that 'Lord Onslow had an Execution in his House last week for an hundred and sixty thousand pounds & is quite ruined.' The execution came as a great shock to Onslow's wife, 'who knew nothing at all of his Debts, & to comfort her he told her it was greatly owing to his having kept two or three Women whose expenses lay very hard on him'.[174] Keeping a mistress often generated expenditure on the purchase or rent and furnishing of another town property and no doubt the sort of attack that Onslow's house fell prey to. Even in the absence of statistics it is clear that mistresses were frequently set up in their own furnished premises, and the often-reported prevalence of kept women in the streets of Marylebone in particular may be another reason why town houses and women were and are so closely linked, often derogatively. The popular press suggested that the capital's demographic make-up reflected the unfaithfulness of husbands in London: 'Scarce a street in this metropolis but contains a lady notoriously known to be kept by some nobleman, gentleman, or tradesman; and many streets, particularly in the new buildings, are inhabited entirely by ladies thus maintained', observed *Town and Country Magazine* in 1773.[175]

In the year of Onslow's embarrassment, seemingly a bad one for executions, Judith's sister Sophia Curzon reported that 'Lord Derby has had sad work in his house; he had four executions all at a time'.[176] Thus a house that had been handsomely, lavishly and prominently refurbished by the Adams only a few years before, at great but unknown expense, was already the subject of physical and verbal attack. Sophie Curzon herself was at the mercy of executioners two years later, when she and her husband had the property in their town house sold for the benefit of creditors. By 1781 the Curzons were obliged to give up the house altogether, and moved in with relatives in town.[177]

One reason why executions happened so frequently in the town house was surely that the creditors themselves were London based, as part of the construction trade or of the wider range of essential and luxury trades. I outlined in Chapter One the role of a good London house in establishing what I will call 'social credit', an aspect of which was the financial credit that a good social 'figure' could attract. Personal security against which credit was offered 'was simply a *belief*, based on an assessment of the individual's creditableness (where issues of character meshed with financial acumen), that repayment would be made. Confidence was a cornerstone of the whole system'.[178] A correspondent to the *London Chronicle* in 1772 (another notable year of financial crisis, principally in private finance) moaned with some justification that unregulated credit was 'an evil of the first magnitude, when applied to the encouragement of . . . forgeries; furnishing men of no property with most fallacious appearances'.[179]

The cyclical link between credit and power may explain a number of purchases of town houses in fashionable areas during this period. Sir Watkin Williams Wynn's initial move to Grosvenor Square followed by his move to St James's Square, the types of additional purchasing he undertook and the level at which he pitched his entertainments, are conceivably evidence of a bid for the type of social power which, incidentally or deliberately, could procure the means to increase purchasing power – which in turn, if correctly managed, further increased the owner's social and/or political power. Where one need ended and another began was sometimes hard to distinguish: if a man decided he needed a London house, then that house not only generated the need for the money to finance it, most likely in the form of credit, but also became the means by which he could attract the credit to support his life there.

During the funding crisis over the rebuilding and decoration of Wynn House, Sir Watkin desired his steward and agent to be as secret as possible about his financial affairs and to take care of his credit, or it would 'be in a strange situation'.[180] Such caution indicates the need to hide the feeble financial base on which much opulence rocked.[181] This secrecy, and the 'masking' displays that it engendered, became part of the vicious circle of luxury, which was well illustrated in Fanny Burney's *Cecilia* (1782). Living well beyond their means in a new property in Portman Square, and entirely devoted to gambling and keeping abreast of fashion, the Harrels are repeatedly threatened with an execution in their house. They are saved by their wealthy visitor, Cecilia, who then looks for some expression of remorse and change in their habits and creed, but is horrified to find that their extreme distress quickly dissipates and is replaced by Mr Harrel's determination not only to visit the Pantheon but also to 'take another measure for removing all suspicion. This was to give a splendid entertainment at his own house to all his acquaintance, to which he meant to invite every body of any consequence he had ever seen, and almost every body he had ever heard of in his life.'[182] The Harrels are quite clear and insistent in their reason for diving back into the pool of luxury so soon after nearly drowning in it: rumours of their financial distress may already be circulating; it is therefore imperative that they counter them by appearing to have their 'credit rating' intact, because it is on that rating that their social credibility depends, and vice versa. Appearances were, for some, the only means of keeping up appearances, and men of '*great* titles with *small* estates' were said to indulge in the fashion for levees 'not because they have *business*, but because they have *creditors*'.[183] Living in the right sort of house in the right sort of place perhaps generated the power to become indebted. As D. Grant Campbell points out, 'the riotous opulence of the Harrels' lives rests upon credit, and flourishes entirely within an extended caesura between purchase and payment. Any movement outside this region of deferral into the world of consequences threatens to bring their glittering lie to pieces'.[184] For this reason, Cecilia is advised against paying any one of the Harrels' creditors, out of sympathy for their plight, because it will only bring all the duns clamouring for payment.

'Private' debt could be a very public matter, often advertised, as I have discussed, by the sale of a town house or its goods. In *Cecilia*, Burney describes the entertainment value of attending sales at the town houses of the financially broken, as advertised by the likes of Mr Christie:

> "I am come," cried [Miss Larolles] eagerly, "to run away with you . . . to my Lord Belgrade's sale. All the world will be there; and we shall go in with tickets, and you have no notion how it will be crowded."
>
> . . .
>
> "And do you intend to buy any thing?"
> "Lord, no; but one likes to see the people's things."[185]

As debt was public, and the town house was often its victim, the house became another London spectacle. As with many entertainments held at private houses, admission was by ticket. The sale for the benefit of creditors was the ultimate public scrutiny to which a town house and its contents could be subjected, and over which the owner had least control of his or her audience. It is possible, therefore, that a grand failure in a well-furnished and tasteful house in a good location was the next best thing to a grand success in the same surroundings.

Whilst credit and debt seem to have been an accepted way of life, Margaret Doody has argued (in connection with *Cecilia*) that 'society itself has invented the concept of "ruin", the great communal sneer. With an "execution in the house" the public identity is annihilated.'[186] Credit and what it afforded therefore combined to create public identity, where true financial substance was wanting. When both substance and credit were wanting, the individual could no longer retain a public identity in the polite West End and the relinquishing of house, contents or both, was symptomatic of its loss.

Rationalising unaffordable expenditure

The question of affording remains a vexed one in two respects. Firstly, the evidence presented here tends to suggest that people could not afford town houses. But we cannot take that to be universally true and, strictly speaking, we have to accept that affording is not simply having spare capital to hand, but also finding ways of raising funds and servicing the debts incurred by buying, building, rebuilding, refurbishing or simply decorating a house in town. At some point, in this sense, these people could 'afford' to have a town house, even if they could not afford to retain it long term. Secondly, it is difficult to draw any universal conclusions from the limited evidence available. Richard Wilson and Alan Mackley found much the same difficulty looking at the financing of country houses in the years between 1660 and 1880, noting that it required the coincidence of a 'set of building accounts with parallel ones disclosing total income and expenditure. Good fits of both are rare', they observe,[187] and even rarer with regard to town houses within a much narrower time period. Nevertheless, the question needs addressing and Wilson and Mackley's work provides a useful background against which to speculate about town houses in the absence of solid information.

Wilson and Mackley look at examples of various types of country-house builder over this longer period, studying those individuals' building finances in the context of their various regular, occasional and one-off sources of income. By this means they gauge how the house-building and refurbishment projects were paid for and account for stops and starts in building, gaps between completing a house and landscaping a garden, and so on. The results of their survey suggest that 'the English country house was seldom built from landed rentals alone'. Houseowners put to use the 'rewards of office', as well as funds raised by 'ground rents, mineral rights, and canal and railway company shares', while 'good marriage settlements, the savings of earlier generations and the sale of outlying lands were also important'.[188] We have already seen examples of marriages and other life events, including inheritance, as well as government office or simply a parliamentary seat, creating the need and sometimes providing the means (as far as we can judge) to purchase a house in town. The happy coincidence of inheriting both house and money allowed for splendid refurbishments, too. In 1762, Thomas Anson inherited his brother's house in St James's Square, together with a large inheritance that enabled him to rebuild it in stone, with the most fashionable interiors, all to James Stuart's designs.[189] Mortgaging or selling off land was certainly used to raise capital for these same purposes, as the case of Sir Watkin demonstrates. 'The benefits of industrial and urban development' could also be put to good use in the country,[190] and no doubt in the town, too.

Thus far we can surmise that the means of funding the purchase, building or refurbishment of a town house were not dissimilar to the means of funding building projects in the country. In cases where a landowner was building or refurbishing in both places, even a good collection of financial records and building accounts does not help us distinguish between the means of funding each project.[191] However, one reason why few housebuilders could rely on landed rentals alone to support country-house projects, Wilson and Mackley suggest, is that rental income was consumed by the need to maintain lifestyles, 'increasingly often in London'.[192] In this analysis, the London house becomes part of that expenditure on maintaining a lifestyle that diverts landed income away from the country house (one of Smollett's gripes). It would not be too rash, therefore, to suggest that landed income was a means by which many householders supported not only house purchases and building projects in town but their London residence generally.

If the building of a country house 'had to wait until the owner's economic circumstances were right',[193] this was not the case with the town house. The need or desire was often immediate: not a moment was to be lost. While in the country there was scope for getting oneself in the financial position to commit to a major project and for proceeding at a pace and in a fashion that matched activity and expenditure levels with income, in town the expenditure was less sporadic, not just because of the initial outlay on house or site, but also because town houses, and the lives conducted in them, did not lend themselves to phased building development. A country house could be constructed in sections, so that although the complete building was always kept in mind, in practice it could proceed in rational fits and starts according to the flow of income necessary to fund it. This approach was less viable in relation to the town house. While in less ambitious schemes rooms and suites could be refurbished as resources allowed, a complete new building or rebuilding project in a terrace house did not allow for sectionalised plans amenable to discrete construction phases. There was time for designs to evolve in the country, but the town house was ideally an all-in-one package.

Delaying payment (rather than work) was a means of 'affording' commissions of country and town houses alike. Wilson and Mackley report how Edwin Lascelles's bills in relation to Harewood House, Yorkshire, 'were paid so leisurely it protected his cash flow while it must have nearly wrecked those of his creditors',[194] while Francis Chambre's entreaties to Sir Watkin Williams Wynn, discussed above, make clear not only that the same tactic was put to use in town, but also that clients knew what they were doing. In their defence, vagueness as to final costs and unforeseen factors complicated the task of predicting and synchronising cash flows and building expenditure. One advantage that the town house had over the country house was that expenditure on the former could quickly be redeemed, by letting or selling the property, whereas expenditure on the country house could be temporarily or permanently halted, but rarely directly recouped, even if the property was let.[195]

Wilson and Mackley identify that the profits of Lord Carlisle's gaming in London contributed 7 per cent of the cost of Castle Howard earlier in the century,[196] and it would be interesting to know if the town house was implicated in the world of gambling in this more positive respect, as well as being the target of betting and other debts, as discussed earlier in this chapter. No doubt there were instances in which a good win helped finance a house purchase, or a major refurbishment project, but without the evidence to point to, we can only surmise that such was the case. However, we do have the certain knowledge that town houses were often directly or indirectly forfeited in games of risk, of which buying and furbishing the house itself was one. Wilson and Mackley suggest that building for the specific purpose of displaying riches was a reason for debt in respect of the country house,[197] but as regards to the town house, debt was often incurred even in connection with relatively modest houses, so it appears that it was not necessarily the desire for display, but the desire for the house itself, that was often the root of the problem. The cases of Lord Derby and Sir Watkin Williams Wynn, financially ill-placed commissioners of lavish houses, were exceptional only in their level of expenditure, not in the act of spending itself.

So why did people make a positive decision to damage their finances in this way? Both contemporaries and historians have accounted for the eighteenth-century consumer's behaviour through notions of luxury, social emulation and conspicuous consumption. And eighteenth-century attributions of blame for overspending invariably involved a villainous role for women. But these blanket explanations prove inadequate for explaining individual consumers' behaviour in respect of the town house.

The review of the town house's uses and values in Chapter One counters any straightforward conception of it as a luxury item. Luxury might be an appropriate framework for studying what people said about what others were doing, but when looking at what people did themselves, and why, it is safer to assume that they were driven by concepts of necessity.[198]

Amanda Vickery rightly observes that 'social emulation and conspicuous consumption are useful concepts for accounting for purchasing motivation under certain circumstances, but as portmanteau descriptions of eighteenth and early nineteenth-century consumer behaviour and material culture they are dangerously misleading'.[199] Neil McKendrick, defining the existence and causes of a purported 'consumer revolution' in the third quarter of the century, takes the eighteenth century at its own word, seeing the consumer as 'spurred on by social emulation and class competition', and implicitly endorses its own view of man as 'a consuming animal with boundless appetites to follow fashion, to emulate his betters, to seek social advance through spending, to achieve vertical social mobility through possessions'.[200] Emulation and fashion must have played a part in some, perhaps many, purchases of town houses by the gentry or town-based middle classes, who arguably had no real need (at least in the eyes of some contemporaries) to be in London or the West End respectively. But even in such cases, the emulation does not account for the house's whole purpose and value to its owner, and neither fashion nor emulation can account either for all instances or for all classes. The trickle-down theory of emulation, even if it does explain some middle- and working-class behaviour, is also an inadequate explication for consumer behaviour among the upper classes, who were more likely driven by a desire to lead the field, or at least to keep up with the front runners. In any case, high expenditure by the upper classes was often deemed 'natural', even appropriate, and only the motives for middle-class purchasing behaviour were under suspicion.

Conspicuous consumption also seems inappropriate or inadequate as an explanation of overspending on town houses. In his general review and critique of the theories of conspicuous consumption, Roger Mason identifies two conflicting explanations for it. The traditional view (prevalent pre-1750 but restated by later commentators) sees such consumption as essentially 'motivated by exclusively personal considerations' and owing 'little or nothing to the social and economic environment in which men live'.[201] The other, 'social' view, that conspicuous consumption is 'generated by specific socio-economic conditions which make the conspicuous display of wealth a necessary activity for those seeking higher personal status and prestige within the community', was expounded in the post-1750 period by Adam Smith, and more famously by Thorstein Veblen at the end of the nineteenth century. According to Mason, status considerations are generally accepted, within this post-1750 'social' framework, to be an important element in motivations for conspicuous consumption, but such consumption may not, in fact, be status-directed, and personality traits will always play a significant part in the decision to consume conspicuously, or not. Mason admits that 'social' theories cannot explain why people with the same or similar backgrounds and circumstances have differing attitudes to conspicuous consumption.[202] Therefore, while Mason, like McKendrick, can characterise eighteenth-century Britain as a fluid society with ample potential for vertical mobility, and expects, on that basis, 'to see the motivation for conspicuous consumption considerably increased . . . as status striving individuals recognise the rewards which are offered for displaying accumulated wealth or high income levels',[203] such an observation can only ever be a generalisation about motivations, and about behaviour itself. The evidence for this period certainly shows that although many people went for impressive houses and interiors, many others, less concerned with show or perhaps more confident in their monetary or social worth, lived decently yet modestly in town, even if they still got into financial trouble by doing so. Some people consumed conspicuously, others just consumed – and some in each party felt financial pain as a result. Mason admits, too, that many purchases will always be prompted by practical necessity and desire to display wealth,[204] and it becomes evident, if we look closely at the information I have presented so far, that 'personal' and 'social' reasons for expenditure on the town house are, in practice, difficult to prise apart.

Many eighteenth-century commentators equated social emulation and conspicuous consumption with a loss of power, control or reason brought on by external forces. Informal explanations, in letters, magazines, novels and other contemporary sources, often cite London itself as an incitement to unnecessary or unaffordable expenditure, because it was the heart of the fashionable world, the marketplace of luxuries and, because of the number of people there, the home of emulation. London was the place where one was exposed to 'every degree of temptation to Vice, Folly, & Extravagance', as Ann Pelham felt that her son should be

17

reminded before his return to town in 1780.[205] Although Smollett's *Humphry Clinker* offers more judgement than explanation, his general implication is that luxury, of which the London house was a representative, was an infection to which visitors to the capital were most susceptible. Burney writes of the Harrels as if they, too, had caught a fever in London, in the grip of which they had lost their reason.

London-based suppliers of 'luxury' goods were cast as proactive agents in financial ruin, sometimes even their own. Subsequent to Sir Watkin Williams Wynn's deep financial involvement in the refurbishment of his house at 20 St James's Square, his agent Francis Chambre astutely noted that 'when Alterations and Additions become a Foible, it cannot be well known where they are to end or what expence will carry them on, so the less they are undertaken the better'. The fault, he perceived, lay not just with the client, but with his advisers, or tempters: 'beware of your Architects and modern Gardiners', he continued.[206] The architect had long been cast as an expenditure-inducing villain, and the same seems to have been true of that 'rascally vamper of crazy moveables' in the ever-shifting world of eighteenth-century interior fashion, the upholsterer.[207] Where creditors clamoured for payment in contemporary plays, the upholsterer is often singled out as their representative, illustrative of the type of unnecessary and vain expenditure on a London house which might have caused this problematic debt.[208]

Some modern economic historians have subscribed uncritically to the eighteenth-century view that consumers' reason was disabled by 'the hypnotic effects of fashion' and the infection of luxury. Neil McKendrick writes of novelty becoming 'an irresistible drug', of frenzied spending among the middle classes, a 'feverish' consumer response to equally feverish commercial activity and of manufacturers exploiting 'this "epidemical madness" to consume, this sickness to buy even at inflated prices, this "universal" contagion to spend'.[209] But, in contrast to the helpless irrationality with which McKendrick and others identify consumer behaviour in this period, other writers, notably the anthropologists Mary Douglas and Baron Isherwood, characterise consumption as a rational exercise in expectation or certainty of calculated benefits.[210] Douglas and Isherwood also argue that 'all goods to some extent emanate messages about rank, sets of goods even more so [and] it is not always easy to separate pure rank marking from practical efficiency'.[211] This argument proves to be especially true of the set of goods that comprises the town house and its contents.

McKendrick cites the importance of the size and character of London in exposing potential consumers to the dangers of the market, in terms of the easy dissemination of new styles and the accessibility of products, for example.[212] Lorna Weatherill, in her book *Consumer Behaviour and Material Culture in Britain 1660–1760*, also suggests that town life encouraged expenditure because 'people were liable to meet others and to learn about consumption and to have the opportunity to present themselves in a variety of situations'.[213] But that was also what they came to London specifically to do: London did not simply encourage expenditure, but expenditure was a given once the decision to come to town had been made, and was surely part of the reason for making that choice. London allowed or facilitated expenditure; that was part of its attraction. As shown in Chapter One, a 'good house' may have had something of a practical function in putting socialites above reproach, but the necessity of such homes as Derby House and Wynn House was created only by a positive wish to be sucked 'into the vortex of extravagance and dissipation, leading . . . a fashionable life in town'.[214] The city did not operate as the great external force on innocent, passive or neutral subjects, but on subjects primed and eager to respond to its opportunities and temptations. A good town house was itself an incitement to go to London, as we have seen, and to behave in a certain way once there, and part of the incentive to buy a house in town was the chance to make a display in it, and one which was different from the type of display possible in a country house. The reasoning behind such moves to or within London is the key to understanding why so much money was spent on town houses, and how it was spent.

The strong link between London and women helps to explain the capital's characterisation as both a beguiler and temptress during this period. London, it was said, attracted and acted on women, whose 'supposedly weaker faculties of reason and heightened emotional susceptibility made them uniquely vulnerable to the glittering allure of the city and urban luxury'.[215] And men fell prey to both: they spent beyond their means on living in town because their women made them do it. Both Smollett and Burney, or at least the characters they created, present luxury and extravagance surrounding the West End house as a female-directed vice. Mrs Baynard's passion for London and a town house precipitated her husband's financial undoing, according to Matthew Bramble, and Mr Harrel accuses his wife of being a 'fool' who has been 'the cause of his ruin'.[216] But did women incite men to overspending on the town house and all that came with it? *Humphry Clinker* and *Cecilia* are fictional accounts, and however accurate they may have been in representing the contemporary perception that women's hankering to make a figure in a London house was the root of men's financial ruin, in practice it was young (and sometimes unmarried) men such as Sir Watkin and Lord Derby, as well as wealthy widows such as Mrs Montagu and the Dowager Countess of Home, who commissioned the most lavish and interesting houses from leading architects in this period.[217] A contemporary print of *Frederick Elegantly Furnishing a Large House* (c.1782) shows the young man himself centre stage, intent on making a 'proper figure', with his wife in a modest supporting role. He is being measured for new clothes, while directing the furnishing of his new house. The particular link between London-based (or induced) luxury and women may have arisen because many women wanted to be in London, but it cannot really be extended to account for why men took London houses, the type of house they chose or the treatment that it was given.

The influence and impact of wives is hard to establish, not least because bills were addressed to their husbands regardless of who had instigated the expenditure. It is difficult, in any case, to distinguish between the drive to spend and the act of spending. Although men may have exercised their own taste in purchases for the house, this does not mean that women were not urging them to make those purchases, and vice versa. Moreover, the stereotyping of women as 'extravagant' may have resulted from the fact that any money spent by married women was only ever notionally their own: legally it was their husband's.[218]

Consumption was itself seen as feminising,[219] so the blame for overspending on luxuries in town may have been projected on to women to 'safeguard' the masculinity of men. Furthermore, the popular presentation of the town house as a characterisation of negative 'female' traits – a drain on finances, parasitic and unproductive, according to Smollett – may have made it seem yet more a feminine zone, emasculating those who got involved in it. Although the distinction between the country house as masculine and the town house as feminine is too simplistic, whether in terms of their use, appearance, or financial impact, it is easy to see how contemporary antagonism towards London houses and their association with luxury arose. This point is discussed further in the concluding chapter.

Town residence was certainly not the economy that some latter-day sources such as Lawrence and Jeanne Stone have suggested. In support of their argument that living in town saved people money because their estate income was no longer offset by expenditure on maintaining a full household in the country, the authors quote César de Saussure, visiting England in the 1720s:

> A curious fact is that many noblemen live in town to economize, and though they are surrounded with great luxury, they declare that in their country seats they are forced to spend far more, having to keep open house and table . . . In the country most of them have sumptu-

ous abodes, or rather palaces, whereas in town they are lodged like citizens.[220]

Contemporary evidence contradicts Stone and Stone's conclusions, raising the question of whether economising by living in London was ever a fact and, if so, whether the balance changed in or by this later period. During these years 'retiring to the country' was an often-cited reason for selling up in London, and many letters refer to abandoning city life for a period in order to recoup finances, a strategy validated by the financial accounts.

It is vital to stress the importance of town houses to their owners and occupiers; what they wanted from them; and the practical and financial lengths to which they would go to acquire this. Susceptibility to over-spending in London was clearly a fact, regardless of who, or what, insti-gated residence or expenditure there. London life was expensive in itself, visitors were often there to spend and the desire or pressure to make a figure led to more expense in the form of the house. The attendant cost of London residence therefore operated at different, incremental levels. First, accommodation was needed; then, security of accommodation was preferred. Attention had to be paid to its quality in terms of location, size, proximity to other people, internal finish and entertainments to make the most of being in London and to show off the house.

The desire (or need) to reside in the West End, permanently or tem-porarily, must have been sufficient to warrant a high level of expendi-ture, in spite of the attendant financial risk. Although both eighteenth-century and twentieth-century writers have styled such expenditure and over-expenditure senseless, it was often a rational gamble in expectation of a profit, not necessarily financial, as long as one did not play too deep. Many did, and the house (and perhaps the public identity it con-tributed to) was the forfeit. The town house was, as Smollett suggested, a drain on finances – in terms of the necessary and incidental purchas-ing that it induced – and it provided nothing tangible in return, beyond its own exchange or rental value. But, even if Smollett omitted to acknowledge as much, the return on the house – its power – lay else-where, as part of the cycles of political, financial and social credit at play in later eighteenth-century London. Many householders showed their awareness of this fact by their willingness to spend money on their West End house. Yet it must have been necessary to strike a nice balance between sufficient expenditure to get a decent property in a good loca-tion, in sound condition, tastefully or fashionably fitted out, and the need to avoid the sort of over-expenditure that might necessitate a sale in which those same qualities came into play.

Part Two

~

From Building to Architecture

In this second part I examine actual architectural practice, and combine this evidence with the anecdotal evidence and findings reported in earlier chapters. I reveal what people wanted from London houses, and why, and how architects and developers responded with both standardised and exceptional houses.

In his discussion of distinctions between 'public' and 'private' in the eighteenth century, Lawrence Klein points out that 'high theory and prescriptive literature represent only one layer of society's knowledge. Even when theory is proscriptive or silent about certain practices, still those practices entail . . . a practical consciousness that orients, guides and provides normative support to the practitioner.'[1] Whilst the standard terrace-house format prevailed and remained popular with purchasers and developers, it remained unpopular with prescriptive critics purportedly writing with the city's, or nation's, best interests at heart. The town house's external appearance, notably its supposedly deceptive façade, particularly troubled such critics. And the town house's apparent inability to meet the formalised requirements of 'architecture' goes some way to explaining its dismissal by theorists and many pattern-book authors.

The average house, especially in its terraced form, was largely disregarded in architectural treatises, manuals and pattern books prior to the 1770s, after which there is some evidence of a rise of interest in its appearance, planning and general architectural potential. But it was in practice that this increase in interest was most evident. Architects, in response to clients' needs, worked with, rather than against, those particularities of the individual town house that others felt inhibited its potential. In this way such designers as Robert Adam moved the terrace house from common practice to exceptional contrivance; that is, from just 'building' to a redefined 'architecture' centred around the house's own peculiar qualities.

Four

Private Contentment, Public Disquiet

Terrace houses constituted by far the greatest proportion of both new and existing building stock in the West End in the later seventeenth and eighteenth centuries, particularly in the period c.1760–90. The standard terrace house satisfied the generic needs and preferences of the town resident; it suited builders, developers and planners; and legislators encouraged it through building regulations. It was for these reasons that houses were generally both similar in form and externally plain. However, more 'disinterested' observers' broad prescriptions for London's domestic architecture were at odds with the actual practice of those buying, commissioning, designing and building houses in the West End. In their eyes the terrace house had certain failings. It was not only its size and attachment to its neighbours that caused disquiet, but also its appearance. As well as being the focus of popular gossip, physical attack and covetous inspection, therefore, the West End terrace house's ubiquity and popularity made it the subject of adverse published criticism.

The popular house

It is clear that people rarely looked for expansive London mansions, detached or not. We know that few were built in this period and we can now guess why. The abandonment of the Adams' scheme for individually designed, insulated palaces in Portland Place suggests that people did not want such big homes, and cared little about distinguishing them-

selves from others by the size of their house. The cost involved in building, purchasing, refurbishing or decorating, in addition to running a big
house must have been one reason for erring on the smaller rather than
the larger side, although Stefan Muthesius suggests that terrace houses
were 'not adopted simply through economic necessity but because of a
positive liking for certain architectural consequences of the plan.'[1]
Muthesius does not elaborate, but a partiality for compactness is certainly evident in the phrasing of house advertisements and elsewhere.
Moreover, the notion of 'completeness' reflects the successful integration of all elements of the house, including accommodation for carriages
and horses, into one narrow, self-contained site. The terrace house was
designed for the most efficient use of space and other economies.
Consequently, William Chambers advised Charles Turner against building further rooms at the rear of his Grosvenor Street house as they would
darken the kitchen and offices, be too small to be useful, and 'the
Expence will greatly exceed the advantage of anything that is done'.[2] In
other words, the optimum had already been reached.

As a house often had to be readily disposable when its cost became
too onerous, and because its disposability increased in accordance with
its general conformity to a norm, the standard terrace house was the
most robust option for a buyer who was also a prospective seller. At
least in this period, it seems that purchasers and tenants generally chose
between houses on the basis of subtle differences within general sameness. The more particular the buyer's requirements, the harder it was to
achieve a good match. For example, Agmondesham Vesey's friends
specifically required 'room for two [sedan] Chairs & a good Eating
room'. Despite the many properties for sale or rent in 1774, a suitable
house proved hard to come by.[3] On the other hand, the effort to match
house and resident also increased if the house were substantially different from others and, as we have seen in Chapter Three, a house could
be hard to sell because its greater-than-average size limited its potential
market. Distinctions between basically similar houses were no doubt
more apparent to the eighteenth-century house-hunter than they are to
the present-day architectural historian, who in any case looks rather for
general patterns and equivalences. Nevertheless, in the process of discrimination, a house's material merits or flaws often counted for little
in the face of factors unrelated to its physical form or fabric, such as its
location or neighbours.

The differentiation of the house itself – the move from homogeneity
to heterogeneity, from the general to the special – was usually something
effected later, rather than sought in the shell of a house at the point of
purchase. It was typically achieved less by changes to the house's form

than by means of applied embellishment and customised fittings, such as fashionable ceilings or chimney pieces. Occasionally these features were decorated with motifs reflecting the owner's interests, as in the pieces John Johnson supplied for the Duke of Dorset in Grosvenor Square, which were embellished with emblems of the theatre and music.[4] Extensive interior and exterior work, or even rebuilding, was an extreme way to adapt a house to one's own particular needs or to keep up with fashion, but a new owner could readily make their mark through furnishings and furniture, and erase the previous occupant's mark just as easily. Even when significant differences were constituted, for example, in the reshaping of rooms, as at Derby House, rather than solely in decoration, this was not a reaction against the typical town-house form, but a reworking of it, often on the site or within the party walls of an older house. In the apparent absence of any client impetus, there was little reason for the 'standard' body of the house to change over the years, and there were no drastic technical changes that might have precipitated developments in its form.[5]

Practical considerations are at the root of both the evident preoccupation with completeness and convenience and the tendency to provide variations on the model, rather than changing the model itself. Nevertheless, David Hume, in *A Treatise of Human Nature* (1739), uses an architectural analogy in his discussion of aesthetics that has some bearing on both matters:

> A man, who shews us any house or building, takes particular care among other things to point out the convenience of the apartments, the advantages of their situation, and the little room lost in the stairs, anti-chambers and passages; and indeed 'tis evident, the chief part of the beauty consists in these particulars. The observation of convenience gives pleasure, since convenience is beauty. But after what manner does it give pleasure? 'Tis certain our own interest is not in the least concern'd; and as this is a beauty of interest, not of form, so to speak, it must delight us merely by communication, and by our sympathizing with the proprietor of the lodging.[6]

Such scrutiny was not, of course, peculiar to the age or place. Writing in fifteenth-century Italy, Leon Battista Alberti had argued that

> when we see other Men's Houses, we immediately set about a careful Examination of all the Proportions and Dimensions, and, to the best of our Ability, consider what might be added, retrenched or altered; and presently give our Opinions how it might be made more compleat and beautiful. And if a Building be well laid out, and justly fin-

ished, who is he that does not view it with the utmost Pleasure and Delight?[7]

The tendency to scrutinise and criticise is a natural one and its corollary is 'Pleasure and Delight' when things are well done. The town-house occupant was particularly well placed to share in his neighbours' satisfaction with enhancements to the convenience and beauty of his own property, and vice versa, because the two houses operated within the same idiom and therefore shared a common aesthetic (as well as common restrictions) with which he could sympathize. In Hume's terms, the utility of the object can only concern the owner, who therefore sees beauty in it, but the spectator can easily imagine and share in that appreciation, so that a 'beauty of interest' becomes in some measure a beauty of 'form'.

Perhaps, therefore, it was partly for reasons of shared appreciation that owners of such exceptional houses as Wynn House and Derby House spent vast sums of money on elaborating the basic plan of an existing terrace house, rather than on a detached town mansion – by this time a dying breed, outmoded and largely defunct as a symbol of greatness, wealth, power or ambition. Clients and architects seem to have realised that they could achieve a greater impact by excelling within the same idiom rather than operating within a different one, as I discuss in more detail in Chapter Six.

Like the individual house-hunter, the speculative builder or developer would have considered the standard terrace house the most robust choice for production in a risky financial world.[8] As well as being most likely to sell, the standard model was easily, infinitely and economically repeatable. There was often, in any case, no requirement, incentive or even licence for the builder or developer to provide anything more elaborate than the minimum specified in his contract with the ground landlord, whose prescriptions often encouraged both loose uniformity and plainness. Building agreements for the Bedford Estate specify only such things as storey heights and wall thicknesses, and basic interior finish, such as dados and wainscot,[9] while in August 1766 James Manley simply agreed with the estate to build three houses on the west side of Duke Street, Bloomsbury, 'in ye same Manner as the 3 houses on ye East Side of the Same Street lately built by Mr Richd Morris'.[10] On a larger scale, the ambitions of town planning fed off the fact that the standard house changed little. With a basic, familiar and popular building unit to work with, planners and designers could focus their attention on rows, squares and more extensive developments without giving much thought to their constituent elements.

Parliamentary legislation also played its part in abetting standardisation of form, as well as external uniformity and plainness. As John Summerson explains, 'the limitation of size and value set out in the ratings tended to create optimum types from which there was no escape and within which very little variation was possible',[11] and ground landlords sometimes used the ratings as prescriptions for building on their estates. The Building Act of 1774, in particular, encouraged both similarity of form and appearance, and flatness, although Frank Kelsall has argued that this act consolidated rather than instigated tendencies towards the latter.[12] In 1847, Benjamin Disraeli looked back to the new buildings of the previous fifty or so years and firmly laid the blame for their timidity, insipidness and uniformity at Parliament's door:

> All the streets resemble each other . . . What an opportunity for Architecture suddenly summoned to furnish habitations for a [big and wealthy population]. Mary-le-bone alone ought to have produced a revolution in our domestic architecture. It did nothing. It was built by Act of Parliament. Parliament prescribed even a façade. It is Parliament to whom we are indebted for your . . . Baker Streets and Harley Streets, and Wimpole Streets, and all those flat, dull, spiritless streets, all resembling each other, like a large family of plain children, with Portland Place and Portman Square for their respectable parents.[13]

But it was not only Parliament that was to blame: the rise of neo-Palladianism in the earlier eighteenth century had done much to dictate a norm of plain classical appearance, to which speculative builders and developers were still happy to adhere in this later period. There are few specifications for façade designs in many surviving building contracts.[14] They focus instead on such basic features as window surrounds and particularly on materials, implying that 'designs' and proportions were so standardised that they did not need spelling out: the default position of the more-or-less Palladian front would suffice in most cases. For example, the articles of agreement drawn up in November 1771 between the Portland Estate and the carpenter John White are detailed regarding the materials and finish of the houses' fronts but not their actual design: 'the fronts should be of red or grey stock bricks; the arches and returns or jambs or the windows in rubbed brick or stone; the parapet walls to be coped with stone and other proper ornaments'.[15] Where proportion is given positive consideration, it is often in the name of uniformity. In July 1768, the Bedford Estate gave permission for the building of a house on the west side of Charlotte Street, and stipulated that the builder should 'put a Portland Block Cornice above the Two pair of Stairs window in a line with the other Houses adjoining', in addition to 'a Portland String and Fascia under the One pair of Stair Windows and Portland Window Stools under all the other Fore Front Windows'.[16] While this contract gave the builder positive instructions, many other building specifications dictated what features were not to be included on façades, such as bay windows, rather than what was. External plainness, like uniformity, happened by default.

Planners, too, were happy to 'maintain existing standards of taste',[17] and were less bothered about innovation in the design of the houses themselves than in their settings. So, while estate planning and design in and around Bedford Square in the 1770s and 1780s, for example, was forward looking, the houses themselves were old-fashioned in style, even within the limited development of house façades, bearing 'a striking resemblance to certain Palladian houses of the 1720s and 1730s'.[18] Within the framework of town planning, therefore, street was differentiated from street, not house from house, and differences between streets became greater as houses stayed the same.

Disraeli may have blamed Parliament, but Dan Cruickshank and Neil Burton ascribe restrained street fronts to a kind of native puritanism, suggesting a positive aesthetic and moral preference for an understated, modest façade. For them, the uniformity of such terraces as Gower Street reflected not just 'the economic advantages offered by mass-produced architecture' but also 'the public's taste for austere and repetitious façades'.[19] The authors use Inigo Jones's prescription that architecture should mimic the outward behaviour of 'every wyse man' who 'carrieth a graviti in Publicke places'[20] as evidence for an 'English preference for undemonstrative and uniform building elevations'.[21] But Jones requires 'graviti'; he does not require façades to be uniformly reticent, just non-whimsical, non-capricious. In any case, for the consumer, the terrace house's appeal derived, as we have seen, from practical considerations such as economy, convenience and compactness, and not, as these and other comments in the modern literature imply, from moral or egalitarian principles.[22] It is unlikely that people positively subscribed to Quatremère de Quincy's contemporary vision 'of a city of sober citizens, living modestly at a private level':[23]

Have you never entered in imagination into any of those cities which were the dwelling of the arts and of liberty? How all the proper houses, commodious and solid, seem to become reconciled under the level of a modest temperance! How happy uniformity in their aspect seems to announce to you citizens equal among themselves, as all appear to announce the same needs, the same means, the same sufficiency, without luxury and without superfluity![24]

Christoph Heyl extends advice found in eighteenth-century conduct books – 'to regulate one's facial expression so as not to betray any particular thought or inclination' when among strangers – to account for the 'expressionless mask' of the terraced house: 'as with people, so with their houses: their facades also studiously avoided expressing anything beyond a broad indication of the social status of their inhabitants'.[25] It may well be that the house's deadpan look happily coincided with this general disposition to lack expression in public, but it seems a step too far to ascribe plainness and sameness wholly or even mostly to this principle. In view of clients' and purchasers' general lack of interest in façades, evident in various contemporary sources, it seems at least as likely that they accepted the norm of plainness as a default position. Likewise, it is all very well to report that legislation was passed (or writers wrote) to the effect that people should be constrained in what they could build, but to extrapolate from those facts that the Englishman's natural propensity was to plainness is nonsensical. There is a big difference between not minding exterior plainness and positively subscribing to it as an ideal. There is also plenty of physical and recorded evidence from earlier periods that 'the aesthetic preferences of the English public' were quite the opposite and that, in fact, they 'traditionally sought in architecture complexity of effects, producing amazement and surprise, rather than clarity, proportion or regularity'.[26] Efforts to impose classical order and rationality into British architecture in the eighteenth century can be seen as attempts to curb such 'natural' enthusiasms.

Thus modern-day architectural historians may have overstated the desire and willingness (and perhaps tendency) to conform. In 1776, Sir John Fielding praised St James's Square for possessing grandeur without pomp, through regularity, and astutely remarked that 'the Houses are built more for the Convenience of their opulent and noble Possessors, than for causing Surprize in the Beholders'.[27] The writer equates regularity with (practical) convenience, and owners' lack of interest in façades leads naturally to simple uniformity. The plain façade was not necessarily a positive choice; it was a non-choice. In terms of the town-house façade, people were generally happy with what other factors dictated they should get, and, in practice, the 'happy uniformity' that Quatremère lauded was most likely to be dictated by the exigencies of speculative building and of legislation.

Sometimes the façade did receive special attention, as demonstrated by the bespoke fronts that some leading architects designed for individual houses (discussed in Chapter Six). Such expressions may have resulted from a desire to stand out, or from a wish to make something of the standard terrace house, which was increasingly likely to be occupied by people distinguished by rank or wealth.[28] But such examples do not affect the general assertion that the London terrace house was 'a refined industrial product brought to perfection through constant selection during repeated serial construction'.[29] Any attention the façade received from ground landlords, builders and developers was most likely to relate not to the individual house but to all or part of a terrace. It was neither necessary nor expected that each house should be an individual work of art.[30]

Despite the basic template shaped by Palladianism and regulation, true uniformity was often lost somewhere between ambition and execution. Fragmentary development of streets militated against strictly uniform elevations and uniformity sometimes happened more by default (where the same builder developed several houses at the same time). For example, seven houses erected by Michael Barrett in Park Street (now Queen Anne's Gate) on a lease dated 1774 'were not designed, nor built as an architecturally coherent composition', although they had several external features in common.[31]

Even more so than the loosely or tightly uniform terrace façade, the true 'palace front' subsumed the individual identities of a number of houses within a group identity, as at the Royal Terrace, Adelphi. Such a front required positive planning, resolution and control,[32] and money, and there were many failed schemes. Some architectural historians have argued that the investment of effort and money in a palace-front treatment reaped benefits by making the development to which it was applied more popular. Cruickshank and Burton, for example, suggest that 'elevational uniformity, when it was achieved, was brought about because the chief undertaker desired it, and he desired it because it became increasingly obvious during the Georgian period that the illusion of living in a palace was highly marketable'.[33] But there seems to be little evidence to support this assumption. James Ralph, writing in 1734, believed that only someone with more money than sense would be deceived by the 'triple house' on the north side of Grosvenor Square, 'a wretched attempt at something extraordinary', bad in itself and in its situation towards the end rather than in the centre of the row. There was no excuse for it 'unless the view of taking in some young heir to buy it, at a great rate, may be allow'd one'.[34] In 1765, John Wood wrote of how his design for the Grand Parade, Bath, to be embellished with Corinthian columns and pilasters, came to nothing because of 'a Scheme contrived by one of the Tenants . . . to lay aside the Ornaments'.[35] John Nash's double house in Bloomsbury Square (c.1777–8) was stuccoed to give the imposing look of a single, large house with one central doorway, and 'an arcaded and pencilled ground floor, giant Corinthian pilasters and alternating triangular and segmental pedimented first floor windows along the principal front', but proved hard to sell.[36] Such evidence suggests that housebuyers were not interested in paying for such embellishment. One of the most prominent palace-front treatments was that given to the Royal Terrace, Adelphi, but it was not enough to prevent the Adams from having to dispose of many of the unlet houses by means of a lottery in 1773. If houses were generally hanging heavy on builders' and developers' hands, a handsome, grand and unifying frontage was not enough to make a difference.

Any changes to a façade were applied rather than integral to the house's form, and even such palace fronts as the Royal Terrace were articulated largely by decoration alone – 'classical architectural details were used . . . in a rather superficial way, both literally and figuratively'.[37] The Adelphi's modishness was largely constituted in its outré external finish; the planning of the houses' interiors, and the development's general layout, were largely conventional.[38] Exterior decoration could be added or omitted without in any way affecting the structure of the individual houses or the row. In fact, in many instances, such as the north side of Bedford Square, the façade design made sense only on its own terms and bore no relation to the divisions of the houses that it fronted. A house's membership of a composed group generally made no difference on the inside, only on the outside, allowing generic house types and plans to be untouched by changing fashions for exteriors.

This manner of external decorative treatment was therefore itself a response to an enduring preference for the three-bay terrace house. As James Lewis argued in 1780 in respect of his country-house-style design for the elevation of three houses in Great Ormond Street, 'if this mode of building were generally adopted . . . our houses would have a more magnificent aspect, and their present conveniences might be retained'.[39] There was no need to sacrifice one for the sake of the other.

The unpopular house

The prevalence and continuing popularity of the terrace house among all classes is scarcely acknowledged and certainly not welcomed in the writings of observers of London architecture at this time. The following discussion is based principally on the two main essays of this type published in this period: John Gwynn's *London and Westminster Improved* (1766) and John Stewart's *Critical Observations on the Buildings and Improvements of London* (1771).[40] These works have a strong affinity with the tradition of the essay on civic taste,[41] and earlier essays in the same architectural vein, such as Ralph's *Critical Review*, first published in 1734 and in an extended, posthumous version in 1783.[42] This affinity, together with their successive dependency, makes it difficult to determine which parts of Gwynn's and Stewart's prescriptions for London were specific to this period. The conservatism of the genre also goes some way to explaining why their observations were largely out of step with contemporary practice.[43] Nevertheless, the essays provide evidence that traditional ideas – for example, that the public sphere should have an influence on private practice and that private individuals should build for public benefit – were still considered, by some, to be valid in this period.

Gwynn and Stewart consider the wider cityscape, and the role of the individual building in that broader context, adopting a long-term perspective in opposition to the short-termism associated with the individual interests that had so far dictated the form and detail of the city. The authors view London houses from a public rather than a private perspective – that of the viewer, not the inhabitant – effectively setting up the city, or even the nation, as the ultimate consumer of domestic building in the capital. The notion of house building as a selfless, public-spirited occupation, a contribution to the city's and nation's grandeur and well-being, was a longstanding one. Alberti writes of the 'Benefit', 'Delight' and 'Glory' architecture has brought to nations, and makes clear that individual and public interest in this respect are inseparable:

> Men of publick Spirits approve and rejoice when you have raised a fine Wall or Portico, and adorned it with Portals, Columns, and a handsome Roof, knowing you have thereby served not only yourself, but them too, having by this generous use of your Wealth, gained an Addition of great Honour to yourself, your Family, your Descendants, and your City.[44]

Gwynn and Stewart therefore voiced a common (and long-held) belief that the architecture of the town house had some role to play in ornamenting the town and that it should be the object of civic and national pride.[45] Stewart felt he had licence to discuss the 'merits and demerits of private undertakings as far as they relate to public ornament',[46] because the fronts of terraces, and the general size and demeanour of larger houses, contributed to the city's appearance and thus its reputation. Likewise, a writer praising the Adelphi in *Town and Country Magazine* (1771) wished 'that there were many such public spirited men of property and genius as Mess. Adam, who would risk a part of their fortunes to increase the beauty, regularity and convenience of this metropolis',[47] and Gwynn complains about the selfish interests more typical of architects, builders, clients and developers. These interests had manifested themselves in two main ways: on the one hand, failure to subscribe to planning and uniformity (and therefore to utility and beauty, respectively), and on the other, the failure of the nobility to distinguish themselves in the size and architecture of their London houses. Stewart, too, desires the nobility to lead the necessary drive from neatness to magnificence.[48]

For both Gwynn and Stewart, therefore, the façade of the house has a duty to the street. There are two ways of fulfilling this obligation: either by blending in to contribute to a greater whole or by standing out magnificently. Noblemen should, preferably, indulge the broader public, and do themselves justice, by building mansions. Exceptional houses should distinguish exceptional people. The homes of ordinary people, on the contrary, should be blended together to provide buildings that had more to do with the ornamentation of the city than with the representation of the individual householders.

Some resistance to the prevailing practice of 'people of quality' living in terrace houses is evident in both essays, although Stewart, writing a few years later than Gwynn, is more realistic than his predecessor. Stewart strongly prefers the insulated town mansion set back from the road beyond a courtyard, but he is aware of the numbers who are now happy with what he calls a 'street house'. He deems this trend acceptable, in some cases, where the house is 'rented for a winter residence, without any idea of property annexed'. 'It is not indeed required', he writes, 'that every nobleman should have a palace in London; all that is contended for, is, that when they think it necessary to build, they at least present us with something elegant in the design'.[49] A good-looking town house, distinguished either by size or external finish, could conflate personal satisfaction and self-aggrandisement with a public expression of civic responsibility.

Given the tendency towards 'street houses', partly accepted by Stewart, both authors argue that individual houses should act together to contribute to the kind of grandeur and beauty achieved by regularity and order. Many descriptions of the eighteenth-century capital similarly single out for praise 'the several beautiful Squares which contribute to the Embellishment and Ornamentation of London'.[50] It was the square, not the individual properties that made the contribution; the 'handsome' and 'elegant' houses had to be grouped for effect. Gwynn's ideal is a circus in which the centre building of each quarter projects slightly, but is 'regularly designed in harmony with the rest of the buildings'.[51] The 'grandeur of the whole' is to be preserved by not suffering any 'innovation' to be made. The Bedford Estate exercised this sort of tight control over developments on its land, and the author of the posthumous passages in the 1783 edition of James Ralph's *Critical Review* praises Bedford Square as 'a proof of the improvement of our taste. It is without exception the most perfect square in town . . . the regularity and symmetry of the sides . . . the great breadth of the pavements, and the neatness of the iron rails.'[52] On the other hand, in the 1734 edition Ralph had called the west and south sides of Grosvenor Square 'little better than a collection of whims and frolicks in building, without anything like order or beauty'.[53] Uniformity was a credit to public taste, but disharmony was a private fault.

Speculative builders and estate landlords went some way towards satisfying Gwynn's requirements for uniformity, although not for disinterested reasons. Gwynn appealed to the mercenary nature of developers in arguing that 'the novelty of the design, the elegance and spaciousness of the area itself, and above all, its magnificent appearance would contrive to render it the most desirable situation for persons of rank and distinction'.[54] Few estate owners believed that architectural unity would attract the sort of 'quality' people who were prepared to pay for the privilege of living behind a palace front. Modern architectural historians peddling this argument may well have derived their assumptions from Gwynn, who was surely no neutral observer in this respect.[55] It is worth noting, too, that Gwynn was 'a pioneer improver and extender of the "publick good" ' and that an essential pragmatism underlies his schemes, however idealistic they might seem. Order and decorum in London's planning could operate against disease, criminality and other real dangers, as well as against the visual distress caused by untidy building stock.[56] Likewise, concerns for safety and legibility, coupled with a desire to make the city a fit representative of the nation, lay behind the Act for Paving, Cleansing and Lighting the Squares, Streets, and Lanes, within the City and Liberty of Westminster, passed in 1762. The act translated houseowners' individual responsibility for maintaining the pavement in front of their homes (and also lighting the stretch of street it fronted) into a tax which allowed the commissioners to do the same for entire streets in a prompt and uniform manner. 'The whole scheme was applauded by Charles Walcot, MP, as successful in creating durable, clean and safe streets with "an elegant uniform appearance," and he deplored the old order with "every one consulting his own interest, or gratifying his own fancy, without the least regard to order, or the safety or convenience of the public".'[57]

Uniformity in paving was one thing, but there were good practical reasons for the general failure of London terrace architecture to live up to its public role. Simple homogeneity in a whole row was achievable, either because of stipulations by the ground landlord, as on the Bedford Estate, or because of a tacit consensus as to what form the individual terrace house should take. But under the same circumstances the application of an overall design scheme, such as a palace front, was much less likely, and only possible where an architect was able to design the whole row, and sacrificed individual façades to an imposed design scheme. Robert Morris blamed 'the unpolite Taste of several Proprietors of that Ground' for preventing Edward Shepherd's proposed design from ornamenting the whole rather than part of the north side of Grosvenor Square,[58] while in rapidly expanding Marylebone speculative builders were 'motivated by an urgent desire to run up houses as quickly as possible and were not interested in palace fronts'.[59]

Neither were they greatly interested in the quality of their buildings. The poor constructional and material standards of speculative houses had been criticised as long as such houses had been around, and would continue to be criticised into the nineteenth century.[60] In 1756, and again in 1767, Isaac Ware explained the problem:

> The nature of the tenures in London has introduced the art of building slightly. The ground landlord is to come into possession at the end of a short term, and the builder, unless his Grace tye him down to articles, does not chuse to employ his money to his advantage. It is for this reason we see houses built for sixty, seventy, or the stoutest of this kind for ninety-nine years. The care they shall not stand longer than their time occasions many to fall before it is expired; nay some have carried the art of slight building so far, that their houses have fallen in before they were tenanted.[61]

Newspapers and magazines reported on these sloppy and dangerous building practices, particularly among the 'new buildings' being rushed up in Marylebone.[62] The architect James Peacock, writing in 1785 under the anagrammatic pseudonym Jose Mac Packe, proposed that those builders trained in the 'Marylebone school' had focused their skill on ensuring that a building fell down six months after the lease expired. 'The Master of Arts', he concluded, 'is he who can manage matters so as to keep up his building till he has sold it.' He claimed to base his own maxim of 'a little stronger than strong enough' on real experience of such buildings collapsing before half finished.[63] A certain amount of fudging was intrinsic to the speculative development process, but shoddy materials and execution came to characterise the terrace house, further tainting its reputation and contributing to its unpopularity in terms of the public interest.[64]

Some individual houses, such as 11 St James's Square, which was given a distinctive new front by Robert Adam for Sir Rowland Winn in 1774–6, clearly presented a good face to the street or square and as such went some way towards satisfying critics such as Gwynn and Stewart, even though the motivations for such work were not disinterested or altruistic. Christopher Sykes argues that the architectural impact of great town mansions such as Bedford House and Newcastle House had, in public opinion, never been as significant as their owners' political affiliations[65] and other magnificent mansions, such as Devonshire House and Burlington House, both in Piccadilly, hid themselves behind blank walls. The latter's celebrated architecture was therefore in no position to embellish the street, as John Stewart griped in 1771: 'How many are there, who have lived half a century in London without knowing that so princely a fabric exists. It has generally been taken for a jail'.[66] Meanwhile, Devonshire House was almost as plain externally as the wall it presented to Piccadilly.[67] There was nothing new, therefore, about individual preferences taking priority over public interests; the rise in popularity of the terrace house amongst the nobility was just the latest, and most obvious manifestation of a longstanding truth in respect of town houses – that individuals did not build with the city's interests in mind.

The dissembling façade

Behind Gwynn's and Stewart's preferences for a mixture of architecturally distinguished noblemen's houses and magnificently uniform terraces lay a desire for legibility – for distinguishing the exceptional resident from the unexceptional. The terrace-house front offered some scope for differentiation and elaboration, to be discussed in Chapter Six, but there seems to have been little correspondence, in general, between a tenant's social standing and the house's external finish. The grandest fronts were neither reserved for, nor the sole choice of, the aristocracy, who might be content with brick and Coade stone. If noblemen chose to live 'anonymously' in terraces, alongside people of lesser rank and means, the inherent duplicity of the uniform terrace front presented a dilemma for the spectator, who had been denied a marker of the owner's status. Complaints about the inability to identify or judge people by their house's external appearance were part of a wider gripe to that effect. As a writer in the *Lady's Magazine* (1777) complained, 'an insipid similarity of manners reigns throughout the fashionable circle; and it is downright affectation to pretend to find out characters amongst those who compose it, when they are making this kind of exhibition'.[68] The palace front was the most deceptive finish of all, despite its advocacy by Gwynn and Stewart, because it deliberately subsumed the identities of individual houses, and therefore their owners, within a single, encompassing finish.

Such illegibility was an offence against 'propriety', which informed many of Gwynn and Stewart's notions about what was right and proper in domestic architecture. The concept of propriety was not new to the age, but depended on architectural writers as far back as Vitruvius. It formed part of the notion of *convenance* or convenience, developed and most clearly expressed earlier in the century by the French architectural theorists Germain Boffrand, Jacques-François Blondel and Marc-Antoine Laugier.[69] For Laugier, propriety (or *bienséance*) 'requires that an edifice should not have more or less magnificence than is agreeable to its destination, . . . [T]he decoration of the building . . . should always be relative to the rank and quality of those that inhabit it', while for Blondel, propriety is 'the decorum one should observe with respect to each type of building, depending upon the rank of the persons for whom one is building it'.[70] On Laugier's terms, the individual, understated terrace-house façade, secreting a nobleman behind a poker face, was insufficiently magnificent, while the even-handedness of the row of houses that treated all its occupants the same way, with or without a palace front, was fine so long as it housed only the middle classes. But that was not always the case. On Blondel's terms, an architect or builder required prior knowledge of the house's occupant, but this, too, was rare in the speculative development of later eighteenth-century London.

Gwynn's and Stewart's writings reveal the overlap between social and architectural principles that typified the period. These principles were most needed in London, where identities were often confused and unreadable, although not always by intent. If houses were not always what they appeared to be, the dissimulation was more incidental than deliberate, unlike the wide use of fine apparel that (supposedly) obscured class distinctions, too. The illegibility may have been inherent in the architectural solution to London's increasing permanent and temporary populations, but that was no excuse, and it came to be part of a general uneasiness about the ability or inability to judge by appearances.[71] What is more, its root cause – London's expansion – was discomfiting in itself; as such the illegibility of London houses was a manifestation of a far greater (and perennial) problem, and the terrace house's reputation suffered for that reason.

A terrace-house façade of any type was, anyway, manifoldly deceptive. It could not indicate a house's layout and might actually hinder any judgements of its likely form. In 1779, Elizabeth Montagu complained not only of the smallness of the houses in the Royal Crescent and Circus at Bath, but of their misleading appearance: 'on ye outside it appears a good stone Edifice, on ye inside a nest of boxes'.[72] Two equally proportioned façades could mask a deviation of the party wall behind, whereby one house borrowed space at the expense of its neighbour, as at 11 and 12 North Audley Street and 14 and 16 Queen Anne's Gate.[73] The front could never be a true indicator of the size of the house, which was largely determined by its extension backwards from the façade; added storeys were more common in the following century. In all but the very largest houses, which had room for symmetry, the façade rarely gave any indication of the house's interior planning or decoration. As discussed below, it could be remarkably aggrandised, either in size or finish, without any readable indication on the façade. Grandeur was therefore exposed only to the occupant's chosen audience; it was not provided for the ornamentation of the city and the benefit of the broader public.

Another of Gwynn's grievances was that the houses' backs were not as regular as their fronts. He complained of the practice 'in many parts of the new buildings' of

> erecting single brick edifices with stone fronts of a regular design, the sides and backs of which being entirely exposed present nothing but absurdity and contradiction, a motley composition of stone and brick walls perforated with holes in order to admit light.[74]

For Gwynn, the terrace house failed not only in terms of quality of construction, but also of design. Regularity of the street façade was not enough, because houses were sometimes viewed from vantage points other than the composed vista. Such sights, he wrote, offended the spectator when he found that the back had no connection with the front but exhibited only 'a heap of confused irregular buildings'.[75]

There are two facets to Gwynn's complaint. Firstly, the terrace house – or row of houses – was not conceived in three dimensions, in the manner of the detached house. The front and back were treated as the unrelated elements that, visually, they were. But Gwynn and others wanted to see a relationship constructed where none naturally existed. Secondly, the house or row allowed meanness to be exhibited. It is unlikely that either complaint would have affected practice. Even if it could be proved that a fancy front treatment was attractive to purchasers, the builder was unlikely to spend, or be required to spend money on elaborating a rear façade.[76] Even the plainest houses distinguished between front and back, perhaps simply by the omission of the cornice.

More importantly, the houseowner, particularly within a speculative development, was unlikely to be concerned about whether the front of his house matched the back. Even the finish of the front façade was extraneous to the needs of the house, or its occupant, as my earlier discussion suggests. If, in the opinions of Gwynn, Stewart and others, the front owed something to the street or square, it owed nothing to the house: it belonged to the view.[77] For example, 13 Hertford Street was distinguished from its high-class but conventional neighbours by a pediment, 'perhaps because it was the only house visible from Oxford Street'.[78] Likewise, Chandos House (1770–1), an individual speculative building by the Adams, may have been treated to a special stone front not for reasons to do with the grandeur of the house itself, but because it could be seen to advantage from Cavendish Square.[79] Tara Draper suggests that the Adams may have intended to provide 'an elegant announcement for the aristocratic enclave [they] planned to build behind it', in Portland Place.[80] The space required for viewing a façade was not often available, so individual or group façades responded where it was: for example, the Royal Terrace, Adelphi (viewable from or across the Thames), the unusually wide Portland Place, and in squares in general.

The palace front, above all, came within the 'jurisdiction' of the street (or the river, in the case of the Adelphi's Royal Terrace), rather than of the houses it fronted, with which its divisions might have no real correspondence. The houses at either end of James Adam's palace-front scheme for the west side of Portland Place had their fronts to Portland Place marked out with a high arch, even though their entrances were on the adjacent side streets.[81] The Portland Place fronts therefore had little logic in terms of the individual houses: the arches terminated the row's overall façade design, and were not intended to mark the fronts of the two houses whose sides they spanned. Arthur Bolton observes that 'Robert Adam's façades, in Fitzroy Square and elsewhere, are often simple negations of the interior structure. He was prepared at any time to sacrifice such facts in the interest of his general composition.'[82] That is, Adam understood the nature of the superadded façade as unrelated to the group of houses it fronts.

The superficiality that Gwynn bemoaned was a natural result of the divided interests in the town house: the owner happy with a standard form of house (and most concerned with the interior) and the developer and/or estate landlord wanting to regularise or embellish a new development (and most concerned with the exterior). The two sets of interests coincided beautifully, or plainly. Whether the individual house or row was left simple or given an elaborate finish, the effect belonged to the street, the square, the vista – not to the house. John Wood believed that his design for the Grand Parade, Bath, would have 'given Pleasure and Satisfaction to Multitudes, among all Rank of People', but the tenants who refused to implement his scheme presumably saw no benefit to themselves, only expense.[83] Housebuyers' apparent reluctance to pay a premium for houses incorporated in a palace front, discussed above, may indicate their perception that such ornamentation clearly did not belong to their houses.

The back, on the other hand, was related to the house. It had no other allegiance, or job to do. As Gwynn bitterly observes, it often reflected, without pretension, the functional mix of smaller rooms and closets at the house's rear. It was rarely given an architectural treatment unless warranted by a particularly large garden, as at Home House, Portman Square (begun 1772), or where it could be viewed from the house, in which case it functioned, visually, as an extension of the interior and was treated accordingly. A mews building to the rear of the north side of Bedford Square has 'a remarkably well-detailed pedimented brick elevation' with better facing work than the main houses,[84] perhaps because it belonged to the private view from the house, whereas the house façade itself belonged to the public view. Likewise, the screen wall and the front to the offices visible from the rear reception rooms of 20 St James's Square, by Robert Adam, were given elaborate architectural finishes that had no relation to the structures they fronted. Behind the screen wall was simply a wall. The applied trimmings did not differentiate between different parts of the wall, and the Portland stone front to the stables and laundry clearly reflected neither the disposition of the rooms within nor the magnificence of their internal finish.[85] The clear distinction between a front and what it fronted, evident in the courtyard at 20 St James's Square, was also at work in terrace house façades, either individually or in combination.

A further element of the front's artifice was the common mismatch between the house's external and internal finishes – 'the former grimy, austere, repetitive – the latter clean, richly decorated and full of variety', a contrariness often remarked upon by visitors to eighteenth-century London, if not by Gwynn and Stewart.[86] Like the mismatch between exterior and occupant, that between inside and outside happened less by contrivance than by circumstance, but was nevertheless the root of further dissatisfaction with the terrace house. In a discussion of convenience and propriety, as part of his study of the use of architectural space in the eighteenth-century English novel, Simon Varey discusses Henry Fielding's objection to the hypocrisy of inverting, on the inside of a house, the impression given by its exterior. The difference between the two is immoral because one is artificially constructed (the exterior)

23

and one is the owner's natural expression (the interior).[87] In the case of the faceless town house, deception was inherent, so long as the upper classes declined to distinguish themselves on the outsides of their homes. Expression of self was normally reserved for the inside.

Congruence between inside and outside sometimes came in the disturbing form of prettified façades. Inigo Jones's arguments for confining the whimsy elements of the house to the interior are another aspect of propriety, one taken up in 1785 by James Peacock, who maintained that a houseowner should be attentive to what seems 'characteristically proper' in his façade, 'if he would not offend against the strictness of propriety'. If he is determined to decorate the outside of his house,

> and thinks nothing can be beautiful, unless it is fine, let him at least be careful to avoid an excess of the peurile [sic] ornaments, as well as the emasculate proportions of the modern school, and not enervate his elevation with filigree work, proper only for his lady's dressing-room . . . let him suffer his exterior to be made in some small degree like antique architecture and be in some measure guiltless of the excess of modern refinement and modern finery.[88]

But what people write may have no relation to what they build. As Harold Kalman points out, members of Peacock's architectural circle did not stop short of prettily embellishing house fronts, as shown, for example, in the upper façade of George Dance's terrace on the west side of Finsbury Square (1777),[89] in which Peacock himself may have had a hand. Dance's shop-front designs also feature fanciful and abundant exterior ornamentation.[90] Perhaps, in domestic buildings, external ornament characterised by frippery rather than magnificence had unacceptable commercial overtones of self-publicity.

In practice, most coincidences of grandness inside and out in an individual house were more indicative of the client's wish to embellish his home externally than to construct a deliberate relationship between interior and exterior. Derby House, where the modest brick façade was retained despite the money and architectural skill lavished on the refurbished interior, demonstrates the separateness of the two concerns. John Soane's judgement that the façade was retained 'in token of the proud "disregard to external appearance" of which English noblemen like to boast' sits uncomfortably with Lord Stanley's propensity for personal display.[91] It seems more likely that Stanley appreciated the impact to be achieved by the contrast of exterior and interior, and the exclusivity served by concentrating all efforts on embellishing the latter. Likewise, despite the extravagantly bespoke interior decoration at Home House, Portman Square, the wide façade, which offered plenty of scope for embellishment, was left relatively plain, adorned only with relieving arches for the ground-floor windows, decorative string courses and Coade-stone panels with swags. But then no fancy façade was necessary to advertise what was effectively a private 'club' inside, an exclusive coterie concerned only with itself.[92] While it would be a mistake to consider the town houses of the Dowager Countess of Home and Lord Stanley as 'typical', in this regard they demonstrate nicely why and how the reality of private interests would always triumph over the idealism of public demands, even in this most public of arenas.

Five

The Town House Dismissed

Gwynn's and Stewart's writings are broadly prescriptive, wide-ranging and ambitious; they concern the effects and role of town architecture, rather than the niceties of building design. Nevertheless, they do imply a distinction between building and architecture – that is, a distinction between common practice and exceptional contrivement. During this period the town house became caught up in a call for architecture, but the way in which it responded was not always what these 'public' campaigners had envisaged. There were other, private petitioners – town-house clients and purchasers – with a much better claim to the architect's attention and often with entirely different interests at heart. I discuss in Chapter Six how leading architects such as the Adams responded to their clients' needs by making 'architecture' out of the house's interior, in particular. But first I stay in the public domain to look at how architecture was formally defined there, and how the town house fell short of its theoretical and practical demands.

In his *Treatise on the Decorative Part of Civil Architecture* (first published in 1759, with subsequent editions in 1768 and 1791),[1] William Chambers talks broadly of architecture's role. He is proud of its permanence:

> fine furniture, rich dresses, brilliant equipages, [and] numerous domestics are only secondary attractions, . . . they soon feel the effect of time; and their value fluctuates, or dies, with the fashion of the day . . . the productions of architecture command general attention; are

monuments lasting beyond the reach of modes; and record to latest posterity, the consequence, virtues, achievements, and munificence of those they commemorate.

Architecture, says Chambers, also gratifies 'a thousand superfluous, a thousand artificial cravings' resulting from successful commerce.[2] It could be argued that the London town house played its part; but architecture's main commemorative function, as described by Chambers, was one that ill suited the terrace house. It would certainly have been easier to link the house with 'fine furniture' and 'rich dresses' of short duration and fluctuating value, than to think of it as a monument to 'consequence', 'virtues' or 'munificence'. Chambers surely had in mind the grander country house and, possibly, the impressive, insulated London mansion. It is unlikely that he thought of his Berners Street houses in this way.

The role Chambers describes for architecture was not that of the terrace house. At best, it would stand as witness to the present-day 'consequence' and 'achievements' of an individual in the eyes of his contemporaries. It lacked, therefore, a monumental, commemorative role for individual or family. Gwynn and Stewart nevertheless envisaged a role for the nobleman's town house comparable with that of his country house. They wanted it to serve the public good by being an accessory to the nation's natural order and decorum and a reflection of family importance and grandeur. They wanted the individual house, or group of houses, to contribute either to the uniformity or the ornamentation of the city, depending on its occupant's status. With the exception of Stewart's qualified acceptance of the 'street house', such ambitions ignored the popularity of the terrace house and the particular ways in which it served its owners.

The terrace house was also largely disregarded both in prescriptive texts on architecture and building and in pattern books of designs, especially prior to the 1770s. The period c.1760–c.1790 produced some influential publications by leading architects, but is characterised more by the continued burgeoning of lesser architectural publications typically providing practical guidance to young architects and builders. Subjects ranged from the architectural orders to the price of bricks in London, and from designs for whole houses to interior details. Some of these publications appeared for the first time, and perhaps also in further editions, in the period. Others were later editions or reissues of earlier publications. In the 1750s to 1770s, known architectural publications amounted to just over a hundred in each decade, of which around half were first editions.[3] Within these texts, both written and pictorial prescriptions reveal a general reluctance (or no perceived need) to address the terrace house as architecture, as opposed to routine building: it was generally not written about or designed for. The town house, as a broader category than the terrace house, receives some attention in these publications, but generally of a negative sort, as writers on the practice of architecture in this period use the country house to draw attention to the town house's relative deficiencies, defining the crippling restrictions facing the designer of the town house by contrast with the freedom and licence enjoyed by the architect of the country house. In short, for both town houses in general and terrace houses in particular, there was no discourse or group of aesthetic principles to match those governing the design of country houses.

The town house in architectural treatises

Of course, the principal reason why the terrace house was not considered to be architecture is that it so rarely involved an architect: with the standard format broadly adhered to – for good reasons – there was generally little requirement for anything beyond the capabilities of the competent builder. The West End town house was very often more akin to vernacular building than to 'polite' architecture.[4] That is, it was essentially conservative and based on recent tradition and standard practice. That the tradition itself was informed by classical/Palladian architectural principles should not be overstated. Palladianism's strength or weakness, depending on your viewpoint, was its accessibility, which 'architectural' publications served to increase.[5] On the ground, those principles were 'vernacularised' – that is, they were not the province of the architect, even if they once had been, as their workaday expression and discussion in a number of builders' manuals attests. Politeness was often constituted in the grouping or arrangement of buildings, in the landlord's or architect's overall scheme – those parts which were beyond the means (including the financial means) of the common builder. In this respect the town house often had a strange dual identity as a vernacular component of polite architecture. Left to its own devices, it was vernacular – and only an architect could make it 'polite'. That is, the newly (and scarcely) defined professional architect, as a repository of architectural theory and history and active arbiter of taste, could bring to bear his skills where they were required.[6] Otherwise, as Robert Campbell noted in 1747, there were 'but few rules to the building of a city house';[7] and a decade later Isaac Ware claimed that 'the common houses in *London* are all built in one way, and that so familiar that it will need little instruction, nor deserve much illustration'.[8] The town house's omission from the prescriptive texts is therefore no real surprise. However, the terms in which it is dismissed in these texts is further evidence of the kind of antipathy towards the town house found in many other sources.

Of the many British architectural treatises published in first or subsequent editions in the second half of the eighteenth century, the most prominent and authoritative were those by Robert Morris and Isaac Ware. Morris's *Lectures on Architecture* and *Essay upon Harmony as it Relates Chiefly to Situation and Building* date from 1734 and 1739 respectively, but a second edition of the *Lectures* was published in 1759. Ware published his *Complete Body of Architecture* in 1756, and a second edition appeared in 1767. Ware in particular also remained a source for other writers later in the century, who lifted passages of his advice almost word for word – not always with due acknowledgement. In fact, a heavy dependence on earlier – sometimes much earlier – authors, whether English or foreign, is a characteristic of many writings in this period. Chief among the later writers offering general rather than simply technical advice to builders and architects were Thomas Skaife, who published *A Key to Civil Architecture* in 1774 (with further editions in 1776 and 1788), and the authors of *The Builder's Magazine*, published in parts from 1774 to 1778. But neither Skaife nor *The Builder's Magazine* made an especially personal or original contribution to the discipline, drawing heavily on their predecessors and making few, if any, concessions to the requirements and fashions of the age.

The discussion here is based on literature published or reprinted in this period, and does not refer to writings of earlier theorists except as re-encountered in either quote or paraphrase. For example, a second edition of James Leoni's English translation of Leon Battista Alberti's *Ten Books of Architecture* was published in weekly parts from 1753 and as a single volume in 1755.[9] It is hard to gauge the extent to which Alberti's guidance, originally offered in fifteenth-century Italy, was read and heeded by eighteenth-century Englishmen, but, like Palladio, he was also cited by some architectural writers in this period, including Morris.[10] What makes his writing interesting in this context, however – and my main reason for including it – is its tone and scope with reference to town houses, which reveal by comparison the shortcomings and prejudices of eighteenth-century English writings. I refer to Robert Morris's *Essay upon Harmony*, despite its publication date of 1739, with the excuse that his advice relating to 'situation' is also prominent in the fifth of his *Lectures on Architecture* but more fully expressed in the *Essay*.[11]

British publications in this period tended to reaffirm some basic, broad and longstanding principles of architectural design. A review of those principles, as expressed by Ware, Morris and others, shows how such writers explicitly or implicitly excluded the town house or set it at a theoretical disadvantage. The default subject for most writings was the country house – the author's and the architect's chief concern – and much of the general advice was in fact specific to that building type. For example, in their directions to the architect and housebuilder, Morris and Ware first consider principles of 'situation', discussing (in order of priority) a site's 'convenience', 'health' and 'beauty'. Although Ware asserts that 'in all buildings we seek convenience and pleasure, and neither the one nor the other can be obtained unless we properly consider the place and situation of the structure',[12] the country house is clearly the main concern of both writers.

The terms in which Morris (and others) describe the qualities of an inconvenient and unhealthy country site – 'dead and stagnant Waters', 'the grossest and most unwholesome Air', 'contagious Vapours', and so on[13] – have much in common with those used by Tobias Smollett in *Humphry Clinker* to characterise London on the whole. These in turn are part of a longstanding tradition of comparing the city's unpleasant and unhealthy sallowness to the country's healthy glow. 'Shall I state the difference between my town grievances, and my country comforts?' Matthew Bramble asks, rhetorically, before letting flow an unstinted rant displaying a shared concern with architectural writers about space and health as qualities of location:

At Brambleton-hall, I have elbow room within doors, and breathe a clear, elastic, salutary air . . . I drink the virgin lymph, pure and crystalline as it gushes from a rock, or the sparkling beveridge, home-brewed from malt of my own making; . . . my bread is sweet and nourishing, made from my own wheat, ground in my own mill, and baked in my own oven; my table is, in great measure, furnished from my own ground . . . My salads, roots, and pot-herbs, my own garden yields in plenty and perfection; the produce of the natural soil . . . Now mark the contrast at London – I am put up in frowzy lodgings, where there is not enough room to swing a cat; and I breathe the streams of endless putrefaction; and these would, undoubtedly, produce a pestilence, if they were not qualified by the gross acid of sea-coal . . . If I would drink water, I must quaff the mawkish contents of an open aqueduct, exposed to all manner of defilement; or swallow that which comes from the River Thames, impregnated with all the filth of London and Westminster . . . The bread I eat in London, is a deleterious paste, mixed up with chalk, alum, and bone ashes, insipid to the taste, and destructive to the constitution . . . [The greens] are produced in an artificial soil, and taste of nothing but the dunghills, from whence they spring.[14]

Bramble's rather extreme articulation of London's deficiencies as a place for healthy and happy living, born of Smollett's own extreme antipathy towards the capital, depicts the city as the absolute antithesis of the ideal 'situation' for building a house, as defined by Morris. In Smollett's analysis, the negative situational qualities against which Morris warns his readers cannot be avoided in choosing a location for a London house, because they are inherent in the city itself. The well-situated, well-managed country house is healthy and self-sufficient, while even the most advantageously situated town house leaves its occupants at the mercy of poorly managed natural amenities and self-serving commercial interests.

Yet it was not, in any case, the site's natural qualities that counted in town, but those imposed on it by existing streets and buildings. Mrs Montagu found better air in Portman Square than Hill Street,[15] and others no doubt found some parts of town healthier than others, but 'good' air was a consequence not just of distance from the river, but also of good town planning in the newer areas, rather than the knots of streets and lanes in the older ones. It is difficult to say whether such qualities were perceived as a bonus rather than sought after in themselves, but it is easy to say that a 'good' situation in town was very different from a 'good' situation in the country. In fact a 'well-situated' town house would be hard to define even on the town's own terms. Qualities of a 'good' location were often particular rather than universal: people sought houses near to friends, family, club, Parliament and social amenities, for example. Ware considers choice of 'neighbourhood' in the country at some length, recommending a balance between retirement and suitable company: the 'meaner sort' of person was to be avoided, and, for the 'man of middling fortune', the lord – who might outshine him.[16] But while avoiding the lower classes was also the ideal in town, residences near 'people of quality' were, on the contrary, much sought after there.

After convenience and health, Morris is concerned with beauty or harmony, with the matching of building and situation in terms of views to and from the house to create 'a Compound of *Art* and *Nature*'. He advocates varied views from the house, such as 'the noble, the grand, and magnificent, the populous, and the busy Prospect', the urban and the rural. Morris is after 'delight' and 'rapture', 'where the Imagination can dwell upon the Object, where the Fancy can be play'd upon, by the Variety of Beauties; and where the Eye is catch'd with different

Attributes to Harmony'.[17] Ware proposes that the country around a house

> even to a great distance, may be understood in some sense as the property of the eye, and its situation and disposition are therefore to be regarded with respect to prospects; the more cultivated it be, always the more cheerful and beautiful. . . . Where it rises in an agreeable manner so that two or three views are seen at once, the object is the more pleasing; and a road at a proper distance, or a navigable river, affords a continual moving picture.

and he agrees with Morris that

> The great articles in prospects are variety and extent; either without the other tires. There is something composed and cheerful . . . in a home view, or limited prospect, but we grow weary of it if in some other part there be not a larger field.[18]

London could rarely compete with the rural location in this respect, even if it offered its occupants visual variety of a different sort. The Thames afforded a busy prospect, but was less salubrious at close quarters than viewed from the outlying hills. Some town houses were advertised as having views to the sort of distant raised sites from where Morris envisaged his country-house builder looking towards the city, so there was some reciprocity in that respect. But views mentioned in house advertisements are often to man-made features of town – 'the new Improvements, the Canal and the Parade',[19] for example – and even a more rustic prospect could be shaped and protected by built development, like the unimpeded and uninterrupted views to Hampstead and Highgate from a house for sale in Portland Street, which would be framed and safeguarded by 'the capacious new street now erecting'.[20] An advantageous prospect was one in which the pattern of built development was already settled, so that the resident could be sure of looking out on to a grand or at least polite and distinctively urban vista. A prospect in town seems to have been of relatively little consequence. General Clerk, at least, believed it to be 'an absurd thought', as it either lacked the proprietorial element of the country view or achieved it at the expense of more essential parts of town life, such as company and convenience.[21]

A house was also to be conceived as a constituent of prospect, and Morris recommends that it should respond to its environs with an appropriate order.[22] But, when introducing his fifth lecture concerning 'what kind of Situations suit with the different *Orders*', he is quick to qualify his terms, making clear that the town house is excluded from such ideal considerations:

When I speak of Situation, it must not be suppos'd that I mean proper Choice of it in Towns or Cities, where every *Order* is promiscuously perform'd, and, perhaps, in the same Pile of Building; but I would be understood, such Situations which are the proper Choice of Retirements [sic], where a Sameness should be preserv'd between *Art* and *Nature*'.[23]

Ware, too, is careful to clarify that

when we speak of a situation we naturally mean that of a house in the country. In cities and great towns business is more regarded than pleasure, and men are confined to do not what they chuse, but what they can. They are cramp'd for room, and must conform to the method of other buildings; what regards a situation therefore in this respect, concerns rather the placing of streets or squares than of private houses.[24]

How different in the country, where the builder or owner 'may have room to spread his edifice over what extent of ground he pleases, and no check upon his fancy as to the disposition of parts'.[25] For Morris, 'Cities and Towns require a just and nice Consistency of Things. The Prospect, it is true, cannot be had, but the Expences of erecting many irregular Buildings might be appropriated to better Taste and Fancy.'[26] In town, therefore, the responsibility is a collective rather than an individual one. There is no scope for the single housebuilder, or house, and even though 'a SPACIOUS Square . . . might give room for Elegance and Design', 'where a proper Distance is wanting to view a building at, it makes an uncouth Figure'.[27] Once again, inherent features of town situations prevent the builder or architect from following ideal prescriptions for architectural design, causing the town house to be condemned, individually or collectively, as substandard or second rate.

On the very few occasions when writers specifically discuss qualities of site in town, other than in the negative respect discussed above, they make limited, vague statements that combine such conventional considerations as good air (again linked with built development), with a few concessions to the particularities of town life. For example, Thomas Skaife recommends that a residence for 'a person of rank, diverted of commercial connections' should be 'in some open airy street, contiguous to some square' with good access to public places.[28] In this way, prescriptions for building for different client types in town are as much related to qualities of the site (or, more accurately, location) as of the house itself, for good reason. Ware (and later *The Builder's Magazine*) advised that a house should 'be suited either to the condition of the person who is to inhabit it, or to the place where it stands'.[29] For the country, Ware could offer particular advice for the seat with columns, the seat without columns, 'common' houses and small and large farm-houses, because (at least in principle) the type of, and often the actual, person to inhabit each would be known in advance. Things were less clear-cut in town where the majority of building was speculative, and the client or even client type unknown. Writers could therefore do little more than make generalised links between location and class. Some distinctions are made between the provision necessary in the houses of merchants and aristocrats respectively – convenience taking priority for the former, and beauty and proportion for the latter group[30] – but these remain, essentially, distinctions between building in the West End or the City. Morris set the merchant firmly in the latter, and required proportion to be 'set aside for Convenience' there; the courtier, on the other hand, resided in 'the more retir'd Parts of the Town, where Spaciousness and Grandeur are the Object of the Designer'.[31] Writers generally ignored the fact that members of the merchant and upper classes had pretty much the same requirements now that they were lodged side by side in a West End street or square, with a shared etiquette, a common lifestyle and similar financial means. Moreover, Morris qualifies the need for grandeur in the town house, as compared with the country seat, on the basis that the courtier's residence in town is 'only a small Part of the Year' during a 'short Attendance on Court or Parliament'. The disparity between what Morris writes in these two instances and what was actually happening in town is understandable given the original publication date of his *Lectures*, but it shows again how architectural publications of the period often failed to keep abreast of the reality of contemporary town life.

Ware recognised that suiting a building 'to the place where it stands', rather than to 'the condition of the person who was to inhabit it', was necessarily 'the common practice in great towns' but argued that

> even in that, there is something to be considered with respect to suiting it to the inhabitant. Though the architect, in this case, will not know who is to live in his edifice, yet he can very well guess of what rank he will be, and this according to the place where it stands: thus much is to be considered in building in this general and random way; the street, or square, the neighbourhood, the conveniences, and the other concurrent circumstances, will instruct the builder; for he would be mad who should build a shed in *Grosvenor Square*, or a palace in *Hedge Lane*; and thus far he will be able to proportion the building to the tenant, or purchaser, though unknown.[32]

Ware clings here to the requirements of propriety and convenience, which were at the root of many architectural prescriptions in this period, and mentioned frequently and glibly in publications offering the London builder limited advice for building according to location or rank of client. *The Builder's Magazine* repeated Ware's advice very nearly word for word in the 1770s.[33] As I discussed earlier, with reference to façades, this commonsense principle of 'convenience' was not new to the age. Like much else in the prescriptive texts, such ideas were truisms, all subscribing to what was right and proper in architecture as in life: everyone in his place and recognisably so. According to Germain Boffrand, for example, it was 'simply common sense that a house should represent the status of its owner, by its site, size, and ornaments'.[34] For Jacques-François Blondel, writing in this instance in 1754, but developing his ideas over previous and subsequent decades, 'it is the spirit of *convenance* which, through the application of constant principles, enables one to give different forms to buildings raised with the same end in view depending upon the rank, dignity or affluence of the owners'. (Blondel's pairing of 'rank' and 'affluence' perhaps excuses the fact that the respective possessors of the two qualities – noblemen and merchants – became equal, at least architecturally, in the West End in this period.) *Convenance* linked this noble end with the practical means of achieving it, and governed choice of site, correctness of proportion, convenience of arrangements and appropriateness of materials and their treatment. In his synthesising work *Cours d'architecture* (published in four volumes between 1771 and 1777), Blondel reiterated that 'all the components of a residence should be selected and arranged so as to suggest a unified character for the whole appropriate to the inhabitant'.[35] *Bienséance* or propriety contributed to the making of the 'convenient' building, which included 'convenient' elements of location, frequently discussed by Morris, Ware and others, as well as the practical conveniences highlighted in house advertisements. Newspaper advertisements make heavy use of the term 'convenient' in their recommendations of houses. Although this use referred more to practical convenience, the accompanying descriptions of the rank or status of the person to whom the house would be suited, combined with the practical commendations, provided a broader notion of convenience, which was conditional rather than absolute, and more in line with the sense in which architectural theorists used the term.

So while the country-house architect had full scope for making the house both 'suitable to the person and adequate to the place',[36] prescribers were obliged to qualify the requirements of convenience when discussing town houses. The exigencies of speculative building, where the architect or builder had to guess the likely class of inhabitant that his house would suit, precluded the proper application of the received wisdom of Blondel and others. The problems of matching inhabitant to habitation in accordance with the principles of convenience may indeed have stumped theorists and other advisers faced with terraces of largely similar houses. While the popularity of such houses for both the middle and upper classes increased in this period, much of the advice framed by the concepts of convenience and propriety was redundant, and aired more out of habit than with any real hope of affecting practice. With successive writers borrowing from other times and places, it is difficult to say what, if anything, in their advice was unique to this period, and not surprising that there was a mismatch between prescribed and actual needs and solutions.

The comparison of architectural constraint in town with licence in the country is, unsurprisingly, common in the prescriptive literature, and coupled with a conviction that both architect and house will – *must* – underperform in town. Only in the country, says Ware, is the architect able to make 'free use of his fancy; for in *London* all is restrained'.[37] The terms on which success is judged are those of the detached house unhindered by its site. The town house is destined to be at best unsatisfactory; at worst a failure. Sometimes its exclusion from the potential to be successful is inadvertent. For example, Morris defines that critical attribute 'Harmony' in terms of the very qualities that the town house was criticised for lacking, such as 'Symmetry', 'Order', 'Exactness', 'Propriety' and 'Perfection'; while that other essential, 'Beauty', springs from 'Proportion': 'the joint Union and Concordance of the Parts, in an exact Symmetry, [forming] a compleat Harmony, which admits of no Medium'.[38] There is no space here for compromise or concession, those principles on which town house architecture was, in practice, based.

At other times the town house's exclusion from the ranks of good architecture is overt. Morris draws his reader's attention to 'the great Disadvantage [that] arises in Buildings which are, or are to be erected in Cities or Towns, that neither Proportion or Convenience can be had' and Thomas Skaife argues that the London architect was often 'confined' in his mode of building 'through the inconvenience of the place' and was therefore less likely to 'strike upon that happy groupe [sic] of consistencies, which, when properly united, will ever render a structure pleasing, of whatever size or dimensions it be'.[39] The ideal practice governing the country house was always compromised by the more difficult practicalities of building in town.

The inadvertent or explicit exclusion of the town house in the writers' generalised remarks on architecture is also to be found in their more specific discussions of house design. For example, Morris considers in detail the proportions of a house not only in respect of achieving a 'more extended Prospect' from it, but also in relation to 'the proper Point of Sight where to view the whole Fabrick distinctly'[40] – something that was rarely a consideration even for a detached house in town, as Morris himself remarked.[41] To satisfy the requirements of both harmony and sound construction, Morris states, 'it will be necessary in Country Seats, to have each Side of the Entrance or Middle of the Building alike'.[42] He makes no mention of town, but while symmetry (and therefore harmony) was possible in a large terrace or detached town house, it could not be accommodated in the regular terrace house except at the expense of optimum planning (and therefore convenience). Nevertheless, in his discussion of doors, Ware criticises the practice 'in the common run of houses in *London*, of placing the door to one side, and making a passage parallel with the fore parlour' which in some houses, 'encroaches on the parlour, and spreads out into a kind of hall; and in others, the parlour encroaches upon that, and squeezes it into an entry'. Ware concedes that 'in those common little houses where the extent of the front is limited to a few feet, and there is a necessity of a certain number of apartments, some excuse may be made for throwing the door to one side', but 'nothing can be said in justification of it', and 'in large and elegant edifices, it is a practice that admits no apology'.[43] Ware therefore insists on a central doorway, an ideal implicitly promoted by neo-Palladianism, and advises giving over the front part of the ground floor to a hall, to avoid the difficult relationship with the front parlour. Consequently, his model town house[44] has a central door leading into a hall on a scale inappropriate to town life. Ware's adherence to principles rather than practicalities is not only out of step with practice and preferences in town, but also, in this respect, with his own advice that 'neither magnitude nor elegance are needful' in a town-house hall, it being a place of reception for servants in the absence of other ways into the house.[45] He recognises that the positioning of the door and stairs has a critical effect on 'the judicious disposition of the rest of the house'.[46] But he cannot conceive of circumstances in which the abandonment of symmetry could be beneficial, in which houseowners' requirements could justify disregarding architectural protocol to this improper extent. A central entrance dictated rather than responded to the plan, and was rarely handled successfully, or even attempted, in a three-bay house. This general disjunction between theory and practice in smaller houses was remarked upon under the heading 'architecture' in the *Encyclopaedia Britannica* (1771). Architects, it says, were always trying to reconcile internal convenience and external regularity in small,

25

The Town House Dismissed 147

private houses, achieving neither,[47] and in his model town house Ware achieves the latter at the expense of the former.

In discussing the proportioning of rooms first to the house and then to each other, Ware again remarks that symmetry 'is the great beauty in building',[48] and he particularly objects to the prevailing custom of building a house 'for the sake of one room', or adding an 'out of proportion room' to an existing house, which disrupts symmetry as it 'hangs from one end, or sticks to one side, of the house, and shews to the most careless eye, that, though fastened to the walls, it does not belong to the building'.[49] 'This,' he continues, 'is the reigning taste of the present time in *London*, a taste which tends to the discouragement of all good and regular architecture.'[50] As with aspects of site, the 'adulterate enjoyments of the town' can never rival the 'genuine pleasures of a country retreat'.[51] Although Ware admits that 'this taste for a great room is not confined to *London*' – he had seen the same gross error committed in a house in Leicestershire – the capital is nevertheless frequently and explicitly the home of specific and general examples of bad practice in these writings, particularly for Ware: as we have seen, doors there were not central, even in larger houses, and the houses themselves were built 'slightly'. The offices of London houses were underground, which was 'unwholesome, inelegant, and inconvenient'.[52] In addition, London was where every popular fancy was followed without regard to propriety or even logic. For example, the bow window

> from its being uncommon, pleased extremely; those who built it where there was a prospect, were followed by people whose houses were situated where there could be none: and at present we see *Venetian* windows that look into stableyards, nay that block up one another in the streets. Nor need we go out of the circuit of the new buildings in *London*, for a house where the architect has made two *Venetians* that block up one another.[53]

Skaife uses the 'new buildings about the town' as evidence for the worrying tendency to omit set-offs on the outside of houses. He believed that 'the builders greatly mistook their interest . . . because a house properly set off on both sides will not require to be so strong by one sixth of the quantity of materials, which would amount to a considerable sum in a large building'.[54] Even the first principle of construction, 'with respect to strength', was violated in London, where solid did not always stand over solid, nor void over void, according to Ware.[55]

Writers do offer some advice specific to building in London, although even in this the town house is often presented as the country house's poor relation. Morris explains that 'Buildings in Town require *Contrivance*

64 (left) 44 Berkeley Square, William Kent, 1742–4, view of the staircase, drawn for Sir John Soane's Royal Academy lectures, c.1809–36.

65 (below) Houses in St James's Square as they looked in 1821.

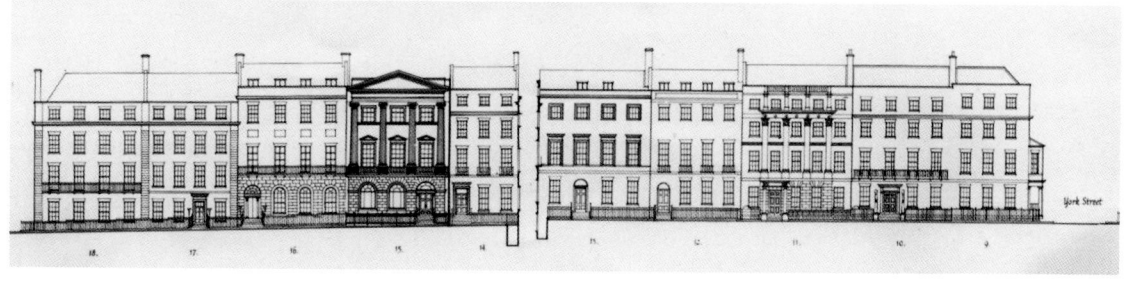

66 (left) 37 King Street, Covent Garden, attributed to James Paine, 1777.

67 (right) 31 and 32 Old Burlington Street, Colen Campbell, 1718–23.

Front of ELY HOUSE in Dover Street.

68 (left) Ely House,
37 Dover Street, Robert
Taylor, 1772–6, front
elevation in an anonymous
aquatint, *c.*1780.

NORTH WEST CORNER OF SOHO SQUARE. 1883

69 (right) 7 Soho Square,
Robert Taylor, 1745–8, in a
watercolour by J. P. Emslie,
1883.

70 (above) View of Soho Square from *The Repository of Arts, Literature, Commerce, Manufactures, Fashions, and Politics*, printed for R. Ackermann, vol. 8, 1812, plate 22.

71 (left) George Dance the Younger, design for the elevation of 6 St James's Square, n.d., unexecuted.

72 (left) 15 St James's Square, James Stuart, 1764–6, view of the front, drawn for Sir John Soane's Royal Academy lectures, c.1809–36.

73 (below) Robert Adam, design for new elevation for Sir William James's house in Gerrard Street, 1781, unexecuted.

74 Adam House, Adam Street, Adelphi, Robert and James Adam, *c*.1770.

75 R. Rushworth, *The Supplemental Magazine*, published by S. W. Fores, 1786, hand-coloured etching. Women, like the town house, disguise their true nature with artificial, dishonest appendages.

76 Robert Adam, Home House, Portman Square, design for a section of the music room, 1775.

PANTHEON MACARONI.

77 Philip Dawe, *Pantheon Macaroni*, *c*.1773, mezzotint. The vain, foppish macaroni, with his overdressed refinements, exaggeratedly slender proportions, and propensity for make up, could be the London town house personified.

more for Convenience than Grandeur' and then concerns himself with practical matters:

> the Chambers of Lodging-Rooms, require to be as far from the noise and Tumult of the Street as conveniently can be plac'd, and so near a Stair-case, that if any Accident by Fire (which too frequently) happens, an easy Access may be had to it; for which Purpose all Back Stair-cases in Town-Houses, as they generally are carried from the lower offices to the Roof, should be of Stone, and the Walls of them Stucco that no danger might prevent the Safety of getting down them, to avoid the Fury of the Flames; and such which are plac'd about the Middle of the Building and illuminated by a Sky-light, are by far the most convenient.

It soon becomes apparent that even this advice mainly relates to particularly large town houses, as Morris goes on to recommend that 'as in Town-houses, so in the Country, the Kitchen should be remote from the House [and] the servile Offices are best always to be some Distance from the main Building'.[56] His examples include Burlington House, Piccadilly, and Montague House, Great Russell Street – houses more analogous with country mansions than with even the grander terrace house in town. Ware, too, uses examples of exceptional town houses, such as his grand Chesterfield House, to illustrate general points about cesspools and drains in town, for example.[57] Of course, both Morris and Ware were writing earlier in the century, when insulated mansions were not quite the white elephants they were later to become. Ware in particular may also have hoped to attract larger architectural commissions.[58] Nevertheless, such mansions were never built in large numbers. The terrace house, even if subdivided for lodgings rather than occupied by a single family, was the most prevalent building form in London even in the 1730s.

The most town-specific architectural writings of the later eighteenth century are those that give an account of the 1774 Building Act, such as *The Builder's Magazine*. The act was only effective within Westminster, and its inclusion in some general publications suggests that either it was considered more broadly valid as a model of good practice, or that authors and publishers anticipated that their audience would be principally London based and likely to be playing some part in the construction boom there. Either way, the juxtaposition in *The Builder's Magazine* of such up-to-the-minute, London-specific technical advice with traditional maxims principally concerned with country-house architecture re-emphasises the discrepancy between theory and practice in the writings published in this period.

Ware does include 'common houses in London' as one of his domestic building categories, yet his words are more descriptive than instructive (with the exception of his repeated petition to make the front part of the ground floor a hall, against common practice or sense). 'The general custom' he writes, 'is to make two rooms and a light closet on a floor, and if there be any little opening behind it, to pave it', and 'nothing will be more familiar, or more proper, than for the young student to begin with a plan and a model of such a house; the subject being perfectly easy, and every part of it familiar in his mind.' Ware concedes that there is scope for improvement even in this, 'the most trivial and most familiar manner of building', in the quest for practical convenience, and acknowledges that it will be to the common builder's advantage to devote his energies to this task and 'recommend himself in the eye of the middle rank of people'.[59] Such a task is clearly below Ware's consideration, and he firmly relegates the town house to the ranks of building, not architecture. He does not concede that there might be people of a higher rank to whom the architect, rather than the builder, could recommend himself, by refusing to equate lack of space with lack of convenience, or grandeur, or style.

Morris clings to the notion that the West End, the home of the courtier, offers the designer more scope, and allows 'spaciousness and grandeur' to be his object: 'here, indeed, he finds generally the most Regularity in his Spot of Ground, and more Space for his Fancy to move in'. He concedes that 'sometimes Nobleness itself may be seen in Miniature' in town, among the architect-designed homes of the upper classes. But even a large town site was often restricted, and Ware explains how elements of the design of a large house intended for Mayfair were executed in response to the plot, which was 'considerably deeper at one end than the other', and its situation 'in a street which it terminated at the corner'.[60] He describes how he disguised and made optimum use of the irregular space to the sides and rear of the regular house so that the negative aspects of the site did not impinge on the house so much as on the offices, gardens and stables.[61] The completed design was an example to the young architect, who 'will see in what manner, on like occasions, a right knowledge of his profession will palliate natural irregularities, or in some cases turn defects to advantages'.[62] While the builder could concern himself with optimising the convenience of the terrace house, the architect's attention was to be diverted to bigger and better (and more lucrative) challenges.

Morris recognises that the West End street or square sometimes had the potential for displaying the 'Magnificence and Proportion', 'Delicacy and Convenience' that could not, it seemed, be achieved in the individual town house. He bemoans the wasted opportunity presented at Grosvenor Square in the 1720s and 30s; this site, being spacious, healthy and convenient, with 'an excellent Foundation', wanted only 'the nice Application of *Design*' to allow it to surpass even Rome. But individual interests had compromised the square's scope for harmony, symmetry, uniformity and other marks of greatness:

> There is a Field for Fancy, the World cannot shew a Spot of Ground built on so Noble, and so capable of producing four magnificent regular Sides; If every Builder had agreed as to the external Part, to have made each Range as regular as the East Side, or with that Grandeur of Esquire *Shepherd*'s on the North, I may affirm, future Ages might boast, that the greatest and most regular Buildings on one Spot of Ground, was erected near the City of *London*, call'd *Grosvenor-Square*.[63]

Edward Shepherd's attempt at grandeur served only as a reminder to future generations that the town house was at the mercy of a multiplicity of other, neighbouring interests, and might be restricted in its bid for architectural greatness by those as much as by its own physical limitations. The individual designer was not necessarily in a position to capitalize even on the broader scope offered by the row or square of houses.

According to Morris and Ware, town houses severely limited the architect's scope for displaying his talents. Morris declares that 'the Irregularity or Littleness of the Spot' prevents the town-house architect from 'shewing his Skill in Designing', and he would need all his judgement to make the best of this bad situation.[64] On the other hand, the 'Advantages of a Rural Situation' are that 'no Impediments lie in the way to Proportion and Convenience' and 'the Care and Skill of the *Architect* is under no Restraint'.[65] As Skaife says, the country-house architect could take 'every advantage to obtain the most pleasing effect, both as to place and prospect' and the site would generally offer 'room enough for invention and no check upon fancy, or restraint to the most pregnant genius'.[66] Skaife's and Ware's assertions were no doubt generally true, but three centuries earlier Alberti had put a slightly different spin on the comparison, admitting that he discussed the design of the country house ahead of the town house because the lack of restrictions made it a simpler task.[67] He did not go so far as to say that a good performance in town, under challenging circumstances, would be a great credit to an architect and a fitting display of genius; it took the Adam brothers to demonstrate this point both in practice and in their *Works in Architecture* after 1773.

Alberti's writings offer a useful point of comparison for the writings of this period, not least because something of his style and scope was lost when later writers picked over his *De re aedificatoria* for aphorisms. Writing in a very different time and place, Alberti gives considerable attention to the town house and particularly to the relationship between the country house and the town house. This relationship is ignored in eighteenth-century English treatises. The nearby town, like the navigable river, may be a resource or facility to be looked for when choosing where to build a country house, but the delineation of close links between life, business and pleasure in both places, evident in Alberti, is missing in the works of Morris and his contemporaries.

After experiencing the rather blinkered approach of many eighteenth-century writers, Alberti comes across as refreshingly pragmatic and reasonable. For example, he recognises that beauty (and, by extension, propriety) is relative to the building type, so that there is a 'Sort of Beauty . . . proper to each Edifice'.[68] What is more, he admits that qualities of situation are relative, too.[69] He does acknowledge, like his eighteenth-century successors, that

> you cannot distribute [the necessary parts of your building] as you would in a City so well as you can in the Country. In building a House in Town, your Neighbour's Wall, a common Gutter, a publick Square or Street, and the like, shall all hinder you from contriving it just to your own Mind; which is not so in the Country, where you have as much Freedom as you have Obstruction in Town.

He therefore begins his discussion with the buildings 'which are most easy': country houses. But he does not equate them with unlimited potential for displaying genius in the way that later English writers do. As he says, they are the easiest sort, because they are 'freest from all Obstructions'. For this and other reasons, he argues, 'the habitation for a private Person must be different in Town from what it is in the Country' – and, he continues, between classes.[70] He talks openly and pragmatically about the relationship between the two properties and their day-to-day and seasonal uses in a way that English writers simply do not.

Alberti also makes a clear distinction between the adorning of private houses in town and country. The ornaments for a town house 'ought to be much more grave than those for a House in the Country, where all the gayest and most licentious Embellishments are allowable' but this advice is not based simply on a whim. 'In Town', he continues, 'you are obliged to moderate yourselves in several Respects according to the Privileges of your Neighbour; whereas you have much more Liberty in the Country. In Town you must not raise your Platform or Basement too high above your Neighbours, nor let your Portico project too far forwards from the line of the adjacent Buildings.' He even argues that 'the Thickness and Height of the Walls at *Rome* anciently were not suffered to be according to every Man's particular Fancy, but by an old Law were all to be made according to a certain Standard', a sound precedent for building legislators in eighteenth-century Westminster if ever there was one.[71] The type and size of town house Alberti had in mind is very different from that erected in Georgian London, but he articulates nicely the link between civic consciousness and some external restraint without resorting to eighteenth-century notions of moral rectitude.

It is not that Alberti does not openly recognise the town house's disadvantages in design terms – for example, he wishes that the need for several floors could be done away with there as it could in the country.[72] But he does not let such observations colour his general attitude to the house. Why, then, didn't eighteenth-century writers take up and develop parts of Alberti's observations and advice that would have been highly relevant to their own time, notably the relationship and distinctions between the country house and the town house? Why were they so dismissive of the town house in general and the terrace house in particular?

The eighteenth-century town-house architect was denied, in prescription and practice, the scope to follow standard guidelines for domestic architectural design, based on the principles of classicism which various parties had been at pains to establish as the polite norm. Those principles were particularly defined in formal writings, which 'conceptualized the visual as contingent on the intellectual'. They were concerned with ideals of beauty, achieved through harmonic and rational means, and had a strongly didactic, even moral flavour.[73] Although Morris is not explicitly anti-town, he clearly articulates the town's (and the town house's) inability to abide by the advice he sets out in his *Lectures* and elsewhere. Town is the place where order (and by implication morality) is lost; and where Art and Nature cannot work together to create Beauty and Convenience – Morris's principal concerns. When a building and its situation are mutually enhancing – when 'a proper Design' blends 'Art and Nature together' – a house will be 'the Delight of the Inhabitant, and give an unspeakable Pleasure to the Eye of every Beholder'.[74] Like William Chambers, Morris makes the link between architecture and reputation in the present and the future: the person who chooses his site well and suits his design to it, 'must doubtless . . . perpetuate his Judgment to his Posterity; it must render his Off-spring a Happiness and

Pleasure which gives a true Relish to Life'.[75] By implication – and by its very nature – urban domestic architecture cannot, therefore, fully satisfy public and private, personal and familial interests.

The town house did not allow the architect to distinguish himself from the builder – neither requiring nor offering scope for 'architectural' skill. It cannot have helped the town house's image that this exceptionally prominent and lively area of building practice, patronised by members of even the highest classes, was therefore dominated by effectual practitioners who fell well short of the definition of an architect which theorists were at pains to construct in this period. These practitioners may not have possessed an architect's full range of skills and knowledge, but they knew enough (helped by the accessibility of codified Palladian principles which governed the basics of most town-house design) to operate successfully in this area, and to the satisfaction of a good proportion of the public.

Much of the generic advice on building was at odds with the physical requirements of the town house and with the ethos of town life in a terrace. While prescriptive texts like Skaife's and Ware's offer some specific advice on how to build in town, the guiding framework within which they discuss the town house is that of the country house. Factors governing choice of site are considered first, even though little choice was available and physical and legal obstacles often encumbered prospective building plots.[76] Next the exterior appearance of the building is considered; and finally the interior, in accordance with priorities that tended to govern the design of country mansions. Writers could spell out what was required in town where there was some correspondence between town and country practice – bringing the insulated town mansion in particular into the fold of good architectural design – but floundered on, or simply ignored, the specifics of building design where needs fell outside the paradigm within which they typically operated. The town house was not given a set of governing principles of its own but borrowed those from the country house, whether this was appropriate or not. Ware tries to adhere to his architectural principles despite the hindrances and qualifications that he clearly recognises in town building. He acknowledges that 'smaller houses in London are naturally cramped for room, and ty'd down to a particular situation; yet even in these,' he continues, 'there will be found use for those rules established upon good practice'. But faced with the problem of making those established principles applicable to the small London house, he is forced to limit his statement only to 'those which are largest and most free'.[77] References to the terrace house in texts typically present it either as the negative to the positive of the country house or identify vague points of loose correspondence. A positive outlook centred on the town house itself is missing.

It is unsurprising that the advice given in prescriptive architectural publications did not keep pace with the rising interest in the town house and its architectural potential given that many publications of this period were either reissues or new editions of earlier texts, or derived their prescriptions from previous writings and commonplaces of architectural guidance. The town house may also have been disregarded in this literature because it did not fit in with standard expectations, and because no substitute prescriptions could be imagined for a situation in which clients and purchasers were neither looking for mansions nor selecting a house type according to their status. A good part of the writers' reticence was probably the lack of anything to say. As I have said, in its standard form the terrace house did not really need designing, just building. Perhaps for this reason John Leadbeater chose a four-storey, three-bay, plain town house of 20-foot frontage as the illustration for a measuring exercise, in *The Gentleman and Tradesman's Compleat Assistant; or, the Whole Art of Measuring and Estimating Made Easy* (1770), the format being so common that the design itself needed neither explanation nor to be regarded as a peculiar element of the exercise.[78]

The town house in the pattern books

Eighteenth-century pattern books and collections of designs offer little that is specific to the terraced property, no doubt because of the limited forms that it could take, especially within the speculative market.[79] Likewise, few designs for town houses of any sort were exhibited at the Royal Academy.[80] Perhaps designers saw little credit in publishing designs that afforded such limited scope for 'invention' and 'fancy' and no apparent outlet for 'pregnant genius'.[81]

In both their selectiveness and their designs, the pattern books reinforce much of what I have argued in relation to the prescriptive texts, and elsewhere. The country house (or the country-house paradigm) dominates. The town house is often either ignored or, in its larger form, considered to be little different from the country house. Width greater than that which the terrace-house site usually allowed for, or the inclusion of side windows, often made such purported 'town house' designs unsuitable for inclusion in a real row, and the real terrace house is largely disregarded altogether or grouped with its neighbours and disguised as a country house. Also evident in the pattern books is the same resistance to 'people of quality' living in three-bay terrace houses which can be discerned in the writings of Gwynn and Stewart and is implied in Skaife's prescriptions.

Many pattern books do not mention town houses at all, some authors reneging on promises to include designs for them. For example, Robert Morris includes no town houses in his *Select Architecture* (1757),[82] despite the claims in the extended title that the publication featured 'regular designs of plans and elevations well suited to both town and country [. . .] from the plain TOWN-HOUSE to the stately HOTEL; and in the country from the genteel and convenient FARM-HOUSE to the PAROCHIAL CHURCH'.

One problem in discussing the coverage of the town house in illustrated architectural publications of this period is that it is very often hard to distinguish the town house from the country house, partly because the text does not indicate which is which, but also because so few designs respond directly to a restricted London site, let alone the typical, narrow site of a London terrace. In addition, almost all fall within the basic prevailing 'country house' format: broader than deep, with basically symmetrical planning on two axes in a double-pile arrangement, and, externally, a plainish façade articulated by a central pediment and perhaps slight recessions and projections, with a central door emphasised by an architectonic treatment such as a portico or porch.

However, there does seem to be a kind of 'town format' for exteriors – typically comprising a deep rusticated ground floor with a virtually flush, understated entrance and windows in relieving arches (or arched openings) topped with a pilaster order over one or two storeys. A 'design for a town-house', illustrated over several plates in William and James Pain's *Pain's British Palladio* (1786), has this appearance, even if it remains essentially a double-pile building symmetrically disposed either side of the axis running backwards from the central front door. In terms of planning, it does not respond to the typical town-house site (long and narrow), and the concessions to fashion that might be expected by this date are limited to a bow window to the substantial rear extension. There is little in the way of the type of circuit of rooms through which, in the new fashion, guests progressed, experiencing different entertainments in each space.

A variation on this format appears in William Pain's earlier publication *The Builder's Golden Rule* (1781). Here it is used as the façade to a pair of basic town houses. The ground floor is not rusticated, but the rectangular windows are set in an arcade embellished with roundels. The giant order is topped with a short attic order, but a run of arches echoing the arcading at ground-floor level maintains the balance between verti-

26

27

cality and horizontality that is a feature of this format – equally suited, it seems, to individual houses or rows.[83]

William Pain's *Practical House Carpenter* (1794, first published in 1788), offers 'Plans, Elevations, and Sections for Town and Country Houses', but we are left to guess which are which among the plates themselves. Again, it is a façade which identifies the most obvious candidate for a town house, rather than any remarkably suitable or different aspects of its plan. The house is broader than deep, but it has no side windows, and fits the 'town format', with its arched, rusticated ground floor with restrained front entrance, and giant order above.

28

The typical town house, in practice, 'was never the country house built small',[84] but many pattern-book designs for town houses seem more or less interchangeable with those for country houses of equivalent size, both in external appearance and planning. John Crunden's *Convenient and Ornamental Architecture*, first published in 1767 and popular enough to warrant four further editions before the turn of the century, includes several designs for town houses. A five-bay house 'calculated for a large family, town situation' could easily be taken for a modest country house, with its pedimented central section and balanced disposition of rooms either side of a corridor running backwards from the central entrance. A side entrance precludes the house's inclusion in a terrace. A larger version, externally, of the same house spreads to seven bays and has more generous storey heights. Crunden describes it as 'intended for a town situation, where the back front commands the river, or some other agreeable object',[85] setting the design firmly within the country-house paradigm which demands a proprietorial outlook at odds, as we have seen, with what was generally possible or even desirable in town. Crunden has taken the trouble to articulate the side walls with blind windows, in addition to various openings, and the house was evidently not intended for a terrace or even a restricted insulated site. Internally, the house is more or less symmetrical on both main axes. The central entrance and the spacious hall into which it leads would have pleased Isaac Ware: the 64-foot frontage necessitates no concessions to town life, or to the reality of relatively narrow building plots sandwiched between other, equally narrow plots.

29

30

Where authors suggest that the same design can be used for a house in town or country, this 'interchangeability' is often questionable. The extended title of William Thomas's *Original Designs in Architecture*, published in 1783, boasts of plans and elevations 'for Villas and Town Houses' but the book nevertheless has little to offer in respect of the latter in its twenty-seven plates. A 'Casino or Box' is 'calculated for a Country Retreat, or the Town House of a small Family'. The house is not evidently suitable for town, in the way we might expect by this period: the end bays of the three-bay, 55-foot frontage project slightly, the entrance has a curved portico and there are side windows. At the centre of the rear, an eating room projects into a three-windowed bay.[86] Similarly, the main feature of a rather strange plan in Crunden's design for a house 'calculated for either town or country' is the half-octagonal bow to the dining room at the rear, which becomes a very large dressing room on the first-floor level. Despite the space with which to play behind the 50-foot façade, Crunden goes no way towards devising the type of 'circuit' over one or two floors that was becoming such a feature of fashionable entertainment in town by this time. His concession to fashion is the bay; there is no concession to town.

In his *Original Designs in Architecture* (1780), James Lewis offers a town variation on a large, winged country house, originally stretching to a total width of around 220 feet. He illustrates the central block of the house (just over 60 feet wide) with porticoes replacing the wings on either side – a variation which, he suggests, makes the design suitable for a town mansion. The house is not hugely out of scale for a London home, but it would have required an insulated site.[87] Like many other pattern-book designs for town houses, it is just 'the country house built small' rather than a direct response to town life and conditions. *The Modern Builder's Assistant* illustrates a building 'designed for a Seat in a pleasant Situation in the Country, or may be adapted to Town'.[88] But it is hard to see how that might happen. The house's nine-bay main block alone is over 80 feet wide and the substantial wings, twice the depth of the house's main block, sweep forwards on either side. Like many other designers, one of the authors, T. Lightoler, deems his design interchangeable in the face of much evidence, in both theory and practice, that houses in town and country were two quite different matters.

Of course, it would not have seemed inconceivable in 1757 for a house with wings to be built in London. But the propensity to offer designs for inappropriately large town houses persisted at least to the end of the eighteenth century, despite the major trend, defining London's architectural and construction practice in this period, for building, rebuilding or refurbishing terrace properties. As late as 1792, George Richardson was offering supposedly interchangeable designs for town and country mansions among his *New Designs in Architecture*. The two town mansions illustrated could, he says, be erected in the country 'with equal propriety'. Richardson does admit that a site suitable for a frontage of 140 feet was both hard to come by and prohibitively expensive in London, which was 'without doubt' a reason why 'so many gentlemen of the first rank and distinction' live in 'town houses of so small dimensions'.[89] Such examples are further evidence of the disparity between theory and practice, or between public and private preferences, and the location of pragmatism in the text rather than the designs reflects the fact that pattern books were often showcases of an architect's talent. Understandably, designers preferred to demonstrate their skills on a canvas broader than the three-bay terrace house, and did not necessarily intend their designs to be realised in the form illustrated.

This combination of self-advertisement and a lack of realism reaches a peak in Crunden's design for 'a mansion for a person of distinction, adapted to either town or country', which shows an elaborate house with a high, rusticated ground floor, and a first floor articulated along its full width with attached Corinthian columns and pediments over the central three bays and each of the end ones. The plans reveal this to be essentially a triple-pile house, with internal courtyards either side of a central staircase space. Again, the design's supposed suitability for either town or country is not only baffling but also denies the fact that the requirements and possibilities in each place were fundamentally different, even for the grandest residents. It is, in any case, hard to imagine where Crunden envisaged this house sitting in any town, with its thirteen bays and frontage approaching 200 feet.

32

Many town-house designs therefore make few or no concessions to London circumstances, such as the expense and availability of ground, and in some cases very specific site requirements restrict the design's application yet further. For example, one 'town mansion' in Crunden's *Convenient and Ornamental Architecture* requires 'the back situation' to be open, preferably 'to the river or Hyde Park', to make it 'as convenient and pleasant a house as any in London', while another 'is calculated for the situation of Piccadilly, commanding Hyde Park, and consequently the serpentine river, with many other beauties which adorn that noble inclosure'.[90] The chances of obtaining such a site must have been slim, and the likelihood of the lucky and wealthy purchaser choosing a house design from a pattern book yet slimmer. Crunden's efforts here to create space and variety are compromised by the restrictions of a town site, and his design flounders in a no-man's-land between best practice in town and country, belonging in neither one place nor the other. Externally, however, both town mansions reinforce the argument for a distinctive 'town format', with their rusticated ground floors with arched openings and unobtrusive front entrances and giant orders over the upper two storeys, even if the second has a pediment providing some central emphasis.

33

34

These collections of designs make few concessions, too, to the broad market for the three-bay terrace house amongst all classes and give very little, if any, explicit coverage to that building type, even where, as in Thomas Rawlins's *Familiar Architecture* (1768), they are purportedly concerned with 'small' houses suited to 'a City or large Town'. Rawlins claims to illustrate 'the many different Conveniences that may be made in a House from Thirty to Sixty Feet in Front, and upwards',[91] but despite his supposedly pragmatic approach, he is against the idea of underground offices, and prefers them to be 'properly disposed in Wings, or, at the most distant Parts of a House'.[92] There is not a terrace house in sight. His houses are typically broader than deep, or square, with plentiful side openings, and sometimes wings and rear courts.

Within the limited coverage given to terrace houses in the pattern books, groups of three houses are popular, perhaps because they offered more scope than a single house front, but did not exceed the number of plots likely to be acquired by an individual builder.[93] *The Modern Builder's Assistant* is more realistic about what was generally desirable, affordable and practicable in town in its inclusion of Robert Morris's unremarkable designs for a row of three houses and his 'small Town House, 20 Feet in Front by 40 Feet deep'. The publication offered several larger, grander town houses, but here it is clearly addressing the lower end of the town-house market – Ware's 'common house in London'. The terrace of three houses 'may be executed in a plain Manner for 40*l. per* Square' making a total of £840 for the group, while the 'small Town House', at £60 per square, costs £480, as compared with £3712 10s for Morris's grander town house in Plate 36 of the same volume. According to the authors, achieving a balance between convenience and uniformity was the guiding principle behind the design of the three terrace houses: the centre house has been made '24 Feet in Front, and the others 18 Feet, otherwise it would be very inconvenient in so small a Plan, the Door being in the middle'.[94] But the central door to the middle house effectively creates two small rooms either side of a narrow corridor. Thus, even in a design so clearly responding to town circumstances, the adherence to conventional Palladian design principles comes at a price.

Externally, these three houses are considered as part of one design, and in this instance that design dictates elements of the plan. We find the same on a grander scale in John Crunden's 'country house' façade applied to another row of three houses 'making one regular elevation',[95] but here the broader width of the central house (around 40 feet), spreading to five bays and topped with a pediment, allows for decent-sized rooms on either side of the central corridor. In fact, the design illustrates well the persistence of the double-pile country-house plan for the (relatively) grander house and the compromise of the town-house plan (one room front and back, and a side passage with stairs) for the lesser one.

The authors of *The Modern Builder's Assistant* clearly envisaged that each of Morris's row of houses would be occupied by more than one family, writing of their lower offices that

> it is not material whether they are disposed of in this Work, for where Families are intermixed, such Places must be rather adapted to the Use and Convenience of them, than if they were designed for private Families, in which the Disposal is often at the Caprice and Humour of the Inhabitant, or the Wants and Necessities of his Employment.[96]

In this way – and like authors such as Morris and Ware – they make a clear distinction between two types of town house: the house responding to choice, and the house responding to necessity. Of course, the distinction was not wholly effective in practice: almost all houses, for all types of people, had to respond to the practicalities and particularities of London and of town life in general. Nevertheless, it is reflected in the designs and plate descriptions in *The Modern Builder's Assistant*, and in many other publications: the large house for the 'quality' person more or less disregards its town location, and the small house for the lesser person responds to it, generally in an unimaginative manner.

The only truly interesting designs of the 1770s for terrace houses, combining inventiveness with an element of realism, appeared in *The Builder's Magazine*, published in monthly instalments between 1774 and 1778. The designs by John Carter for two individual houses illustrate 38–41 in their treatment of the façade and planning what could be done with the terrace house if allowed to operate outside of the country-house idiom. Sections of the elaborate 'great stair-case' of one of the houses 39 show the anticipated interior finish and indicate that these houses for gentlemen were superior to the common terrace, though distinguished neither by size nor detachment. The treatment and details of their façades set them apart from the other published designs for terrace houses in the pattern books, while the later house's plan removes it far 40, 41 from the 'standard' plan or any of its close relations. The detailed coverage of these two designs is evidence of a rising interest in the terrace house's architectural potential, perhaps stimulated by the boom in rebuilding and refurbishing existing houses, where there was more scope for inventiveness than in new, speculative developments. The publishers advertised that a town-house design for a 'private Gentleman' was to be featured in their magazine, presumably confident of public interest.[97] The illustrations showed builders and their clients how the individual terrace house could be 'architecture' and not just 'building', by working with rather than against the restrictions of the narrow site, and by providing variety in plan and elevation which went far beyond builders' routine offerings of one room at the front and back and a plain façade. The later house has a commendably novel façade, although the central entrance in the fairly narrow frontage results in a wastefully large hall. At least on the first-floor level, Carter has given thought and space to a fashionable circuit, making good use of the central circular staircase. Only the oval-shaped hall and the shallow rear bay window of the earlier house distinguish it from its many built predecessors, plan-wise, but the elevation, while simple, reveals a consideration of detail rare in previously published designs for terrace houses.[98] Nevertheless, the designs were probably not intended for direct imitation in practice. What they demonstrate most is a willingness to do something different with the three-bay terrace, even if they are not an entirely good example of what should be done.

On the whole, though, the pattern books do not reflect the increasing partiality for terrace houses, nor the declining interest in larger, freestanding town houses. Carter's designs are really an anomaly rather than the first step in a new direction. In their grander designs, the authors of *The Modern Builder's Assistant* disregard their own advice that 'the Design of Town Houses should be to contrive as many Conveniences as may be on a small Plan, because the Front of Ground in Streets is valuable',[99] echoing Ware, Morris and others: at least in the pattern books, designers seem reluctant to acknowledge that such contrivance was as important in all but the very largest, detached London homes, as it was in the smallest. In some cases, 'town house' designs which make few, if any, concessions to London sites may have been intended for provincial towns, where space was perhaps cheaper and more plentiful and wider-than-average houses were built for prominent citizens.[100] Such clear correlation between a house's size and its occupant's social standing was the exception rather than the rule in London by this period, but pattern books seem nevertheless to cling to this principle in general. Designs are labelled according to prospective client types, and whereas the better three-bay town houses are typically for 'a gentleman', suggested designs for a 'nobleman's town house' or that of 'a person of distinction' are more likely to be for houses of five to seven bays or more. Such classifications therefore reveal that same concern with 'legibility' that we have seen in the prescriptive writings of Gwynn and Stewart, and expressed in more general theoretical terms in the works of Morris, Ware and others.

Where designs for mansions and some more modest town houses are, intentionally or incidentally, interchangeable with those for country houses, the governing paradigm remains that of the country house. But this paradigm and the practical advice that upheld it were largely inapplicable to the terrace house. The typical terrace house could not conform to standardised design principles. Ambitious designers of such houses, and their clients, therefore began to develop alternative principles that took as their starting point the particularities of the London terrace house, in terms of both physical restrictions and customer preferences. Within the pattern books, this development was expressed in *The Builder's Magazine*, in which the town house came into its own in a limited way.

To find any serious and realistic attention paid to town houses, and terrace houses in particular, in pattern books prior to *The Builder's Magazine* we need to go back to Pierre Le Muet's *Maniere de bien bastir pour toutes sortes de personnes*, first published complete in 1647, and later in an English translation as *The Art of Fair Building* (1670, with an augmented edition in 1675). Le Muet offers an abundance of terrace-house designs starting with houses only 12 feet wide and little more than 20 feet deep, and provides choice even for such small plots.[101] While the smallest houses are mean in scale, they are nevertheless treated individually rather than as part of an encompassing design for a row. There are no palace fronts or other unifying treatments. Rather than trying to make the smaller house conform to a set of 'universal' rules, Le Muet acknowledges that its main referents must be its own restrictions and its occupants' requirements. But this does not mean dismissing the smaller house as unworthy of the architect's attention. Like elements of Alberti's *Ten Books on Architecture*, Le Muet's *Bien bastir* shows what English architectural theory and pattern books avoided dealing with, for whatever reason. Le Muet's designs belie Ware's implication that the common town house did not really need designing. It may be that the meaner London houses were 'all built in one way, and that so familiar that it will need little instruction, nor deserve much illustration',[102] but Le Muet shows that this need not be the case. The town house's dismissal, particularly in its smaller variety, as unworthy of the designer's attention seems almost a conscious policy on the part of eighteenth-century English theorists and pattern-book authors.

42, 43

What, then, were the 'negative' aspects of the terrace house that led to its general neglect by architectural writers and pattern-book designers? First was the site, the comparatively small size and narrowness of which limited the architect's scope for demonstrating his usual architectural rather than decorative skills. He had limited play with either the modelling and finish of the outside or the planning and disposition of rooms on the inside. Even an unusually large plot could not always be exploited to the full. Much of the site of Shelburne House, Berkeley Square (1762–8), had to be devoted to the garden because of agreements not to build immediately north of Devonshire House.[103] It was not only the narrowness of the site that hampered the town-house architect. James Paine had to handle an irregular corner plot in his design for a house for the Earl of Scarborough, providing an admirable performance under the circumstances, as discussed further in the next chapter. Many houses were rebuilt within existing party walls, which sometimes followed the plans of an earlier building on the site. No. 13 St James's Place, for example, was rebuilt around 1781 to the plans of its seventeenth-century predecessor, and its concession to new fashions was limited to inferior imitations of the 'Adam style' in moulded plaster ceilings.[104] These various factors conspired to restrict or discourage developmental changes, or displays of architectural skill.

Secondly, the town house's size offered limited scope for grandeur in its façade. This limitation was explicitly recognised by John Stewart, who recommended the architect to aim for beauty instead.[105] Plainness was not associated purely with the three-bay terrace house: even the greater scope for elaboration offered by a wider frontage was not always exploited in practice, as the restrained decoration of Home House's five-bay façade demonstrates. James Lewis, in the text accompanying his *Original Designs* of 1780 sees the architect's 'abundant latitude to exercise his talents upon the external parts of an edifice' as the key to his artistic input.[106] With this scope severely limited or absent in the terrace house, the architect was restricted in his capacity to display talent and taste – those two essential qualities that, as Blondel says, distinguish him from the common builder (and indeed differentiate architecture from building).[107] Furthermore, partly because of this limiting narrowness, it was harder for three-bay terrace houses to reflect the status of their inhabitants. However, only observers like Gwynn and Stewart, and the theorists from whom they and other architectural writers derived their prescriptions, seem to have lamented this deficiency.

The country-house exterior offered the broader public varied views, both distant and close, and incorporated surrounding parkland and its physical and symbolic function as the central motif to a much bigger entity. But the London town house's true public was not the broader one on whose behalf Gwynn and Stewart claimed to speak, but the owner's circle of acquaintance. It is true that the exterior was more visible (and consequently worth the careful attention of the architect in its capacity to reflect well or badly on him), but it was what visitors thought about the house that counted, and they saw its inside. Moreover, because of the size restrictions, the house's front was likely to be drafted into the service of the street or square, through general conformity or as a contributor to a palace-front treatment. Not even the palace-style front fully replicated the idiom of the insulated town or country mansion, however; it was literally a superficial solution, having no influence on interior planning.

The third and related negative aspect of the terrace house was that there was no possibility of a relationship between its front and back façades. The detached house, typically the country house, was conceived in three dimensions. The viewer could anticipate relationships between façades and details of one merged into those of the next, with the result that there was some architectural continuity between the four fronts, even if they looked different. But even in the largest terrace house only the front could be comprehended at a glance. Viewing the back and the front of the house were two separate experiences. Nor could the glance reveal much about the house's interior. Generally a doorway in the right- or left-hand bay simply confirmed the asymmetrical arrangement inside. Deprived of its function as contributory indicator of form or interior arrangement, the front façade therefore took on a new role.

General principles often could not be applied to the terrace house, as demonstrated by the consequences of Isaac Ware's adherence to the ideal of a central doorway in his model town house.[108] The central entrance to the later town-house design in *The Builder's Magazine* induces the same wastefulness: an unnecessarily large hall. The success of Thomas Leverton's 1 Bedford Square (*c.* 1778) is exceptional. Here, as Andrew Byrne notes, 'the façade is inextricably related to the interior by its central entrance', from where the whole interior flows.[109] Leverton's 45, 46 house was in no way typical, acting rather as a show house to demonstrate the differences a talented architect could make, if a client was prepared to pay the price.

In practice, forward-looking designers recognised that these 'failings' or differences required the terrace house, or group of houses, to adopt its own aesthetic in order to move from building to architecture. As shown in the next chapter, leading architects achieved distinction in this field precisely by allowing the town house's design to respond positively to those very particularities that others felt inhibited its potential.

Six

Making a Town House Architecture

In the later eighteenth century there was clearly a general disparity between what clients wanted and what self-styled arbiters of taste and practice recommended. Purchasers' general and specific needs led the way, rather than any established aesthetic (or moral) principles, and both exceptional and unexceptional practice sat outside the sorts of framework codified in prescriptive texts and pattern books. The prevailing building practice which satisfied most real, private needs (rather than purported public ideals) was governed instead by habit and consensus, and even demands for something beyond the habitual are scarcely evident in print, despite what was happening in practice. John Carter's designs for individual terrace houses in *The Builder's Magazine* in the mid-1770s are rare evidence of a desire to raise the town house's architectural status, but it is in the executed designs of leading architects, obliged to address real needs, rather than those conveyed in pattern books, that this desire and its gratification are most apparent.

James and Robert Adam's descriptions and illustrations of their executed town projects in their *Works in Architecture* is the first instance where written 'philosophy' and built object concur. The Adams were at the forefront of the movement to establish a town house architecture. Their philosophy in this respect is well demonstrated in their bespoke construction and refurbishment projects, discussed below, but they also conveyed it through the publication of their *Works* (1773–9)[1]. The *Works* and James Paine's *Plans, Elevations, and Sections of Noblemen and Gentlemen's Houses* (published in two volumes, 1767 and 1783) are further evidence of rising interest in the town house, particularly the terrace house, among architects and clients in this period. A close examination of the *Works* in particular helps explain how there came to be a new architectural context for the town house, one which centred on the individual house's interior planning and finish, and how the Adams thereby raised its status through words and actions. The Adam philosophy and practice clarifies both the nature of the town house and its treatment as architecture rather than building from the 1770s onwards.

The virtue of difference

Unlike the aesthetic principles governing the freestanding country house, those governing the terrace house's design were less the province of the architect or theorist and more client driven, deriving principally from the distinctly different uses and values that such houses had for their occupants. In practical terms, and in contrast to the writers discussed in Chapters Four and Five, owners and occupants did not compare their town house with their country house; they compared it with other terrace houses, and noted its qualities and limits within that context. Individuals were concerned with the accommodation that the house provided and other aspects of the interior, but generally much less bothered, it seems, about the house's outward appearance or any external signifiers of quality or of grandeur expressed in the house's size or detachment.

A general overview of the prescriptive writings of Robert Morris and others reveals an outward-looking rather than an inward-looking focus. For example, the first considerations to which the architect must give his attention are all things external to the house, things that must be thought about even before the house itself is designed: 'we are to consider the Extent of the Spot, its Beauties and Fertility; what Improvements may be made in each of these; before the Design can be form'd agreeable to this'.[2] Morris implies here and elsewhere that the country house's architectural merit and its symbolic role alike were embodied primarily in its external demeanour, incorporating not only its form and exterior appearance but also the surrounding land and views to and from the building. Its symbolism was necessarily inclusive: addressed to the broadest public from workers and tenants on the surrounding estate to visiting nobility. A considerable part of the country house's aesthetic appeal derived from its successful performance of this role, and a principal part of the architect's task was to give the country seat a form and finish redolent of lineage, tradition and power and the unassailable links of family, land and nation.

The form and exterior of even the grandest terrace house had no comparable function. Any symbolic role the house played was quite different, and this was performed by its interior arrangement and finish in addition to its position within London and proximity to, rather than distance from, other houses. These were things that did not largely, if at all, concern the building's exterior appearance or form, and therefore denied the architect a large part of his role as defined by Morris and other architectural theorists. The provision, planning and finish of the accommodation was therefore the essence of the design task, and the Adams' ability and willingness to embrace this critical difference between town and country houses is evident in the presentation and description of the former in the *Works* and in their practice. An architect of the rank and ability of Robert Adam could move the terrace house from mere building to a form of architecture by effectively turning it inside out, so that (in contrast to the prescriptions of Morris, Ware, Skaife and others) the principal and 'practical' issues were not grounded in external factors – soundness of construction, location and site – but internal disposition.

Adam articulates his grasp of this difference and its virtue in the *Works*, which offers both a rare concurrence of textual philosophy and practice and is a further example of the rising interest in the terrace house's potential during the 1770s. Like John Carter, Adam and Paine no doubt anticipated an interested audience when including terrace houses in their published designs. In the *Works*, the Adams give prominent placing to two grand and remarkable terrace houses: Derby House, Grosvenor Square (refurbished 1773–4), and Wynn House, 20 St James's Square (rebuilt 1771–4), indicating the importance that they attached to the two projects. The coverage of Derby House is exclusively and comprehensively concerned with the house's interior, which is discussed in the very first paragraph of the preface to volume two. Plates show the ground and principal floors, interior details and decorative schemes (in six plates) as well as designs for furnishings and furniture (one plate). The front elevation, which was left in its original plain form, does not feature. The Adams declare that 'many persons of rank and fortune [have] been struck and pleased with the taste' displayed in the Derby House reception rooms – and some, such as Earl Bathurst and the 'Countess Dowager of Home in Town' and the wealthy Mr Child at Osterley Park had already commissioned the Adams to construct their own 'Etruscan' rooms, based on the designs and colouring of ancient Etruscan pottery.[3] The Adams present the town as the site of innovation: the town house has a promotional function and, as with other fashions, the new style spreads first within London and then out into the country.

47, 48
49

50

The Adams also draw attention to their planning achievements in mastering the inherent problems of the narrow, long site of the London terrace house. The ground and principal floors of Derby House are used, they say, to illustrate 'an attempt to arrange the apartments in the French style, which . . . is best calculated for the convenience and elegance of life'. Lord and Lady Derby's apartments could not be accommodated on the same floor, but the architects boast that their first-floor reception rooms are suitable for 'every occasion of public parade'.[4] This claim makes the London town house the subject of favourable comparisons with Parisian hotels, as well as a display of their skill as architects to enable such comparisons to be made.[5] The Adams therefore introduced an international dimension, which set the scene for the wider arena in which they viewed their town-house architecture, and in which they wanted it to be assessed. They are intent, it seems, on defining what lifts this house out of the ordinary and creates a new variety of town residence: the terrace house in which ingenuity and magnificence of planning and design are enhanced rather than defeated by the site's restrictions.

The second part of volume two of the *Works* is devoted to Wynn House. In this instance, there is an embellished front to show off, but the plates still begin with floor plans to demonstrate that although this house, too, is 'considerably circumscribed with regard to scite [*sic*] . . . great care has been taken to make the apartments spacious, and even magnificent'.[6] The authors then list those rooms 'thought to merit these appellations',[7] introducing an element of external endorsement and setting up the town-house interior as subject to the interest and scrutiny of a wider body of people than just simply the architect and the client. After the plans, the new front of Wynn House is shown and the text again emphasises, this time through rather heavy-handed false modesty, the impressive feat the Adams have pulled off in trying circumstances:

> It is not in a space of forty-six feet . . . that an architect can make a great display of talents. Where variety and grandeur in composition cannot be obtained, we must be satisfied with a justness of proportion and an elegance of style.[8]

The front itself, being a masterful handling of the particular requirements and restrictions of a terrace-house front, cleverly belies what the Adams write here, demonstrating far more than a 'justness of proportion' or 'an elegance of style'. (Of course they would not have selected it for illustration if it did not.) The brothers take as their starting point the restrictions that others saw as blighting the terrace house. They do not see 'the Irregularity or Littleness of the Spot' as preventing the architect from 'shewing his Skill in Designing'.[9] In fact they define talent in terms of a response not to absolute licence but to such limitations, and they regard the town house rather than the country house as the site of that talent's display. A difficult task was not to be shied away from, but welcomed as an opportunity to show off.

A further indication of the rising interest in the potential of the town house in this period is the inclusion of a designated 'Town Houses' section in the second part of James Paine's *Plans, Elevations and Sections* (1783). Paine illustrates two terrace houses: Dr Heberden's house of 1769–71 and the Hon. Thomas Fitzmaurice's house of 1779–80, both in Pall Mall. As in the *Works*, the floor plans come first, but unlike the Adams, Paine provides as much detail about the office floor as he does about the main reception rooms. A comparison of Paine's two sets of plans shows how both he and the terrace house had moved on during the period separating the commencements of the Heberden and Fitzmaurice houses in 1769 and 1779 respectively. More space was required, as well as variety, and more imaginative ways of achieving both had been devised.

53–56

This change is also brought out in volume one of the *Works*, where the Adams pay particular attention to problems and solutions directly or indirectly related to town-house design. They write, for example, that 'the skilful . . . will easily perceive, within these few years, a remarkable improvement in the form, convenience, arrangement, and relief of apartments . . . and in the decoration of the inside an almost total change'.[10] This claim was not specifically about town houses, but the coverage of Wynn and Derby Houses in volume two appears designed to substantiate it. In the preface to part four of volume one, the Adams state, too, that the architectural master

> who has not an opportunity to distinguish himself by displaying his abilities in works of real greatness will naturally betake himself to other resources, and . . . call forth the admiration of mankind by the richness of his invention, and by the elegance and dedication of his ornamental decorations. All these may be adopted with great propriety in small rooms and private apartments.[11]

The preface to part five of the first volume of the *Works* also focuses tellingly on interiors and the broadened intellectual and practical scope that they offer the architect:

> Architecture has already become more elegant and more interesting. The parade, the convenience, and social pleasures of life, being better understood, are more strictly attended to in the arrangement and dis-

position of apartments. Greater variety of form, greater beauty in design, greater gaiety and elegance of ornament, are introduced into interior decoration.[12]

In such passages, the Adams may well have been preparing their readers to accept the town-house interior as an arena for both performance and praise.

'And in . . . the inside an almost total change'

The particularities of the terrace house certainly put its interior in the limelight, and some of the best town-house architects of this period, notably Robert Adam and James Paine, understood the importance of the interior to the fame of their buildings, their clients and themselves. It certainly seems that people wanted to operate and, in some cases, excel within the same framework as others – the 'standard' terrace house of three to five bays. A wider-than-average frontage could offer more potential for planning according to Palladian or other standard principles, but that was not necessarily the sort of scope or difference that people wanted. Prestige and width of frontage ceased to be linked as a matter of course and the houses of Derby, Wynn and Fitzmaurice confirm that it was what could be achieved within the plot's depth that mattered. The house generally addressed a 'private public' – one privy to its interior – rather than indiscriminately impressing any passer-by. Where the terrace house's typical format did not satisfy, then exceptional solutions were brought into play. The architect's task, which was also the means of displaying his skill, was to maximise differentiation within the standard form, principally in the interior. As Tara Draper points out, 'Adam never denied the usual terrace house plan of one front and one back room per floor, but instead used it as the backbone for his designs'.[13]

Adam first applied his planning ideas at Chandos House (1770–1). Arthur Bolton suggests that Chandos House, Wynn House and Derby House 'form an ascending series of high importance and value, one which illuminates the development of Robert Adam's ideas in house planning and decoration'.[14] The Adams had plenty of space to play with at Chandos House. The house itself had a four-bay frontage of around 50 feet and extended backwards around 60 feet in its main body and a further 55 feet in the wing extension to the right-hand side at the rear. There was ample space, too, for a large stable block with accommodation for coachmen and groomsmen. But even this relatively large

57

plot did not relieve the Adams of 'the problem of providing spacious reception rooms without compromising accommodation and service areas', and it was the wing, rather than the house's size, which was the key to the innovative planning that would also influence the most prominent of the Adams' later town-house commissions.[15] Rather than accommodating both reception and private rooms in the main body of the house, the Adams stretched the typical 'closet' extension at the rear of the basic town house into a range of private apartments, incorporating a mezzanine level for servants' rooms. The main body of the house was thereby left free for a circuit of reception rooms, culminating in the second drawing room at the rear of the first floor. As Draper writes, 'while the wing was conceived as distinct and separate from [the] circuit, the doorways were arranged so that private rooms could also be added to the "processional route" if necessary'.[16] So, Chandos House was the first development of the Adams' 'wing' solution to the balance of public and private spaces in the terrace house.[17]

The Adams articulated their reasoning for this planning, retrospectively, in volume two of the *Works*. Their text, discussed above, clarifies that no sacrifice has been made. They will not admit to such a notion; they have taken equally good care of 'public' and private needs, achieving a near perfect balance between the two principal requirements of the town house – show and convenience. They admit it would be preferable to have the lady's and gentleman's apartments on the same floor, as in France; but as it cannot be done, they let it go. After all, the vital balance has been accomplished, despite the limitations of the town-house site.

There are other ways in which we can articulate the Adams' achievement. The reception rooms on the ground and particularly the first floor of a town house typically constituted what Erving Goffman, in his study of *The Presentation of Self in Everyday Life*, calls 'frontstage'. They might be distinguished simply by more elaborate or fashionable decoration than that on other floors.[18] Or, in the hands of Adam, the decorative scheme might be graded 'in a carefully developed crescendo, which reaches its climax in the grand drawing-room on the first floor', as at Chandos House and later at Wynn and Derby Houses.[19] In these houses, because the main body of the building was given over to the reception rooms and private apartments were tucked away in the wing, the architect and his client created the appearance of a house devoted to frontstage. The London house was not simply for display, but it could be made to look as if it were.

It is worth remembering, however, that despite the Adams' innovative contrivances of interior decoration and planning, Chandos House was a speculative project and took two years to sell.[20] It seems that innovation in this field was generally client led or responsive, rather than anticipated. The Adams guessed wrong at Chandos House, which was speculative fbut looked bespoke. The potential offered by its large site was used to create a few, large reception rooms in the main body, and a grand staircase. Perhaps the Adams were gambling that a purchaser would be prepared to devote so much space to frontstage. Yet it appears that the more exceptional the house, the harder it was to match it to a buyer and the architect or builder was perhaps better off with the basic town-house model unless a client commissioned something more. Both innovation and tradition therefore responded to clients' needs. Most people just wanted what was routinely provided for them, while some were looking and prepared to pay for something more or different. These were the clients who stimulated their architects to come up with imaginative treatments of the basic house plan. But innovations and variations within the standard format did not permanently transform plans from this point onwards – there was no call for them to do so.

The Adams continued their development of the upmarket terrace-house plan at Wynn House, 20 St James's Square (1771–4). At Chandos House, the architects had done little to the shape of individual rooms, remaining content with a bowed end to the principal room on each of the main floors. But the Wynn House plans show the unusual, though not unprecedented feature of paired main rooms on each floor with 'large segmental apses set back to back'.[21] These apses allowed for the formation of recesses in the staircase hall, which gave it a sense of spaciousness at no cost to the principal rooms.[22] John Martin Robinson writes that the use of these spaces, 'to mitigate the somewhat straitened feeling of such a high, narrow, rectangular space' as this hall, is characteristic of Robert Adam's genius.[23] The hall consequently has the effect of an inner court, perhaps helping visitors believe they were at the centre of a bigger building, rather than the right-hand boundary of a terrace house.[24]

Such means of transcending the sense of circumscribed space were employed throughout the ground and first floors of the house. On the latter, the rooms 'are given additional spatial magnificence by groined or barrel-vaulted ceilings'.[25] Here the second drawing room, the climax of the 'parade', has a segmental arched ceiling, given a banded design which appears to repeat and thus emphasise the curve, making the rise of the arch seem higher than it actually is.[26] Decorative means therefore supplement constructional and planning ones to give a sense of movement and variety, which undermines any residual notions of restraint or circumscription. As at Chandos House, the first rooms of the private

51

58

59

apartments housed in the wing on each main floor could be included in the circuit as required, as 'a coda to the parade of grand reception rooms, thrown open to the public at big assemblies'.[27]

Derby House also displays such complexity, even though the remodelling did not require many structural alterations. Here Adam focused on creating on each floor a sequence of public rooms 'progressively increasing in size and importance'.[28] As at Wynn House, the library on the ground floor and the countess's dressing room on the first were intermediate spaces defining the end of the 'frontstage' and the beginning of the 'backstage', which again occupies the wing. The remodelling included the creation of liminal spaces on the ground floor, such as those between the hall and anteroom and the anteroom and parlour. Together with the contrived circuit, these spaces must have contributed to a sense of travelling 'through', in contrast to the town house's natural disposition to provide an 'up and down' spatial experience. In *Cecilia* and *Evelina*, Fanny Burney uses the experience of travelling through rooms to indicate the grandeur of houses in two great squares. Cecilia is 'ushered with great pomp through sundry apartments, and rows of servants', before coming into Mr Delvile's presence in his St James's Square home, while Branghton junior, in *Evelina*, is unnerved by being 'led through such a heap of servants and so many rooms', when paying an inappropriate visit to Lord Orville in Berkeley Square.[29] At Derby House, the visitor's disorientation through changing vistas and directions must have created a sense of depth and penetration at odds with the site's true shape and dimensions.

Nevertheless, the significant difference between the earlier house and its Adamatic successor was less the layout and more the management of contrasting room spaces and particularly the variety of wall treatments, which achieved 'a lively contrast of light and shadow and a diversity of contours, proportions and character expressly intended to please and entertain the observer'.[30] The third drawing room provided the climax, and Eileen Harris writes of it:

> There were very few domestic interiors of the period in which the spirit of Roman antiquity was so successfully introduced and so completely transfused with novelty, variety and gaiety: not only by surface decoration, but also by modelling the walls in relief, as it were, bringing them forward from the flat plane and raising the ceiling to create an impressive groin vault in the centre, with barrel vaults at either end.[31]

It is significant that this unusual interior was in a town house, not just because it increases Adam's achievement but also because it put that achievement at the centre of the fashionable world, where people could see it. And in case they failed to register its significance, he drew particular attention to it in the *Works* with a dramatic illustration.

Such extremes of decorative and planning contrivance were clearly responsive to very specific and exceptional needs. Adam's client at Derby House was Lord Stanley, later Earl of Derby, 'one of the most profuse and ostentatious party-givers in London'.[32] Few other people required, or could afford, this level of 'architectural' input in their town house. A simple comparison of Derby House's floor plans with those of a similar-size house in the same square, remodelled by John Johnson for the Duke of Dorset around 1776, demonstrates the different lengths to which clients were prepared to go. Dorset's house makes just a nod in the direction of the (by then) not-so-new style, with the bowed front to the centre room of the wing extension.

47
60

The manner of Adam's work at Derby House diverged sharply from the additive nature of the regular town house's interior decoration, where an architect's contribution might be fragmentary – comprising perhaps only isolated designs for chimney pieces and ceilings. Adam introduced a degree of complexity in planning and integrated decor that was the antithesis of replication and standardization. Derby House was emphatically bespoke.

At Home House, where he was involved from 1775, Adam mitigated the inevitably sharp, vertical movement up and down the town-house staircase by giving the traveller a sequence of changing views. Although the house was on a wider site than many others, Adam was constrained by the existing building, already half completed by James Wyatt. He excelled himself in his response to the task and, as Eileen Harris notes, 'it is particularly ironic that the ingenious planning of the interior should in the past have been credited to the freedom afforded by the unusual width of the site'.[33] Adam was permitted to remove his predecessor's staircase, and rose to the challenge of providing a superior replacement within the same, confined space. Within a nearly square, top-lit shell Adam constructed 'an extraordinary circular staircase hall and imperial stair'.[34] The optimum position for such a staircase would have been on the axis of the entrance, but Adam turned the predetermined position at the right-hand side of the house to his advantage. As Harris explains, 'his alignment of the projecting first flight with the vestibule to the ground-floor reception rooms defines the important cross axis and helps to direct the circuit'.[35] The success of Adam's arrangement here can be compared with the under-exploitation of the centrally placed, circular stairwell in the later terrace-house design in *The Builder's Magazine* (1777), which fails to create or direct a true circuit on either ground or first floor.

61

62

Making a Town House Architecture 175

As at Wynn House, the Home House staircase stops at the first floor, contributing to the demarcation of front from back spaces; and a balcony at the second-floor level allows the frontstage space below to be surveyed from a fresh angle. Home House is exceptional in the group of Adam houses discussed here because its site was sufficiently wide not to require a rear extension. Nevertheless, the squarish body was still given over to frontstage on ground and first floors, with the Etruscan room on the latter acting as an intermediate space. This was never designed as a family home, and bedrooms and servants' accommodation could therefore be limited to one floor.[36]

Not every client required of Adam the brilliance shown at Wynn, Derby and Home Houses. At 33 St James's Square (1770–2), a four-bay house very similar externally and in size to Chandos House, Adam mixed the private and public areas. On the ground floor, to the left of a largish hall, is a dressing room, conveniently sited for conducting business. A powdering room and valet's room link the dressing room to the large parlour at the rear. On the first floor, an anteroom links two large drawing rooms, and another dressing room is incorporated in the circuit. Much space is devoted to the 'great stair' in the centre, with its Palladian 'window' and column screen, but its prominence is at odds with what the room designations and connections suggest. Neither floor displays a fully formed circuit; the house, it seems, was not predominantly for show, despite its position in the illustrious St James's Square.

On occasion, no doubt, clients were prepared to forgo artistry to save money, as William Gerard Hamilton did in the villa Adam remodelled for him at Brighton. Hamilton declared 'warmth and comfort' to be his 'principal Objects'; 'Elegance, though a desirable, is only a secondary one'. Consequently, Hamilton suggested that 'the Recess part of the Dining Parlor instead of being Circular might be made strait and in that case the Door in the Centre of the Dining Parlor might be shut up'. As Chris Miele writes, the plan therefore 'shows the architect taking difficult decisions, compromising, thinking, tinkering, reconciling rigorous, abstract notions of the villa, of how it appears in the mind's eye, with the indisputable givens of the real world, of budgetary constraints and awkward sites, of a world where architecture is a luxury which can only just be afforded'.[37] There must have been many similar exchanges regarding town houses: turning one's house from building to architecture was certainly a costly business, as Sir Watkin's papers confirm.

James Paine's illustration and description of Dr Heberden's house in his *Plans, Elevations, and Sections* suggest that the ground and first floors were not both devoted to show, but were, respectively, the principal and the chamber floor. Unlike at Chandos, Wynn and Derby Houses, the private apartments were incorporated into the body of the house, rather than pushed back into an extended wing. Paine's house for the Hon. Thomas Fitzmaurice, begun ten years later, answers very different requirements, but still keeps the public rooms for business and entertainment principally on the ground floor. A large extension to the original house, at the side and rear of the site, houses the reception rooms, without aspiring to a circuit, while the main body of the house, on this floor, accommodates two offices for business, the hall and the staircase. Paine's plan is an interesting though not ingenious solution to a patron's particular needs.

55

At Fitzmaurice House, Paine or his client may not have wished to tamper much with the main body of the existing house, but a new building on a virgin site presented Paine with more exacting challenges. He had to contrive a house for the Earl of Scarborough on a plot of four unequal sides, with a frontage of around 44 feet to Chesterfield Street and extending over 90 feet to the rear.[38] The previously unpublished ground-floor plan, the only one to survive, shows a vaulted hall leading to an impressive oval staircase hall with deep niches, and a sequence of three rooms down the right side. The position of the staircase, tucked into the inside centre of the house, ensures a clear run of space for the splendid first-floor room, which, according to a note on the plan, would stretch 38 feet along the front.

63

The cleverest feature of the plan is Paine's use of the light afforded by a corner plot to set three rooms side by side, all facing the street, each echoing the shape of the others, yet slightly different. Their shapes are not expressed on the outside wall, except that of the front room, whose bay to the street catches the perimeter of the plot (of which a corner is lost to soften the exterior angle). The other two rooms are symmetrical across their east–west axes, spared from expressing the irregularity of the site's western border (incorrectly marked as 'east' on the plan). In Adam's houses the rooms are shaped to counter the effect of a sequence of box-like spaces, but here the shapes stop the exigencies of the site from impinging on the interior. Paine maximises the space by setting the rooms side by side, rather than end on end, thereby fitting in three decently sized spaces without resorting to a wing, which the site could barely have accommodated. His disregard for the resulting irregular fenestration on the west front reveals him to be more concerned here with the interior arrangements than with their expression, or effect, on the outside.

Other architects played with space in the town house, either out of necessity or fancy; and the play was admired. Sir Robert Taylor's obituary describes his own house at 34 Spring Gardens as 'a great curiosity for the economy of space, fanciful shapes and multiplied accommodations'.[39] Elsewhere, Taylor had performed well under trying circumstances. In his intriguing account of the development of Grafton Street, Richard Garnier shows how James Paine's scheme of *c.*1764 for the Earl of Albemarle for a row of five houses was superseded by Taylor's designs for the Duke of Grafton. Although Paine's group was noteworthy for some subtleties of planning (including suites of 'intercommunicating geometrical-shaped rooms with curved inner ends'), its design assumed that an existing road would be moved, thereby creating a more regular plot and allowing for fairly conventional house plans. Taylor, on the other hand, was stuck with 'Grafton's undertaking not to disturb the road pattern', and therefore 'worked through the difficulties of the site to produce a revolutionary set of town house plans'.[40] Each of those plans responded to the particular exigencies of its site, including property boundaries and restraining covenants with regard to the obstruction of 'lights' (windows). The houses in the northern arm of Grafton Street 'had tighter and more intricate plans as the individual house plots diminish in size, top-lit geometrical staircases and octagonal rooms crowding together towards the east' as a response to an existing building abutting the rear of No. 14 and an order 'effectively preventing Grafton from building right up to his back boundary' in Nos. 11–13.[41] The more restricted the site, the greater ingenuity required to provide a convenient yet fashionable residence in keeping with the remainder of the development.

Sir Robert Taylor also worked with the site's particularities where there was more space. At 3 Grafton Street he capitalized on the sloping ground at the back of the site and the potential of views incorporating part of Berkeley Square, Charles Street and the front and garden of Lansdowne House by including a canted, six-storey bay at the rear.[42] Like Adam, Taylor also understood how to make the spatial experience of moving through a terrace house more exciting than it naturally tended to be, and included at No. 3 his idiosyncratic device of 'dividing off a small vaulted section of lower height separated by a short-columned screen from the main space, which could thus be experienced as though from an external viewpoint'. Here it not only confuses the 'parading' visitor, but also manipulates their entry into the grand first-floor room at the culmination of the circuit so that they enter the room's main space boldly on its central axis, facing the apse at the far end, rather than uncomfortably and timidly at the corner.[43] Taylor used this device elsewhere, including at the Bank of England;[44] but its inclusion here, in company with several other interesting features, demonstrates a lack of restriction in how the interior space of the terrace house could be handled, and a desire to make as much of this building type as of the country house, villa or public building.

I discussed in Chapter Five the problems arising from a central door in a narrow house front, but at 1 Bedford Square Thomas Leverton displayed invention and talent in overcoming the danger of wasting the whole ground-floor front of the house on a hall. He divided the space   46 into three parts: the central forming a hall, that on the left housing an elegant staircase rising to the second floor, and the right-hand side forming an anteroom. Unlike the hall in the later of the two *Builder's Magazine* terrace-house designs, where only the central portion serves any real purpose, there is no dead space – an unaffordable luxury in a town house. Both side spaces here are oval, distinguishing them from the rectangular hall proper, and each has access through the spine wall to the rear room stretching the full width of the house.

Paine, Leverton and, in particular, Adam, surpassed the previous level of ingenuity displayed by town-house designers even in those earlier houses that are considered to be examples of architecture rather than building, as the examples of 44 Berkeley Square (1742–4) and 12 North Audley Street (*c*.1725–30) demonstrate. At the first house, William Kent had provided a famously beautiful and striking staircase for Lady Isabella Finch. Horace Walpole remarked on its theatricality: 'as beau-   64 tiful a piece of scenery, and considering the space, of art, as can be imagined'.[45] Walpole's linkage of contrivance in a limited space with 'art' has great significance for my argument here. There is no art in the standard terrace-house layout, so the house itself is an instance of 'building' rather than 'architecture'. But 'art', in Walpole's sense, is what makes 'architecture' of the exceptional town house. At Lady Isabella Finch's house the architectural achievement and appeal is largely limited to the staircase and the grand saloon to which it leads, both of which derive from generic or specific country-house models. The staircase is a development, in miniature, of an earlier design of Kent's, the hall at Holkham,[46] while, as Christopher Sykes writes, the saloon 'gave an impression of great splendour and guests must have felt they were in the ante-room of some palace'.[47] The aesthetic effect at 44 Berkeley Square, it seems, relied on its associative links with great country houses. By contrast, Adam's achievement in his principal terrace-house projects was to look to the format itself for inspiration. By that means he was able to move well beyond the application or inclusion of an individual feature like a staircase to embrace the whole house in a composite design, where nothing is evidently sacrificed for the sake of anything else. At Home House, the staircase, though magnificent, is subordinated to or integrated with the overall plan, with little evidence of sacrifice except a narrow entrance to the stair that, after all, increases its impact. At 44 Berkeley Square, however, the staircase dictates to the house. The accommodation is made subservient to the staircase, thereby disrupting conventional London town-house planning,[48] and much of the second floor is taken up by the deep, coved ceiling of the first-floor saloon 'on the model of the Double Cube [room] at Wilton'.[49] If anything, the scale and appearance of these two key features – the staircase and the saloon – draw attention to the smallness of the house itself. It may be that later clients, asking much more of their houses and architects, were unwilling or unable to make such compromises and looked for a more satisfactorily integrated solution.

Christopher Hussey calls 12 North Audley Street (c.1725–30) 'a most interesting example' of a 'small' West End town house built before the practice of lengthening the closet wing to provide extra accommodation was introduced by Adam and others. The house has a single-storey gallery at the rear (marked 'drawing room'), which extends into the rear space of the next house. This gallery has a central coffered dome, and there is also an octagonal library on the ground floor, top lit through another dome. Hussey suggests that the house 'presents many advantages over the later convention' of the rear extension to one side,[50] but the great reception room at the rear was only provided at the expense of the neighbouring house and much accommodation on the upper floors was lost for the sake of the two domes. Not only did the 'later convention' not require such sacrifices, it was also better suited to the new patterns of entertainment of the second half of the century, which required a succession of rooms, and, at least in Adam's hands, it also offered more opportunity for serial surprise and delight.

It was almost wholly by adjustments to the interior that Adam turned the basic town-house model from building into architecture. It is clear that innovation was mostly a response to particular client needs, which were primarily focused on the inside of the house. Other than practical considerations, what else led clients to focus their interest, and their architect's talents, on their house's interior?

The interior was the place for making a 'figure': for displaying taste and wealth, or modesty and restraint. Extensive remodelling or decoration, particularly decoration as idiosyncratic as Adam's, represented the investment of much time, money and skill. It was a gesture of extravagance and evinced a degree of commitment to a house (and to a presence in London). In any case, the town house relied on its interior to summarize its owner's personality, interests and ambitions. The carcass could not help in this respect, not least because the town house was so often a faceless box. However, it was amenable to internal change. It was generally in its interior that the house revealed itself to be modern or old-fashioned, stylish or tasteless. In the absence of a stylistic relationship between inside and out, the inside became the principal target for differentiation between houses, and for exploring fashion; both differentiation and fashion were as easily applied as removed.

Clients themselves therefore looked to the interior to exercise their own taste and genius, as well as for diversion. In fact James Peacock (in what is surely a critique of the 'Adam style') made clear how far removed from the governing hand, or interests, of the 'serious' architect the interior could be – so far, in fact, that it might as well be left to a woman:

> Let [the owner] suffer his exterior to be . . . in some measure guiltless of the excess of modern refinement and modern finery; on the contrary, in the interior let him not be afraid to copy the architects of the present day, (unless he shall rather choose to leave the whole to the direction of his lady, which, perhaps, after all, is the best and wisest way). Here let the nicknackery of the Cabinetmaker, Toy-man, and Pastry-cook preside with impunity. Here let the light and elegant ordonnance of the bed-post triumph over the clumsy orders of old Greece. Here let Pilasters rival the substances and ornaments of figured ribbons . . .[51]

The distinction between the demands made on the outside and the inside of a house is explicit: while the exterior is to be serious, proper and well managed, the interior gives licence to waywardness and whimsicality, qualities with which the architect should be reluctant to associate himself. For Peacock at least, the 'nicknackery' that characterises the 'modern' interior is as far removed from architecture proper as its purveyors are from the architect. But because the town-house architect, too, relied chiefly on the interior to display his talent and genius, the balance of his interest necessarily lay inside rather than out.

Integrity versus integration

In spite of this inevitable attention to interiors, architectural practice in this period does show an increased interest in individualised town-house façades, where 'modern refinement and modern finery' were also displayed – particularly from the 1770s onwards. As Pierre-Jean Grosley noted of Grosvenor Square houses following a visit in 1765, some 'are quite plain and simple in front' while others 'have ornaments according to the taste and caprice of the owner'.[52] The practice of giving the front of a house a finish that differentiated it from its neighbours was – like singular interior decoration or planning – another means of manipulating the common framework to emphasise difference, and a further example of the client-led inventiveness displayed in this period.

The option of elaboration (or plainness) typically arose not in new developments – where some degree of uniformity, not necessarily aspiring to grandeur, was likely – but in the rebuilding or refronting of an existing house as part of a discrete refurbishment project. This practice was more common in established parts of the city, such as Grosvenor and St James's Squares, where individual leases fell in at different times and where there was no question of conformity.[53] Such areas therefore offered the most scope for individuality in façades, and the rising interest in the exterior look of terrace houses may have developed partly to cater for the needs of that specific market: the refronted terrace house in an established location.

Differentiating designs for individual fronts defined the 'integrity' of the house front as a unit of design rather than its integration into a wider scheme. By integrity I mean a certain self-sufficiency and completeness and, by implication, a lack of relation to built surroundings. Integrity was a natural feature of the country house, or insulated town mansion, which was clearly defined by its own four walls and its surrounding land. But, where desired, it had to be created in the terrace house. Integrity can be opposed to integration, which involves acknowledging a context and making concessions to it. An individual house could be demarcated within a palace front, but the latter's decorative articulation was not necessarily, or usually, linked to the divisions of the houses that it fronted. In some instances a single house owned the whole of a pedimented central, temple-front section (as on the west side of Portland Place), but did not thereby achieve integrity because of the temple front's integral contribution to a wider design. The individual façade's distinction was most powerful in its contextual relationship with the other, undistinguished façades that sat either side of it, as part of a total composition.

The individual town-house façade, taller than wide, has a natural verticality, which palace-front and other integrating treatments, as well as 'country house' designs for groups of town houses, negate. Integrating fronts emphasise both membership of a group and horizontality, by such means as continuous cornices, string courses and regular window levels. They deny a critical difference between the aesthetic idiom of the terrace house and that of the classical town or country mansion. However, many contemporary façade designs, such as Robert Adam's for Wynn House and 11 St James's Square (1774–6) and James Paine's design for Fitzmaurice, emphasise and celebrate the verticality of the terrace house. In 56 this respect they hark back to a pre-Palladian tendency of the late seventeenth and very early eighteenth centuries to give vertical emphasis to the façade, by the narrow piers which framed it and by linking windows by their dressings and aprons.[54] In particular, Adam's design for Sir Rowland Winn at 11 St James's Square shows how even a five-bay house could be drawn visually inwards and upwards to replicate the impact of a tall and narrow house. Adam accentuates the middle three bays with pilasters and rustication and emphasises their verticality with roofline statues. The superimposition of verticality, usually in the form of pilasters, was often an important part of creating the façade's integrity. Winn's house had earlier shared a very plain front with two others. A drawing of the group's appearance in 1821 shows how Adam's 65 treatment of the façade pulled the house away from its immediate neighbours, not only by drawing it in visually towards its centre three bays but also by disrupting the continuous, heavy moulding above the second-floor windows which previously bound the three houses together and stressed the horizontality of their combined street façade.[55]

Those three designs – for the houses of Wynn, Winn and Fitzmaurice – also illustrate a closely related tendency to follow the 'town format' described in Chapter Five with regard to some pattern-book designs: the rusticated ground floor with arched openings, surmounted by a grand pilaster order strapping the house in and pulling it up straight and tall, and no pediment. Visual associations with Renaissance urban palazzi – most obvious in larger buildings such as John Nash's paired houses in Bloomsbury Square (c.1777–8) – may or may not have been intentional, but the format certainly contributes to a distinctive town look or aesthetic well suited to the building type and its location, which resolutely disregards the 'country house' aesthetic that dominates the prescriptive writings and pattern-book designs. The façade of Paine's house for Fitzmaurice at 105 Pall Mall expresses this independent 'town aesthetic' to perfection.

There were other methods of achieving integrity and individuality: most of Paine's terrace houses had a roof ridge running at right angles to the front, 'which was crowned by his characteristic device of a silhouetted pediment across its whole width so that the individual character of the single house was stressed'.[56] As Peter Leach points out, this 66 device 'decisively rejected' the standard Palladian model represented by Colen Campbell's development in Old Burlington Street: 'a significant feature of [Campbell's] buildings was that the individual houses were subordinated to the effect of the street as a whole'.[57] The tall, narrow 67 proportions of the buildings that Paine's pediments topped prevented them from mimicking the classical country mansion, operating instead as a marker of difference from the surrounding houses. In this respect the pediment was assertively anti-horizontal and anti-integration. The device is, in fact, more gable end than pediment, and perhaps represents a wistful glance back to earlier, differentiated City houses rather than the imitation of an unrelated house type.[58]

68   Robert Taylor's celebrated façade of Ely House, Dover Street (1772–6), is an excellent example of integrity at work without the assistance of an applied order.[59] A stone façade was a straightforward, if expensive, way of demarcating a house from its brick-fronted neighbours.[60] The façade at Ely House was unusual for its time in being faced entirely in Portland stone and in resembling 'a miniature palazzo rather than a routine London terrace house', with its suggestion of an arcade at ground-floor level. But the integrity was also assured in more subtle ways, such as 'the contrivance of a small, shallow recess on either side of the elevation which allows all the mouldings – rustication, string course and cornice – to be returned and fully silhouetted rather than cut off in the manner of a normal terrace house'.[61] The first and second storeys also suggest, by means of a double return, that the house does not share a party wall with its neighbour but has its own sides, running back from the street front.[62] These two upper storeys therefore appear narrower than the rusticated ground floor and 'the parapet is set back a further degree at its ends, so that the whole elevation tapers gradually as it goes upwards, an unexpected architectural refinement'.[63] The façade of Ely House therefore states its difference from its neighbours not just by its stone front but also by such subtleties of design.

Taylor was seemingly long-practised in differentiating a single house front from its terrace neighbours. In the eighteenth century, examples of clear distinction before the 1760s are unusual, but the *Survey of London* volume on the parish of St Anne Soho features a distinctive house by

69   Taylor in Soho Square, dated to the mid-1740s. This house has a Palladian window at first-floor level set in a tall, relieving arch that fills and defines the house front over its upper two storeys. The house is topped with a pediment behind which the roof space rises – not a gable end in this case, but still a clear marker of the house's distinction from its neighbours. The verticality in this instance is somewhat stilted, because the arch clips the second-floor windows, counteracting the upward thrust. But in the mid-1770s Taylor produced a similar design

70   that let verticality go unhampered. This house, also in Soho Square, featured a Palladian window at second-floor level immediately above a tripartite first-floor window, again set within an arch spanning the house's front. The upward thrust is unequivocal, suggesting that unstinted ver-

ticality had become allowable by the 1770s. Only the broad width of the entrance fanlight keeps the house grounded in the square.[64]

Such façade designs operated on the terms of the terrace house, rather than relying uncomfortably on those borrowed from the detached town or country mansion. Only the front needed the treatment for integrity to be achieved; nothing of the sort was required at the back (another reason for the mismatch of front and rear façades). This integrity was hardly an essential aspect of the terrace house, but the increased interest in such differentiation in this period indicates not only a better understanding and appreciation of the nature of the house itself but also pleasure in defining and responding to the aesthetic principles which governed its design. An undated (and unexecuted) design by the younger George Dance for the elevation to 6 St James's Square turns its back on the country-house aesthetic more than most. It features rustication over the first two storeys, paired and individual pilasters subjugating all horizontals, above and below cornice level, and a pattern of three, deep, superimposed voids on either side tied together and pulled to the centre at the top by a row of three Diocletian attic windows. Once again, the combination of opportunity and wealth made St James's Square a hot-bed of innovation.

In bespoke houses, differentiation was ultimately the client's not the architect's choice, as shown by the mix of plain and more elaborate town-house façade designs produced by Robert Adam.[65] No doubt the client's budget had a major part to play in the decision to elaborate a façade or not. John Stewart fondly believed that 'the expense of adorning a front, can never be an object of consideration with a man of high rank, who finds himself in a condition to build a house',[66] but many houseowners would not have agreed with him. The cost of pilasters, columns and other ornament was easily reckoned. At 11 St James's Square, the Adams offered Winn a choice of stuccoed fronts – either a more restrained, yet tasteful and cheaper version at £180, or the more elaborate one for which he opted at £500.[67] At 18 Cavendish Square, in the late 1750s, Henry Keene offered Thomas Bridges a choice between two fairly plain elevations, one with fewer trimmings, indicating that the additional cost for dressing the architraves, friezes and cornice, rather than just the cills, would be £56.[68] Neither version offered integrity, in the sense of defining the house's distinction from its neighbours, but the choice presented to Bridges confirms the importance of financial and other non-aesthetic considerations when making such decisions. Stewart nevertheless clung to his principle that a 'street house' was only permissible if its noble owner expressed his altruism in a worthy façade. He proposed two houses recently erected in Cavendish

Square by Mr Tufnell, and 15 St James's Square by James Stuart, to be good examples of this.[69] The terrace house with an adorned front could become, in Stewart's eyes, a marker of rank (and taste) and such a front substituted for grandeur and size, the former being ruled out by a lack of the latter.

Integrity was not always desired and rarely required as such, although it may sometimes have compensated for a neighbourhood's lack of elegance or fashionableness. Baron Grant, whose house in unfashionable Soho Square was remodelled and refronted by Robert Adam in 1771–2, may have sought such redress. It might have been looked for, too, by Sir William James in nearby Gerrard Street, although the Adam design for his house (1781) was not executed.[70] James's front was of five bays; like the design for 11 St James's Square, the central three bays are emphasised, in this instance with arcading at ground-floor level and a pediment above the second-floor windows with an attic order rising behind. By these means the design also emphasises the house's verticality, particularly in this middle section, rather than its expanse over five bays. Grant's house was even wider, but integrity was never the exclusive prerogative of the three- to five-bay house, although the wider house did not answer the requirements of the fully expressed town-house idiom, which required integrity and verticality. The Adams' front to 20 Soho Square merely used elaboration in the form of pilasters, a balustrade and ground-floor rustication to distinguish the house from its plainer neighbours.

Escape from the binding force of a newly planned square might offer the opportunity for differentiation in an individual façade. No. 1 Bedford Square falls 'outside the self-contained symmetry' of the square's east side,[71] and was not therefore obliged to share in the square's architectural treatment (although it could still borrow from its prestige). Perhaps Sir Lionel Lyde, Leverton's client here, chose the house for that reason. Certainly he exploited his opportunity for a distinctive façade. The house was widened at the cost of the adjacent house in Charlotte Street (now Bloomsbury Street), although it remains relatively small. The entrance's decoration and centrality make it the house's most distinguishing external feature. The façade's individualism, a product of vision, invention and talent, leads to a further display of ingenuity inside. It is significant that it took an enlightened patron, as well as a very capable architect, to achieve such individuality not repeated elsewhere in the square.

Learning from the Adams

The Adams' practice exposes certain key aspects of the London terrace house's nature in this period. The house came to be treated as architecture, rather than just a building, because many West End residents wanted a terrace house, and some wanted it to do more for them than it had been required to do in the past. The house remained popular not just because most people were happy with the standard product, but because those who wanted something different recognised the benefits of expressing that difference in the context of the standard format. At Wynn and Derby Houses, the Adams showed just how successfully and impressively this could be done.[72]

Theorists and prescribers clung to ideals inspired by such abstract notions as London's 'needs', far removed from the town-house owner's personal and practical requirements. Unsurprisingly, explicit demands from the likes of Gwynn and Stewart were defunct in the face of private interests, which inevitably dominated the architectural (and building) scene. Houseowners did not expect the house to be comparable in purpose or symbolic function to the country house; it was required to be different. All those things prescriptive writers advocated were the things seemingly of least interest to house buyers and architects' clients. Prescriptive writers on architecture saw many of the terrace house's distinctive qualities (narrowness of site; lack of scope for symmetrical or axial planning; no relation between interior and exterior dispositions; and proximity to its neighbours, for example) as failings, because they judged the house by its degree of approximation to an ideal defined by the country house. Architectural publications betray a pervading sense of disappointment that the circumstances in which the London house was built impinged on its ability to attain the sort of perfection promoted by such theorists as Robert Morris and Isaac Ware, a perfection to which the country house could more readily aspire.

Like their clients, however, the Adams took the town house's actual rather than relative nature as their starting point, and framed the distinction between the town house and the country house in a positive way in both practice and text. In the *Works* they emphasise variety, invention, elegance and ornamental decoration, and single out interiors (and explicitly town interiors) as the arena in which these qualities can be displayed. The town-house architect has no want of opportunities in this redefinition of architecture, and the discrepancy between the respective roles of architecture and the town house, as evident in William Chambers's definition, is no longer relevant. The town-house architect's necessary reliance on the town-house interior as a vehicle for displaying talent and genius was problematic, as James Peacock's remarks suggest, but the Adams and others turned such imperatives to their clients' advantage.

In both the Adams' and general practice, the town house was defined by its interior. Whereas in the country house the interior was the finish to the building, in the town house the building was simply the container for the interior. The interior was often the only indicator of the town-house owner's personality, standing, taste or wealth; as such, it came to represent the house as a whole in a manner far removed from the joint show staged by the country house, its exterior, its surrounding gardens and its estate. This is not the place to reconsider the specifics of town-house interiors in the light of this understanding: that would be an entirely new project. As I said in my introduction, I hope that the arguments presented here will both contextualise existing writings and inform future research. What is important in the context of this book is the impact of the interior's role on perceptions of the town house past and present, and I discuss this further in the concluding chapter.

The Adams' practice did not initiate a pervasive or permanent change: most people were happy with the general product the market provided, and few could have afforded anything better. Nevertheless, the Adams offered the terrace house a wider stage, allowing comparisons to be made not with the 'ideal' standards of the freestanding town or country mansion but with the best of continental practice, exemplified by Parisian hôtels. In the Adams' hands, the house was no longer a compromise or failure but free to operate and excel within its own idiom. As Roy Porter neatly explains, 'thanks to Adam brilliance, town living became stylish: smart, classy and exhilarating . . . The art of London living was to make a virtue of necessity'[73] – and, we might add, of difference.

Conclusion

The Town House Reassessed

Anecdotal and other documentary evidence brings to light a wide variety of uses and values attached to the town house – some practical, others more abstract, with many of both sorts being unforeseen by the modern-day scholar. Through such evidence it is clear to see why many people pursued a life in London and required a house there, and the financial investment and risks that they were prepared to make to that end. (It is equally easy to see why others avoided residence in the capital.) The town house's new importance in this period is readable not only in its vastly increased numbers, but also in the rising interest in its exterior appearance and interior manipulation. Its importance to many individuals and families was also expressed in its treatment as a piece of property, revealed in wills and settlements, which included efforts to keep a good, well-placed house in the family. Most people, however, chose rather than inherited a house, and evidence and accusations of discrimination and over-discrimination show how much attention they paid to this choice. It is clear by this reckoning that even the nondescript, standard town house often had a greater significance for its owner or tenant than we could possibly gauge by just looking at it. Whether the landed classes set more store by their country houses and whether real property was the only sort 'that mattered in a symbolic sense',[1] is beside the point when we know that the town house nevertheless had significant non-utilitarian uses, values, or 'meanings', as I hope I have proved.

Armed with a new appreciation of the broader social and financial contexts in which houses and their owners operated, we can return to the built form and conceive why the town house took the forms it did, both standard and exceptional. The general absence of this broader appreciation partly explains the house's representation in much of the literature to date as inconsequential to its owners, and to architectural history as a whole. However, it remains only a part explanation, and I identify and revisit below some other factors which further account for the dismissive and even disapproving tone adopted with regard to the town house in contemporary, as well as some subsequent, literature. It is worth noting on the way, in the light of the bad press the house has often received, the irony that 'far from inhibiting development as originally intended [in the seventeenth-century legislation], the orderly pattern of facades, streets and above all the amenity of all those well-planted squares, about which so many of the foreign visitors to London in the eighteenth century enthused, actually increased the attractions of living in London and have remained a sound investment in environmental planning which continues to pay dividends three centuries later'.[2]

My reassessment of the West End house has focused primarily on what the house meant and was worth to its eighteenth-century owners and occupants, with some surprising revelations. If we pursue to its logical conclusion Martin Locock's argument for 'the analysis of buildings primarily in terms of their role in the constructing society, as a mode of creating and transmitting social statements',[3] then we must incorporate into the town house's composite 'meaning' not only occupants' perceptions, intentions and expectations, but also external observations. I have also explored, therefore, the ways in which diverse other parties perceived the house. It is these private and public assessments and judgements that explain why the house attracted specific, often derogatory comments in this period, some of which have persisted to the present day. The misalignment between this negative press – past and present – and the town house's evident popularity is this concluding chapter's principal concern.

Scrutiny and spectacle

Disinterested observers made demands on the house and its occupants simply by virtue of its location in the West End, although householders were more responsive to requests for displays of civic conscience accompanied by immediate threats of window-breaking than they were to Gwynn and Stewart's more distant petitions. The house's fashionable location also brought private judgements and attendant responsibilities for its finish and furnishing. Consumers plundered it for ideas, and sometimes for goods, with the auctioneer rather than the owner over-seeing the ultimate scrutiny to which the house and its contents could be exposed: the sale for the benefit of creditors. The town house, its finish and its acquisition and disposal were indicators eagerly read or misread by other West End residents.

In this respect, the 'good' house had an incalculable value in con-structing and maintaining an identity in the West End – a 'proper figure', attracting social and financial credit. To extend my earlier gaming analogy of gamble and forfeit, the house could be used in the manner of a trump card, to better others, or a wild card, to compensate for lack in other areas. For example, Lady Derby's splendid house in Grosvenor Square excused her marital indiscretions and no doubt also made amends, in some eyes, for her husband's want of refinement. Derby's public image was hardly sophisticated, and he and his friends took plea-sure 'in being overtly crude, as the following wager illustrates: "Ld Cholmondeley has given two guineas to Ld Derby, to receive 500Gs. whenever his lordship fucks a woman in a Balloon one thousand yards from Earth" '.[4] An earlier 'Letter to Lord Stanley' from 'Gentlemen of Lancashire', printed in the *Public Advertiser* in 1775, revealed his con-stituents' more general concerns about Stanley's want of maturity and judgement:

> Your Youth and Inexperience, in some measure, shield you from the Severity with which your Conduct would otherwise be treated; but it is necessary to give you a hint to your Vanity . . . Your personal Character hath hardly yet budded. I wish the Twig may be so bent, that the Tree may be well inclined. You was pruned indeed by an able Hand, but you tell us too plainly that your Uncle is not now with you.[5]

In fact Stanley's uncle, General John Burgoyne, had 'supervised the works at Derby House . . . making comments on decorative features and ensuring the construction progressed on schedule, until he left for America in February 1775'.[6] But his supposedly steadying influence was not enough to counter Stanley's own social ambition as expressed in the house's unrivalled finish. Stanley and Wynn were true 'players' in this social and ultimately financial game of risk and reward. They fully embraced the notion of the house as 'spectacle', contriving with their architect to give its main body over to 'frontstage'.

Perhaps Wynn, Derby and others like them were also unwittingly rising to the challenge set down by Alberti in the first book of his writ-ings on architecture, published in English in 1755:

[I]t will be a Scandal to you, if as far as in you lies, you suffer any other Building with the same Expence or Advantages to gain more Praise and Approbation than your own. . . . Therefore we ought to be as severe and diligent as possible in our Scrutiny of every Particular, as well to suffer nothing but what is excellent and elegant, as to have all Things mutually concur to make the whole Handsome and Beautiful, insomuch that whatever you attempted to add, or retrench, or alter, should be for the Worse . . .

On the other hand, these exceptionally ambitious young men did not wholly follow Alberti's guidance to

let your moderator be the Prudence and Counsel of the most experienced Judges, whose Approbation is founded upon Knowledge and Sincerity: Because by their Skill and Directions you will be much more likely, than by your own private Will and Opinion, to attain Perfection or Something very near it.[7]

Alberti's succinct observations on the competitive nature of building and the importance of external judgement were still relevant in this period. They were particularly so in this area of architectural practice, given the West End house's proximity to its competitors, its shared form and its potential for scrutiny. There is no doubt that West End residents were keenly interested in the homes of others and particularly observant of new decorative and architectural work, including purely practical innovations, such as new fireproofing methods.[8] In 1764, Lady Holland reported to her sister in Ireland on Lady Fludyer's new house in town. She found the plan 'very handsome and convenient' (praise indeed, as we have seen) but wished that Lady Fludyer 'had a better taste in fitting it up and finishing'.[9]

Some people held assemblies and parties specifically to show off new interiors. In 1774, William Chambers reported that Lord Melbourne, whose house he had recently completed, gave

two public morning concerts to show his house, which meets with more general Applause than I ever expected; or could possibly [have] hoped for, but fashion governs all things in London; my Lord says it is fashionable to like his house, and all the world is delighted with it, because the few that give the Ton are pleased.[10]

Architects' work was showcased in London homes for the benefit of potential clients and even other architects; Robert Adam reportedly visited Spencer House to see his rival James Stuart's work in progress.[11] Mrs Montagu's Portman Square house 'was open to the visiting public for much of its construction', and in 1782, the year she moved in, Mrs Montagu remarked that 'it is much ye fashion to go and see my House, and I receive many compliments upon its elegance and magnificence'.[12] In March 1768, Lady Shelburne wrote of her 'vast pleasure' in seeing a house she admired 'improved as much as possible', noting such details as colours and new locations of pictures,[13] while in 1787 *The World*, a London newspaper, kept the fashionable West End abreast of the progress and details of Samuel Wyatt's work on William Weddell's house in Upper Brook Street:

> Mr Weddell's improvements, which Wyatt is doing with so much taste are chiefly these: – a new staircase of stone – an enlargement of the dining parlour – and turning the two back rooms into one – the dimensions of which are to be 33 by 18. The front room is about 23 feet.[14]

There must have been a considerable and wide interest to warrant such public and detailed coverage of this long-running private event. In November 1789, William Palgrave, a friend of Weddell's, reported on the 'rising glories in Brook Street':

> The Cornice in the Drawing Room *comes out* beautifully. But the Trunk ceiling in the other room! Oh! no words can describe, no fancy paint the striking effect that will be produced from the last, beauty and elegance so happily united to set the astonished World at gaze![15]

Even allowing for some element of flattery on Palgrave's part, his enthusiasm for Weddell's house seems matched only by the Adams' praise for their own work at Derby and Wynn Houses in the *Works*. As in those two houses, it is the interior which astonishes the world. Most transformations took place within the fairly standard framework of the terrace house. Exceptional ones were thus to be marvelled at.

Clients, purchasers and occupants seem to have liked the terrace house for what it was, and what it could be made to be. The house's capacity for successive and speedy changes behind an inscrutable façade may have been dictated by the exigencies of estate development and speculative building, but it was well suited to sequential owners, with their propensity to refurbish and redecorate. The clear distinction between the interests governing the house's interior and exterior meant that the shell and the inside operated in different, largely unrelated fields. Façades were often subject to regulation or other factors tending to conformity, and did not often express changes of fashion, despite an evident interest in prettifying the terrace-house façade in this period. But the interior was the space of latitude and licence, even if it was subject to the often-critical scrutiny of visitors.

Aside from non-physical qualities such as location, the interior was therefore the only indicator of its proprietor's wealth, taste, character and standing. A country house was more likely to be described or judged by a wider range of attributes. For example, a description of Mr Andrew's house at The Grove, near Newbury, Berkshire, in the *Gentleman's Magazine* (1772) focuses on the taste displayed in its exterior (castellated Gothic) form, the 'natural' features of its situation, its picturesque outlook onto fields, its well-managed grounds, neat lawns, garden follies and so on, the 'whole place' being 'laid out with great taste'.[16] The town house was already on shaky ground as far as architectural aspirations were concerned. It was more so when, in the absence of any other indicators (such as façade, size and grounds), the characteristics of its interior – whether attention-seeking, self-assured, cultured, unrefined, fashionable, affluent, prudent or penurious – came to be representative of the 'whole place', and of its owner. In this way, Fanny Burney's Cecilia sees the prime qualities of her two guardians embodied in the interiors of their respective town houses: 'vulgarity seemed leagued with avarice to drive her from the mansion of Mr Briggs, and haughtiness with ostentation to exclude her from that of Mr Delvile'.[17] Such equivalencies were registered in real life, too: Mrs Carter was pleased to find Lady Robert's 'manner of filling and ornamenting her rooms' to be 'perfectly agreeable to the turn of her conversation'.[18]

The house was criticised with regard to the quality of its design and construction, outside and in. The contingent reality of town-house design disrupted ideals of harmony, rationality and order. As theorists implied, the town house therefore lacked the moral dimension of classicism. It was prey not only to peculiarly urban constraints, but also to the mutability of fashion and whim, and to a lack of sound judgement on the part of the designer or his client. Ware and Peacock, among many others, bemoaned the 'art of slight building', and Gwynn despaired at the disregard for uniformity and correspondence between a house's front and back and the general detachment of exterior and interior from public interest. Such criticisms persist to this day, and while they are largely justified in terms of quality of construction, they are tinged with the same disappointment in the potential of the terrace house. For example, Cruickshank and Wyld criticise what they call the 'facadism' which dictated the design and construction of Georgian terrace houses, and blame the 'curious relationship' between interior and exterior on 'the eighteenth-century acceptance of superficial effects' – the way that it was, they say, 'socially acceptable to cover an ageing face and bosom with white lead-based paint'.[19]

Yet a concern with appearances over substance was surely a symptom not just of the times or of the construction and development processes, but also of the use to which owners or tenants sometimes put their London house. The Duke of Dorset, for example, ran his Grosvenor Square home for his own convenience and for entertaining others – not evidently as an investment, nor as the seat of family interests and values. Around 1776 the interior was 'gutted throughout and refashioned with features of greater delicacy and lightness: a stone staircase with a lively iron balustrade and oval toplight, drawing rooms with voluptuous marble chimney-pieces and plasterwork ceilings incorporating inset allegories painted in the fashionable manner of Carracci'.[20] A survey of 1781 nevertheless revealed serious structural and superstructural faults, noting that 'the Plaistering of the Great Staircase is on Brick, instead of Lath on Battens – and the painting is all mildewed'. The same went for the breast of the chimney in the dining parlour, where the 'Smoaky Bricks' showed through.[21] The Duke of Dorset's use of the house was itself temporary and superficial, and perhaps the finish applied to it shared those traits for that reason: it was not required to be permanent or substantial. William Davenant described London houses as 'fantastical works . . . so slight and prettily gaudy, that if they could move, they would pass for pageants'.[22] If changeability and impermanence were chief characteristics of the West End domestic interior, a degree of insubstantiality was perhaps the inevitable corollary – and not universally conceived as a problem.

The town house 'failed' on so many fronts. While Gwynn, Stewart and others wanted to be able to judge by external appearances, in practice viewers scrutinised the interior, and judged the house and its owner on that basis. Internal appearances were what mattered; and these were not only changeable but also contrived by insubstantial means. Consequently, the house was, for many, not only physically suspect but also ideologically unsound.

The womanish town house

Various real and perceived connections between women and the town house have emerged in the course of this book. However, to these might be added some further, implicit connections which, though not necessarily articulated fully either in the eighteenth century or afterwards, may nevertheless account for attitudes towards the West End terrace house since 1760.

Many women, and especially widows, had a strong desire to be in town. They often had sound motives for being there, such as the need to find society or medical expertise. Widows were very often left town houses in wills, or provided with them by marriage settlements. In addition, men often – and reproachfully – cast women firstly as the instigators of moves to and within London, and secondly as responsible for extravagant spending on the house. While there may be some truth in these two assertions, it is clear that the latter, at least, stemmed partly from the long-standing association of women and luxury. Women are represented in the fictional and journalistic literature of the period as possessors of irrational desires, which lead them to drive the last remnants of consumer sanity from men's minds. If we combine the association of women, luxury and excess with women's propensity to prefer the town life, and the town house's status as 'luxury' and container of luxury goods, we find a circle of links between women, luxury and the town house. This circle may help explain the many subsequent negative, womanish connotations attaching to the town house.

Many of these connotations are explicit, as I have shown – and show further below – but others are more implicit. For example, Smollett's portrayal of the town house as an expensive liability, devoted to show and easily done without, was undoubtedly a feminizing characterisation, if not spelt out as such. His representation of the town house as parasitic and unproductive closely coincides with representations of women elsewhere in eighteenth-century literature as 'both agents of corruption and idle ornament',[23] consuming all and giving nothing. The house is therefore identified not just with women but also with womanish qualities, in contrast to the perceived maleness of the patrimonial country seat. In such an analysis, the former is a marker of short-sighted selfishness, the latter of long-term family interests. Smollett is a handy and entertaining witness – but again his real role in this context is to stimulate the search for corroborative evidence elsewhere. Real-life reckonings of how much money was being spent in town and on town houses affirm the perception of London life as self-interested and self-centred.[24] The leasehold house's ambiguous property status may also have contributed to this perceived division between the role of town and country properties within the wider family, as well as the gendered shadings attached to them as a result. The house was very often evidence of an individual family member branching out on his or her own, and could be bought and sold pretty much at the owner's whim. Expediency rather than investment seems generally to have been the name of the game. And due to its leasehold status, the house was not so easily tied into longer-term patriarchal family concerns, but was, in practice, closely aligned with chattels – the more slippery form of property and the usual province of female or lesser male dependents. What is more, like so many other 'new' goods in the later eighteenth century, it was generally acquired through consumption rather than inheritance, as were its contents. This commercial world in which it was embroiled was also responsible for the house's inherent physical weakness and its concern for appearance over substance and the shorter term over the longer. The masculine country house stood aloof from such feminine vagaries and frailties, at least notionally. Such a clear differentiation between the two property types is inaccurate, but it is easy to see why the simple division between feminine town house and masculine country house nevertheless prevailed in the period.

It was not simply the town house as an entity that attracted such a negative, even misogynistic press. Many comments on the architectural and decorative treatments given to houses in this period had comparable overtones of a lack of reason and restraint, which was often by implication effeminate or childish. In 1768, Mrs Carter declared she would 'as soon be tempted to cry for a doll or a coral' as to covet the overdose of ornament she beheld in a town-house room 'adorned with the utmost profusion of expensive elegance'.[25] The 'Adam style', best exemplified in its genuine form at Derby House, was the worst offender, and attracted belittling criticisms couched in terms of sweet foods, whimsies, toys and trinkets. Chambers called Adam's interior style 'filigrane toywork',[26] while Walpole associated it with 'gingerbread', 'sippets of embroidery' and 'harliquinades'.[27] Such decoration was declared to be bad not only in itself but also in its ability to mask other more fundamental attributes. Over-refined ornament arouses suspicion and creates unease because it disguises the true nature of the things and people to whom it is applied. It is surely significant that the host of the masquerade in David Garrick's comedy *Bon Ton; or, High Life above Stairs* (1775) is called Lady Filigree, making a clear link between elaborate or over-elaborate decoration and the disruption of legibility which was a masquerade's purpose and pleasure.[28] In his famous description of Derby House as 'filigreed into puerility',[29] Walpole went a step further, linking the excess and excessive fineness of ornament with a lack of sophistication and maturity. For Walpole, the very ornamentation that is intended to mask these qualities is itself the strongest evidence of their presence, as only a child would fail to realise. The fault lies not simply in the decoration, or its designer, but in the sort of person to whom it is deemed to appeal. Both Derby and his house were the antithesis of masculine maturity, sobriety and restraint.

As with disappointment related to the town house's structural substance, such inferences that 'Adam style' decoration catered for feminine or childish tastes persist into the present. John Harris writes of

Chambers's town-house interiors at the unusually large Gower and Melbourne Houses that 'although not so inventive as Adam's [they] were in their unpretentious way just as elegant and perhaps, because they were more masculine, more satisfying'.[30] The implication that the Adam or Adam-style decoration so fashionable after 1760 is feminine, is no sooner viewed than consumed and gives no lasting mental or visual gratification, derives from the eighteenth century itself. For example, Mrs Carter found that she grew 'tired and vacant' after the 'first slight impression' of a room in which 'there was no moving to any situation, or turning one's eyes to any spot without being struck by some *bijou* of fancy',[31] while James Peacock emphasised the importance of not enervating elevations with 'peurile ornaments' and 'filigree work, proper only for [a] lady's dressing room'.[32]

Summerson describes the 'new feeling for the externals of architecture' after Adam's arrival on the London scene as 'the delicacy of a feminine "make-up" '. He sees stucco and Coade stone (both pioneered by Adam in the 1760s and 1770s) as having 'a slightly cosmetic character', suggesting 'faintly and agreeably, the artificiality of powder and rouge'.[33]

74   His characterisation of the Adam-style town-house façade as feminine might be couched in kinder terms than Cruickshank and Wyld's discussed above, but it nevertheless reinforces the links between the town house, women and insubstantiality – as well as dissimulation and unnaturalness. Peacock was concerned that façades should not 'offend against

75   the strictness of propriety';[34] according to Joseph Spence in 1752, the 'unwillingness to act in accordance with the dictates of prudence or propriety' was evidenced in 'the excesses of an over-dressed femininity'.[35] Like the connections between women, luxury and the town house, those between women, superfluity and impropriety in appearance abound in the later eighteenth century, as both ideology and snide remark.[36]

Criticisms levied at the real Adam style and its imitations were not made in connection with London houses alone. Yet the style's most

76   refined examples, such as the music room at Home House, were often to be found in town. The West End house, at the centre of the fashionable world, was more likely to display the latest Adam-style interior fashions, especially given its habitual redecoration by successive owners. Peacock argued that the interior was so far removed from the architect's interests that it might as well be left to a woman.[37] If, as I have suggested, the house was represented by its interior, then such light, insubstantial and whimsical decoration came to characterise the house as a whole, which thus became by implication feminine at best, and emasculate at worst. In any case, the terrace house's notorious structural flim-

siness coincided with ubiquitous literary portrayals of women as perennially infirm and constitutionally deficient.[38]

Penny Sparke argues that the masculinity of modernism relegates to the margins all that sits outside it – notably 'feminine culture, linked with the everyday, the commercial and the aesthetically "impure" '.[39] While I would not go so far as to say that the town house's relatively deficient coverage in the literature reflects the masculine framework of modernity as represented in the traditional architectural historiography, nevertheless its commercial, contingent, compromising, mutable nature make it the antithesis of 'male' classicist (or modernist) ideals. It is certainly the case that the individual town house and its owner are often subsumed within such all-encompassing, large-scale, 'male' stories as speculative development, urban planning, or classicism (in the form of residential squares and palace fronts, for example). After all, as criticisms of Adam-style decoration suggest, small details are female (and therefore inconsequential); big schemes are male (and therefore important).

The unflattering association of women and the town house stems from the concurrence of the house's real, inescapable characteristics and the perceived, 'innate' characteristics of women. If there was one thing worse than a woman, it was an effeminate man; and the town house could also be described as 'foppish'. Robert Morris uses the analogy to warn clients and their architects of the dangers of over-dressing a house: 'if you will be lavish in Ornament, your Structure will look rather like a Fop, with a Superfluity of gaudy Tinsel, than a real Decoration'.[40] The fop was 'over nice and affected in his Dress, Speech and Behaviour', 'a whimsical empty fellow . . . whose mind is totally taken up with modes and fashions', and 'a man of small understanding and much ostentation'.[41] In physical terms he had an 'unimpressive physique', which both resulted from 'the degenerative effect of over-refinement' and was disguised by an excess of finery 'symptomatic of a superficial and trivial character'.[42] The town house's appearance, like the fop's, could be read as evidence of a lack of responsibility, integrity, substance and self-command; like the fop himself, it was characterised as irrational and undisciplined, contrived and artificial, conspicuous and attention seeking – and even detrimental to the public interest. In short, the fashionable house displayed in the most public of arenas the emasculate and foppish characteristics of 'puniness, vanity and foolishness'.[43] And like the fop, it was used as a scapegoat. Many criticisms of the London house and the style of decoration associated with it in this period derive from uneasiness about the current state of the capital itself, its rapid growth and unwieldiness and the crisis of differentiation and legibility (to say

77

nothing of disease and crime) that came with it. The London house was therefore used as both evidence and a metaphor for a loss of control and reason.

In a variety of ways, therefore, the town house was particularly susceptible to unflattering associations with childish or effeminate impermanence, inconstancy, insubstantiality, impropriety, dissimulation and intemperance. And Adam-style decoration exemplified these emasculating traits. For all that Robert Adam marketed his own work in this field as something more substantial, as something closer to architecture, the manner in which he transformed some town houses ultimately played into the hands of his and the town house's critics. To many observers, the town house was fundamentally flawed, and no amount of genius was going to change that. Nevertheless, public critical reception had little or no impact on private practice and opinion. The town house's enduring ability to respond to its inhabitants' diverse needs ultimately accounts for its lasting popularity and success.

Notes

Abbreviations

The following abbreviations are used in this book:

BL   British Library
SL   *Survey of London* – all endnote references to the *Survey* give the volume and page number only. Full details of each volume can be found in the bibliography.

Introduction Questioning the Town House

1   John Summerson, *Georgian London*, 3rd edn (London: Barrie and Jenkins, 1978), p. 111.
2   John Stewart, *Critical Observations on the Buildings and Improvements of London* (London: J. Dodsley, 1771), pp. 27–8.
3   Damie Stillman, *English Neo-classical Architecture*, 2 vols (London: Zwemmer, 1988), vol. 1, 196 (all references to Stillman in this book are to volume one). See also Stefan Muthesius, *The English Terraced House* (New Haven and London: Yale University Press, 1982), p. 7: 'The lack of demand [for

great palaces in London] stemmed from the fact that, unlike many of their continental brethren, the English nobility saw their main task to be in managing the land and embellishing their country seats, and they were content with a comparatively moderately sized house in town.'
4   Tobias Smollett, *The Expedition of Humphry Clinker* (Harmondsworth: Penguin, 1985; first published 1771), p. 118.
5   Dan Cruickshank and Peter Wyld, *London: The Art of Georgian Building* (London: The Architectural Press, 1975).
6   Roderick J. Lawrence, 'Integrating Architectural, Social and Housing History', *Urban History* 19 (April 1992): 39.
7   Matthew Johnson, *Housing Culture: Traditional Architecture in an English Landscape* (London: UCL Press, 1993), p. xii.
8   See, respectively, Stillman, *English Neo-classical Architecture*; Summerson, *Georgian London*; Stefan Muthesius, *English Terraced House* and Donald J. Olsen, *Town Planning in*

London: The Eighteenth and Nineteenth Centuries (New Haven and London: Yale University Press, 1964).

9 Julie Schlarman draws attention to the way in which some architectural histories 'neglect to place the eighteenth-century townhouse in either a formal construct or a social setting', citing Worsley's *Classical Architecture in Britain: The Heroic Age* (New Haven and London: Yale University Press, 1995) as an example. She also cites John Summerson's *Architecture in Britain, 1530–1830* (New Haven and London: Yale University Press, 1953), where, as she points out, the discussion is limited to the works of John Wood in Bath and John Nash in London. See Julie Schlarman, 'The Social Geography of Grosvenor Square: Mapping Gender and Politics, 1720–1760', *London Journal* 28 (2003): p. 8. See also the discussion below regarding how classicism as a methodology shunts certain building types and traditions out of the picture.

10 Tim Keirn, 'Monopoly, Economic Thought and the Royal African Company', in *Early Modern Conceptions of Property*, ed. John Brewer and Susan Staves (London and New York: Routledge, 1995), p. 430, quoted in Craig Clunas, 'Modernity Global and Local: Consumption and the Rise of the West', *American Historical Review* 104 (1999): p. 1501.

11 A. A. Tait, 'Home House', *Apollo* 126 (1987), p. 80.

12 See, for example, Jules Lubbock, *The Tyranny of Taste: The Politics of Architecture and Design in Britain, 1550–1960* (New Haven and London: Yale University Press, 1995), p. 4.

13 See, also, Muthesius, *English Terraced House*; Dan Cruickshank and Peter Wyld, *London: The Art of Georgian Building* (London: Architectural Press, 1975); Dan Cruickshank and Neil Burton, *Life in the Georgian City* (London: Viking, 1990); and Frank Kelsall, 'The Architect as Speculator', in *Georgian Architectural Practice*, papers given at the Georgian Group Symposium 1991, ed. Giles Worsley (London: Georgian Group, 1992), pp. 32–8.

14 See Barbara Arciszewska and Elizabeth McKellar, eds, *Articulating British Classicism: New Approaches to Eighteenth-century Architecture* (Aldershot: Ashgate, 2004), preface, for a useful summary of this and other abiding methodological frameworks for writing the general architectural history of the eighteenth century, including their roots and drawbacks.

15 See John Martin Robinson, 'Samuel Wyatt, Architect', D.Phil. diss., University of Oxford, 1973, p. vii.

16 See, for example, Stillman, *English Neo-classical Architecture*, and many *Country Life* articles published over a century, together with features in other art and architectural history journals such as the *Journal of the Society of Architectural Historians*, the *Georgian Group Journal*, the *Architectural Review* and *Apollo*.

17 Arciszewska and McKellar, p. xx; Barbara Arciszewska, 'Classicism: Constructing the Paradigm in Continental Europe and Britain', in Arciszewska and McKellar, p. 1.

18 Arciszweska and McKellar, p. xxiii.

19 Ibid., p. xx. Carol Watts's essay on Bath in that collection ('A "Rarie-shew System of Architecture": Bath and the Cultural Scenography of Palladianism', pp. 119–41), takes a step towards rectifying this absence.

20 Peter Guillery, *The Small House in Eighteenth-century London* (New Haven and London: Yale University Press, 2004), p. 1.

21 Raphael Samuel, *Island Stories: Unravelling Britain, Theatres of Memory* (London: Verso, 1998), vol. 2, pp. 367–8, quoted in Guillery, p. 1.

22 Guillery pp. 1–2.

23 See Jill Low, 'French Taste in London: William Weddell's Town House',

Country Life, 27 December 1979, p. 2470. See further discussion in Chapter Seven below.

24 Letter from Francis Chambre to Wynn, 17 September 1774, National Library of Wales, Wynnstay papers, 122, fols. 239–40.

25 'Principal' residents tend to be selected on aristocratic and meritocratic criteria.

26 Damie Stillman (p. 184) was able to identify only sixteen large houses set in their own grounds which were built or substantially remodelled in London between 1756 and 1800. Much of this study, therefore, is necessarily concerned with terrace houses, although some generalised references embrace both terraced and detached properties, which will be evident from the context.

27 Adrian Forty, *Objects of Desire: Design and Society 1750–1980* (London: Thames and Hudson, 1986), p. 8.

28 Ibid., pp. 7–8.

29 See Anthony D. King, 'Introduction', in *Buildings and Society: Essays on the Social Development of the Built Environment*, ed. Anthony D. King (London: Routledge and Kegan Paul, 1980), p. 1. See, also, Amos Rapoport, *House Form and Culture* (1969), as discussed by King, for more on architectural history's selective approach, which means, 'to use Rapoport's terms, that only "high style", architect-designed buildings are deemed appropriate for attention' (Anthony King, p. 1). The essays in Arciszewska and McKellar's edited volume on *Articulating British Classicism* draw, as the editors say, 'on current thinking about the period from other disciplines' as part of a move to shake off the shackles of classicism 'as a pervasive methodology'. Likewise, the questions I posed myself in researching this book were stimulated by research and writing in other non-architectural areas, such as property and consumption history, as discussed below.

30 Johnson, pp. x–xi.

31 In defining my approach to answering the questions I had raised, I found three texts particularly useful, all of which I make explicit and implicit reference to in this introduction. These are, Martin Locock, 'Meaningful Architecture', in *Meaningful Architecture: Social Interpretations of Buildings*, ed. Martin Locock (Aldershot: Avebury, 1994), pp. 1–13; Roderick Lawrence, 'Integrating Architectural, Social and Housing History'; and Colin Campbell's chapter on 'Understanding Traditional and Modern Patterns of Consumption in Eighteenth-century England: A Characteraction Approach', in *Consumption and the World of Goods*, ed. John Brewer and Roy Porter (London: Routledge, 1993), pp. 40–57. I also found Mary Douglas and Baron Isherwood's *The World of Goods: Towards an Anthropology of Consumption* (Harmondsworth: Penguin, 1979) very useful for framing my ideas of what broader meanings and uses the town house could have; Locock, pp. 1, 7.

32 Alice T. Friedman, 'The Way You Do the Things You Do: Writing the History of Houses and Housing', *Journal of the Society of Architectural Historians* 58, no. 3 (1999), p. 407.

33 Douglas and Isherwood, pp. 64–5. Locock, too, writes of the multiplicity both of a building's meanings in the past and of views from the present (pp. 7–8).

34 T. H. Breen, 'The Meaning of Things: Interpreting the Consumer Economy in the Eighteenth Century', in *Consumption and the World of Goods*, ed. John Brewer and Roy Porter (London and New York: Routledge, 1993), p. 258. See also Clunas (p. 1500) for a discussion of recent authors who express this view in opposition to the notion that material goods have inherent meanings.

35 Stana Nenadic, 'Middle-rank Consumers and Domestic Culture in Edinburgh and Glasgow 1720–1840', *Past*

and *Present* 145 (November 1994), p. 138.

36 Eileen Harris, *The Genius of Robert Adam: His Interiors* (New Haven and London: Yale University Press, 2001), p. 278.

37 Lawrence, p. 42.

38 Alastair Owens and Jon Stobart, 'Introduction', in *Urban Fortunes: Property and Inheritance in the Town, 1700–1900*, ed. Jon Stobart and Alastair Owens (Aldershot: Ashgate, 2000), p. 13.

39 Clunas, p. 1497.

40 See, for example, David Solkin, *Painting for Money: The Visual Arts and the Public Sphere in Eighteenth-century England* (New Haven and London: Yale University Press, 1993).

41 Although later authors have challenged some of the premises in Neil McKendrick, John Brewer, and J. H. Plumb's *Birth of a Consumer Society: The Commercialization of Eighteenth-century England* (London: Europa, 1982), it remains the foundation stone of the consumption literature, with Lorna Weatherill's *Consumer Behaviour and Material Culture in Britain, 1660–1760* (London and New York: Routledge, 1988) as its only near competitor (see Clunas, p. 1498). Most significant in the subsequent literature is the trilogy which forms the focus of Clunas's review, comprising John Brewer and Roy Porter, eds, *Consumption and the World of Goods* (1993); John Brewer and Susan Staves, eds, *Early Modern Conceptions of Property* (1995) and Ann Bermingham and John Brewer, eds, *The Consumption of Culture, 1600–1800: Image, Object, Text* (London and New York: Routledge, 1995). I refer to all of these volumes in the course of this book, and the latter three in particular have been a treasure trove of ideas and information, which have stimulated and informed my thinking.

42 Campbell, 1993, p. 43.

43 Ibid., p. 44.

44 For the purposes of this study, I take anecdotal evidence to be, firstly, any comments on life in London, London houses, or their occupants, written in a private capacity, and intended principally for private consumption, such as personal correspondence and diaries. Secondly, I consider personal reports, freely made, on London, its residents or houses, published at the time, but not presented by its authors as didactic or prescriptive material.

45 For a fuller discussion of the dangers inherent in the use of anecdotal evidence in architectural history, as well as arguments in its favour, see Rachel Stewart, 'Telling Tales: Anecdotal Insights into the West End House c.1765–c.1785', *Transactions of the Royal Historical Society* 13 (2003): pp. 319–27.

46 The problems of finding comparable documentary evidence among the personal papers of even the wealthier members of the middling classes would make the equivalent exercise for that group extremely difficult.

47 Lawrence (p. 46) promotes the use of both descriptive and prescriptive texts for complementing studies of the physical or documentary evidence about houses with 'a contextual study of the interrelations between the physical, societal and personal ideas and values that people attribute to domestic space and daily life'.

48 *Gentleman's Magazine* (1771, vol. 41, p. 317) remarks that *Humphry Clinker* 'abounds with satire that is equally sprightly and just', while in a letter of September 1782 Hannah More writes to Mary Hamilton of Burney's characterisations in *Cecilia*: 'She has certainly caught the manners of the day. The characters . . . are strong likenesses of life, tho' perhaps a little over charged.' (*Mary Hamilton, Afterwards Mrs John Dickenson, at Court and at Home. From Letters and Diaries, 1756–1816*, ed. Elizabeth and Florence Anson (London: John Murray, 1925), p. 119).

49 *The Georgian Country House: Architecture, Landscape and Society*, ed. Dana Arnold (Stroud: Sutton, 1998), p. xiii; Dana Arnold, 'The Country House: Form, Function and Meaning', in ibid., pp. 16, 19.

50 See, for example, Lubbock, p. 4. The West End was 'a completely new town of squares and streets built to a uniform design for people of quality'.

51 Miles Ogborn, *Spaces of Modernity: London's Geographies 1680–1780* (New York and London: Guilford Press, 1998), p. 38.

52 See Francis Sheppard, Victor Belcher and Philip Cottrell, 'The Middlesex and Yorkshire Deeds Registries and the Study of Building Fluctuations', *London Journal* 5 (1979): pp. 176–217 (p. 184). For the planning and architectural development of London after the Great Fire see, for example, Summerson, *Georgian London*, Olsen, *Town Planning in London*, and Roy Porter, *London: A Social History* (Harmondsworth: Penguin, 1994). The financial and economic impetuses for London's development in this period are disregarded here as neither directly affecting client choices, nor contributing to the uses and values of individual houses for their owners.

53 Sheppard, Belcher and Cottrell, p. 186. The authors identify peaks in 1767, 1772 and 1777, on the basis of the number of deeds registered. They take levels of deed registrations to give some indication of building activity, a hypothesis that they substantiate with evidence from other primary and secondary sources.

54 See, for example, *The Craftsman*, 16 September, 7 October 1769. The phrase 'rage of building' is used in both places, and elsewhere.

55 Smollett, p. 117.

56 Horace Walpole to Sir Horace Mann, 16 July 1776, *Horace Walpole's Correspondence*, ed. W. S. Lewis and others (London: Oxford University Press, 1937–83), vol. 24 (1967), 228.

57 *Town and Country Magazine* 4 (1772), 542.

58 Over the century as a whole, Westminster's population more than doubled, from around 70,000 to somewhere in the region of 150,000.

59 Marylebone Road, built in 1757 as part of the 'New Road from Paddington to Islington' which had been required by an Act of Parliament. See *The London Encyclopaedia*, ed. Ben Weinreb and Christopher Hibbert (London: Macmillan, 1995), s.v. 'Marylebone Road'.

60 Summerson, *Georgian London*, pp. 105, 110, 163.

61 Ibid., pp. 164–5; Stillman, p. 230.

62 Porter, pp. 110–12.

63 For example, evidence from Grosvenor Square, built in the 1720s and 1730s, suggests a first widespread wave of renovation in the 1760s and 1770s (*SL*, vol. 40, 114).

64 Stillman, p. 196.

65 Andrew Byrne, *Bedford Square: An Architectural Study* (London and Atlantic Highlands, NJ: Athlone Press, 1990), p. 9.

66 John Wood had more complete and earlier success in Bath, beginning with Queen Square (1729–36).

67 Kelsall, 1992, p. 36, where further information on the history of the palace front is given. For more on the terrace in Percy Street, see Dan Cruickshank, '29 Percy Street', *Country Life*, 21 November 1991, pp. 92–5.

68 Letter from Robert Grews to Robert Palmer, 4 February 1784, quoted in full in Byrne, p. 156.

69 Letter from Robert Brettingham to his aunt, 19 August 1784, MS Eng misc c504, Bodleian Library, University of Oxford.

70 Horace Walpole to Lady Ossory, 17 September 1785, *Horace Walpole's Correspondence*, vol. 33 (1965), 500.

71 Steen Eiler Rasmussen, *London: The Unique City* (Harmondsworth: Penguin, 1960), p. 160. In 1773, the

Adams resorted to a lottery to raise funds for completing the Adelphi scheme, their finances and income severely depleted by both the ambitiousness of the project and other factors beyond their immediate control.

One   Occupying the West End

1   Summerson, 1978, p. 24.
2   John Gwynn, *London and Westminster Improved* (London: self-published, 1766; repr. Farnborough: Gregg International, 1969), pp. 16–17.
3   The post-Fire Act for Rebuilding the City (1667) had classified houses into four sorts and provided for street widths and building heights, relating size to location (an important factor in standardising appearances, as I discuss further in Chapter Four). The Building Act of 1774 was 'the first comprehensive Act covering all of central London and establishing seven rates or classes of houses based upon their size' and called for greater standardisation of houses and row, streets and even districts (James Ayres, *Building the Georgian City* (New Haven and London: Yale University Press, 1998), p. 231, which also provides a useful summary of seventeenth- and eighteenth-century building legislation). For further details of the 1774 act see Muthesius, pp. 33–4; Summerson, 1978, pp. 125–30; or Cruickshank and Wyld, 1975, pp. 29–33.
4   See Summerson, 1978, p. 24; Stillman, p. 176; and Muthesius, p. 7, for more on the middle-class impetus behind the demand for housing after the Peace of Paris (1763). Although there were 'very many urban gentlemen who did not own country estates', as Penelope J. Corfield, *Power and the Professions in Britain, 1700–1850* (London and New York: Routledge, 1995), p. 228, makes clear, the evidence used in this chapter is

almost exclusively concerned with the landed classes, for reasons given in the Introduction.

5   See, for example, ratebook entries for the 1770s for Chandos Street, Queen Anne Street, Dover Street, Harley Street and Hertford Street in the City of Westminster Archives.
6   Michael H. Port, 'West End Palaces: The Aristocratic Town House in London, 1730–1830', *London Journal* 20 (1995): 17–46.
7   Stillman, p. 194.
8   See Port, 1998, p. 19.
9   Guillery, p. 3.
10 Dorset Record Office, Fox-Strangways papers, D/FSI, Box 241A (uncatalogued), various solicitors' bills and abstracts of bills.
11 See, for example, entry for 26 January 1781 relating to a mortgage of £3000, in A[lbert] E. Richardson, *Robert Mylne, Architect and Engineer 1733–1811* (London: Batsford, 1955), p. 115.
12 Dorset Record Office, Fox Strangways papers, D/FSI, Box 241A (uncatalogued), letter of 24 July [1770s].
13 See John Brewer, *The Sinews of Power: War, Money and the English State, 1688–1783* (London: Unwin Hyman Ltd, 1989), pp. 116–22, 204.
14 Ibid., pp. 44–5, 75–82, 205.
15 Elaine Chalus, 'Elite Women, Social Politics, and the Political World of Late Eighteenth-century England', *Historical Journal* 43, no. 3 (2000), p. 675. As Chalus makes clear, it was not only society but also politics themselves that brought many women to town – see discussion later in this chapter.
16 Paul Langford, *Public Life and the Propertied Englishman 1689–1798* (Oxford: Clarendon Press, 1991), pp. 378–9.
17 Smollett, pp. 119, 150–5.
18 Ian Donaldson, 'The Satirists' London', *Essays in Criticism* 25 (1975), p. 101.
19 See Chalus, 2000, p. 687.
20 Jane Austen, *Pride and Prejudice*

(Harmondsworth: Penguin, 1996. First published 1813), p. 38. Neither Darcy nor Mr Bingley's sisters are impressed by Mrs Bennet's claim to dine with 'four and twenty families' (p. 39); Joyce Ellis, ' "On the Town": Women in Augustan England', *History Today* 45, no. 12 (Dec. 1995), pp. 21–2.

21 Smollett, p. 154.

22 John Brewer, *The Pleasures of the Imagination: English Culture in the Eighteenth Century* (London: Harper Collins, 1997), p. 103.

23 Cruickshank and Burton, 1990, note the likelihood of differences in the format and etiquette of the formal dinner in town and in the country (p. 35). See also Roy Porter, p. 95.

24 Mrs Montagu to Mrs Robinson, 3 October 1778, BL, Montagu correspondence, Add MS 40663, fol. 80.

25 *The Early Journals and Letters of Fanny Burney*, ed. Lars E. Troide, 2 vols (Oxford: Clarendon Press, 1988 and 1990), vol. 1, 83–4, entry for 21 July 1769.

26 Mary Noel to Judith Milbanke, 25 January 1787, *The Noels and the Milbankes: Their Letters for Twenty-five Years, 1767–1792*, ed. Malcolm Elwin (London: Macdonald, 1967), pp. 312–13.

27 Anna Barbauld to Dr Aikin from Caroline Street, London, 31 January 1787, *The Works of Anna Laetitia Barbauld. With a Memoir by Lucy Aikin*, 2 vols (London: Longman & Co., 1825), vol. 1, pp. 151.

28 *Reminiscences of Henry Angelo with Memoirs of his Late Father and Friends*, 2 vols (London: Henry Colburn and Richard Bentley, 1830), vol. 1, 368–9.

29 Penelope J. Corfield, 'The Georgian Town: New Perspectives', in *Life in the Georgian Town*, papers given at the Georgian Group Symposium, 1985 (London: Georgian Group, 1986), p. 13.

30 Frances Burney, *Evelina; or, the History of a Young Lady's Entrance into the World*, ed. with an introduction and notes by Margaret Anne Doody (Harmondsworth: Penguin, 1994; first published 1778), p. 65. See also Evelina's mortification at Madame Duval's improper participation in a minuet at the Hampstead assembly rooms: 'She danced in a style so uncommon; her age, her showy dress, and an unusual quantity of *rouge*, drew upon the her eyes, and, I fear, the derision of the whole company' (p. 249). See, too, John Brewer's discussion of the cultural realm in the eighteenth century, which 'was loathed for the possibilities that it afforded for social dissembling and disguise' (' "The Most Polite Age and the Most Vicious": Attitudes Towards Culture as a Commodity, 1660–1800', in *The Consumption of Culture 1600–1800: Image, Object, Text*, ed. Ann Bermingham and John Brewer (London and New York: Routledge, 1995), p. 349. Also, Iain Pears, *The Discovery of Painting: The Growth of Interest in the Arts in England 1680–1768* (New Haven and London: Yale University Press, 1988), pp. 5–6.

31 Brewer, 1995, p. 348.

32 Letters from Anna Barbauld to Dr Aikin from London and Palgrave, 2 and 21 January 1784 and letter to Mrs Beecroft from Hampstead, May 1789, *The Works of Anna Laetitia Barbauld*, vol. 2, pp. 22–4. The trial was presumably that of Warren Hastings, then in the second of its seven years. William Hastings, 1st Governor General of India, was impeached in 1787 in relation to standards of conduct in India under his governorship. The trial began in 1788 and ended with his acquittal in 1795. Eleanor Elliot reported a similar interest in the Duchess of Kingston's trial for bigamy in 1776, which, she reported to her brother Hugh, 'fills the mind of all the inhabitants of this great metropolis; people seem much more sincerely interested

in this cause than in the American war.' See Countess of Minto, *A Memoir of the Right Honourable Hugh Elliot* (Edinburgh: Edmonstron and Douglas, 1868), p. 86.

33 Helen Berry, 'Prudent Luxury: The Metropolitan Tastes of Judith Baker, Durham Gentlewoman', in *Women and Urban Life in Eighteenth-century England: 'On the Town'*, ed. Rosemary Sweet and Penelope Lane (Aldershot: Ashgate, 2003), pp. 136–7, 146–7.

34 *Works of Anna Laetitia Barbauld*, vol. 2, pp. 295–6.

35 General Mostyn to the Duke of Newcastle, 7 November 1776, University of Nottingham, Hallward Library, Newcastle papers, Ne C 2690.

36 *Works of Anna Laetitia Barbauld*, vol. 2, p. 296.

37 *Lady's Magazine* 8 (1777), 532.

38 *Noels and Milbankes*, p. 60.

39 Low, p. 2470.

40 Lady Caroline Fox to Marchioness of Kildare, 9 March 1762, *Correspondence of Emily, Duchess of Leinster (1731–1814)*, ed. Brian Fitzgerald (hereafter *Leinster letters*), 3 vols (Dublin: Dublin Stationery Office, 1949, 1953, 1957), vol. 1 (1949), 231.

41 Lawrence Stone and Jeanne C. Fawtier Stone, *An Open Elite? England 1540–1880* (Oxford: Clarendon Press, 1984), p. 323.

42 Badminton, Badminton muniments, sequence of letters at FmL 4/3/2.

43 Various letters between Thomas Pelham and his wife, Ann, dating from the 1770s, BL, Pelham papers, Add MS 33092.

44 Stone and Stone, p. 323. Both girls and boys went off to school. See *The Francis Letters, by Sir Philip Francis and Other Members of his Family*, ed. Beata Francis and Eliza Keary, with a note on the Junius controversy by C. F. Keary (hereafter *Francis Letters*), 2 vols (London, Hutchinson, 1901), vol. 1, 289, where the London-based

Mrs Francis remarks in her journal for 1777 on the need for a bigger house now that her two elder girls have left school.

45 Corfield, 1985, p. 12. See also Susan Skedd, 'Women Teachers and the Expansion of Girls' Schooling in England, *c.*1760–1820', in *Gender in Eighteenth-century England: Roles, Representations and Responsibilities*, ed. Hannah Barker and Elaine Chalus (Harlow: Addison Wesley Longman Ltd, 1997), pp. 101–25: 'London predominated [in fashionable girls' schooling], not only on account of the size of its populations, but also because of the Season, which brought many families to the capital and provided a convenient opportunity for daughters to be educated at one of the many schools or by the specialist masters' (p. 104).

46 Lady Winn to her sister-in-law, Charlotte Winn, 25 May 1785, West Yorkshire Archive Service, Nostell Priory papers, NP A1/5A/10.

47 *Town and Country Magazine* 1 (1769), 576.

48 Stone and Stone, p. 323; Port, 1995, p. 24; Philip Jenkins, *The Making of a Ruling Class: The Glamorgan Gentry 1640–1790* (Cambridge: Cambridge University Press, 1983), p. 241.

49 Long-term career opportunities afforded by almost continuous warfare, as well as the enticements of half-pay in intermittent peacetimes after 1714, meant that both army and navy 'became a reputable calling for genteel members of society'. Brewer, 1989, pp. 55–6.

50 Lady Sarah Bunbury to Duchess of Leinster, 29 November 1774, *Leinster Letters*, vol. 2, 25–6.

51 See, for example, Mrs Caroline Howe to Lady Spencer, [1767], BL, Althorp papers, F 42: Lady Howe has brought little Mary to town this morning in order to be inoculated'; Mrs Howe to Lady Spencer, 19 April [1773], F 43: 'Mr Poyntz brings his little boy to

town this morning to have him inoculated'; Mrs Howe to Lady Spencer, 12 October [1776], F 44: 'Lady Holland is in town to inoculate her son'.

52 *Noels and Milbankes*, pp. 301–5, correspondence between Judith Milbanke and Lady Scarsdale in October and November 1786.

53 Badminton, Badminton muniments, sequence of letters at FML 4/3/2.

54 Sophia Curzon to her aunt Mary Noel, 30 November 1781, *Noels and Milbankes*, p. 184.

55 Letter to 3rd Duke of Portland, 6 November 1781, University of Nottingham, Hallward Library, Portland papers, PW F 1289; letters of 1 April and 18 April 1783, Newcastle papers, Ne C 2976, 2971.

56 Mrs Caroline Howe to Lady Spencer, letters of 4 June and 21 July 1773, BL, Althorp papers, F 43.

57 Mrs Caroline Howe to Lady Spencer, 10 November [1772], BL, Althorp papers, F 42.

58 Letter from Dowager Duchess of Beaufort to Duke of Beaufort, 16 June 1771, Badminton, Badminton muniments, FML 4/3/1/27.

59 Lord Nuneham to Lord Spencer, October 1756, BL, Althorp Letters, F 114.

60 Mrs Caroline Howe to Lady Spencer, 8 and 16 September [1771?], BL, Althorp papers, F 42. Post was also gathered at Spencer House for forwarding to Lady Spencer while she was travelling abroad (letter from Caroline Howe to Lady Spencer, 29 October [1772], F 42).

61 London, 22 December 1788, *Betsy Sheridan's Journal: Letters from Sheridan's Sister 1784–1786 and 1788–1790*, ed. William LeFanu (London: Eyre & Spottiswoode, 1960), p. 138.

62 Lady Carlow to Lady Louisa Stuart, October 1781; note from Miss Herbert to Lady Louisa Stuart, [October] 1781, *Gleanings from an Old Portfolio Containing some Correspondence between Lady Louisa Stuart and her Sister Caroline, Countess of Portarlington and Other Friends and Relations*, ed. Mrs Godfrey Clark, 3 vols (Edinburgh, 1895–8), vol. 1, 155–6.

63 See Elaine Chalus, ' "That Epidemical Madness": Women and Electoral Politics in the Late Eighteenth Century', in *Gender in Eighteenth-century England: Roles, Representations and Responsibilities*, ed. Hannah Barker and Elaine Chalus (Harlow: Addison Wesley Longman Ltd, 1997): 'For someone who lived in Scotland, like Lady Galloway, being in close contact with connexions in London was vitally important: "I trouble You My Dear Lady Gower to inquire what You hear, *or rather think*, relative to the time it is probable the Parliament may, or may not be dissolved, such intelligence wou'd be of material Consequence, as the success of the Stewartry Election will much depend upon that epoch. . . .' (Lady Galloway to Lady Gower, Galloway House, 27 Aug. [1780], Granville Papers, PRO 30/29/4/3/93, f. 451, quoted p. 167). See also, Chalus, 2000.

64 Chalus, 2000, pp. 680–1, quoting from Lady Anson to Lady Grey, Admiralty, 24 Oct. [1758], Bedfordshire Record Office, Wrest Park (Lucas papers), L30/9/3/83.

65 BL, Althorp papers, F 42, F 43, F 44 and F 45 various letters dated 1767–80; F 42, Caroline Howe to Lady Spencer (abroad), 9 August [1772]. Taylor was also architect of Mrs Howe's Grafton Street house (between 1768 and 1775).

66 Ann Pelham to Thomas Pelham, from Stratton Street, 2 April 1783, BL, Pelham papers, Add MS 33092, fol. 153.

67 Amanda Foreman, *Georgiana, Duchess of Devonshire* (London: HarperCollins, 1999), pp. 48, 142, 156, 213.

68 Corfield, 1986, p. 9.

69 Smollett, p. 327.

70 Henry Fielding, *Amelia*, ed. David Blewett (Harmondsworth: Penguin, 1987; first published 1751), p. 461.

71 Ellis, 1995, pp. 20–2.

72 Ibid.

73 Fielding, p. 163.

74 Lord Bracebridge to the Rt. Hon. Lord Bruce, 11 April 1796, Wiltshire Record Office, Brudenell-Bruce (Ailesbury) papers, 9/35/81.

75 Sarah Lennox to Lady Susan O'Brien, 26 October 1778, *The Life and Letters of Lady Sarah Lennox 1745–1826: Daughter of Charles, 2nd Duke of Richmond, and Successively the Wife of Sir Thomas Charles Bunbury, Bart., and of the Hon. George Napier; also a Short Political Sketch of the Years 1760 to 1763 by Henry Fox, 1st Lord Holland*, ed. Countess of Ilchester and Lord Stavordale, 2 vols (London: John Murray, 1902), vol. 1, 283.

76 Caroline Howe to Lady Spencer, 29 December [1772], BL, Althorp papers, F 42.

77 Countess of Bute to Lady Louisa Stuart, 22 September 1783, *Gleanings from an Old Portfolio*, vol. 1, 226.

78 Sir Gilbert to Lady Elliot, Pall Mall Court, 20 Jan. 1789, in *Life and Letters of Sir Gilbert Elliot First Earl of Minto from 1751 to 1806*, ed. Countess of Minto, 3 vols (London: Longmans, Green and Co., 1874), vol. 1, p. 267, quoted in Chalus, 2000, p. 680. Chalus also cites the examples of Sir Roger Newdigate and James Boswell, from the 1750s and 1760s respectively.

79 Lady Holland to Marchioness of Kildare, 20 September 1764, *Leinster Letters*, vol. 1 (1949), 413. Lady Holland remarked that Lady Fludyer had 'the spending of her fortune herself more than any married woman ever had before, to be sure', so perhaps this level of independence in acquiring and overseeing the design and construction of a new town house was somewhat exceptional in a married woman (although not in a widow).

80 Duchess of Portland to Miss Dewes, May 1768, *The Autobiography and Correspondence of Mary Granville, Mrs Delany: with Interesting Reminiscences of King George the Third and Queen Charlotte*, ed. Lady Llanover, 2nd series, 3 vols (London: Richard Bentley, 1862), vol. 1, p. 142, editor's note; p. 146.

81 Mary Noel to Judith Milbanke, 2 February 1787, *Noels and Milbankes*, pp. 317–18.

82 Judith Milbanke to Mary Noel, 28 January 1785, ibid., p. 258.

83 See Ellis, 1995, pp. 21–2. Country society was less restricting for men, who could mix with men not their equals, while women were expected to mix with others of their own class.

84 Schlarman, 2003, p. 18.

85 A woman lost her legal persona on marriage: 'stripped . . . of a separate identity and autonomous property' (Linda Colley, *Britons: Forging the Nation 1707–1837* (London: Pimlico, 1994), p. 238), but regained her legal status on her husband's death (Amy Louise Erickson, *Women and Property in Early Modern England* (London and New York: Routledge, 1993), p. 5).

86 Quoted in Erickson, p. 153.

87 David Green, 'Independent Women, Wealth and Wills in Nineteenth-century London', in *Urban Fortunes: Property and Inheritance in the Town, 1700–1900*, ed. Jon Stobart and Alastair Owens (Aldershot: Ashgate, 2000), p. 221.

88 Christopher Simon Sykes, *Private Palaces: Life in the Great London Houses* (London: Chatto & Windus, 1985), p. 219. See Chapter Two for more discussion of the relation of women to property, and for the way in which a town house might be insisted on, or protected, by a father signing over his daughter in a marriage settlement.

89 Mrs Caroline Howe to Lady Spencer, 6 December 1776, BL, Althorp papers, F 44.

90 See, for example, the tale of Will Brazen in *Town and Country Magazine* 2 (1770): 687.

91 *Mary Hamilton, Afterwards Mrs John Dickenson, at Court and at Home. From Letters and Diaries, 1756–1816*, ed. Elizabeth and Florence Anson (London: John Murray, 1925), pp. 196–7. Some town-house bequests to widows were only effective until the woman remarried. See my further discussion of bequests of town-house property in Chapter Two.

92 Countess of Minto, 1868, p. 225.

93 *Gleanings from an Old Portfolio*, vol. 1, 227.

94 Stone and Stone, p. 350.

95 Letter to Rev. Mr Townson, 24 May 1776, Staffordshire Record Office, Bagot papers, D5121/1/12/34.

96 Letter to Sir George Jerningham, 12 April 1764, Staffordshire Record Office, Jerningham/Stafford papers, D641/3/P/5/3.

97 Mr Whistler to William Shenstone [London], 13 April [n.d.], in Frances Seymour, *Select Letters Between the Late Duchess of Somerset . . . and Others* (2 vols, London, 1778), vol. 2, p. 31, quoted in Chalus, 2000, p. 681.

98 *Town and Country Magazine* 3 (1771), 429.

99 Samuel Rudder, *New History of Gloucestershire* (Cirencester, 1779), p. 420, quoted in John Habakkuk, *Marriage, Debt and the Estates System: English Landownership 1650–1950* (Oxford: Clarendon Press, 1994), p. 296; C. Bruyn Andrews (ed.), *The Torrington Diaries*, 4 vols (London: Eyre and Spottiswoode, 1934), vol. 2 (1935), pp. 75–6, 87–8, both quoted in Michael H. Port, 'The Town and Country House: Their Interaction', in *The Georgian Country House: Architecture, Landscape and Society*, ed. Dana Arnold (Stroud: Sutton, 1998), p. 117. Regarding John Byng's testimony, it is wise to bear in mind that he was, as Richard Wilson and Alan Mackley put it, 'a jaundiced

younger son', possibly disgruntled at eminent landowners not valuing their inheritance (Richard Wilson and Alan Mackley, *Creating Paradise: The Building of the English Country House, 1660–1880* (London: Hambledon and London, 2000), p. 41).

100 Stillman, p. 196 (my emphasis); Mark Girouard, *Cities and People: A Social and Architectural History* (New Haven and London: Yale University Press, 1985), p. 224.

101 Port, 1995, p. 19.

102 Information from the steward's accounts, Badminton, Badminton muniments, RA 2/1/13-4.

103 Information from the kitchen accounts in the steward's book, National Library of Wales, Wynnstay papers, 115/2.

104 Letter of 23 October 1781, Staffs Record Office, Hand Morgan papers, D1798, bundle 129.

105 See, for example, Hertfordshire Archives and Local Studies, Grimston of Gorhambury, Earls of Veralum papers, D/EV F41, printed almanac for 1783 with notes added.

106 See Countess of Minto, 1874.

107 Mary Noel to Judith Milbanke, 3 July 1789; Wentworth to Judith Milbanke, 26 July 1789, *Noels and Milbankes*, pp. 341, 345.

108 See Peter Howell and T. W. Pritchard, 'Wynnstay, Denbighshire', *Country Life*, 23 March 1972, p. 688.

109 While Sir Watkin was building up his 'interest' in London, he and his wife were demonstrating their disdain for their Welsh neighbours and disregard for their 'interest' in that country, as reported to the Duchess of Beaufort by Lady Granby in 1778: 'Sr. Watkin has lost almost all his interest in Wales merely by his & Ly. Williams in particular behaving rudely to their country neighbours . . . they say Lady Williams makes it a rule not to speak to any of the County Squires; & in short Sr. Watkin who was King of Wales & whose Family has been so for a long time is now nothing very

great.' 24 Sept. [1778?], Badminton Muniments, FMK, 1/2/7.

110 *Torrington Diaries*, vol. 2, 14, quoted in Port, 1998, p. 120. Byng sees noblemen's fortunes sacrificed at 'the shrine of politics', leaving them unable to maintain a country residence. In such cases, a house in town is not an economy measure; it is a necessity, and the country house becomes surplus to requirements, given the lack of time spent there and the cost of running it.

111 See Stone and Stone, p. 295; Roy Porter, p. 115; and Olsen, p. 4.

112 Louisa Stuart to Lady Carlow, May 1785, *Gleanings from an Old Portfolio*, vol. 2, 25.

113 Isaac Ware, *A Complete Body of Architecture, Adorned with Plans and Elevations from Original Designs . . . in which are Interspersed some Designs of Inigo Jones, Never Before Published* (London: T. Osborne and J. Shipton, 1756; later edition 1767), p. 433. All references are to the 1756 edition unless otherwise stated.

114 Louisa Stuart to Lady Portarlington, 6 April 1787, *Gleanings from an Old Portfolio*, vol. 2, 73.

115 Frances Burney, *Cecilia; or, Memoirs of an Heiress*, ed. Peter Sabor and Margaret Anne Doody, with an introduction by Margaret Anne Doody (Oxford: Oxford University Press, 1988; first published 1782), p. 53.

116 Lady Louisa Conolly to Duchess of Leinster, 8 March 1777, *Leinster Letters*, vol. 3 (1957), 255.

117 Richard Hurd to Mrs Warburton, Kew, 21 August 1776, BL, Hurd papers, Egerton MS 1958, fol. 68.

118 *Secret Comment: The Diaries of Gertrude Savile, 1721–1757*, ed. Alan Savile, assisted by Marjorie Penn (Kingsbridge History Society, Devon, with The Thoroton Society of Nottinghamshire, 1997), p. 296, entry for 23 April 1751.

119 Schlarman, p. 18.

120 See Marcus Binney, 'Sir Robert Taylor's Grafton Street – 1', *Country Life*, 12 November 1981, pp. 1634–7, for links between early occupants of Grafton Street, including shared business interests in London banking, the East India Company and West Indian plantations. See Schlarman, p. 23 for a discussion of politics and the Grosvenor estate in the period 1720–60.

121 See Chalus, 2000, especially pp. 678–9, 684–5.

122 Ibid., p. 685, with reference to letter from Lady Waldegrave to Lady Gower, Whitehall, 30 Oct. 1780, PRO, 30/29/5/2/55, fol. 205, and pp. 686–9.

123 Ibid., p. 684, with reference to the diary of George Grenville, 20 May 1765, BL, Add. MS 42,083, fols 172v–3.

124 Tara Draper, 'No. 10 Hertford Street', *Georgian Group Journal* 9 (1999), p. 119.

125 Letter from Thomas Noel to Judith Milbanke, 30 November 1774, *Noels and Milbankes*, pp. 45, 229.

126 Wilson and Mackley, 2000, p. 78.

127 *SL*, vol. 29, p. 112.

128 *SL*, vol. 40, p. 119.

129 Lawrence Stone, *Broken Lives: Separation and Divorce in England 1660–1857* (Oxford: Oxford University Press, 1993), pp. 142–8.

130 Caroline Howe to Lady Spencer, 30 April [1773], BL, Althorp papers, F 43. See also Colonel James's use of residence in the country as a threat to his wife, in Fielding's *Amelia*, discussed above.

131 Countess of Minto, 1868, p. 198.

132 *Town and Country Magazine* 4 (1772).

133 A full divorce, allowing remarriage, was only available through an Act of Parliament, which required proof of adultery or life-threatening cruelty. A legal separation was available from the ecclesiastical court or damages for adultery from the civil court.

134 See Stone, pp. 139–61 and 117–38 for fuller accounts of the marital breakdowns of the Graftons and Beauforts respectively.

135 Philip Francis to Alexander Mackrabie, 5 December 1767, *Francis Letters*, vol. 1, 79.

136 *The Life and Times of Frederick Reynolds, Written by Himself*, 2 vols (London: Henry Colburn, 1826), vol. 1, 65.

137 Amanda Vickery, *The Gentleman's Daughter: Women's Lives in Georgian England* (New Haven and London: Yale University Press, 1998), p. 37, referring to letter of 4 October 1782, W. Stanhope to W. Spencer, in the West Yorkshire County Record Office, Bradford, Sp St/5/21/59.

138 Richard Hurd to Mrs Warburton, December 1774 and 22 December 1774, BL, Hurd papers, Egerton MS 1958, fols 18–19, 24. Nevertheless, *The Survey of London* lists Hurd as the occupant of another Grosvenor Square house, the then No. 38, from 1778–80, so perhaps he later succumbed to pressure, temptation or obligation. Whether or not he was resident there is unclear, as he was still writing from Great Russell Street in 1779 (*SL*, vol. 40, p. 154).

139 Lady Hervey to Rev. Edmund Morris, 25 September 1759, *Letters of Mary Lepel, Lady Hervey: with a Memoir, and Illustrative Notes* (London: John Murray, 1821), p. 261.

140 Sarah Lennox to Lady Susan O'Brien, 9 March 1779, BL, Holland House papers, Add MS 51354.

141 Lady Charlotte Finch to Dowager Duchess of Beaufort, undated, Badminton, Badminton muniments, FMK 1/3/20, letter no. 15.

142 Mrs Montagu to Mrs Robinson, 17 January [1782] and 2 March 1782, BL, Montagu correspondence, Add MS 40663, fol. 110 and fol. 112.

143 See letter from Mrs Montagu to Mrs Robinson, 19 December [1779], BL, Montagu correspondence, Add MS 40663, fol. 97.

144 Mrs Montagu to Mrs Robinson, 4 December [1781], BL, Montagu correspondence, Add MS 40663, fol. 104.

145 Anna Barbauld to Dr Aikin, Palgrave, 19 January, 1778, *Works of Anna Laetitia Barbauld*, vol. 2, p. 19.

146 Northamptonshire Record Office, Finch Hatton papers, FH 4208, undated document with first three pages missing.

147 Mrs Montagu to Mrs Robinson, 18 August [1779] and 1 December [1781], BL, Montagu correspondence, Add MS 40663, fol. 92 and fol. 104.

148 Lady Holland to Duchess of Leinster, 6 October [1768], *Leinster Letters*, vol. 1 (1949), 544.

149 Roy Porter, p. 114.

150 Richard Hurd to Mrs Warburton, 8 November 1773, BL, Hurd papers, Egerton MS 1958, fol. 8.

151 See Corfield, 1995, pp. 21, 76; Julius Bryant, *Robert Adam: Architect of Genius* (London: English Heritage, 1992), p. 15; and John Fleming, *Robert Adam and his Circle in Edinburgh and Rome* (London: John Murray, 1962), pp. 246–7.

152 Lady Sarah Lennox to Lady Susan O'Brien, 20 November 1777, BL, Holland House papers, Add MS 51354.

153 Lady Sarah Lennox to Lady Susan O'Brien, 30 December 1777, BL, Holland House papers, Add MS 51354.

154 Mrs Caroline Howe to Lady Spencer, 9 November 1774, BL, Althorp papers, F 43.

155 Mrs Caroline Howe to Lady Spencer, 12 October [1776], BL, Althorp papers, F 44.

156 Foreman, pp. 68–9.

157 General Robert Clerk to the Earl of Shelburne from Paris, 14 May 1765, quoted in Arthur T. Bolton, *The Architecture of Robert and James Adam*, 2 vols (London: Country Life, 1922), vol. 2, 3.

Two   Owning, Using, Passing On

1 See, for example, Stone and Stone, *An Open Elite?*; M. R. Chesterman, 'Family Settlements on Trust: Landowners and the Rising Bour-

geoisie', in *Law, Economy and Society: Essays in the History of English Law*, ed. David Sugarman and G. R. Rubin (Abingdon, Oxfordshire: Professional Books, 1984), pp. 124–67; John Habakkuk, 'Economic Functions of English Landowners in the Seventeenth and Eighteenth Centuries', in *Essays in Agrarian History*, ed. W. E. Minchinton, 2 vols (Newton Abbot: David & Charles, 1968), 1, 187–201; Susan Staves, *Married Women's Separate Property in England, 1660–1833* (Cambridge, Mass. and London: Harvard University Press, 1990); and various essays in Brewer and Staves, eds, *Early Modern Conceptions of Property*, especially David Sugarman and Ronnie Warrington, 'Land Law, Citizenship, and the Invention of "Englishness": The Strange World of the Equity of Redemption', pp. 111–43.

2 Owens and Stobart, pp. 13, 14, 16.

3 Burney, 1782, p. 458.

4 I am grateful to Alastair Owens for this argument and for his helpful comments on a draft of this chapter.

5 Letters from Sir Watkin Williams Wynn to Francis Chambre 9 and 15 June 1775; National Library of Wales, Wynnstay papers, 122, 129.

6 See, for example, J. G. A. Pocock, *Virtue, Commerce, and History: Essays on Political Thought and History, Chiefly in the Eighteenth Century* (Cambridge: Cambridge University Press, 1985), p. 103. Land was intrinsically valuable and because of the various types of security afforded by its ownership, the landowner's personality was, in a tradition deriving from Aristotle, considered stable and disinterested. His independent means, it was thought, made him at least capable of holding impartial views, and therefore well placed to manage the nation's affairs in an equitable manner. Moreover, his own interests and his country's interests were as one. On the other hand, the 'personality' of the monied man who dealt in

invisible, mobile and market-dependent property forms, such as stocks, shares, mortgages and other financial speculations, was characterised as rootless, unsure and self-interested.

7 Day book of Sir Edward Littleton 1782, reference to payment of Riot Duty for 1780, Staffordshire Record Office, Littleton/Hatherton papers, D260/M/E/28.

8 Sir William Bagot to Rev. Mr Townson(?), 20 February 1779, Staffs Record Office, Bagot papers, D5121/1/13/10A.

9 Mrs Francis's journal entry for 11 February 1779, *Francis Letters*, 1, 328.

10 Countess of Minto, 1874, vol. 1, pp. 281–2.

11 Copy letter Thomas Pelham (later 1st Earl of Chichester) to Ann Pelham, 7 June 1780, BL, Pelham papers, Add MS 33092, fol. 73.

12 The Hon. Mrs E. Stuart Wortley, ed., *A Prime Minister and his Son, from the Correspondence of the 3rd Earl of Bute and Lt.-General the Hon. Sir Charles Stuart, K.B.*, with an introduction by the Rt. Hon. Sir Rennell Rodd, G.C.B., G.C.M.G., G.C.V.O. (London: John Murray, 1925), p. 221. Bute resigned in April 1763.

13 I am grateful to Steven Parissien for enlightening me about the significance of attacks on glass in this period.

14 Howard M. Colvin, *A Biographical Dictionary of British Architects, 1660–1840*, 3rd edn (New Haven and London: Yale University Press, 1995), p. 551; *Dictionary of National Biography*, 1895, vol. 43, s.v. 'Sir Hugh Palliser'.

15 Susan Staves defines an equity of redemption as 'the right of a mortgagor, after a non payment or breach of the condition of the mortgage, to redeem property from the forfeiture by discharging the obligation within a reasonable period' (Staves, 1990, p. 45). See also Sugarman and Warrington, p. 142.

16 *Morning Post and Daily Advertiser*, 4 September 1775 and 24 May 1776.

17 Centre for Kentish Studies, Sackville papers, U269 E148.

18 Counterpart of reconvenance or assignment of mortgage, 26 January 1774, Yorkshire Archaeological Service, Duke of Leeds's papers, DD5/26/2.

19 Various solicitors' bills and abstracts of bills, Dorset Record Office, Fox-Strangways papers, D/FSI, Box 241A (uncatalogued).

20 Leonore Davidoff and Catherine Hall, *Family Fortunes: Men and Women of the English Middle Class, 1780–1850* (London: Routledge 1992), pp. 205–6.

21 Mrs Carter to Mrs Vesey, 19 August 1782, *A Series of Letters between Mrs Elizabeth Carter and Miss Catherine Talbot, from the year 1741 to 1770. To which are Added, Letters from Mrs Elizabeth Carter to Mrs Vesey, between the Years 1763 and 1787*, ed. Montagu Pennington (hereafter *Carter Letters*), 4 vols (London: F. C. and J. Rivington, 1809), vol. 4, 314–15.

22 J. H. Habakkuk, 'England', in *European Nobility in the Eighteenth Century*, ed. A. Goodwin (1953), quoted in James Raven, 'Defending Conduct and Property', in *Early Modern Conceptions of Property*, ed. John Brewer and Susan Staves, p. 306.

23 Raven, 1995, p. 306.

24 The Real Property Commissioners were dismayed to find this to be the case in 1833. I am grateful to Alastair Owens for giving me this information and confirming its applicability to the earlier period with which I am here concerned.

25 They were not necessarily hard done by in comparison with the men who inherited land; moveables had a higher value relative to land than they do now, and depreciated as slowly as land prices appreciated. See Amy Louise Erickson, *Women and Property in Early Modern England* (London and New York: Routledge, 1993), p. 64.

26 Abstract of title to house in Upper Grosvenor Street, Derbyshire Record Office, Harpur-Crewe papers, D2375M/281/3.

27 Probate copy of will of William Weddell of Newby, Esq. Will date 30 May 1789; probate date 21 July 1792, West Yorkshire Archive Service, Ramsden papers, 46/4.

28 Erickson, p. 24.

29 See table 2 in Schlarman, p. 20.

30 Letter from Caroline Howe to Lady Spencer, 22 October 1772, BL, Althorp papers, F 42.

31 Julie Schlarman's research relating to Grosvenor Square in the reign of George II (1727–60) shows not only a significant number of widows among the ratepayers, but also many of them letting their houses at the time of their death. See table 1 in Schlarman, p. 19.

32 Instructions for the will of Richard Benyon, 5 December 1781, Berkshire Record Office, Benyon papers, D/EBY, F 5.

33 Lawyer's bill dated 12 October 1786, Dorset Record Office, Fox-Strangways papers, D/FSI, Box 241A.

34 Copy will of Sir Richard Lyttleton, 11 October 1770, Hertfordshire Archives and Local Studies, Ashridge 11 collection, AH 1349.

35 Probate of will and codicil of Sir Henry Harpur, 16 February 1789 (will and codicil dated 1777), Derbyshire Record Office, Harpur-Crewe papers, D2375M/147/5.

36 Codicil to Cecilia Isabella Finch's will of 1766, Northamptonshire Record Office, Finch Hatton papers, FH 797.

37 Green, p. 222.

38 Letter from Lady Caroline Fox to Marchioness of Kildare, 4 February 1762, with reference to the marriage of Lady Sarah Lennox and Thomas Charles Bunbury, *Leinster Letters*, vol. 1 (1949), 312.

39 *SL*, vol. 39, p. 81. The term 'Bills of Mortality' was used to refer to the Cities of London and Westminster, and other parts of Surrey and Middlesex,

for which mortality statistics were gathered under the London Bills.

40 Warwickshire Record Office, Seymour of Ragley papers, CR114 Rag III/4 Pt 3/1.

41 University of Nottingham, Hallward Library, Newcastle papers, Ne A 166.

42 *SL*, vol. 29, p. 180.

43 Marcus Binney, *Sir Robert Taylor: From Rococo to Neoclassicism* (London: Allen & Unwin, 1984), p. 33. Research relating to the Grosvenor Estate in the reign of George II confirms the tendency for non-landed residents to bequeath their town houses to their sons rather than widows. I am grateful to Julie Schlarman for this information from her unpublished research. On the other hand, the lists of residents for properties on the Grosvenor Estate in Mayfair, in the relevant *Survey of London* volume (vol. 40) confirm, as I have said, the high numbers of widows on the estate, many of whom succeed their husbands in the chronological lists.

44 Information from lists of residents for Harley Street, for example, compiled from ratebooks held at City of Westminster Archives. Admittedly, this is no certain evidence that houses were not bequeathed to relatives, as they may subsequently have been let to tenants.

45 See, for example, Alastair Owens's discussion of the middling classes in early nineteenth-century Stockport in 'Property, Gender and the Life Course: Inheritance and Family Welfare Provision in Early Nineteenth-century England', *Social History* 26, no. 3 (2001): 299–317.

46 *SL*, vol. 39, pp. 81, 82, 123, 161.

47 Letter from Francis Chambre to Sir Watkin Williams Wynn, 17 September 1774: 'this House will (with what Charges are yet to come) cost near £40,000', National Library of Wales, Wynnstay papers, 122.

48 Sykes, p. 21.

49 Suffolk Record Office, Grafton (Fitzroy) papers, HA 513/4/31;

Northants Record Office, Grafton papers, G3882, fols 101–2. Although Grafton's story suggests that his grandfather was determined to establish a patrimonial home in London, this assumption is somewhat undermined by the fact that Grafton's hold on the Bond Street property in any case was conditional on him raising, within six months, sufficient money to provide a £1500 annuity for his younger brother, who would otherwise himself have 'absolute' entitlement to the property.

50 Christopher Hussey, 'An Historic London House: No. 45 Berkeley Square', *Country Life*, 2 January 1937, p. 14.

51 Undated document with first three pages missing, but relating to Lady Finch's will, Northants Record Office, Finch Hatton papers, FH 4208.

52 Draft wills of Richard Benyon of Gidea Hall, wills of 1781 and 1789, Berks Record Office, Benyon papers, D/EBy, F5.

53 Will of 2nd Earl of Ilchester, 8 February 1778, copy case with margin notes, Dorset Record Office, Fox-Strangways papers, D/FSI, Box 241 (uncatalogued).

54 *SL*, vol. 40, pp. 42, 123.

55 Ibid., p. 154.

56 Letter to Lady Carlow, November 1784, *Gleanings from an Old Portfolio*, vol. 1, 288.

57 G. R. Foley to Mrs Palmer, 1772, Lincolnshire Archives, Stubton papers, II D/1/4.

58 *SL*, vol. 40, p. 132.

59 Centre for Kentish Studies, Milles (Watson) papers, U791 E53 Bundles 1–4, various documents.

Three   Buying and Affording the West End House

Parts of this chapter were originally published in Rachel Stewart, 'The West End House *c*.1765–*c*.1785: Gamble and Forfeit', *Georgian Group Journal*, vol. XII, 2002, pp. 135–48.

1 Owens and Stobart, p. 10.
2 See Julian Hoppit, 'Financial Crises in Eighteenth-century England', *Economic History Review*, 2nd series, vol. 39, no. 1 (1986), pp. 44–5.
3 Robert Brettingham to Miss Anne Brettingham, 23 June 1772, University of Oxford, Bodleian Library, MS Eng misc c504.
4 Mrs Carter to Mrs Vesey, 21 May 1778, *Carter Letters*, vol. 4, 203.
5 Confusingly, both arrangements were referred to as leasing. I shall make a distinction here between the capital-outlay approach, which I shall call buying, and the periodic-outlay approach, which I shall call renting.
6 Caroline Howe to Lady Spencer, 27 and 28 January 1780, BL, Althorp papers, F 45.
7 Memorandum of 12 October 1763, bound into booklet including inventory of fixtures and fittings and plans of each floor, Warwickshire Record Office, Seymour of Ragley papers, CR114A/254.
8 William Bagot to ?Rev. Mr Townson, 24 May 1776, Staffordshire Record Office, Bagot papers, D5121/1/12/34.
9 Building accounts for 'Sundry works done for Sir W Bagot, Upper Brook Street', 1776–7, Staffs Record Office, Bagot papers, D5121/3/216.
10 It is difficult to provide average costs for building country houses, but R. G. Wilson and A. L. Mackley provide estimates of the average cost an houses by estate size in the period 1770–1800. Houses on smaller estates (3,000–5,000 acres) cost an estimated average of £7000 (R. G. Wilson and A. L. Mackley, 'How Much did the English Country House Cost to Build, 1660–1880?', *Economic History Review*, vol. 52, no. 3 (1999), pp. 436–68; see table 10, p. 464). A modest country house could cost considerably less, and Wilson and Mackley note elsewhere that Salle Park, Norfolk, a seven-bay brick house built in the mid-1760s, cost £2470, while the 'case' of Honing Hall, a five-bay, two-and-a-half storey, red-brick house, also in Norfolk, cost no more than £500 in the 1740s, the interior finish probably a little more (Wilson and Mackley, 2000, p. 39).
11 Tenancy agreement book, entry for 26 May 1773, Guildhall Library, Christ's Hospital archives, MS 12853, vol. 1, fol. 193; *Public Advertiser*, 2 August 1775; memorandum of 12 October 1763, attached to plans and inventory for the Earl of Hertford's house in Grosvenor Street, Warwickshire Record Office, Seymour of Ragley papers, CR114/A/254.
12 Letter from Elizabeth Montagu to Mrs Robinson, 10 February 1779, BL, Montagu correspondence, Add MS 40663, fol. 85. The Duke of Hamilton had offered Mrs Montagu 300 guineas for a four-month stay in her Hill Street house.
13 Mrs Carter to Mrs Vesey, 29 October 1779, *Carter Letters*, vol. 4. 238. In 1774, William Chambers reported to Sir Charles Bingham that a house advertised at £36 per annum, of which £4 was accounted for by ground rent, could not be worth more than £400 or £500 at most. 'I would not advise you as a friend to give more for the whole house [i.e., for the house and land] than 1700£s whereas they ask even now 2500 for it & their 1st Demand was above 3000.' Letter dated 5 February [1774], BL, Chambers letterbooks, vol. 1, Add MS 41133, fol. 112.
14 The development of actuarial science in the eighteenth century and the publication of tables for calculating discounts no doubt helped the valuation of leases and aided the sophisticated operation of the leasehold system (James Anderson, 'The Lawyer, the Investor and the Property Speculator: How Urban Development was Financed in Georgian England', unpublished paper presented at The Georgian Group, 19 January 1999).
15 William Chambers to Agmondesham

Vesey, 30 December [1773], BL, Chambers letterbooks, vol. 1, Add MS 41133, fol. 119.

16 Letter to Lady Caroline Dawson, 21 November 1778, *Gleanings from an Old Portfolio*, vol. 1, 107. Lady Emily was the daughter of Lady Lothian, who had recently died leaving her financially independent.

17 Henry Bridgeman to Sir William Lee, 13 July 1763, Buckinghamshire Record Office, Hartwell papers, D/LE/D1/44.

18 Princess Amelia, daughter of George II, was resident in Cavendish Square.

19 Agmondesham Vesey to William Chambers, 28 September 1774, BL, Chambers letterbooks, vol. 3, Add MS 41135, fol. 47v. Robert Mylne, too, viewed, surveyed and valued houses for his clients. In June 1773, for example, he 'surveyed a house and offices in Grosvenor Place for Lord Abingdon and gave an opinion thereon for the purchase thereof'. Richardson, p. 94, diary entry for 12 June 1773.

20 The *Craftsman* magazine reported in October 1769 how the many recent bankruptcies among the Marylebone builders had not abated the 'rage of building in that parish . . . carcases which cost the builders . . . at first hand, from £600 to £1000 each, have lately been sold from only £90 to £200'. See also Olsen, p. 15: 'the supply in particular of the more expensive type of house did usually exceed demand'.

21 *Public Advertiser*, 10 August 1775.

22 William Chambers to Agmondesham Vesey, 8 October 1774, BL, Chambers letterbooks, vol. 3, Add MS 41135, fol. 48. This Grafton Street house would cost them around £100 more than they had budgeted for, being available at 400 guineas for the year or 12 guineas a week if taken for a shorter period.

23 Lady Louisa Stuart to Lady Carlow, July 1784, *Gleanings from an Old Portfolio*, vol. 1, 260, 262.

24 Journal entries for 13 and 15 March 1777, *Francis Letters*, vol. 1, 290–1.

25 *Lady's Magazine* 8 (1777), 532–3.

26 Charles Bragge Bathurst to Duke of Beaufort, 19 May 1769, Gloucestershire Record Office, Badminton muniments, D421 C3.

27 William Chambers to ?Paul Sandby, 27 August 1772, BL, Chambers letterbooks, vol. 1, Add MS 41133, fols 82–82v.

28 Letter of 29 November 1792, Wiltshire and Swindon Record Office, Brudenell-Bruce (Ailesbury) papers, 9/35/81.

29 Mary Noel to Judith Milbanke, 28 December 1784, *Noels and Milbankes*, p. 252.

30 William Chambers to Henry Errington, 3 August 1770, BL, Chambers letterbooks, vol. 1, Add MS 41133, fol. 19v.

31 Elizabeth Montagu to Mrs Robinson, 21 February [1778], BL, Montagu correspondence, Add MS 40663, fol. 74.

32 What follows is based principally on a review of advertisements placed in the *Public Advertiser* throughout 1775. I also studied other, similar publications (including the *Morning Chronicle and London Advertiser* for 3 January 1770; *Morning Post and Daily Advertiser* for 30 January 1779; the issues of the *London Courant and Westminster Chronicle* for November 1779 to December 1780; various issues of *St James's Chronicle; or, British Evening-post* for 1764 and 1772–4; and the *Gazetteer and New Daily Advertiser* for 1779) to check for any variations in coverage between papers and across the decade. There seems to have been little variation in either respect.

33 See Stephen Porter, *The Great Fire of London* (Godalming: Bramley Books, 1998), p 107.

34 Documents in the BL (Hamilton and Greville papers, vol. 1, Add MS 40714, fols 110–16) show that the final account was not settled until

June 1776, although David King, *The Complete Works of Robert and James Adam* (Oxford: Butterworth Architecture, 1991), p. 264, suggests an end date of 1771. Colvin, s.v. 'Robert Adam', states that the house was damaged by fire in that year, and subsequently rebuilt between then and 1775. Both King and Colvin state that the house was built for General Clerk, even though the accounts (fols 113–14) refer to 'cash received of the Countess of Warwick' in July and December 1768, and the estimate (fols 110–12) is marked on the outside as referring to 'the New House built by My Mother The Countess Dow^r of Warwick in Mansfield Street'. The advertisement, in the *St James's Chronicle; or, British Evening-post* for 30 December 1773 to 1 January 1774, is for 'a most elegant and spacious House, 100 Feet in Front, situate in Mansfield-street, and looking South towards Queen Ann-street, Cavendish Square, between a Court and a Garden'. Further particulars were available from 'Mr John Grierson, at Mess Adams's, in the Adelphi'.

35 Lease of 1 March 1775, Caernarfon Record Office, Newborough collection, XD2/7224; BL, Hamilton and Greville papers, vol. 1, Add MS 40714, fols 115–16.

36 *Public Advertiser*, 19 April 1775 and 6 January 1775; SL, vol. 40, p. 18.

37 SL, vol. 33, p. 45.

38 Lady Caroline Fox to Marchioness of Kildare, 21 March 1763, *Leinster Letters*, vol. 1 (1949), 362.

39 Bolton, 1922, vol. 2, 4, quoting letter from Clerk to Earl of Shelburne, 14 May 1765.

40 Judith Gibbison makes this argument with regard to Bath in 'The Bath Town House: An Eighteenth-century Perspective' (BA diss., University of Reading, 2004), p. 16.

41 *Public Advertiser*, 2 January 1775.

42 *Public Advertiser*, 16 March 1775.

43 Letter from Lord Bracebridge to Lord Bruce, 11 April 1796, Wilts and Swindon Record Office, Brudenell-Bruce (Ailesbury) papers, 9/35/81. Letter from Elizabeth Montagu to Mrs Robinson, 29 December 1779, BL, Montagu correspondence, Add MS 40663, fols 96–7. Advantages of location were not limited to the West End; a house in Billiter Square, off Fenchurch Street, in the City, could boast being 'within four Minutes Walk of the "Change and Custom-House"' (*Public Advertiser*, 2 June 1775).

44 SL, vol. 39, p. 120. Thomas Noel to Judith Noel, 1 December 1774, *Noels and Milbankes*, p. 45.

45 General Robert Clerk to Earl of Shelburne, 14 May 1765, Bolton, 1922, vol. 2, 4.

46 SL, vol. 40, p. 114.

47 It is no surprise that Mrs Montagu said of the laying out of her garden in Portman Square that 'in this puny age I think it will make a figure' (University of Manchester, John Rylands Library, Thrale-Piozzi papers, Eng MS 551/9, n.d.).

48 *Public Advertiser*, 28 May 1772, advertisement for auction of Chandos House by Mr Christie.

49 *Public Advertiser*, 22 April and 17 May 1775. Other advertisements that mention bow windows clearly relate to shop premises. It is worth noting here that Sir Robert Taylor made good use of bow windows where the view warranted, most notably at the rear of No. 3 Grafton Street (c. 1770–1), which had a rear-canted bay rising through six storeys, the upper five offering 'an extensive view west across the south arm of Berkeley Square and along the length of Charles Street, Mayfair', encompassing the garden and front of Lansdowne House. As Richard Garnier writes, this 'must have been one of the best urban vistas anywhere in London at the time, as heady in its day as the view from an upper-floor apartment overlooking Central Park in New York today' ('Grafton Street, May-

fair', *Georgian Group Journal* 13 (2003), p. 231).

50 Mrs Carter to Miss Talbot, 30 June 1764, *Carter Letters*, vol. 3, 99–100.

51 General Clerk believed that 'a prospect is well in your own Park, but is an absurd thought for a town house for it cannot well be obtained but at the expense of more essential pleasures & at any rate is a trifling consideration . . . Not only is the ground not yours, but the pleasures such as they are of such a situation are not dependent upon you . . . The whole prospects may be taken away in one week by an order of the Court.' General Robert Clerk to the Earl of Shelburne from Paris, 14 May 1765, quoted in Bolton, 1922, vol. 2, 3–4.

52 Ibid., vol. 2, 20.

53 *Public Advertiser*, 24 March 1775. The advertiser overestimated the street's width (it is closer to 110 ft), but it was nevertheless unusually broad, due to 'an undertaking given to Lord Foley that the view northwards from the windows of his house, which blocked the southern end of the street, should never be obscured' (*The London Encyclopaedia*, ed. Ben Weinreb and Christopher Hibbert (London: Macmillan, 1995), s.v. 'Portland Place').

54 James Paine to Lord Scarborough, 24 March 1757, Sandbeck Park, Yorkshire, Scarborough papers. I am grateful to the late 12th Earl for bringing this letter to my attention.

55 *Dr Campbell's Diary of a Visit to England in 1775*, ed. James L. Clifford, with an introduction by S. C. Roberts (Cambridge: Cambridge University Press, 1947), p. 84.

56 Elizabeth Montagu to Mrs Robinson, 26 November 1783, BL, Montagu correspondence, Add MS 40663, fol. 130.

57 Mrs Montagu to William Pepys, October 1780, *Mrs Montagu, 'Queen of the Blues': Her Letters and Friendships from 1762 to 1800*, ed. Reginald Blunt (London: Constable, 1923), p. 103.

58 *Morning Post and Daily Advertiser*, 24 May 1776.

59 Suffolk Record Office, Grafton (Fitzroy) papers, HA 513/4/31; Northamptonshire Record Office, Grafton papers, G3882, fols 101–2, and see, also, the discussion of this house in Chapter Two, p. 66.

60 *Public Advertiser*, 28 May 1772.

61 *Morning Post and Daily Advertiser*, 30 January 1779.

62 *St James's Chronicle; or, British Evening-post*, 30 December 1773 to 1 January 1774.

63 *Morning Post and Daily Advertiser*, 30 January 1779; *Public Advertiser*, 7 November 1775.

64 *Letters and Journals of Lady Mary Coke*, ed. J. A. Hume, 4 vols (Edinburgh: 1889–96), vol. 2, 220, quoted in Port, 1995, p. 27.

65 Peter Leach, *James Paine* (London: Zwemmer, 1988), p. 193.

66 William Chambers to Agmondesham Vesey, 30 December [1773], BL, Chambers letterbooks, vol. 1, Add MS 41133, fol. 119.

67 Caroline Howe to Lady Spencer, 22 January [1773], BL, Althorp papers, F 43.

68 Judith Milbanke to Mary Noel, 24 February 1778, *Noels and Milbankes*, pp. 92–3.

69 In her study *Hospitality in Early Modern England* (Oxford: Clarendon Press, 1990), Felicity Heal has little to say regarding individual, private hospitality (as opposed to corporate, 'public' hospitality) in London, although with reference to the Elizabethan period, she notes that 'for all the enthusiasm that townsmen might show for feasting, their daily entertainment of guests was constrained by space and habit, so that short visits and few meals were the approved modes in London and other "good towns" ' (pp. 353–4).

70 *Public Advertiser*, 24 March 1775.

71 Closets had a variety of functions (and sizes) in this period, and could be used in the modern-day sense of a

supplementary or storage space as well as the more specifically eighteenth-century sense of a place to be 'closeted'.

72 David King, p. 270.

73 *St James's Chronicle; or, British Evening-post*, 30 December 1773 to 1 January 1774. The documents recounting the Adams' estimates and payments made to them by the Countess Dowager of Warwick and General Clerk (BL, Hamilton and Greville papers, vol. 1, Add MS 40714, fols 110–16) refer to 'repairs after the fire', suggesting that the measure was not an effective one.

74 University of Nottingham, Hallward Library, Portland papers, Pw F 7991.

75 *Public Advertiser*, 28 May 1772.

76 *Public Advertiser*, 3 February 1775.

77 Tara Draper, 'Chandos House', *Georgian Group Journal* 7 (1997), p. 137. *SL*, vol. 33, pp. 69–72, 74–9.

78 *SL*, vol. 33, 70–1.

79 *Public Advertiser*, 3 February 1775.

80 John Adam to Sir Rowland Winn, 6 July 1774, Nostell Priory Archives, C3/1/5/2. Robert Adam to Sir Rowland Winn, 15 February 1776, C3/1/5, quoted in Stillman, p. 198.

81 *SL*, vol. 29, p. 124. The house was apparently sold by late March 1785 for £6930, but it stood empty until it was occupied in 1787, when it was finally conveyed by Sir Rowland's widow in trust for Sir Richard Hoare.

82 *SL*, vol. 33, pp. 69–72, 74–9.

83 *Public Advertiser*, 27 May 1775.

84 Port, 1995, p. 27.

85 Ian Doolittle, 'The City's West End Estate: A "Remarkable Omission"', *London Journal* 7 (1981): p. 21.

86 *Public Advertiser*, 28 October 1775; 25 January 1775.

87 It is difficult to determine the impact of the Window Tax, introduced in 1696, on the saleability of houses, but the Grosvenor Estate agent Edward Boodle used the additional expense it would incur as an argument against a corner property he viewed on behalf of the Dowager Duchess of Beaufort in 1798 (letter of 10 February 1798, Gloucestershire Record Office, Badminton papers, D2700, QJ 6/4).

88 Letter from the Adams in *St James's Chronicle; or, British Evening-post*, 29 October to 31 October 1772.

89 *Public Advertiser*, 10 June 1775.

90 Mrs Montagu to Mrs Robinson, 20 November 1780, BL, Montagu correspondence, Add MS 40663, fol. 102.

91 For the purposes of comparison, I studied advertisements for York houses in the *York Courant* for the periods May 1763–June 1764 and January to December 1775. The figures refer only to houses which clearly had been owned or leased by a nobleman, gentleman or lady, or which were not evidently associated with a tradesperson or a business.

92 Of the forty-one houses advertised in May 1763–June 1764 and in 1775 (eighteen to let, twenty to sell and three to sell or let), nine advertisements give prominence to stabling and coach-houses; seventeen refer to gardens. Only four refer explicitly to size, and six outline the range and number of rooms.

93 Four of the eleven houses for sale in York in 1763–4 and seven of the nine houses for sale in 1775 were to go to the highest bidder or be sold at auction.

94 Letter from Mrs Montagu to Mrs Robinson, 11 April 1778, BL, Montagu correspondence, Add MS 40663, fol. 78.

95 Therese Parker to her brother, 5 March 1773, BL, Morley papers, vol. 1, Add MS 48218, fol. 129.

96 Unsurprisingly, there were far fewer houses advertised to sell or let in York, reflecting a smaller building stock but also, perhaps, less movement in and out of the city and fewer abrupt changes of mind. In York, as in London, auctions were a common means of disposing of a property within a short space of time, especially in the 1770s.

97 *Public Advertiser*, 27 December 1775.

98 Staffs Record Office, Jerningham/ Stafford papers, D641/3/P/3/5/3, Edward Jefreys to Sir George Jerningham, 12 April 1764; letter from Mary Noel to Judith Milbanke, 16 October 1783, *Noels and Milbankes*, p. 224, 'Mrs Bland told me she knew for a certainty that Sir T[homas] C[lavering] has positively said he shall decline being again in Parliament, that he is parting with his House in Town, & intends to live intirely [sic] in the Country, being in *very* bad Circumstances'.

99 Letter from Lady Caroline Fox to the Marchioness of Kildare, 9 March 1762, *Leinster Letters*, vol. 1 (1949), 321.

100 Wilson and Mackley, 2000, p. 339. Mrs Francis volunteered, in 1777, to sub-let her Harley Street house and retire to the country if her husband thought her annual expenditure too much, and he himself reportedly claimed that 'even with the strictest economy' he found it difficult to live in London on what was a substantial income of £3000 per annum (journal entry for 19 May 1777, *Francis Letters*, vol. 1, 294, vol. 2, p. 347, editors' note). Likewise, in 1787 Louisa Stuart believed that 'fifteen or sixteen hundred a year would not do much for two people who must live in London and appear in fine clothes at St James's twice a week' (Louisa Stuart to Lady Portarlington, 13 March 1787, *Gleanings from an Old Portfolio*, vol. 2, p. 69).

101 Smollett, p. 327.

102 *The Gentleman's Magazine* (1771, p. 317) identifies the passage about Bramble's visit to Baynard as 'among the pictures of life, which may serve as monitors to the supine and thoughtless, the extravagant and the vain'.

103 Smollett, pp. 363–4.

104 See John Sekora, *Luxury: The Concept in Western Thought, Eden to Smollett* (Baltimore and London: John Hopkins University Press, 1977), p. 109. Nevertheless, Smollett's perpetuation of an old approach to luxury in the face of new ones does not alter the fact that he identifies the London town house as a specific example of a luxury and thereby inspired, in part, this investigation into the financial relationship between owner, or tenant, and house. In so far as the period under study saw a move away from the blanket term 'luxury' towards its application to specific objects and actions, Smollett's specification of the town house is in line with contemporary approaches, even if his disregard for the 'benefits' or innocuousness of luxury is out of step with the reasoning of such contemporaries as David Hume and Adam Smith.

105 While this practice was not universal, numerous examples were found in the course of this research. Sir Robert Burdett, among others, also included in his London accounts the spending money given to his family members as well as that he allowed himself, so that even their personal expenditure in London can be tracked (household accounts for Sir Robert Burdett, 1764–71, Derbyshire Record Office, Burdett papers, D5054/14/1).

106 Of the 'extraordinary expence' of £111 4 s 6 d in 1778–9, £102 9 s 6 d was accounted for by 'taking care of House and 11 weeks Housekeeping in London'. In the following year, 1779–80, £156 17 s out of extraordinary expenses of £217 4 s was incurred during fourteen weeks in London (Bucks Record Office, Hartwell papers, D/LE/E4/3). The Duke of Dorset kept track of bills for entertainment at his Grosvenor Square house during the period 1779–83, including sums paid to the fishmonger, confectioner, butcher, poulterer and greengrocer for dinners there between December 1782 and May 1783, which alone totalled £70 (Centre for Kentish Studies, Sackville papers, U269 A241, bills for entertainment at Grosvenor Square 1779–83, including 1241/3,

'Abstract of Bills for Dinners at Grosvenor Square from December 17th to May the 8th 1783').

107 Badminton, Badminton muniments, RA 2/1/14.

108 Langford, 1991, p. 380. Langford cites James Burgh's *Political Disquisitions* (3 vols, London: 1774–5, vol. 3, 45) as evidence. Concern about the neglect of country estates, and the hospitality associated with them, was not new in this period. As Felicity Heal notes, 'both the conventional *rus/urbs* dichotomy, and the evolving role of London and other provincial capitals in the experience of the English élite, suggest that town was commonly identified with the break-up of households and the failure of hospitality' (Heal, p. 301).

109 Badminton, Badminton muniments, RA 2/1/14.

110 For example, Sir Robert Burdett included the purchase of chimney pieces and Chippendale chairs in his figures for London expenditure, but clearly marked them as meant for his country property at Foremark, Derbyshire (Derbys Record Office, Burdett papers, D5054/14/1, entry for 4 February 1768).

111 Essex Record Office, Audley End Estate papers, D/DBy A205-10, monthly general accounts.

112 London Metropolitan Archives, Ashburnham papers, Acc 524/23, 15 August 1786.

113 Hampshire Record Office, Clarke-Jervoise papers, 6M59/1/33.

114 Hertfordshire Archives and Local Studies, D/ECd F99.

115 English Heritage, Historians' files, WM 209, notes on 45 Berkeley Square. Clive had bought the remainder of the lease of the house, which he had previously rented, for £1050 in 1764. John Harris puts the total cost of refashioning the London house at about £6000, possibly including the addition of a low attic storey (John Harris, *Sir William Chambers: Knight of the Polar Star*, with contributions by J. Mordaunt Crook and Eileen Harris (London: Zwemmer, 1970), p. 216).

116 *SL*, vol. 40, p. 147 (information from Sheffield Central Library, Spencer Stanhope Muniments 64781).

117 These figures are based on estimates made by his agent, Francis Chambre. Letter from Francis Chambre to Sir Watkin, 17 September 1774, National Library of Wales, Wynnstay papers, 122, fols 239–40. The purchase price of the house included interest to the time of payment.

118 Bucks Record Office, Drake papers, e.g., 'Abstract of Sundry Bills for Alterations and Repairs done to a House in Grosvenor Square for Wm Drake Esqr under the Direction of Jas Wyatt', D/DR/5/69; *SL*, vol. 40, p. 130. A further £896 was spent in 1785–6.

119 Guildhall Library, Christ's Hospital archives, tenancy agreement books; Woburn Abbey, Bedford Estate Office, Bedford Estate proposal books. This and other information from the papers of the Bedford Estate is included here by kind permission of the Duke of Bedford and the Trustees of the Bedford Estate.

120 Woburn, Bedford Estate Proposal Book D, fol. 166.

121 Ibid., fol. 280.

122 Woburn, Bedford Estate Proposal Book E, fols 2, 30.

123 See, for example, ibid., fol. 61 regarding the lease of a house in Tavistock Row, 4 August 1774, which was increased from twenty-four to thirty-one years.

124 Surrey History Centre, Frederick papers, 183/33/14–15, account books for London 1760–72 and 1772–81, see, for example, entries for 13 December 1770, 26 August 1772, 2 April 1773 and 21 April and 22 October 1777.

125 Staffs Record Office, Hand Morgan papers, note with questions and answers in two different inks and dated 21 March 1769, loose inside lease agreement at D1798, bundle 129, dated 23 June 1769.

126 Staffs Record Office, Littleton/Hatherton papers, D260/M/E/118.

127 Bucks Record Office, Hartwell papers, D/LE/11/36, agreement dated 26 December 1778.

128 National Library of Wales, Wynnstay papers, 115/3.

129 *SL*, vol. 40, 118.

130 English Heritage, Historians' Files, WM 209, notes on 45 Berkeley Square. The total cost of the extensive refurbishment was £3718.

131 Entries for 17 and 18 March, 19 May 1777; 2 June, 13 November 1778; 23 June 1779 in Mrs Francis's journal, *Francis Letters*, vol. 1, 292, 322, 328, 330.

132 Lady Louisa Conolly to Countess of Kildare, 4 March 1770; Lady Louisa Conolly to William Ogilvie, 10 March 1776, *Leinster Letters*, vol. 2 (1953), 51, 189.

133 Entry for 26 November in Mrs Francis's journal, *Francis Letters*, vol. 1, 299.

134 19 January [1764], BL, Adair papers, vol. 9, Add MS 53808.

135 Low, p. 2470.

136 For example, in August 1775 an advertiser offered that 'a considerable Part of the Purchase Money will be allowed to remain upon the Mortgage of the House for a Term of Years'; and in January 1779 another vendor allowed that 'the greatest part of the money may remain in the hands of the purchaser during pleasure' (*Public Advertiser*, 28 August 1775; *Morning Post and Daily Advertiser*, 30 January 1779). Similarly, in 1764 Sir John Frederick allowed Lord George Sutton a mortgage for a year to pay the £5000 purchase price of his house in Grosvenor Street, receiving half-yearly interest payments at 5 per cent in the meantime (Surrey History Centre, Frederick papers, 183/26/2, agreement dated 2 February 1764, and 183/33/14 account book entries for 23 October 1764, 25 March 1765).

137 For discussions of Taylor's diverse but wholly reputable operations in the London housing market, and his client network, see Richard Garnier, 'Speculative Housing in the 1750s', *Georgian Group Journal* 12 (2002): 163–214 and Garnier, 2003, especially p. 250.

138 Quoted in Garnier, 2003, p. 250.

139 William Chambers to Henry Errington, 15 May 1770, BL, Chambers letterbooks, vol. 1, Add MS 41133, fol. 14.

140 William Chambers to Earl Fitzwilliam, [1770], BL, Chambers letterbooks, vol. 1, Add MS 41133, fol. 30.

141 BL, Hamilton and Greville papers, vol. 1, Add MS 40714, fols 110–12.

142 Information kindly supplied by the late 12th Earl from papers held at Sandbeck Park, Yorkshire.

143 Leach, p. 192.

144 Charles Townley's agreement with the builder Michael Barrett for his house in Park Street stipulated that Barrett would be paid £500 'when he shall have built the said house to the dining room floor – another sum of £1000 when the said house shall be covered in, and the remainder [of £3650] when the said Michael Barrett shall have completely finished the said house according to the above agreement' (Dan Cruickshank, 'Queen Anne's Gate', *Georgian Group Journal* 2 (1992), p. 66).

145 Elizabeth Montagu to Mrs Robinson, 9 July [1782], BL, Montagu correspondence, Add MS 40663, fol. 117: 'till ye whole was completed I would only pay on account, so that there was not a possibility of a final settlement between me and these gentry . . . I had ye satisfaction of getting a receit [sic] in full of all demands from ye various artificers . . . My house never appear'd to me so noble, so splendid, so pleasant, so convenient, as when I had paid off every shilling of debt it had incurred.'

146 Mrs Montagu to Mrs Robinson, 9 July [1782], BL, Montagu correspondence, Add MS 40663, fol. 117.

147 *SL*, vol. 33, p. 70.

148 *Public Advertiser*, 20 November 1775.

149 Samuel Johnson, *A Dictionary of the English Language*.

150 Francis Chambre to Sir Watkin, 17 September 1774, National Library of Wales, Wynnstay papers, 122, fols 239–40. Chambre's extensive comments on Sir Watkin's direct and indirect expenditure on his new house can be found in correspondence in 122, fols 31–3, 47, 239–40, 289–92, 295, 307–9, 421, 501. According to the *Survey of London* the house in St James's Square was bought for £18,500, and in excess of £29,000 was spent on rebuilding it (vol. 29, p. 164).

151 Sir Watkin to Francis Chambre, 9 June 1775, National Library of Wales, Wynnstay papers, 122, fols 307–9. The phenomenon of delayed payments, often amounting to thousands of pounds, was not exclusive to this period, but formed part of annual and perennial patterns of aristocratic expenditure. Robert Campbell offered advice to the London tradesman on this subject in 1747, observing that the seller of luxury goods 'must have Confidence to refuse his goods in a handsome Manner to the extravagant Beau who never pays, and Patience as well as stock to bear the Delays of the sharping Peer who pays but seldom' (p. 148).

152 For example, Samuel Sidebotham to Francis Chambre, 3 February 1774, National Library of Wales, Wynnstay papers, 122, fol. 47.

153 William Chambers to Henry Errington, 12 October 1770, BL, Chambers letterbooks, vol. I, Add MS 41133, fol. 22v.

154 William Chambers to Lord Weymouth, n.d., BL, Chambers letterbooks, vol. I, Add MS 41133, fol. 29.

155 William Chambers to Lord Melbourne, 14 August 1773, BL, Chambers letterbooks, vol. I, Add MS 41133, fol. 22v. Melbourne still owed

Chambers £3000 when he sold the house in 1792 (Port, 1995, p. 45).

156 See, for example, BL, Chambers letterbooks, vol. I, Add MS 41133, fols. 41, 44v, 51v, and 54v.

157 See, for example, *Town and Country Magazine*, in which very lengthy lists of bankrupts appear in December 1778 and January 1779 (vols 10 and 11), a period suggested by other sources as particularly bad for patrons, too. In respect of tradesmen, Julian Hoppit, *Risk and Failure in English Business 1700–1800* (Cambridge: Cambridge University Press, 1989), remarks that 'at the centre of fashion, London businessmen were open to a constantly changing range of opportunities making for success and a constantly changing pattern of uncertainty making for failure. Fashion heightened opportunities and risks' (p. 72). The proportion of bankrupts from London, as listed in the *London Gazette*, was as high as 50.2 per cent in 1769–71 and 52.6 per cent in 1772, dropping slightly to a still substantial 45.2 per cent in 1775–8 (see Hoppit, 1986b, especially table 2, p. 51).

158 Mr King, of Brompton Grove, near Knightsbridge, was unusual in selling his household furniture and letting his house and stabling in order to retire into the City (*Public Advertiser*, 14 January 1775).

159 If we are to believe the 'letter', even death, the fifth reason for sale, might not always be taken at face value, for another overspender is a macaroni officer who had been reported as killed in America. *Town and Country Magazine* 10 (1778), 208.

160 The same is not true of house advertisements in the *York Courant* in the same period (judging by issues for the periods May 1763–June 1764 and January–December 1775) – see note 163 below.

161 See, for example, *Town and Country Magazine* 3 (1771), 334: 'Mr. Thomas Bradshaw, minister to the Junto, has

just bought of the duke of Athol for four thousand pounds, a house for his town residence, opposite to Lord Bute's, in South Audley-street'; and, *Noels and Milbankes*, p. 407, Mary Noel to Judith Milbanke, 1 January 1792: 'Mr Lambton has bought the Dss of Ancaster's house in Berkeley Square, & given six thousand pounds for it.'

162 Caroline Howe to Lady Spencer, undated letter (1767?), BL, Althorp papers, F 42.

163 The York advertisements give no reasons for sale – there is no effort to account for a property's disposal and presumably, therefore, no unwelcome inferences of the kind that plagued the Duke of Manchester, and many other sellers in London. It was, in any case, cheaper to live in provincial towns and cities than in the capital, so there may well have been both fewer sales on account of financial difficulty and less likelihood that anything would be read into a sale, and therefore less reason to excuse it. The York town house clearly did not function as an indicator in quite the same way as the West End house.

164 Peter M. Briggs, ' "News from the Little World": A Critical Glance at Eighteenth-century British Advertising', *Studies in Eighteenth-century Culture* 23 (1994): p. 44, note 19.

165 Henry Bridgeman to Sir William Lee, 13 July 1763, Buckinghamshire Record Office, Hartwell papers, D/LE/D4/8. Surrey History Centre, Frederick papers, 183/3/14, fol. 55, entries for 25 and 27 March 1765.

166 Sir William Lee to Lord Harcourt, 25 August 1765, Bucks Record Office, Hartwell papers, D/LE/D4/8.

167 Of this figure, around 75 per cent was accounted for by work undertaken at or in connection with Hartwell House, Buckinghamshire, where extensive work was done in the 1760s by Henry Keene, whose building accounts were not settled until 1773.

168 Act 1, Scene 1. *Sheridan: Plays*, edited with an introduction by Cecil Price

(London: Oxford University Press, 1975), p. 236.

169 Dorset Record Office, Fox-Strangways papers, D/FSI Box 240B, Bundle 11.

170 *21 Arlington Street: A Brief History of the Building* (n.d.), leaflet at Dept of Woodwork, Victoria and Albert Museum, architecture files, box A.

171 H. Stanley to Charles Jenkinson, 1 August 1778, BL, Liverpool papers, Add MS 38470.

172 In his study of business failures in the eighteenth century, Julian Hoppit recognises the problems with definitions of bankruptcy in the period. The layman's definition was similar to our own, but in law 'only some of those who were insolvent were dealt with as bankrupts; others were dealt with by alternative legal mechanisms; and some escaped the law altogether, though not necessarily their creditors.' It is likely that executions in town houses were instigated by agents appointed to act on behalf of assorted creditors, within the type of alternative legal mechanism mentioned by Hoppit, and by individual creditors operating alone. Outside of bankruptcy, the creditor who chased his debts first was most likely to succeed (Hoppit, 1989, pp. 18, 29). In practice, the balance between chasing hard and soon enough to get paid and being flexible enough to attract essential business, must have been difficult for tradesmen and professionals, including those involved in construction, to achieve.

173 Caroline Howe to Lady Spencer, 13 March [1773], BL, Althorp papers, F 43: 'Sr G. Colebrook's House in Arlington Street is I hear to be sold, and it is imagined the call upon him is so great, that he will be obliged to part with Gatton [his country house].' The house was not sold until 1775, as reported in the *Public Advertiser* on 28 April: 'We hear that Sir George Colebrooke has sold his House in Arlington-street to the Female Coterie for £13,000.'

174 Judith Milbanke to Mary Noel, 3 February 1778, *Noels and Milbankes*, p. 91.

175 *Town and Country Magazine* 5 (1773), p. 256. Contemporary comic plays are a good indication of both the prevalence and the knowledge of trends, as their humour rested largely on their topicality. See, for example, *The First Floor: A Farce*, by James Cobb (London: 1787), Act II, Scene 1; and, *The Heiress*, by General John Burgoyne (London: 1786), Act I, Scene 3. In real life, William Hickey's acquaintance Fanny Temple 'inhabited an excellent house in Queen Anne Street', all paid for by 'a gentleman of rank and fashion', while Bob Potts's then mistress, Emily Warren, was installed in 'a handsome, well-furnished house', in Cork Street, dubbed by Hickey 'as complete a one as ever I saw in every respect' (*Memoirs of William Hickey*, ed. Peter Quennell (London and Boston: Routledge and Kegan Paul, 1975), pp. 54, 269, with reference to the late 1760s and 1780 respectively).

176 Sophia Curzon to Mary Noel from London, 18 May 1778. *Noels and Milbankes*, p. 103.

177 Letter from Judith Milbanke to Mary Noel, 26 December 1781, *Noels and Milbankes*, p. 172; editorial note, pp. 184–5. The Curzons had been spending on the certainty of an inheritance on Lord Scarsdale's death. However, the promise of money in the future was not always sufficient to overcome shortages in the present, or to maintain the confidence of creditors.

178 Hoppit, 1986a, p. 43. Elizabeth McKellar draws attention to the dual meaning of the word 'credit' in the seventeenth century, 'encompassing both the notion of personal credibility and the concept of creditworthiness' (*The Birth of Modern London: The Development and Design of the City 1660–1720* (Manchester: Manchester University Press, 1999), p. 84).

179 *London Chronicle*, 28–30 April, 1772; quoted in Hoppit, 1989, p. 134.

180 Sir Watkin to Samuel Sidebotham, 23 March 1775; Sir Watkin to Francis Chambre, 9 June 1775, National Library of Wales, Wynnstay papers, 122, fols 295, 307–9.

181 In his discussion of credit in the eighteenth century, B. L. Anderson confirms that there is evidence that 'the enthusiasm for credit led contemporaries to serious over-extension and failure, occurring when the size of a man's assets could no longer support the volatility of his credit . . . At worst the outcome involved abscondment, the debtors' prison, or a suicide, all were common enough.' ('Money and the Structure of Credit in the Eighteenth Century', *Business History* 12 (July 1970), p. 97). See also Samuel Foote, *The Bankrupt* (first performed 1773; new edition printed 1782), Act II, Scene 2. City man Sir Robert Riscounter recognises that feigning bankruptcy might be a useful short-term measure for regaining a good financial footing, but also that any damage to his reputation for solvency must threaten not only his own ability to operate within a market which depends on credit, and therefore trust, but ultimately that market's very existence.

182 Burney, 1782, pp. 273, 300.

183 *Town and Country Magazine* 4 (1772), 544. Fictitious bills of exchange, as discussed by Julian Hoppit in 'The Use and Abuse of Credit in Eighteenth-century England', in *Business Life and Public Policy: Essays in Honour of D.C. Coleman*, ed. Neil McKendrick and R. B. Outhwaite (Cambridge: Cambridge University Press, 1986b), p. 70, meant that credit was not only the means by which appearances could be deceptive, but often derived from things that were not what they seemed.

184 D. Grant Campbell, 'Fashionable Suicide: Conspicuous Consumption and the Collapse of Credit in Frances

Burney's *Cecilia'*, *Studies in Eighteenth-Century Culture* 20 (1990), p. 136.

185 Burney, 1782, p. 31.

186 Margaret Doody, *Frances Burney: The Life in the Works* (New Brunswick: Rutgers University Press, 1988), p. 133.

187 Wilson and Mackley, 2000, p. 229.

188 Ibid., p. 346.

189 Kerry Bristol conjectures to this effect in 'James Stuart and the London Building Trades', *Georgian Group Journal* 13 (2003), p. 6.

190 Wilson and Mackley, 2000, p. 346.

191 See Wilson and Mackley's discussion of Sir John Griffin Griffin's restoration of Audley End, Essex, between 1762 and 1797, which ran concurrently with the refurbishment (by the Adams) of his town house in New Burlington Street in the 1770s. The figures for work in town (£8157 plus £2255 on furniture), while substantial in themselves, seem insignificant in comparison with the £72780 spent on work and £13424 on furniture at Audley End (Wilson and Mackley, 2000, pp. 308–13).

192 Ibid., p. 346.

193 Ibid., p. 319.

194 Ibid., p. 327.

195 See ibid., p. 351: 'Net rental income was sharply reduced by the cost of repairs and the replacement of furniture. Rental income was a contribution to unavoidable costs, not a return on investment.'; and p. 354: 'The value of a house was not viewed primarily in economic terms. It might, in adverse circumstances, be rented out, but generally owners wrote it off as an item of exceptional consumption, possessing, however, considerable social and political benefits.'

196 Ibid., p. 303.

197 Ibid., p. 26.

198 In any case, a luxury is not simply that which is expensive and/or strictly unaffordable. In fact, there *is* no definition or 'grand synthesising theory' of luxury (Christopher Berry, p. 231), but a succession of different defini-tions and critiques prior to, contemporary with, and subsequent to this period. More consistent is the default 'definition' of luxury as the obverse of necessity: the notion of luxury therefore changes in line with adjustments to the notion of necessity.

199 Vickery, p. 194. See also Clunas, p. 1499.

200 Neil McKendrick, 'The Consumer Revolution of Eighteenth-century England', in *The Birth of a Consumer Society: The Commercialization of Eighteenth-century England*, ed. Neil McKendrick, John Brewer and J. H. Plumb (London: Europa, 1982), pp. 11, 25. See Clunas (p. 1498) for a commentary on the subsequent lack of agreement among economic and cultural historians about the existence and nature of the eighteenth-century 'consumer revolution', including Jan de Vries's argument in 'Between Purchasing Power and the World of Goods: Understanding the Household Economy in Early Modern Europe', in *Consumption and the World of Goods*, ed. John Brewer and Roy Porter (London and New York: Routledge, 1993), pp. 85–132, that 'the viability of an eighteenth-century "consumer revolution" seems to depend on a studied vagueness in definitional statements and a careful removal of most of the concept from the economic to the cultural sphere: desire, attitude, fashion and emulation furnish the vocabulary of this discourse' (de Vries, p. 89).

201 Roger S. Mason, *Conspicuous Consumption: A Study of Exceptional Consumer Behaviour* (Farnborough: Gower, 1981), p. 17.

202 Ibid., pp. ix, 26–7.

203 Ibid., p. 68; McKendrick, 1982, p. 20.

204 Mason, pp. 143–4.

205 Ann Pelham to Thomas Pelham, 15 May 1780, BL, Pelham papers, Add MS 33092, fol. 72. See, also, James Raven, *Judging New Wealth: Popular Publishing and Responses to Commerce in England, 1750–1800* (Ox-

ford: Clarendon Press, 1992), p. 186: 'Handbooks warned of the economic ruin facing those who were tempted by the fashionable life of the city.'

206 Howell and Pritchard, p. 783, with reference to a letter of 1776.

207 James Cobb, *The First Floor*, Act II, Scene 1.

208 See, for example, Thomas Holcroft, *The Deserted Daughter: A Comedy in Five Acts* (London: 1795), in which the 'insolent' upholsterer threatens to have an execution in the house (Act III, Scene 1), and Cobb, *The First Floor*, in which Furnish, the upholsterer, attends with the bailiff (Act II, Scene 1).

209 McKendrick, 1982, pp. 10–12.

210 Douglas and Isherwood, *The World of Goods*.

211 Ibid., p. 118.

212 McKendrick, 1982, p. 21.

213 Lorna Weatherill, *Consumer Behaviour and Material Culture in Britain 1660–1760* (London and New York: Routledge, 1988), pp. 89–90.

214 Smollett, p. 327.

215 Rosemary Sweet, *The English Town 1680–1840: Government, Society and Culture* (Harlow: Pearson Education Limited, 1999), p. 204.

216 Smollett, pp. 325–7; Burney, 1782, p. 364.

217 Wynn House, 20 St James's Square (Robert Adam, 1771–4); Derby House, Grosvenor Square (Robert Adam, 1773–4); Montagu House, Portman Square (James Stuart, 1777–82); and Home House, Portman Square (James Wyatt, 1772–5; Robert Adam, 1775–7).

218 G. J. Barker-Benfield, *The Culture of Sensibility: Sex and Society in Eighteenth-century Britain* (Chicago and London: University of Chicago Press, 1992), p. 30.

219 See, for example, J. G. A. Pocock, *Virtue, Commerce, and History: Essays on Political Thought and History, Chiefly in the Eighteenth Century* (Cambridge: Cambridge University Press, 1985), p. 114: 'economic man' in the eighteenth century 'was seen as on the whole a feminised, even an effeminate being, still wrestling with his own passions and hysterias and with interior and exterior forces let loose by his fantasies and appetites, and symbolized by such archetypically female goddesses of disorder as Fortune, Luxury, and most recently Credit herself'.

220 Stone and Stone, pp. 350, 299, quoting César de Saussure, *A Foreign View of England in the Reigns of George I and George II* (London: John Murray, 1902), pp. 208–9.

Part Two   From Building to Architecture

1 Lawrence E. Klein, 'Gender and the Public/Private Distinction in the Eighteenth Century: Some Questions about Evidence and Analytic Procedure', *Eighteenth-Century Studies* 29 (1996), p. 101.

Four   Private Contentment, Public Disquiet

1 Muthesius, pp. 6–7. Less convincingly, Sykes, *Private Palaces*, suggests that lack of money rather than inclination explains why so few great London houses were built from the late seventeenth century onwards, because the building of many great mansions was linked with sudden increases in personal or estate fortunes or incomes (pp. 21–2).

2 William Chambers to Charles Turner, Esq., n.d., BL, Chambers letterbooks, vol. 1, Add MS 41133, fol. 53v.

3 Letter from Agmondesham Vesey to William Chambers, 28 September 1774, BL, Chambers letterbooks, vol. 3, Add MS 41135, fol. 47v.

4 *SL*, vol. 40, 150.

5 Cruickshank and Burton, p. xv; Cruickshank and Wyld, 1975, p. 1.

6 David Hume, *A Treatise of Human Nature*, 3 vols (London: 1739 and 1740), vol. 2, 54–5, quoted in Simon Varey, *Space and the Eighteenth-century English Novel* (Cambridge: Cambridge University Press, 1990), p. 22.

7 *The Architecture of Leon Battista Alberti. In Ten Books. . . . Translated into Italian by Cosimo Bartoli. And into English by James Leoni, Architect* (London: printed by Edward Owen for Robert Alfray, 1755), preface (unpaginated). Alberti's *De re aedificatoria* was written in 1452 and first fully published in Italy in 1485.

8 Similarly, Neil Jackson has suggested that the third-rate house in the nineteenth century was 'intended to offer the speculative builder the greatest economy, and the middle-class house-buyer the greatest value' ('Views with a Room: Taxation and the Return of the Bay Window to the Third Rate Speculative Houses of Nineteenth-century London', *Construction History* 8 (1992), 58). For details of the operations of the speculative building system, see, for example, Cruickshank and Burton, pp. 111–17).

9 Various building agreements for construction on the Bedford Estate in Bloomsbury, e.g., LE BC/95, 31/12/64, regarding houses on the south side of Great Russell Street, Woburn Abbey, Bedford Estate Office.

10 Agreement of 9 August 1766, Woburn, Bedford Estate Proposal Book D, fol. 245.

11 Summerson, 1978, p. 126. See also Stillman, p. 180: 'In the hands of a sensitive designer, the first-rate and even the second-rate house could, within limits, be given a distinctive appearance, and the third-rate and fourth-rate would have a refined sense of proportion and an artful reticence. In the hands of speculative builders without recourse to a skilled architect, on the other hand, certain minimum standards were assured but interpreted in a relatively dull manner.'

12 Summerson, 1978, pp. 128–9; Frank Kelsall, 'The London Building Acts and their Influence', unpublished paper presented at The Georgian Group, 20 February 1999.

13 Benjamin Disraeli, *Tancred: or, the New Crusade*, 'new edition' (London: Longmans, Green and Co., n.d.; first published 1847), p. 113. I am grateful to Neil Jackson for bringing this passage to my attention.

14 McKellar, *The Birth of Modern London* notes the same lack of interest in elevations in agreements for speculative building in seventeenth-century London (p. 132).

15 Notes on 85 Harley Street, English Heritage, Historians' Files, WM 250.

16 Woburn, Bedford Estate building contract LE BC/25, July 1768.

17 Olsen, p. 17. See Olsen for further discussion of town planning, particularly on the Bedford Estate, in the eighteenth and nineteenth centuries.

18 See Byrne, pp. 9, 23–4: 'There is little or no genius in the design of the plain brick houses in Bedford Square. They are plagiarized from designs that were first seen about forty or fifty years before.'

19 Cruickshank and Burton, pp. 128–9.

20 Entry dated Friday 20 January 1614 [1615] in Jones's sketchbook, quoted in J. Alfred Gotch, *Inigo Jones* (London: Methuen, 1925), pp. 81–2.

21 Cruickshank and Burton, p. 13.

22 See, for example, John Harris, 'William Kent's 44 Berkeley Square', *Apollo* 126 (1987), p. 101: 'the nobs in London were surprisingly democratically accommodated'.

23 Tanis Hinchcliffe, 'The Enlightenment Project in Restoration France: Quatremère de Quincy and the Romantics', in *Plus ça change . . . Architectural Interchange between France and Britain*, papers from the Annual Symposium of the Society of Architectural Historians of Great Britain, 1999, ed. Neil Jackson (Society of Architectural Historians of Great Britain, 2000), p. 34.

24 A. C. Quatremère de Quincy, 'Caractère', *Architecture, encyclopédie méthodique*, 3 vols (Paris, 1788–1825), vol. 1, quoted by Hinchcliffe, who suggests that he may 'have had in mind some of the new districts, such as Bedford Square, arising at the

time around the City of London which he visited during the late 1780s' (p. 34).

25 Christoph Heyl, 'We are Not at Home: Protecting Domestic Privacy in Post-Fire Middle-class London', *London Journal* 27, no. 2 (2002), p. 14. In common with many other architectural historians, Heyl makes extensive (almost exclusive) use of foreigners' reports in his arguments. While these provide a useful insight into an external view of London in this period, and its differences from continental cities, what foreigners considered notable is not necessarily indicative of the priorities or motives of London's houseowners. For further arguments against the injudicious use of this type of anecdotal evidence, see Rachel Stewart, 'Telling Tales: Anecdotal Insights into the West End House *c*.1765–*c*.1785', *Transactions of the Royal Historical Society* 13 (2003): 319–27.

26 Barbara Arciszewska, 'Classicism: Constructing the Paradigm in Continental Europe and Britain', in *Articulating British Classicism: New Approaches to Eighteenth-century Architecture*, ed. Barbara Arciszewska and Elizabeth McKellar (Aldershot: Ashgate, 2004), pp. 14–15.

27 Sir John Fielding, *A Brief Description of the Cities of London and Westminster* (1776), quoted in *SL*, vol. 29, p. 73.

28 See Port, 1995.

29 Rasmussen, p. 182.

30 Donald Olsen remarks that it was more important to the Foundling Hospital governors when developing their London estate that the houses were substantially built, rather than works of art (p. 116).

31 Cruickshank, 1992, 58–9.

32 For more on the palace front and its history see Kelsall, 1992, p. 36; Muthesius, pp. 6–7, 12–13; Stillman, pp. 263–6; and Cruickshank and Burton, p. 137.

33 See discussion of John Gwynn below for eighteenth-century arguments to this effect. For modern-day arguments, see Cruickshank and Burton, p. 125. The latter authors offer no supporting evidence, although they do provide further information about the way elevational uniformity was achieved, and by whom. See also, Olsen, p. 19: 'The initiative for making a range of houses or an entire square an imposing architectural unit often came from the builders themselves, who well understood the value of such devices in promoting a quick sale of house property.'

34 James Ralph, *A Critical Review of the Publick Buildings, Statues, and Ornaments, in and about London and Westminster* (London: 1734), pp. 108–9, repeated in the posthumous edition of 1783. Robert Morris, in his *Lectures on Architecture* (London: printed for J. Brindley, 1734), takes Ralph to task for the 'intended Satire' of this remark, suggesting that Ralph only makes the observation to set his own judgement in a good light. Morris argues that 'it is only Proportion and Beauty than can affect the Eye of the Judicious or the Ignorant, so as to please' (unpaginated preface). The satisfaction felt on viewing such a front is purely an aesthetic one, unrelated to worldly aspirations or vanity. If the trio of houses were more marketable as a result (which Morris does not go so far as to suggest), it would have nothing to do with any 'illusion of living in a palace'.

35 John Wood, *An Essay towards a Description of the City of Bath*, 2nd edn (London: 1765; repr. Bath: Kingsmead, 1969), p. 350.

36 Stillman, pp. 209–10.

37 Rasmussen, pp. 191–2.

38 Stillman, p. 228.

39 James Lewis, *Original Designs in Architecture: Consisting of Plans, Elevations and Sections, for Villas, Mansions, Town-houses, &c.*, 2 vols (London: self-published, 1780), vol. 1, 55.

40 *Town and Country Magazine* (1771) refers to the 'judicious observation and just satire' of the *Critical*

Observations by Mr Stewart, 'a young gentleman who is going to India in the company's service'. His performance was so 'ingenious' that 'it has been ascribed to Mr Horace Walpole', the paper reports (vol. 3, 102). More recently, the essay was supposed to be by the architect James Stuart (see Dianne Sigler Ames' introduction to James Stuart [John Stewart], *Critical Observations on the Buildings and Improvements of London* (1771; repr. Los Angeles: The Augustan Reprint Society, 1978)), particularly as the author writes in praise of Stuart's work at 15 St James's Square (p. 32).

41 Stuart [Stewart], 1771, p. iii.

42 Ralph's *Critical Review* is discussed at length in Matthew Craske, 'From Burlington Gate to Billingsgate: James Ralph's Attempt to Impose Burlingtonian Classicism as a Canon of Public Taste', in Arciszewska and McKellar, pp. 97–118. While Ralph, Gwynn and Stewart agree that the city's architecture should be in some measure answerable to public opinion and flatteringly representative of the nation, Ralph's particular target (in respect of London's domestic architecture) is ill-designed houses of noblemen. The aristocrat should better represent the public interest by setting good examples and high standards. As such, Ralph's criticism was more 'bottom up' than 'top down' (and controversial for that reason).

43 I have therefore based my discussion here on those comments which were directed at the individual house, its builder, or owner, or clearly of contemporary interest, such as references to the new buildings in Marylebone, at the expense of the authors' wider schemes for introducing beauty, uniformity, magnificence and regularity to the capital.

44 *The Architecture of Leon Battista Alberti*, preface (unpaginated).

45 The licence for Covent Garden (begun 1630) 'called for building that would serve to ornament the town' (Olsen, p. 39). Marc-Antoine Laugier, whose *Essay on Architecture* was published in London in 1755, was equally certain that, for a city to be well built, 'we must not abandon to the caprice of particulars [i.e., individuals] the forefronts of their houses. All that is done in the street should be determined and subject to the public authority, to the design that shall be fixed upon for the entire street' (*An Essay on Architecture* (London: T. Osborne & Shipton, 1755), p. 252).

46 Stewart, 1771, p. 1.

47 *Town and Country Magazine* 3 (1771), 305. The author of the posthumous passages in *A Critical Review of the Publick Buildings, Statues and Ornaments, in and about London and Westminster, originally written by — Ralph, Architect, and now Reprinted with very Large Additions* (London: John Wallis, 1783) also praises the Adelphi as doing 'great credit to the professional abilities of the architects, at the same time that it is an ornament to the metropolis' (p. 79).

48 Gwynn, pp. 3–5; Stewart, 1771, pp. 22–4.

49 Ibid., pp. 24, 27–9.

50 *A Companion to the Plan of London* (London: T. Kitchin and H. Parker, [1765?]). See also, for example, the description of Middlesex in the 'Account of England', *Town and Country Magazine* 5 (1773), 507–8.

51 Gwynn, p. 80; in France, Laugier recommended 'regularity and great variety', rather than 'vicious uniformity', with a different design applied to each row of houses, creating contrasts of plainness and enrichment between streets (*Essay on Architecture*, p. 253).

52 Ralph, 1783, p. 167.

53 Ralph, 1734, p. 108.

54 Gwynn, p. 80.

55 See earlier discussion, and Muthesius, p. 11: 'a row has an architectural unity which provides a heightened

social image and which speaks of a special achievement on the part of those who planned and built it and those who bought and rented it'.

56 Guillery, pp. 280–1. Arguments connecting London's planning with matters of health and safety were longstanding. In 1661, John Evelyn associated the atmospheric pollution in the city with physical and psychological harm, including incitement to rebellion, believing that bad air attacks rational capabilities. As part of his recommended measures, Evelyn 'desired the enforcement of the early Stuart proclamations against London's expansion'. See Lubbock, p. 175, discussing Evelyn's *Fumifugium: Or the Inconvenience of the Aer and Smoake of London* (1661).

57 Ogborn, pp. 91–104, including (p. 98) quote from Charles Walcot, *Considerations for the More Speedy and Effectual Execution of the Act, for Paving, Cleansing, and Lighting the City and Liberty of Westminster, and for Removing Annoyances Therein* (London, 1763), p. 7.

58 Morris, 1734, unpaginated preface.

59 Cruickshank and Wyld, 1975, p. 2.

60 See, for example, Nicholas Hawksmoor's comments on the poor quality of London housing in a letter of 17 February 1715 to Dr George Clarke, quoted in McKellar, p. 30; and a letter to *The Builder*, 15 December 1849 (I am grateful to Neil Jackson for drawing my attention to this letter, and providing a transcript).

61 Ware, p. 291. Although Ware's complaint was specifically directed at London builders, such concerns about the strength of modern building, and the reasons for its failings, were expressed in earlier times and different places. See, for example, Laugier, pp. 129–30.

62 See, for example, *St James's Chronicle; or, British Evening-post*, 31 May–2 June 1764, regarding the 'the continual Accounts given in the Papers of the Numbers of half-built

Houses that tumble down before they can be finished'.

63 [James Peacock], *Oikidia; or, Nutshells: being Ichnographic Distributions for Small Villas; Chiefly upon Œconomical Principles. In Seven Classes. With Occasional Remarks. By Jose Mac Packe, a Bricklayer's Labourer* (London: self-published, 1785), pp. 65–6. Some problems may have arisen more out of ignorance than design. Elizabeth McKellar points out that even though Isaac Ware understood the relative qualities of stocks and place bricks, 'the strongest bricks were . . . used for the non-load bearing façade, while the weakest bricks were doing all the structural work on the inside. This paradoxical construction concept would seem to suggest that it was the illusion that the façade presented to the world, rather than the inherent strength of the building, which was of primary concern' (p. 72). But Ware says that stocks 'are used in front in building being the strongest and handsomest', while the weaker place bricks are 'used out of sight and where less stress is laid upon them' (*A Complete Body of Architecture*, p. 59), implying a misunderstanding of the stresses in construction rather than simply a desire to hide less attractive bricks. The strong and handsome stock bricks were used where they performed, Ware believed, an aesthetic and structural function. Cruickshank and Wyld (1975, p. 181) also quote this passage, calling Ware's recommendations 'a rather structurally dangerous example of the 18th-century obsession with good appearances or "facadism" '.

64 McKellar is more charitable, and perhaps more accurate, than most in suggesting that 'we might get nearer the spirit in which these houses were conceived if we consider them as temporary or short-life housing for an unstable and uncertain market' (p. 85).

65 Sykes, p. 21.

66 Stewart, 1771, p. 24.

67 Sykes, p. 100. In 1783, an observer commented that one would never believe from the bland exterior of Devonshire House whom or what it contained.

68 'Thoughts on the Similarity of Manners among People of Fashion', *Lady's Magazine* 8 (1777), 64.

69 For a fuller discussion of the nature and principles of *convenance*, and its theorists, see Antoine Picon, *French Architects and Engineers in the Age of Enlightenment*, trans. Martin Thom (Cambridge: Cambridge University Press, 1992), especially pp. 85–95, which, together with Simon Varey, and John Archer, 'Character in English Architectural Design', *Eighteenth-Century Studies* 12 (1979): 339–71, I found useful for my discussions of *convenance* and propriety.

70 Laugier, p. 101; Jacques-François Blondel, *Discours sur la nécessité de l'étude de l'architecture* (Paris: 1754), p. 42, quoted in Picon, p. 89.

71 See Pears, pp. 5–6.

72 Elizabeth Montagu to Mrs Robinson, 13 June 1779, BL, Montagu correspondence, Add MS 40663, fol. 89.

73 Christopher Hussey, 'No. 12 North Audley Street, London', *Country Life*, 15 November 1962, pp. 1212–16, fig. 7; Cruickshank, 1992, p. 62.

74 Gwynn, p. 13.

75 Ibid., with reference to the backs of houses in the Circus at Bath.

76 The building agreements for Bedford Square, for example, specified front window cills to be of Portland stone but said nothing about the back ones (Byrne, p. 37).

77 This feature of the town house is not, of course, exclusive to this period, but I draw attention to it here in the light of Gwynn's writings, and because, as I shall explain below, other prescriptive writers, and designers, also had difficulty in accepting the terrace house on its own terms.

78 *SL*, vol. 39, 119. The group of houses was built by John Crunden from 1773.

79 Notes on Chandos House by Roger Bowdler, 21 February 1996, English Heritage, Historians' Files, WM 324. The house was faced with a grey-pink Craigleith stone, which may have come from Aberdeen quarries with a connection to the Adam family. The use of this stone, imported from such a distance, was an unusual expense in a speculative house and perhaps intended to draw attention to the Adams and the resources at their disposal, or to widen the market for their stone. The stone front was not enough, however, to make the house sell quickly: see Tara Draper, 'Chandos House', *Georgian Group Journal* 7 (1997): 130–9, especially pp. 132, 133, 137 and note 20, p. 138.

80 Draper, 1997, p. 130. It is notable, therefore, that private, commercial interests, rather than the public interest championed by Gwynn and Stewart, were at the root of Chandos House's contribution to the townscape.

81 Stillman, p. 230.

82 Bolton, 1922, vol. 1, 76. Bolton observes, too, that Adam 'has thereby incurred the bitterest censures of the logical and serious minded historians of architecture'.

83 Wood, p. 350.

84 Byrne, p. 49.

85 Clients were not always prepared to go to the extra expense of elaborating a rear façade. Arthur Bolton ('No. 17 Hill Street, W.', *Country Life*, 17 March 1917a, pp. 2*–6*) suggests that at 17 Hill Street Sir Abraham Hume declined to carry out Robert Adam's plan design for the elevation of the back wing, because it could not be seen well from the house (p. 6*).

86 Cruickshank and Burton, p. 51.

87 Varey, p. 157.

88 [Peacock], p. 73.

89 Harold D. Kalman, 'The Architecture of Mercantilism: Commercial Buildings by George Dance the Younger', in *The Triumph of Culture: 18th Century Perspectives*, ed. Paul Fritz

and David Williams (Toronto: Hakkert, 1972), p. 78.

90 Ibid., pp. 75–8.

91 *SL*, vol. 39, p. 124.

92 The house's present use as an exclusive club perpetuates this tradition. See Lesley Lewis, 'Elizabeth, Countess of Home, and her House in Portman Square', *Burlington Magazine* 109 (1967): 443–53, for a thesis that the house was originally a surrogate 'royal palace' for the reception of the Duke and Duchess of Cumberland and their circle at the time of their banishment from the court.

Five   The Town House Dismissed

1 The passages quoted and discussed here are taken from the third edition (London: Joseph Smeeton, 1791; repr. Farnborough: Gregg International, 1969).

2 Ibid., pp. i–ii.

3 There was a sharp decline in the 1780s and 1790s both in numbers of publications and the percentage of first editions. Information extracted from Eileen Harris, *British Architectural Books and Writers, 1556–1785* (Cambridge: Cambridge University Press, 1990).

4 Jill Lever and John Harris define vernacular architecture as 'Designed by one without any training in design guided by a tradition based on local needs, materials and construction methods. Unconcerned with national or international styles, vernacular architecture is essentially local and conservative' (*Illustrated Dictionary of Architecture 800–1914* (London, 1993), p. 42), quoted in Guillery, p. 2. Guillery also observes there that 'Recently, new emphasis has been given to the complex interplay of the traditional, or vernacular, with the innovative, or polite, in the rise of speculative building', notably in Cruickshank and Burton's *Life in the Georgian City* (1990) and McKellar's *The Birth of Modern London* (1999).

5 See Arciszewska, pp. 18–19.

6 See John Wilton-Ely on 'The Rise of the Professional Architect in England', in *The Architect: Chapters in the History of the Profession*, ed. Spiro Kostof (New York and Oxford: Oxford University Press, 1977), pp. 180–208, regarding the development of this new role of 'architect' in the later eighteenth century, with Chambers and Adam at the forefront of 'this new breed of professionals' advancing 'personal philosophies of design fashioned by aesthetic judgment from the widest range of visual sources' (pp. 190–1).

7 Robert Campbell, *The London Tradesman, being a Compendious View of All the Trades, Professions, Arts . . . in the Cities of London and Westminster* (London: T. Gardner, 1747; repr. New York: Augustus M. Kelley, 1969), p. 158.

8 Ware, p. 345. He repeated these observations on 'common houses in London' in the 1767 edition.

9 *The Architecture of Leon Battista Alberti*. The first edition had appeared in 1739. All subsequent references are to the 1755 edition of Leoni's translation, unless otherwise indicated.

10 Morris, 1734, p. 66. See also John Aheron's self-confessedly unoriginal *A General Treatise of Architecture in Five Books* (Dublin: self-published, 1754).

11 The two publications overlap in content so closely in this and other respects as to allow the attribution of the former, anonymous work to Morris. See Eileen Harris, 1990, p. 317.

12 Ware, p. 95.

13 Morris, 1734, pp. iv–v.

14 Smollett, pp. 150–2.

15 Letter from Mrs Montagu to William Pepys, October 1780, *Mrs Montagu, 'Queen of the Blues'*, p. 103.

16 Ware, p. 97.

17 Morris, *An Essay upon Harmony as it Relates Chiefly to Situation and*

Building (London: printed for T. Cooper, 1739), pp. 13, 15, 26.

18 Ware, p. 96.

19 *Public Advertiser*, 17 May 1775.

20 *Public Advertiser*, 24 March 1775.

21 General Robert Clerk to the Earl of Shelburne from Paris, 14 May 1765, quoted in Bolton, 1922, vol. 2, 3.

22 Morris, 1734, pp. 67–70; see also in Morris, 1739, pp. 33–5.

23 Morris, 1734, pp. 63–4.

24 Ware, p. 95.

25 Ibid.

26 Morris, 1734, p. 70.

27 Ibid., p. 71.

28 Thomas Skaife, *A Key to Civil Architecture; or, The Universal British Builder* (self-published, 1774), p. 31.

29 Ware, p. 291.

30 See, for example, ibid., p. 293.

31 Morris, 1734, pp. 83–4.

32 Ware, p. 291.

33 *The Builder's Magazine* (London: self-published, 1774–8), pp. 240–1.

34 Varey, p. 20, with reference to Germain Boffrand's *Livre d'architecture contenant les principes généraux de cet art* (Paris, 1745), p. 11.

35 Jacques-François Blondel, *Discours sur la nécessité de l'étude de l'architecture* (Paris: 1754), p. 42, quoted in Picon, p. 89; Archer, p. 345, with reference to volume 2 of the *Cours*. For further discussion of the concept of 'character' as developed in France and England in the eighteenth century, and its relation to *convenance*, see Archer; Varey, pp. 18–21; and Picon, pp. 85–92.

36 Skaife, 1776, p. 33.

37 Ware, p. 299.

38 Morris, 1739, p. 7; Morris, 1734, p. 81.

39 Skaife, 1776, pp. 33–4.

40 Morris, 1734, p. 90.

41 Ibid., p. 71.

42 Ibid., p. 104.

43 Ware, p. 319.

44 Ibid., and plate 34.

45 Ibid., p. 335. The same advice had been trotted out over the decades, and was not, therefore, specific to the period (even though it was repeated in *The Builder's Magazine* in the 1770s, p. 238) or, necessarily, the building type.

46 Ibid., p. 325.

47 *Society of Gentlemen: Encyclopaedia Britannica* (1771), ed. Terence M. Russell, vol. 5 of *The Encyclopaedic Dictionary in the Eighteenth Century: Architecture, Arts and Crafts*, 5 vols (Aldershot: Ashgate, 1997), p. 37. More recently, Dan Cruickshank and Neil Burton have observed that 'even the most adamant of Palladian designers seemed unequal to the task of applying their theories of proportional relationships to the interior [of the terrace house] when faced by the daunting practical problems of fitting a delicately balanced mix of rooms . . . into a constricted site' (Cruickshank and Burton, p. xv).

48 Ware, p. 294.

49 Ibid., p. 295.

50 Ibid.

51 Smollett, p. 150.

52 Ware, p. 322.

53 Ibid., p. 300.

54 Skaife, 1774, p. 36.

55 Ware, p. 315.

56 Morris, 1734, pp. 111–12.

57 Ware, p. 279; Plate 30, p. 287.

58 I am grateful to Steven Parissien for this suggestion.

59 Ware, pp. 345–7.

60 Morris, 1734, pp. 82, 83–4; Ware, p. 421.

61 Ware, p. 423–6.

62 Ibid., p. 421.

63 Morris, 1734, p. 85.

64 Ibid., p. 82.

65 Ibid., p. 85.

66 Skaife, 1776, p. 33.

67 *The Architecture of Leon Battista Alberti*, p. 100.

68 Ibid. (unpaginated).

69 Ibid., p. 10.

70 Ibid., p. 100; see also Leon Battista Alberti, *On the Art of Building in Ten Books*, trans. Joseph Rykwert, Neil Leach and Robert Tavernor

(Cambridge, Mass.: MIT Press, 1988), p. 140.

71 Alberti, p. 188. See also Rykwert, Leach and Tavernor, p. 294: 'the ornament to a town house ought to be far more sober in character, whereas in a villa the allures of license and delight are allowed . . . with a town house the boundary of the neighboring property imposes many constraints that may be treated with greater freedom in a villa.'

72 'A building will gain in comfort and even more in delight, if there is no need to go up and down a great deal. Those who say that stairs disrupt a building are quite right . . . But with a villa there is no need to add story above story. The greater openness allows the villa to take up the most appropriate distribution of space, with one part leading off another, all on the same level; I would also be delighted to find this in a city, if only it were possible.' (Rykwert, Leach and Tavernor, p. 294.)

73 Arciszewska, p. 2.

74 Morris, 1734, p. 65.

75 Ibid.

76 For example, in 1757 James Paine reported disagreements with ground landlords and their neighbours, as well as obstruction by their agents, in his search for a suitable site for the Earl of Scarborough's house (letter from Paine to Scarborough, 24 March 1757, in the archives at Sandbeck Park, Yorkshire. I am grateful to the late 12th earl for bringing this letter to my attention).

77 Ware, p. 322.

78 Leadbeater, 1770.

79 For the purposes of this chapter, I looked at each edition of pattern books published or republished in this period, and available for study in the Bodleian Library, the British Library and the National Art Library at the Victoria and Albert Museum. I have listed in the bibliography only those publications referred to in the text, rather than the many books that only proved the town house's general neglect through an absence of appropriate designs.

80 Stillman, pp. 179, 215–16.

81 Skaife, 1776, p. 33.

82 Robert Morris, *Select Architecture*, 2nd edn (London: 1757). This publication was a later edition of Morris's *Rural Architecture* (1750).

83 William Pain, *The Builder's Golden Rule; or, The Youth's Sure Guide* (London: self-published, 1781).

84 Tait, p. 80.

85 John Crunden, *Convenient and Ornamental Architecture, Consisting of Original Designs for Plans, Elevations, and Sections* (London: self-published, 1770), p. 7. There are no relevant differences, if any, between the coverage of the London town house in the editions of 1767, 1770 and 1785. All references are to the 1770 edition unless otherwise indicated.

86 William Thomas's *Original Designs in Architecture* (London: self-published, 1783) appeared in only this edition, but it had an impressive subscriber list among architects, including Robert Adam, William Chambers, Henry Holland, Robert Mylne, James Stuart, and both Samuel and James Wyatt.

87 James Lewis, *Original Designs in Architecture: Consisting of Plans, Elevations, and Sections, for Villas, Mansions, Town-houses, &c.*, 2 vols (London: self-published, 1780).

88 William and John Halfpenny, Robert Morris and T. Lightoler, *The Modern Builder's Assistant* (London, 1757; repr. Farnborough: Gregg International, 1971), p. 45 and plates 54 and 55.

89 George Richardson, *New Designs in Architecture Consisting of Plans, Elevations, and Sections for Various Buildings* (London: self-published, 1792), p. ii.

90 Crunden, p. 19; pp. 25–6.

91 Thomas Rawlins, *Familiar Architecture; Consisting of Original De-*

signs for Houses for Gentlemen and Tradesmen, Parsonages and Summer Retreats &c. (self-published, 1768), p. iii.

92 Ibid., p. iv.

93 See Guillery, p. 286: 'In 1775 nearly 77 per cent of London builders built five or fewer houses in the year, only 9 per cent erected more than 10.'

94 Halfpenny et al, p. 36.

95 Crunden, p. 13.

96 Halfpenny et al, p. 36.

97 See Public Advertiser, 4 January 1775.

98 Builder's Magazine, 1774–8, pp. 10, 31, 33, 64; plates 20, 56, 60, 97.

99 Halfpenny et al, p. 36.

100 Geoffrey Tyack, 'Architecture and Planning in the Provincial Town', unpublished paper presented at The Georgian Group, 20 February 1999. Stillman (p. 193) notes that five- to seven-bay houses, perhaps partially freestanding, but with little surrounding space, were more common in other cities and large towns.

101 See Pierre Le Muet, Maniere de bien bastir, Paris, 1664, with the addition of a new introduction by Sir Anthony Blunt (Gregg International Publishers Ltd, 1972).

102 Ware, p. 345.

103 Port, 1995, p. 31.

104 SL, vol. 30, 515.

105 Stewart, 1771, p. 31.

106 Lewis, p. 5.

107 Blondel, Cours, vol. 4, p. xlvi, as discussed by Picon, p. 93.

108 Ware, 1767, p. 319, and plate 34.

109 It is not certain that Leverton designed the house, but Andrew Byrne provides considerable evidence to support his assertion in Bedford Square: An Architectural Study.

Six   Making a Town House Architecture

1 The first volume is dated 1778 on the title page, but was published in parts from 1773. The second volume was published in parts from 1777. A third, posthumous volume appeared in 1822. As Julius Bryant explains, it 'amounts to a publisher's miscellany of engravings not used in the earlier editions' (Bryant, p. 23). The following discussion and analysis of the Works excludes this last volume.

2 Morris, 1739, pp. 31–2.

3 Robert and James Adam, The Works in Architecture, 3 vols (London: self-published, 1773, 1779, 1822), vol. 2, preface (unpaginated).

4 Ibid., vol. 2, Part 1, explanation of plate 1.

5 See Eileen Harris, 2001, p. 5, for discussion of the influence of early eighteenth-century French planning on Robert Adam's practice.

6 Adams, vol. 2, Part 2, explanation of plate 1.

7 The eating room, music room and library on the ground floor, the two withdrawing rooms and Lady Wynn's dressing room on the first floor, and the great staircase.

8 Adams, vol. 2, Part 2, explanation of plate 2.

9 Morris, 1734, p. 82.

10 Adams, vol. 1, p. 3.

11 Ibid., vol. 1.

12 Ibid., vol. 1.

13 Tara Draper, 'The London Townhouses of Robert Adam 1761–1792: The Redefinition of a Building Type' (unpublished MA dissertation, University of London, 1992), p. 19.

14 Bolton, 1922, vol. 2, p. 48.

15 Draper, 1997, p. 133. Wings with stairs had appeared in earlier town houses, such as 43 Brook Street (c.1725). 'Adam's innovation was to make it into a private suite, the stair connecting the Lord's and Lady's rooms' (Draper, 1992, p. 27, n. 51). See also Richard Garnier's cogent argument (Garnier, 2002, p. 182) that 'the origins of the fully-developed 1770s grand town house plan' are to be found in the 1750s, and should be credited to Sir Robert Taylor on the basis of evidence from houses in Artillery Lane (1756–7) and elsewhere.

16 Draper, 1997, p. 134.

17 See Draper, 1992, pp. 11–16 for a discussion of the development of the split between private and public spaces in Adam's earlier designs for larger town houses, especially Bute (later Shelburne, then Lansdowne) House, Berkeley Square (begun 1762), and Shelburne's proposed house at Hyde Park Corner. See also Garnier, 2002, especially p. 182, regarding Sir Robert Taylor's contribution to this development.

18 For example, the dining room at 29 Percy Street (c.1765) is still panelled in the manner of the 1740s, while the drawing room on the first floor has fashionable plastered walls (Cruickshank and Burton, p. 70).

19 Arthur Oswald, 'The Preservation of an Adam House: No. 20 St James's Square', *Country Life*, 5 August 1939b, p. 120.

20 Draper, 1997, p. 137.

21 Harris, 2001, p. 258; Harris notes the precedents of the Temples of the Sun and Moon near the Arch of Titus in Rome, published by Palladio, and William Chambers's unexecuted designs for York House, Pall Mall, exhibited at the Society of Artists in 1761. Adam is likely to have known both. See Harris for a full description of the house and the evolution of its planning; and Draper, 1992, p. 33. John Olley ('20 St James's Square, Part 1', *Architect's Journal*, 21 February 1990, pp. 34–57) suggests that the house's shell was well under way before Adam became involved with the project (p. 52).

22 Eileen Harris, 2001, p. 259.

23 John Martin Robinson, 'No. 20 St James's Square, London', *Country Life*, 2 November 1989, p. 156.

24 Draper, too, suggests that Adam's 'great achievement' in his prominent terrace-house commissions 'was to make the viewer forget they were within the narrow confines of a London townhouse' (Draper, 1992, p. 49).

25 Robinson, 1989, p. 156.

26 Eileen Harris, 2001, p. 261.

27 Ibid., p. 265.

28 Ibid., p. 280.

29 Burney, 1782, p. 97; Burney, 1778, p. 277.

30 Eileen Harris, 2001, p. 282.

31 Ibid., p. 287.

32 Ibid., p. 279.

33 Ibid., p. 315.

34 Ibid., p. 300.

35 Ibid.

36 Tait, p. 80.

37 Chris Miele, ' "The First Architect of the World" in Brighton: Robert Adam, Marlborough House, and Mrs Fitzherbert', *Sussex Archaeological Collections* 136 (1998), p. 164.

38 The undated plan is among papers including correspondence between Paine and the Earl of Scarborough, held at Sandbeck Park, Yorkshire, regarding the search for suitable building sites in London in the late 1750s. The shapes of the rooms on the plan suggests a date in the 1760s or later. The late 12th earl believed that the plan was unexecuted, at least for his family, and had not been published. I am very grateful to him for bringing this plan to my attention.

39 *London Chronicle*, 27–30 September 1788, quoted in Stillman, pp. 181–2. The house was still admired in the next century, although the writer was less convinced of the 'economy of space', suggesting that the price for 'artistical feeling' was 'a greater sacrifice of room and convenience than we would be willing to make' (*The Builder*, 1846, quoted in Binney, 1984, p. 59).

40 Garnier, 2003, pp. 208–9, 213.

41 Ibid., p. 232.

42 Ibid., p. 231. See also for further, detailed discussion and illustration of the planning of the Grafton Street houses, especially pp. 230–42, and Fig. 13.

43 Ibid., p. 241.

44 Ibid.

45 Quoted in Arthur Oswald, 'No. 44 Berkeley Square: The Residence of Wyndham Damer Clark, Esq.', *Country Life*, 8 July 1939a, p. 15.

46 Mark Girouard, '44 Berkeley Square, London', *Country Life*, 27 December 1962, p. 1648, and Oswald, 1939a, p. 15.

47 Sykes, p. 111.

48 Neil Burton, unpublished paper on Georgian town-house plans, presented at The Georgian Group, 19 January 1999.

49 Oswald, 1939a, p. 15.

50 Christopher Hussey, 'No. 12 North Audley Street', *Country Life*, 11 April 1925, p. 566.

51 [Peacock], 1785, pp. 73–4. Peacock's publication chiefly concerns small villas, but he declared his musings to have a broader application (p. 51).

52 Pierre-Jean Grosley, *A Tour to London; or, New Observations on England, and its Inhabitants*, trans. Thomas Nugent, 2 vols (London: Lockyer Davis, 1772), vol. 1, 41.

53 The original façades of St James's Square, begun in the late 1660s, appear to have conformed to a pattern, but subsequent rebuildings had destroyed any sense of uniformity by this time.

54 Dan Cruickshank and Peter Wyld, *Georgian Town Houses and their Details*, rev. edn (London: Butterworth Architecture, 1990), p. 47.

55 The drawing shows the house with only the centre three bays rusticated at ground-floor level, whereas Adam's own drawing has the rustication pencilled in on one of the outer bays. The 1821 image also shows the house without roofline statues; David King assumes they were erected and later removed, as one of many changes made to the front over the years (King, p. 291).

56 Leach, p. 105. An exception to this trend was the front to the Hon. Thomas Fitzmaurice's house at 105 Pall Mall (1779–80), in which 'the refacing was entirely in the Adam manner, with rustication to the ground floor, a giant pilaster order to the first and second, and the third treated as a pilastered attic with a sec-ondary entablature crowned by vases' (Leach, p. 196). It would be interesting to know whether this change was stimulated by the other options for creating integrity demonstrated by the Adams at, for example, 20 St James's Square (which itself depended on James Stuart's earlier façade at 15 St James's Square), or a result of the Adam firm's involvement in executing the façade.

57 Ibid., p. 105. Leach's observations, prompted by his close study of Paine's practice, are exceptional in the literature on the town house in noting the distinction between integrity and integration, although not in those terms.

58 See ibid., pp. 105–10, for more discussion, and illustrations, of Paine's treatment of individual façades beneath this pediment. The gable was a traditional feature of northern architecture and naturally divided up houses into units, at least at roof level. Paine's pedimented roofs reinstate this tradition, and its visual effect, within the classical idiom.

59 Christopher Hussey says that the front at Ely House solves in an unusually satisfactory manner the problem faced by architects of making the façade both self-contained and part of the street elevation (quoted in Binney, 1984, p. 67). But it is only the latter in a physical sense; the visual balance is in favour of its integrity and a viewer would have singled out the façade for special scrutiny rather than incorporating it in a composite view of the street.

60 Stucco was a cheaper means of achieving the same effect. Draper suggests that the use of stone in the fronts of 15 and 20 St James's Square, by Stuart and Adam, respectively, is deliberately intended to give the buildings something of a public character (Draper, 1992, p. 35).

61 English Heritage, Historians' Files, WM 749, report by Historic Buildings Consultants [?John Martin Robinson], August 2000.

62 Binney, 1984, p. 67, quoting Christopher Hussey.

63 English Heritage, Historians' Files, WM 749, report by Historic Buildings Consultants [?John Martin Robinson], August 2000.

64 For a detailed description of the façade, see *SL*, vol. 33, 118–19. Arthur Bolton attributed this design to the Adams, but the *Survey* believes him mistaken in this.

65 See Bolton, 1922, vol. 2, *Topographical Index to the Collection of Adam Drawings Now in the Sir John Soane Museum*, pp. 33–51.

66 Stewart, 1771, p. 32.

67 *SL*, vol. 39, 124.

68 English Heritage, Historians' Files, WM 170, copies of documents formerly at the Greater London Record Office, reference 85/223–64, now at the London Metropolitan Archives.

69 Stewart, 1771, p. 32. The author of the posthumous passages to the 1783 edition of James Ralph's *Critical Review*, while thinking the former houses beautiful 'when singly considered', found them 'exceedingly deficient' as potential parts of a greater whole he believed the builder had intended (Ralph, 1783, p. 172).

70 Stillman, p. 194.

71 Byrne, p. 76.

72 Tara Draper reaches the same conclusion in her dissertation on Robert Adam's redefinition of this building type: Adam was 'the first architect to fully comprehend the changing function of the terrace house and to redefine its shape' (Draper, 1992, p. 49).

73 Roy Porter, p. 114.

Conclusion   The Town House Reassessed

1 Summerson, 1978, p. 111; Clunas, p. 1501, with reference to arguments presented in essays in Brewer and Staves, *Early Modern Conceptions of Property*.

2 Lubbock, p. 39.

3 Locock, p. 1.

4 Foreman, p. 45.

5 *Public Advertiser*, 24 October 1775.

6 Draper, 1999, p. 120.

7 *The Architecture of Leon Battista Alberti*, p. 24.

8 See discussion of the attention paid to a new method of fireproofing in Chapter Three, p. 83.

9 Lady Holland to Marchioness of Kildare, 20 September 1764, *Leinster Letters*, vol. 1 (1949), p. 413.

10 William Chambers to Lord Grantham, 29 April 1774, BL, Chambers letterbooks, vol. 3, Add MS 41135, fol. 17v.

11 Bristol, p. 2.

12 Ibid., Mrs Montagu to Mrs Robinson, 2 March 1782, BL, Montagu correspondence, Add 40663, fols 112–13.

13 Arthur T. Bolton, '19 Arlington Street', *Country Life*, 17 September 1921, p. 354.

14 *The World*, 2 August 1787, quoted in Low, p. 2470.

15 William Palgrave to William Weddell, 8 November 1789, quoted in ibid., p. 2471.

16 *Gentleman's Magazine* 42 (1772), 61–2.

17 Burney, 1782, p. 100. Jules Lubbock discusses how in Daniel Defoe's *Roxana* (1724) the eponymous heroine's 'very identity appears to be continuously shifting and changing as she changes her lovers, her clothes and her houses' (Lubbock, p. 181).

18 Mrs Carter to Miss Talbot, 12 January 1760, *Carter Letters*, vol. 2, 311.

19 Cruickshank and Wyld, 1975, pp. 35, 181.

20 *SL*, vol. 39, 122.

21 Kent, Sackville papers, U269/E146/3.

22 From Davenant's description of London, given in James Peller Malcolm's *Anecdotes of the Manners and Customs of London during the Eighteenth Century* (London: Longman, Hurst, Rees and Orme, 1808), p. 455. No date is given for Davenant's writings, but several aspects of them suggest a date in the second half of the eighteenth century.

23 Robert Jones, *Gender and the Formation of Taste in Eighteenth-century Britain: The Analysis of Beauty* (Cambridge: Cambridge University Press, 1998), p. 6.

24 See Langford, 1991, p. 380 and discussion in Chapter Three above. This was a very longstanding notion; see Lubbock (p. xiv) regarding seventeenth-century worries to this effect: 'It was argued that the gentry and nobility flocked [to London] on their shopping sprees, and lived there *privately*, neglecting their *public* duties, draining their districts of the benefit of their expenditure and, insofar as the luxuries that they bought were foreign, the whole country as well.'

25 Mrs Carter to Mrs Vesey, 18 January 1768, *Carter Letters*, vol. 3, 327.

26 Christopher Gotch, 'Mylne and Adam', *Architectural Review* 119 (1956), p. 121.

27 *Horace Walpole's Correspondence*, ed. W. S. Lewis and others, 48 vols (London: Oxford University Press, 1937–83), vol. 33 (1965), 500, letter to Lady Ossory, 17 September 1785; vol. 29 (1955), 184, letter to Revd William Mason, 14 February 1782.

28 David Garrick, *Bon Ton; or, High Life above Stairs. A Comedy in Two Acts*, 1775.

29 *Horace Walpole's Correspondence*, vol. 32 (1965), 371, letter to Lady Ossory, 8 August 1777.

30 John Harris, 1970, p. 76.

31 Mrs Carter to Mrs Vesey, 18 January 1768, *Carter Letters*, vol. 3, 328.

32 [Peacock], p. 73.

33 Summerson, p. 132.

34 [Peacock], p. 73.

35 Sir Harry Beaumont [Joseph Spence], *Crito; or, a Dialogue on Beauty* (London: 1752), quoted in Jones, p. 94.

36 See Jones, *Gender and the Formation of Taste*, for more on connections drawn between taste and gender in eighteenth-century Britain.

37 [Peacock], pp. 73–4.

38 For more on this characterisation of women, see Barker-Benfield, especially pp. 26 and 29–32.

39 Penny Sparke, *As Long as it's Pink: The Sexual Politics of Taste* (London: Pandora, 1995), p. ix.

40 Morris, 1757, preface (unpaginated).

41 Definitions from Nathan Bailey's *Universal Etymological English Dictionary* (1721), Thomas Dyche's *New General English Dictionary* (1735) and Samuel Johnson's *Dictionary of the English Language* (1755) respectively, quoted in Philip Carter, 'Men About Town: Representations of Foppery and Masculinity in Early Eighteenth-century Urban Society', in *Gender in Eighteenth-century England: Roles, Representations and Responsibilities*, ed. Hannah Barker and Elaine Chalus (Harlow: Addison Wesley Longman Limited, 1997), p. 41.

42 Carter, 1997, pp. 41, 54.

43 Ibid., p. 55. Other characteristics of foppishness are also taken from Carter, especially pp. 41, 53–5.

Bibliography

Manuscript sources

This list gives the location of manuscript collections consulted for the purposes
   of this book. Full references relating to individual documents explicitly
   referred to are given in the endnotes.

Badminton, Gloucestershire, Badminton muniments

Berkshire Record Office, Reading, Benyon papers, D/EBY

——, Downshire papers, D/ED

——, Radley Estate papers, D/EB 1089 Bo

British Library, London, Adair papers, Add MS 53808

——, Althorp papers, F 42–45, 104, 114–116

——, Chambers letterbooks, 3 vols, Add MSS 41133–41135

——, Hamilton and Greville papers, vol. 1, Add MS 40714

——, Holland House papers, Add MSS 51342–3, 51352, 51354, 51357

——, Hurd papers, Egerton MS 1958

——, Liverpool papers, Add MS 38470

——, Montagu correspondence, Add MS 40663

——, Morley papers, vol. 1, Add MS 48218

——, Newcastle papers, Add MS 33071

——, Pelham papers, Add MS 33092

Buckinghamshire Record Office, Aylesbury, Drake papers, D/DR

——, Hartwell papers, D/LE

Caernarfon Record Office, Caernarfon, Newborough collection, XD2

Centre for Kentish Studies, Maidstone, Milles (Watson) papers, U791

——, Maidstone, Sackville papers, U269

——, Sackville Tufton papers, U455

City of Westminster Archives, London, various ratebooks
Derbyshire Record Office, Matlock, Burdett papers, D5054
——, Harpur-Crewe papers, D2375
Dorset Record Office, Dorchester, Fox-Strangways papers, D/FSI
Essex Record Office, Colchester, Audley End Estate papers, D/DBY
——, Petre papers, D/DP
Gloucestershire Record Office, Gloucester, Badminton papers, D2700
Guildhall Library, London, Christ's Hospital archives, tenancy agreement books, MSS 12853, 12879, 12811
——, MS 11936/202-4, Sun Insurance Office, policy registers, old series, 1770-1, 290901-293800
Hampshire Record Office, Winchester, Clarke-Jervoise papers, 6M59
Hertfordshire Archives and Local Studies, Hertford, Brand papers, D/Ehm
——, D/ECd
——, Lamb/Melbourne papers D/ELb
——, Ashridge II collection, AH
——, Grimston of Gorhambury, Earls of Veralum papers, D/EV
——, Radcliffe family of Hitchin Priory papers, D/ER
Lincolnshire Archives, Lincoln, Ancaster papers
——, Stubton papers
London Metropolitan Archives, London, Ashburnham papers, ref. GLRO, MRO, Acc 524
Manchester, University of, John Rylands Library, Thrale-Piozzi papers, Eng MS 551
National Library of Wales, Aberystwyth, Wynnstay papers
Northamptonshire Record Office, Northampton, Bateman-Hanbury papers, BH (K)
——, Finch Hatton papers, FH
——, Grafton papers, G
——, Stowe papers, T (S)
Nottingham, University of, Hallward Library, Newcastle papers, Ne A, Ne C
——, Portland papers, Pw F
Oxford, University of, Bodleian Library, MS Eng misc c504
Sandbeck Park, Yorkshire, Scarborough papers
Staffordshire Record Office, Stafford, Bagot papers, D5121
——, Hand Morgan papers, D1798
——, Jerningham/Stafford papers, D641/3
——, King family of Stourbridge papers, D648
——, Legge/Dartmouth papers, D1501
——, Littleton/Hatherton papers, D260
Suffolk Record Office, Bury St Edmunds, Grafton (Fitzroy) papers, HA 513
Surrey History Centre, Woking, Frederick papers, 183
Warwickshire County Record Office, Warwick, Seymour of Ragley papers, CR 114
West Yorkshire Archive Service, Leeds, Newby Hall papers, NH

———, Nostell Priory papers, NP

———, Ramsden papers

Wiltshire and Swindon Record Office, Trowbridge, a'Court papers, WRO 635

———, Brudenell-Bruce (Ailesbury) papers, WRO 9, 111, 1300

Woburn Abbey, Bedford Estate Office, Bedford Estate building contracts, LE BC

———, Bedford Estate proposal books, D-E

Yorkshire Archaeological Service, Leeds, Dukes of Leeds' papers, DD

Other primary sources

Adam, Robert and James, *The Works in Architecture*, 3 vols. London: self-published, 1773, 1779, 1822

Aheron, John, *A General Treatise of Architecture in Five Books*. Dublin: self-published, 1754

Alberti, Leon Battista, *On the Art of Building in Ten Books*, trans. Joseph Rykwert, Neil Leach and Robert Tavernor. Cambridge, Mass.: MIT Press, 1988

The Architecture of Leon Battista Alberti. In Ten Books. . . . Translated into Italian by Cosimo Bartoli. And into English by James Leoni, Architect. London: printed by Edward Owen for Robert Alfray, 1755

Austen, Jane, *Pride and Prejudice*. Harmondsworth: Penguin, 1996. First published 1813

The Autobiography and Correspondence of Mary Granville, Mrs Delany: with Interesting Reminiscences of King George the Third and Queen Charlotte, ed Lady Llanover, 2nd series, 3 vols. London: Richard Bentley, 1862

The Builder's Dictionary (1734), ed. Terence M. Russell, vol. 3 of *The Encyclopaedic Dictionary in the Eighteenth Century: Architecture, Arts and Crafts*, 5 vols. Aldershot: Ashgate, 1997

The Builder's Magazine; or, Monthly Companion for Architects, Carpenters, Masons, Bricklayers, &c. as well as for Every Gentleman who would Wish to be a Competent Judge of the Elegant and Necessary Art of Building. Consisting of Designs in Architecture, in Every Stile and Taste, from the Most Magnificent and Superb Structures, Down to the Most Simple and Unadorned; Together with the Plans and Sections, Serving as an Unerring Assistant in the Construction of Any Building, From a Palace to a Cottage. London: self-published, 1774–8

Burgoyne, General John, *The Heiress: A Comedy in Five Acts*. London: 1786

Burney, Frances, *Cecilia; or, Memoirs of an Heiress*, ed. Peter Sabor and Margaret Anne Doody, with an introduction by Margaret Anne Doody. Oxford: Oxford University Press, 1988; first published 1782

———, *Evelina; or, the History of a Young Lady's Entrance into the World*, ed. with an introduction and notes by Margaret Anne Doody. Harmondsworth: Penguin, 1994; first published 1778

Campbell, R[obert], *The London Tradesman, being a Compendious View of*

All the Trades, Professions, Arts, both Liberal and Mechanic, now Practised in the Cities of London and Westminster. London: T. Gardner, 1747; repr. New York: Augustus M. Kelley, 1969

Chambers, William, *A Treatise on the Decorative Part of Civil Architecture*, 3rd edn. London: Joseph Smeeton, 1791; repr. Farnborough: Gregg International, 1969

Cobb, James, *The First Floor: A Farce, in Two Acts*. London: 1787

A Companion to the Plan of London. London: T. Kitchin and H. Parker, [1765(?)]

Correspondence of Emily, Duchess of Leinster (1731–1814), ed. Brian Fitzgerald, 3 vols. Dublin: Dublin Stationery Office, 1949, 1953, 1957

Countess of Minto, *A Memoir of the Right Honourable Hugh Elliot*. Edinburgh: Edmonstron and Douglas, 1868

——, ed., *Life and Letters of Sir Gilbert Elliot First Earl of Minto from 1751 to 1806*, 3 vols. London: Longmans, Green and Co., 1874

Court and City Magazine, vols 1–2 (1770–2)

Craftsman; or, Say's Weekly Journal, various issues, 1767, 1769

Crunden, John, *Convenient and Ornamental Architecture, Consisting of Original Designs for Plans, Elevations, and Sections: Beginning with the Farmhouse, and Regularly Ascending to the Most Grand and Magnificent Villa; Calculated both for Town and Country, and to Suit All Persons in Every Station of Life*. London: self-published, 1770; first published 1767

Daily Advertiser, 24 May 1776; 31 January 1777

Disraeli, Benjamin, *Tancred; or, the New Crusade*, 'new edition'. London: Longmans, Green and Co; n.d.; first published 1847

Dr Campbell's Diary of a Visit to England in 1775, ed. James L. Clifford, with an introduction by S. C. Roberts. Cambridge: Cambridge University Press, 1947

The Early Journals and Letters of Fanny Burney, ed. Lars E. Troide, 2 vols. Oxford: Clarendon Press, 1988 and 1990

Entick, John, *A New and Accurate History and Survey of London, Westminster, Southwark, and Places Adjacent*. London: Edward & Charles Dilly, 1766

Everyman's Magazine; or, the Monthly Repository of Science, Instruction and Amusement, vol. 2 (July 1772–April 1773)

Fielding, Henry, *Amelia*, ed. David Blewett. Harmondsworth: Penguin, 1987; first published 1751

Foote, Samuel, *The Bankrupt*. London: 1782

The Francis Letters, by Sir Philip Francis and Other Members of his Family, ed. Beata Francis and Eliza Keary, with a note on the Junius controversy by C. F. Keary, 2 vols. London, Hutchinson, 1901

Garrick, David, *Bon Ton; or, High Life above Stairs. A Comedy in Two Acts* (1775)

Gazetteer and New Daily Advertiser, various issues, 1779

Gentleman's Magazine, vols 38–55 (1768–85)

Gleanings from an Old Portfolio Containing some Correspondence between Lady Louisa Stuart and her Sister Caroline, Countess of Portarlington and

Other Friends and Relations, ed. Mrs Godfrey Clark, 3 vols. Edinburgh, 1895–8

Grosley, Pierre-Jean, *A Tour to London; or, New Observations on England, and its Inhabitants*, trans. Thomas Nugent, 2 vols. London: Lockyer Davis, 1772

Gwynn, John, *London and Westminster Improved, Illustrated by Plans. To which is Prefixed, a Discourse on Publick Magnificence; with Observations on the State of Arts and Artists in this Kingdom, wherein the Study of the Polite Arts is Recommended as Necessary to a Liberal Education: Concluded by some Proposals Relative to Places not Laid Down in the Plans.* London: self-published, 1766; repr. Farnborough: Gregg International, 1969

Halfpenny, William and John, Robert Morris and T. Lightoler, *The Modern Builder's Assistant.* London, 1757; repr. Farnborough: Gregg International, 1971

Holcroft, Thomas, *The Deserted Daughter: A Comedy, in Five Acts.* London: 1795

Horace Walpole's Correspondence, ed. W.S. Lewis and others, 48 vols. London: Oxford University Press, 1937–83

Johnson, Samuel, *A Dictionary of the English Language*, 3rd edn, 2 vols. London: 1766

The Lady's Magazine; or, Entertaining Companion for the Fair Sex, Appropriated Solely for their Use and Amusement, vols 1–11 (1770–80)

[Laugier, Marc-Antoine], *An Essay on Architecture, in which its True Principles are Explained, and Invariable Rules Proposed, for Directing the Judgment and Forming the Taste of the Gentleman and the Architect with Regard to the Different Kinds of Buildings, the Embellishments of Cities, and the Planning of Gardens.* London: T. Osborne & Shipton, 1755

Leadbeater, John, *The Gentleman and Tradesman's Compleat Assistant; or, the Whole Art of Measuring and Estimating Made Easy*, 'new edition'. A. Webley and W. Todd, 1770

LeFanu, William, ed., *Betsy Sheridan's Journal: Letters from Sheridan's Sister 1784–1786 and 1788–1790.* London: Eyre & Spottiswoode, 1960

Le Muet, Pierre, *Maniere de bien bastir pour toutes sortes de personnes*, Paris, 1664 (first published 1647) with the addition of a new introduction by Sir Anthony Blunt. Gregg International Publishers Ltd, 1972

Letters of Mary Lepel, Lady Hervey: with a Memoir, and Illustrative Notes. London: John Murray, 1821

Letters of Sarah Byng Osborn, 1721–1773, from the Collection of the Hon. Mrs McDonnel, with an introduction and further notes by John McClelland, The Stanford Miscellany, vol. 2. London: Humphrey Milford, Oxford University Press, 1930

Lewis, James, *Original Designs in Architecture: Consisting of Plans, Elevations, and Sections, for Villas, Mansions, Town-houses, &c. and a New Design for a Theatre with Descriptions and Explanations of the Plates, and an Introduction to the Work*, 2 vols. London: self-published, 1780

The Life and Letters of Lady Sarah Lennox 1745–1826: Daughter of Charles, 2nd Duke of Richmond, and Successively the Wife of Sir Thomas Charles Bunbury, Bart., and of the Hon. George Napier; also a Short Political Sketch of the Years 1760 to 1763 by Henry Fox, 1st Lord Holland, ed. Countess of Ilchester and Lord Stavordale, 2 vols. London: John Murray, 1902

The Life and Times of Frederick Reynolds, Written by Himself, 2 vols. London: Henry Colburn, 1826

London Courant and Westminster Chronicle, November 1779–December 1780

Malcolm, James Peller, *Anecdotes of the Manners and Customs of London during the Eighteenth Century; Including the Charities, Depravities, Dresses, and Amusements, of the Citizens of London, during that Period; with a Review of the State of Society in 1807. To which is Added a Sketch of the Domestic and Ecclesiastical Architecture, and of the Various Improvements in the Metropolis*. London: Longman, Hurst, Rees and Orme, 1808

Mary Hamilton, Afterwards Mrs John Dickenson, at Court and at Home. From Letters and Diaries, 1756–1816, ed. Elizabeth and Florence Anson. London: John Murray, 1925

Memoirs of William Hickey, ed. Peter Quennell. London and Boston: Routledge and Kegan Paul, 1975

Morning Chronicle and London Advertiser, various issues, 1770, 1785

Morning Post and Daily Advertiser, various issues, 1775–81

Morris, Robert (attrib.), *An Essay upon Harmony as it Relates Chiefly to Situation and Building*. London: printed for T. Cooper, 1739

——, *Lectures on Architecture, Consisting of Rules Founded upon Harmonick and Arithmetical Proportions in Building*. London: printed for J. Brindley, 1734

——, *Select Architecture: being Regular Designs of Plans and Elevations Well Suited to both Town and Country; in which the Magnificence and Beauty, the Purity and Simplicity of Designing, for Every Species of that Noble Art, is Accurately Treated, and with Great Variety Exemplified, from the Plain TOWN-HOUSE to the stately HOTEL; and in the Country from the Genteel and Convenient FARM-HOUSE to the PAROCHIAL CHURCH*, 2nd edn. London: 1757

Mrs Montagu, 'Queen of the Blues': Her Letters and Friendships from 1762 to 1800, ed. Reginald Blunt. London: Constable, 1923

The Noels and the Milbankes: Their Letters for Twenty-five Years, 1767–1792, ed. Malcolm Elwin. London: Macdonald, 1967

Pain, William, *The Builder's Golden Rule; or, The Youth's Sure Guide*. London: self-published, 1781

——, *The Practical House Carpenter; or, Youth's Instructor*. London: printed for I. and J. Taylor, 1794; first published 1788

—— and James, *Pain's British Palladio, or, The Builder's General Assistant*. London: 1786; repr. Farnborough: Gregg International Publishers Ltd, 1969

Paine, James, *Plans, Elevations, and Sections of Noblemen and Gentlemen's Houses*, 2 vols. London: self-published 1767, 1783

[Peacock, James], *Oikidia; or, Nutshells: being Ichnographic Distributions for Small Villas; Chiefly upon Œconomical Principles. In Seven Classes. With Occasional Remarks. By Jose Mac Packe, a Bricklayer's Labourer. Part the First, Containing Twelve Designs*. London: self-published, 1785

Public Advertiser, various issues 1753, 1755, 1772; all issues January–December 1775

Ralph, James, *A Critical Review of the Publick Buildings, Statues, and Ornaments, in and about London and Westminster*. London: 1734; rev. edn, 1783

Rawlins, Thomas, *Familiar Architecture; Consisting of Original Designs for Houses for Gentlemen and Tradesmen, Parsonages and Summer Retreats, &c*. Self-published, 1768

Reminiscences of Henry Angelo with Memoirs of his Late Father and Friends, Including Numerous Original Anecdotes and Curious Traits of the Most Celebrated Characters that have Flourished during the Last Eighty Years, 2 vols. London: Henry Colburn and Richard Bentley, 1830

Richardson, George, *New Designs in Architecture Consisting of Plans, Elevations, and Sections for Various Buildings*. London: self-published, 1792

Secret Comment: The Diaries of Gertrude Savile, 1721–1757, ed. Alan Savile, assisted by Marjorie Penn. Kingsbridge History Society, Devon, with the Thoroton Society of Nottinghamshire, 1997

A Series of Letters between Mrs Elizabeth Carter and Miss Catherine Talbot, from the Year 1741 to 1770. To which are Added, Letters from Mrs Elizabeth Carter to Mrs Vesey, between the Years 1763 and 1787; Published from the Original Manuscripts in the Possession of the Rev. Montagu Pennington, M. A. Vicar of Northbourn, in Kent, her Nephew and Executor, ed. Montagu Pennington, 4 vols. London: F. C. and J. Rivington, 1809

Shanhagan, Roger [Robert Smirke], *The Exhibition; or, a Second Anticipation, being Remarks on the Principal Works to be Exhibited Next Month, at the Royal Academy*. London: Richardson and Urquhart: [1779]

Sheridan, Richard Brinsley, *The School for Scandal: A Comedy*. London: 1779
——, *Plays*, edited with an introduction by Cecil Price. London: Oxford University Press, 1975

Skaife, Thomas, *A Key to Civil Architecture; or, The Universal British Builder*. Self-published, 1774; 2nd edn. London: R. Baldwin, 1776

Smollett, Tobias, *The Expedition of Humphry Clinker*. Harmondsworth: Penguin, 1985; first published 1771

Society of Gentlemen: Encyclopaedia Britannica (1771), ed. Terence M. Russell, vol. 5 of *The Encyclopaedic Dictionary in the Eighteenth Century: Architecture, Arts and Crafts*, 5 vols. Aldershot: Ashgate, 1997

St James's Chronicle; or, the British Evening-Post, various issues, 1764, 1772–4

Stewart, John, *Critical Observations on the Buildings and Improvements of London*. London: J. Dodsley, 1771

Stuart, James [John Stewart], *Critical Observations on the Buildings and*

Improvements of London, with an introduction by Dianne Sigler Ames. London: 1771; repr. Los Angeles: The Augustan Reprint Society, 1978

Swan, Abraham, *A Collection of Designs in Architecture, Containing New Plans and Elevations of Houses for General Use, with a Great Variety of Sections of Rooms; from a Common Room, to the Most Grand and Magnificent*, 2 vols. London: self-published, 1757

Thomas, William, *Original Designs in Architecture*. London: self-published, 1783

Town and Country Magazine; or, Universal Repository of Knowledge, Instructions and Entertainment, vols 1–8, 10–11 (1769–76, 1778–9)

Universal Magazine of Knowledge and Pleasure . . . Instructive and Entertaining to Gentry, Merchants, Farmers and Tradesmen, vols 46–7 (1770)

Ware, Isaac, *A Complete Body of Architecture, Adorned with Plans and Elevations from Original Designs . . . in which are Interspersed some Designs of Inigo Jones, Never Before Published*. London: T. Osborne and J. Shipton, 1756; later edition 1767

Westminster Magazine; or, the Pantheon of Taste, vols 6–8 (1778–80)

Wood, John, *An Essay towards a Description of the City of Bath*, 2nd edn. London: 1765; repr. Bath: Kingsmead, 1969

The Works of Anna Laetitia Barbauld. With a Memoir by Lucy Aikin, 2 vols. London: Longman & Co., 1825

Wortley, The Hon. Mrs E. Stuart, ed., *A Prime Minister and his Son, from the Correspondence of the 3rd Earl of Bute and Lt.-General the Hon. Sir Charles Stuart, K.B.*, with an introduction by the Rt. Hon. Sir Rennell Rodd, G.C.B., G.C.M.G., G.C.V.O. London: John Murray, 1925

The York Courant, various issues, May 1763–June 1764 and January–December 1775

Secondary sources – unpublished

Anderson, James, 'The Lawyer, the Investor and the Property Speculator: How Urban Development was Financed in Georgian England', paper presented at The Georgian Group, 19 January 1999

Burton, Neil, paper on Georgian town-house plans, presented at The Georgian Group, 19 January 1999

Draper, Tara, 'The London Townhouses of Robert Adam 1761–1792: The Redefinition of a Building Type', MA diss., University of London, 1992

English Heritage, London, Historians' Files, various files for Westminster streets and houses

Gibbison, Judith, 'The Bath Town House: An Eighteenth-century Perspective', BA diss., University of Reading, 2004

Kelsall, Frank, 'The London Building Acts and their Influence', paper presented at The Georgian Group, 20 February 1999

Robinson, John Martin, 'Samuel Wyatt, Architect', D.Phil. diss., University of Oxford, 1973

Tyack, Geoffrey, 'Architecture and Planning in the Provincial Town', paper presented at The Georgian Group, 20 February 1999

Secondary sources – published

21 *Arlington Street: A Brief History of the Building*, leaflet. Copy in the Furniture Archives, Victoria and Albert Museum, n.d.

Anderson, B. L., 'Money and the Structure of Credit in the Eighteenth Century', *Business History* 12 (July 1970): 85–101

Archer, John, 'Character in English Architectural Design', *Eighteenth-Century Studies* 12 (1979): 339–71

Arciszewska, Barbara, 'Classicism: Constructing the Paradigm in Continental Europe and Britain', in Barbara Arciszewska and Elizabeth McKellar (eds), *Articulating British Classicism: New Approaches to Eighteenth-century Architecture*. Aldershot: Ashgate, 2004, pp. 1–33

—— and Elizabeth McKellar, eds, *Articulating British Classicism: New Approaches to Eighteenth-century Architecture*. Aldershot: Ashgate, 2004

Arnold, Dana, 'The Country House: Form, Function and Meaning', in *The Georgian Country House: Architecture, Landscape and Society*, ed. Dana Arnold. Stroud: Sutton, 1998

——, ed., *The Georgian Country House: Architecture, Landscape and Society*. Stroud: Sutton, 1998

Ayres, James, *Building the Georgian City*. New Haven and London: Yale University Press, 1998

Barker, Hannah and Elaine Chalus, eds, *Gender in Eighteenth-century England: Roles, Representations and Responsibilities*. Harlow: Addison Wesley Longman Ltd, 1997

Barker-Benfield, G. J., *The Culture of Sensibility: Sex and Society in Eighteenth-century Britain*. Chicago and London: University of Chicago Press, 1992

Bermingham, Ann and John Brewer, eds, *The Consumption of Culture 1660–1800: Image, Object, Text*. London and New York: Routledge, 1995

Berry, Christopher J., *The Idea of Luxury: A Conceptual and Historical Investigation*, Ideas in Context 30. Cambridge: Cambridge University Press, 1994

Berry, Helen, 'Prudent Luxury: The Metropolitan Tastes of Judith Baker, Durham Gentlewoman', in *Women and Urban Life in Eighteenth-century England: 'On the Town'*, ed. Rosemary Sweet and Penelope Lane. Aldershot: Ashgate, 2003, pp. 131–55

Binney, Marcus, *Sir Robert Taylor: From Rococo to Neoclassicism*. London: Allen & Unwin, 1984

——'Sir Robert Taylor's Grafton Street – 1', *Country Life*, 12 November 1981, pp. 1634–7

Bolton, Arthur T., *The Architecture of Robert and James Adam*, 2 vols. London: Country Life, 1922

——, 'No. 17 Hill Street, W.', *Country Life*, 17 March 1917a, pp. 2*–6*

——, 'Nos 18 and 20 New Cavendish Street', *Country Life*, 13 October 1917b, pp. 2*–6*

——, 'No. 19 Grosvenor Square – II', *Country Life*, 18 March 1919a, pp. 267–8

——'19 Arlington Street', *Country Life*, 17 September 1921, pp. 350–5

——, 'Town Houses of England – Home House, No. 20 Portman Square, London, Robert Adam Architect 1775–7', *Country Life*, 15 November 1919b, pp. 624–9

Borsay, Peter, *The English Urban Renaissance: Culture and Society in the Provincial Town 1680–1770*. Oxford: Clarendon Press, 1989

——, 'Politeness and Elegance: The Cultural Re-fashioning of Eighteenth-century York', in *Eighteenth-century York: Culture, Space and Society*, ed. Mark Hallett and Jane Rendall. York: York University Press, 2003, pp. 1–12

Breen, T. H., 'The Meaning of Things: Interpreting the Consumer Economy in the Eighteenth Century', in *Consumption and the World of Goods*, ed. John Brewer and Roy Porter. London and New York: Routledge, 1993, pp. 249–60

Brewer, John, ' "The Most Polite Age and the Most Vicious": Attitudes Towards Culture as a Commodity, 1660–1800', in *The Consumption of Culture 1660–1800: Image, Object, Text*, ed. Ann Bermingham and John Brewer. London: Routledge, 1995, pp. 341–61

——, *The Pleasures of the Imagination: English Culture in the Eighteenth Century*. London: HarperCollins, 1997

——, *The Sinews of Power: War, Money and the English State, 1688–1783*. London: Unwin Hyman Ltd, 1989

—— and Roy Porter, eds, *Consumption and the World of Goods*. London and New York: Routledge, 1993

—— and Susan Staves, eds, *Early Modern Conceptions of Property*. London and New York: Routledge, 1995

Briggs, Peter M., ' "News from the Little World": A Critical Glance at Eighteenth-century British Advertising', *Studies in Eighteenth-century Culture* 23 (1994): 29–45

Bristol, Kerry, 'James Stuart and the London Building Trades', *Georgian Group Journal* 13 (2003): 1–11

Bryant, Julius, *Robert Adam: Architect of Genius*. London: English Heritage, 1992

Burnett, John, *A History of the Cost of Living*. London: Penguin, 1969

Byrne, Andrew, *Bedford Square: An Architectural Study* (London and Atlantic Highlands, NJ: Athlone Press, 1990)

Campbell, Colin, 'Understanding Traditional and Modern Patterns of Consumption in Eighteenth-century England: A Character-action Approach', in *Consumption and the World of Goods*, ed. John Brewer and Roy Porter. London and New York: Routledge, 1993, pp. 40–57

Campbell, D. Grant, 'Fashionable Suicide: Conspicuous Consumption and the Collapse of Credit in Frances Burney's *Cecilia*', *Studies in Eighteenth-Century Culture* 20 (1990): 131–45

Cannadine, David, *Lords and Landlords: The Aristocracy and the Towns 1774–1967*. Leicester: Leicester University Press, 1980

Carter, Philip, 'Men about Town: Representations of Foppery and Masculinity in Early Eighteenth-century Urban Society', in *Gender in Eighteenth-century England: Roles, Representations and Responsibilities*, ed. Hannah Barker and Elaine Chalus. Harlow: Addison Wesley Longman Ltd, 1997, pp. 41–57

Chalus, Elaine, 'Elite Women, Social Politics, and the Political World of Late Eighteenth-century England', *Historical Journal* 43, no. 3 (2000): 669–97

——, ' "That Epidemical Madness": Women and Electoral Politics in the Late Eighteenth Century', in *Gender in Eighteenth-century England: Roles, Representations and Responsibilities*, ed. Hannah Barker and Elaine Chalus. Harlow: Addison Wesley Longman Ltd, 1997, 151–78

Chesterman, M. R., 'Family Settlements on Trust: Landowners and the Rising Bourgeoisie', in *Law, Economy and Society: Essays in the History of English Law*, ed. David Sugarman and G. R. Rubin. Abingdon, Oxfordshire: Professional Books, 1984, pp. 124–67, plus notes on pp. i–xii

Clunas, Craig, 'Modernity Global and Local: Consumption and the Rise of the West', *American Historical Review* 104 (1999): 1497–511

Colley, Linda, *Britons: Forging the Nation 1707–1837*. London: Pimlico, 1994

Colvin, Howard M., *Biographical Dictionary of British Architects 1660–1840*, 3rd edn. New Haven and London: Yale University Press, 1995

Corfield, Penelope J., 'The Georgian Town: New Perspectives', in *Life in the Georgian Town*, papers given at the Georgian Group Symposium, 1985. London: Georgian Group, 1986, pp. 7–14

——, *Power and the Professions in Britain, 1700–1850*. London and New York: Routledge, 1995

Craske, Matthew, 'From Burlington Gate to Billingsgate: James Ralph's Attempt to Impose Burlingtonian Classicism as a Canon of Public Taste', in *Articulating British Classicism: New Approaches to Eighteenth-century Architecture*, ed. Barbara Arciszewska and Elizabeth McKellar. Aldershot: Ashgate, 2004, pp. 97–118

Crossick, Geoffrey, 'Meanings of Property and the World of the Petite Bourgeoisie', in *Urban Fortunes: Property and Inheritance in the Town, 1700–1900*, ed. Jon Stobart and Alastair Owens. Aldershot: Ashgate, 2000, pp. 50–78

Cruickshank, Dan, '29 Percy Street, London', *Country Life*, 21 November 1991, pp. 92–5

——, 'Queen Anne's Gate', *Georgian Group Journal* 2 (1992): 56–67

—— and Neil Burton, *Life in the Georgian City*. London: Viking, 1990

—— and Peter Wyld, *Georgian Town Houses and their Details*, rev. edn. London: Butterworth Architecture, 1990

——, *London: The Art of Georgian Building*. London: The Architectural Press, 1975

Davidoff, Leonore and Catherine Hall, *Family Fortunes: Men and Women of the English Middle Class, 1780–1850*. London: Routledge, 1992

De Vries, Jan, 'Between Purchasing Power and the World of Goods: Understanding the Household Economy in Early Modern Europe', in *Consumption and the World of Goods*, ed. John Brewer and Roy Porter. London and New York: Routledge, 1993, pp. 85–132

Donaldson, Ian, 'The Satirists' London', *Essays in Criticism* 25 (1975): 101–22

Doody, Margaret, *Frances Burney: The Life in the Works*. New Brunswick: Rutgers University Press, 1988

Doolittle, Ian, 'The City's West End Estate: A "Remarkable Omission" ', *London Journal* 7 (1981): 15–27

Douglas, Mary and Baron Isherwood, *The World of Goods: Towards an Anthropology of Consumption*. Harmondsworth: Penguin, 1979

Draper, Tara, 'Chandos House', *Georgian Group Journal* 7 (1997): 130–9

——, 'No. 10 Hertford Street', *Georgian Group Journal* 9 (1999): 116–38

Earle, Peter, 'The Middling Sort in London', in *The Middling Sort of People: Culture, Society and Politics in England 1550–1800*, ed. Jonathan Barry and Christopher Brooks. Basingstoke and London: Macmillan, 1994, pp. 141–58

The Eighteenth-century Town: A Reader in English Urban History 1688–1820, ed. Peter Borsay. London and New York: Longman, 1990

Ellis, Joyce M., *The Georgian Town 1680–1840*. Basingstoke: Palgrave, 2001

——, ' "On the Town": Women in Augustan England', *History Today* 45, no. 12 (Dec. 1995): 20–27

Erickson, Amy Louise, *Women and Property in Early Modern England*. London and New York: Routledge, 1993

Esdaile, Katherine, 'The Small House and its Amenities in the Architectural Hand-books', *Transactions of the Bibliographical Society* 15 (October 1917–March 1919), 115–32

Fleming, John, *Robert Adam and his Circle in Edinburgh and Rome*. London: John Murray, 1962

Foreman, Amanda, *Georgiana, Duchess of Devonshire*. London: Harper-Collins, 1999

Forty, Adrian, *Objects of Desire: Design and Society 1750–1980*. London: Thames and Hudson, 1986

Friedman, Alice T., 'The Way You Do the Things You Do: Writing the History of Houses and Housing', *Journal of the Society of Architectural Historians* 58, no. 3 (1999): 406–13

Garnier, Richard, 'Grafton Street, Mayfair', *Georgian Group Journal* 13 (2003): 201–72

——, 'Speculative Housing in the 1750s', *Georgian Group Journal* 12 (2002): 163–214

Girouard, Mark, '44 Berkeley Square, London', *Country Life*, 27 December 1962, pp. 1648–51

——, *Cities and People: A Social and Architectural History*. New Haven and London: Yale University Press, 1985

——, *The English Town: A History of Urban Life*. New Haven and London: Yale University Press, 1990

——, *Life in the English Country House: A Social and Architectural History*. New Haven and London: Yale University Press, 1978

Goffman, Erving, *The Presentation of Self in Everyday Life*. Harmondsworth: Penguin, 1990; first published 1959

Gordon, Robert W., 'Paradoxical Property', in *Early Modern Conceptions of Property*, ed. John Brewer and Susan Staves. London and New York: Routledge, 1995, pp. 95–110

Gotch, Christopher, 'Mylne and Adam', *Architectural Review* 119 (1956): 121–3

Gotch, J. Alfred, *Inigo Jones*. London: Methuen, 1925

Green, David, 'Independent Women, Wealth and Wills in Nineteenth-century London', in *Urban Fortunes: Property and Inheritance in the Town, 1700–1900*, ed. Jon Stobart and Alastair Owens. Aldershot: Ashgate, 2000, pp. 195–222

Guillery, Peter, *The Small House in Eighteenth-century London*. New Haven and London: Yale University Press, 2004

Habakkuk, John, 'Economic Functions of English Landowners in the Seventeenth and Eighteenth Centuries', in *Essays in Agrarian History*, ed. W. E. Minchinton, 2 vols. Newton Abbot: David & Charles, 1968, vol. 1, 187–201

——, *Marriage, Debt and the Estates System: English Landownership 1650–1950*. Oxford: Clarendon Press, 1994

Harris, Eileen, *British Architectural Books and Writers, 1556–1785*, assisted by Nicholas Savage. Cambridge: Cambridge University Press, 1990

——, *The Genius of Robert Adam: His Interiors*. New Haven and London: Yale University Press, 2001

Harris, John, *Sir William Chambers: Knight of the Polar Star*, with contributions by J. Mordaunt Crook and Eileen Harris, Studies in Architecture 4. London: Zwemmer, 1970

——, 'William Kent's 44 Berkeley Square', *Apollo* 126 (1987): pp. 100–4

—— and Michael Snodin, eds, *Sir William Chambers, Architect to George III*. New Haven: Yale University Press, 1996

Heal, Felicity, *Hospitality in Early Modern England*. Oxford: Clarendon Press, 1990

Heyl, Christoph, 'We are Not at Home: Protecting Domestic Privacy in Post-Fire Middle-class London', *London Journal* 27, no. 2 (2002): 12–33

Hinchcliffe, Tanis, 'The Enlightenment Project in Restoration France: Quatremère de Quincy and the Romantics', in *Plus ça change . . . Architectural Interchange between France and Britain*, papers from the Annual Symposium of the Society of Architectural Historians of Great Britain, 1999, ed. Neil Jackson. Society of Architectural Historians of Great Britain, 2000, pp. 33–42

Hoppit, Julian, 'Financial Crises in Eighteenth-century England', *Economic History Review*, 2nd series, vol. 39, no. 1 (1986a): 39–58

——, *Risk and Failure in English Business 1700–1800*. Cambridge: Cambridge University Press, 1989

——, 'The Use and Abuse of Credit in Eighteenth-century England', in *Business Life and Public Policy: Essays in Honour of D. C. Coleman*, ed. Neil McKendrick and R. B. Outhwaite. Cambridge: Cambridge University Press, 1986b, pp. 64–78

Howell, Peter and T. W. Pritchard, 'Wynnstay, Denbighshire', *Country Life*, 23 and 30 March 1972, pp. 686–9 and 782–6

Hussey, Christopher, 'The Courtauld Institute of Art: 20, Portman Square', *Country Life*, 15 and 22 October 1932, pp. 428–33 and 462–8

——, 'An Historic London House: No. 45 Berkeley Square', *Country Life*, 2 January 1937, pp. 14–18

——, 'No. 12 North Audley Street', *Country Life*, 11 April 1925, p. 564–70.

——, 'No. 12 North Audley Street, London', *Country Life*, 15 November 1962, pp. 1212–16

Jackson, Neil, 'Views with a Room: Taxation and the Return of the Bay Window to the Third Rate Speculative Houses of Nineteenth-century London', *Construction History* 8 (1992): 55–67

Jenkins, Philip, *The Making of a Ruling Class: The Glamorgan Gentry 1640–1790*. Cambridge: Cambridge University Press, 1983

Johnson, Matthew, *Housing Culture: Traditional Architecture in an English Landscape*. London: UCL Press, 1993

Jones, Robert W., *Gender and the Formation of Taste in Eighteenth-century Britain: The Analysis of Beauty*. Cambridge: Cambridge University Press, 1998

Kalman, Harold D., 'The Architecture of Mercantilism: Commercial Buildings by George Dance the Younger', in *The Triumph of Culture: 18th Century Perspectives*, ed. Paul Fritz and David Williams. Toronto: Hakkert, 1972, pp. 69–96

Kelsall, Frank, 'The Architect as Speculator', in *Georgian Architectural Practice*, papers given at the Georgian Group Symposium 1991, ed. Giles Worsley. London: Georgian Group, 1992, pp. 32–8

——, 'The London House Plan in the later 17th century', *Post-medieval Archaeology* 8 (1974): 88

——, 'Stucco', in *Good and Proper Materials: The Fabric of London since the Great Fire*, ed. Hermione Hobhouse and Ann Saunders. The Royal Commission on the Historical Monuments of England in association with the London Topographical Society, Publication no. 140, 1989, pp. 18–24

King, Anthony D., 'Introduction', in *Buildings and Society: Essays on the Social Development of the Built Environment*, ed. Anthony D. King. London: Routledge and Kegan Paul, 1980, pp. 1–33

King, David, *The Complete Works of Robert and James Adam*. Oxford: Butterworth Architecture, 1991

Klein, Lawrence E., 'Gender and the Public/Private Distinction in the Eighteenth Century: Some Questions about Evidence and Analytic Procedure', *Eighteenth-Century Studies* 29 (1996): 97–109

——, 'Property and Politeness in the Early Eighteenth-century Whig Moralists: The Case of the *Spectator*', in *Early Modern Conceptions of Property*, ed. John Brewer and Susan Staves. London and New York: Routledge, 1995, pp. 221–33

Lane, Penelope, 'Women, Property and Inheritance: Wealth Creation and Income Generation in Small English Towns, 1750–1835', in *Urban Fortunes: Property and Inheritance in the Town, 1700–1900*, ed. Jon Stobart and Alastair Owens. Aldershot: Ashgate, 2000, pp. 172–94

Langford, Paul, *Public Life and the Propertied Englishman 1689–1798*. Oxford: Clarendon Press, 1991

Lawrence, Roderick J., 'Integrating Architectural, Social and Housing History', *Urban History* 19 (April 1992): 39–63

Leach, Peter, *James Paine*, Studies in Architecture, vol. 25, ed. John Harris and Alistair Laing. London: Zwemmer, 1988

Lewis, Lesley, 'Elizabeth, Countess of Home, and her House in Portman Square', *Burlington Magazine* 109 (1967): pp. 443–53

Lieberman, David, 'Property, Commerce and the Common Law: Attitudes to Legal Change in the Eighteenth Century', in *Early Modern Conceptions of Property*, ed. John Brewer and Susan Staves. London and New York: Routledge, 1995, pp. 144–58

Locock, Martin, 'Meaningful Architecture', in *Meaningful Architecture: Social Interpretations of Buildings*, ed. Martin Locock, World Archaeology Series 9. Aldershot: Avebury, 1994, pp. 1–13

The London Encyclopaedia, ed. Ben Weinreb and Christopher Hibbert, rev. edn. London: Macmillan, 1995

Low, Jill, 'French Taste in London: William Weddell's Town House', *Country Life*, 27 December 1979, pp. 2470–2

Lubbock, Jules, *The Tyranny of Taste: The Politics of Architecture and Design in Britain, 1550–1960*. New Haven and London: Yale University Press, 1995

Mason, Roger S., *Conspicuous Consumption: A Study of Exceptional Consumer Behaviour*. Farnborough: Gower, 1981

McKellar, Elizabeth, *The Birth of Modern London: The Development and Design of the City 1660–1720*. Manchester: Manchester University Press, 1999

McKendrick, Neil, 'The Consumer Revolution of Eighteenth-century England', in *The Birth of a Consumer Society*, ed. Neil McKendrick, John Brewer and J. H. Plumb. London: Europa, 1982, pp. 9–33

——, John Brewer, and J. H. Plumb, *The Birth of a Consumer Society The Commercialization of Eighteenth-century England*. London: Europa, 1982

Miele, Chris, ' "The First Architect of the World" in Brighton: Robert Adam, Marlborough House, and Mrs Fitzherbert', *Sussex Archaeological Collections* 136 (1998), pp. 149–75

Muthesius, Stefan, *The English Terraced House*. New Haven and London: Yale University Press, 1982

Nenadic, Stana, 'Middle-rank Consumers and Domestic Culture in Edinburgh and Glasgow 1720–1840', *Past and Present* 145 (November 1994): pp. 122–56

Ogborn, Miles, *Spaces of Modernity: London's Geographies 1680–1780*. New York and London: Guilford Press, 1998

Olley, John, '20 St James's Square – Part 1', *Architect's Journal*, 21 February 1990, pp. 34–57

Olsen, Donald J., *Town Planning in London: The Eighteenth and Nineteenth Centuries*. New Haven and London: Yale University Press, 1964

Oswald, Arthur, 'No. 44 Berkeley Square: The Residence of Wyndham Damer Clark, Esq.', *Country Life*, 8 July 1939a, pp. 12–17

——, 'The Preservation of an Adam House: No. 20 St James's Square', *Country Life*, 5 August 1939b, pp. 116–20

Owens, Alastair, 'Property, Gender and the Life Course: Inheritance and Family Welfare Provision in Early Nineteenth-century England', *Social History* 26, no. 3 (2001): 299–317

—— and Jon Stobart, 'Introduction', in *Urban Fortunes: Property and Inheritance in the Town, 1700–1900*, ed. Jon Stobart and Alastair Owens. Aldershot: Ashgate, 2000, pp. 1–25

Pears, Iain, *The Discovery of Painting: The Growth of Interest in the Arts in England 1680–1768*. New Haven and London: Yale University Press, 1988

Picon, Antoine, *French Architects and Engineers in the Age of Enlightenment*, trans. Martin Thom. Cambridge: Cambridge University Press, 1992

Pocock, J. G. A., *Virtue, Commerce, and History: Essays on Political Thought and History, Chiefly in the Eighteenth Century*. Cambridge: Cambridge University Press, 1985

Port, Michael H., 'The Town and Country House: Their Interaction', in *The Georgian Country House: Architecture, Landscape and Society*, ed. Dana Arnold. Stroud: Sutton Publishing, 1998, pp. 117–38

——, 'West End Palaces: The Aristocratic Town House in London, 1730–1830', *London Journal* 20 (1995): 17–46

Porter, Roy, *London: A Social History*. Harmondsworth: Penguin, 1994

Porter, Stephen, *The Great Fire of London*. Godalming: Bramley Books, 1998

Rasmussen, Steen Eiler, *London: The Unique City*. Harmondsworth: Penguin, 1960

Raven, James, 'Defending Conduct and Property', in *Early Modern Conceptions of Property*, ed. John Brewer and Susan Staves. London and New York: Routledge, 1995, pp. 301–21

——, *Judging New Wealth: Popular Publishing and Responses to Commerce in England, 1750–1800*. Oxford: Clarendon Press, 1992

Richardson, A[lbert] E., *Robert Mylne: Architect and Engineer 1733–1811*. London: Batsford, 1955

Robinson, John Martin, 'Home House, Portman Square, London W.1', *Country Life*, 17 December 1998, pp. 32–9

——, 'No. 20 St James's Square, London', *Country Life*, 2 November 1989, pp. 152–7

Saumarez Smith, Charles, *Eighteenth-century Decoration: Design and the Domestic Interior in England*. London: Weidenfeld and Nicolson, 1993

Scammell, Lorna, 'Town Versus Country: The Property of Everyday Consumption in the Late Seventeenth and Early Eighteenth Centuries', in *Urban Fortunes: Property and Inheritance in the Town, 1700–1900*, ed. Jon Stobart and Alastair Owens. Aldershot: Ashgate, 2000, pp. 26–49

Schlarman, Julie, 'The Social Geography of Grosvenor Square: Mapping Gender and Politics, 1720–1760', *London Journal* 28 (2003): 8–28

Schofield, John, 'Social Perceptions of Space in Medieval and Tudor London Houses', in *Meaningful Architecture: Social Interpretations of Buildings*, ed. Martin Locock, World Archaeology Series 9. Aldershot: Avebury, 1994, pp. 118–206

Schwarz, L. D., 'Income Distribution and Social Structure in London in the Later Eighteenth Century', *Economic History Review* 32 (1979): 250–9

——, 'Social Class and Social Geography: The Middle Classes in London at the End of the Eighteenth Century', *Social History* 7 (1982): 167–85

Sekora, John, *Luxury: The Concept in Western Thought, Eden to Smollett*. Baltimore and London: John Hopkins University Press, 1977

Sheppard, Francis, Victor Belcher and Philip Cottrell, 'The Middlesex and Yorkshire Deeds Registries and the Study of Building Fluctuations', *London Journal* 5 (1979): 176–217

Skedd, Susan, 'Women Teachers and the Expansion of Girls' Schooling in England, c.1760–1820', in *Gender in Eighteenth-century England: Roles, Representations and Responsibilities*, ed. Hannah Barker and Elaine Chalus. Harlow: Addison Wesley Longman Ltd, 1997, pp. 101–25

Solkin, David, *Painting for Money: The Visual Arts and the Public Sphere in Eighteenth-century England*. New Haven and London: Yale University Press, 1993

Sparke, Penny, *As Long as it's Pink: The Sexual Politics of Taste*. London: Pandora, 1995

Staves, Susan, *Married Women's Separate Property in England, 1660–1833*. Cambridge, Mass. and London: Harvard University Press, 1990

——, 'Resentment or Resignation? Dividing the Spoils among Daughters and Younger Sons', in *Early Modern Conceptions of Property*, ed. John Brewer and Susan Staves. London and New York: Routledge, 1995, pp. 194–218

Stewart, Rachel, 'Telling Tales: Anecdotal Insights into the West End House c.1765–c.1785', *Transactions of the Royal Historical Society* 13 (2003): 319–27

Stillman, Damie, *English Neo-classical Architecture*, 2 vols. London: Zwemmer, 1988

Stobart, Jon and Alastair Owens, eds, *Urban Fortunes: Property and Inheritance in the Town, 1700–1900*. Aldershot: Ashgate, 2000

Stone, Lawrence, *Broken Lives: Separation and Divorce in England 1660–1857*. Oxford: Oxford University Press, 1993

—— and Jeanne C. Fawtier Stone, *An Open Elite? England 1540–1880*. Oxford: Clarendon Press, 1984

Sugarman, David and Ronnie Warrington, 'Land Law, Citizenship, and the Invention of "Englishness": The Strange World of the Equity of Redemption', in *Early Modern Conceptions of Property*, ed. John Brewer and Susan Staves. London and New York: Routledge, 1995, pp. 111–43

Summerson, John, *Architecture in Britain 1530–1830*, 9th edn. New Haven and London: Yale University Press, 1993

——, *Georgian London*, 3rd edn. London: Barrie and Jenkins, 1978

Survey of London, The Parish of St James Westminster, Part I: South of Piccadilly, gen. ed. F. H. W. Sheppard, vols 29 and 30. London: Athlone Press, 1960

——, *The Parish of St James Westminster, Part II: North of Piccadilly*, gen. ed. F. H. W. Sheppard, vols 31 and 32. London: Athlone Press, 1963

——, *The Parish of St Anne Soho*, gen. ed. F. H. W. Sheppard, vols 33 and 34. London: Athlone Press, 1966

——, *The Grosvenor Estate in Mayfair, Part I: General History*, gen. ed. F. H. W. Sheppard, vol. 39. London: Athlone Press, 1977

——, *The Grosvenor Estate in Mayfair, Part II: The Buildings*, gen. ed. F. H. W. Sheppard, vol. 40. London: Athlone Press, 1977

Sweet, Rosemary, *The English Town 1680–1840: Government, Society and Culture*. Harlow: Pearson Education Limited, 1999

—— and Penelope Lane, eds, *Women and Urban Life in Eighteenth-century England: 'On the Town'*. Aldershot: Ashgate, 2003

Sykes, Christopher Simon, *Private Palaces: Life in the Great London Houses*. London: Chatto & Windus, 1985

Tait, A. A., 'Home House', *Apollo* 126 (1987): 75–80

Tillyard, Stella, *Aristocrats: Caroline, Emily, Louisa and Sarah Lennox 1740–1832*. London: Vintage, 1995

Varey, Simon, *Space and the Eighteenth-century English Novel*, no. 7 in Cambridge Studies in Eighteenth-Century Literature and Thought, ed. Howard Erskine-Hill and John Richetti. Cambridge: Cambridge University Press, 1990

Vickery, Amanda, *The Gentleman's Daughter: Women's Lives in Georgian England*. New Haven and London: Yale University Press, 1998

Waterfield, Giles, 'The Town House as Gallery of Art', *London Journal* 20 (1995): 47–66

Watkin, David, *Athenian Stuart: Pioneer of the Greek Revival*. London: Allen and Unwin, 1982

Weatherill, Lorna, *Consumer Behaviour and Material Culture in Britain 1660–1760*. London and New York: Routledge, 1988

Williams, Peter, 'Constituting Class and Gender: A Social History of the Home, 1700–1901', in *Class and Space: The Making of Urban Society*, ed. Nigel Thrift and Peter Williams. London and New York: Routledge and Kegan Paul, 1987, pp. 154–284

Williams, Raymond, *The Country and the City*. St Albans: Paladin, 1975; first published 1973

Wilson, Richard and Alan Mackley, *Creating Paradise: The Building of the English Country House, 1660–1880*. London: Hambledon and London, 2000

——, 'How Much Did the English Country House Cost to Build, 1660–1880?', *Economic History Review* 52, no. 3 (1999): pp. 436–68

Wilton-Ely, John, 'The Rise of the Professional Architect in England', in *The Architect: Chapters in the History of the Profession*, ed. Spiro Kostof. New York and Oxford: Oxford University Press, 1977, pp. 180–208

Worsley, Giles, *Classical Architecture in Britain: The Heroic Age*. New Haven and London: Yale University Press, 1995

——, 'Entertaining Architecture', *Country Life*, 6 October 1988, pp. 142–3

Index

Page numbers in *italic* indicate where plate numbers are shown in the margin; all places are sited in London unless otherwise stated

funding building projects 104–5
links with family 56, 60–1
as paradigm 162–3
perceived as masculine 36–7, 110–11,
    196–7, 199
in property literature 14, 54
sale to finance town house purchase 57
as status symbol 16
symbolic function of 167, 187
country versus city life 30–1, 37, 42–3
court 44
    attendance at 29
Covent Garden 26, 232n45
Coventry, 6th Earl of 79
Craven, 6th Lord 47
credit, obtaining and giving 28–9, 102–4,
    191
Crewe, Mrs John 36
Crunden, John, *Convenient and Ornamental
    Architecture* 157, 157, 158, 159, 159,
    160, 160
Cumberland, Duke of 46
Curzon, Sophia 34, 101

Dance, George jnr. 134, 134, 185, 185
Darnley, earls of 66
Dartmouth, 2nd Earl of 64
Dartmouth, earls of 65
Davenant, William 195
Dean Street 97
debt 60, 96–104
    concealing 98–9
    gambling 100
decoration
    exterior 124, 132, 133–5
    interior 21, 118, 134, 170–81, 188, 194
    new styles of 2
deed registrations 203n53
Defoe, Daniel, *Roxana* 241n17
Delany, Mary 38
Derby, 12th Earl of 13, 42, 47, 51–2, 100–2,
    106, 110, 134–5, 169, 175, 191, 197
Derby, Countess of 51, 169, 191
Derby House, 26 Grosvenor Square 7, 9, 10,
    13, 42, 47, 51, 52, 110, 118, 119, 134,
    168, 168, 169, 170, 171, 174–5, 175,
    187, 191, 193, 197
    great drawing room 51, 168
detached houses 86, 202n26
Devonshire, Duchess of 45, 51–2
Devonshire House 79, 129, 164
Dimsdale, Baron 34
Disraeli, Benjamin 120, 121
distress, financial 97–9, 100

divorce 47, 212n133
Dolling, James 93
domestic architecture, analysis of 12
doors, positioning 147, 165, 179
Dorset, 3rd Duke of 51, 118, 175, 195,
    222n106
Dover Street 92
    No. 37 *see* Ely House
dower, rights of 62–3, 64
Downing Street 37–8, 96
Drake, William 92
drawing rooms 173–4
Dudley and Ward, Viscountess 93
Duke Street, Bloomsbury 119
dynastic disposal 64

Eden, Mrs William 45
education, town 33
Edwards Street, Portman Square 33, 74
Egremont, Countess of 95
Elliot, Sir Gilbert 37, 41, 58
Elliot, Hugh 47
Elliot, Isabella 39
Ely House, 37 Dover Street 184, 184
emulation, social 107–8
entails 57, 60, 81
equity of redemption 59, 214n15
Errington, Henry 76, 96
estate records 92–3
Evans, Charles 93
Evelyn, John 233n56
executions (seizure of property by creditors)
    100–2
expenditure on houses 89–96
    town and country 106
    unaffordable 104–12

façades 86, 115, 121, 122–4, 126, 128, 129–
    35, 156, 157, 162, 164, 165, 181–6, 298
    deceptiveness of 129–31
    and differentation 182, 193
    exceptional 85
    integrity and integration 182
    uniformity in 21, 182, 240n53
facadism 3, 194, 233n63
fashion 35, 107, 181
Fielding, Henry and Sir John 99
Fielding, Henry 133–4
    Amelia 36, 37
Fielding, Sir John 122
'figure, proper', making a 81, 88, 102, 110–
    12, 180, 191
financial problems 9, 17, 22, 71
    see also debt

Thanet, 8th Earl of 37
Thomas, William, *Original Designs in Architecture* 157–8
Titchfield, Marquess of 34
Town and Country Magazine 20, 33, 40, 47, 99, 101, 125–6
'town format' in pattern books 156, 157, 159, 183
town houses
   absence from cultural discussions and literature 8, 115, 138–9, 146–7
   architectural and decorative projects 42, 49–50, 65, 71
   in architectural treatises 138–55
   business conducted at 44
   buying and affording 70–112
   characterised as feminine 111, 195–200, 197
   cost of 95–6
   criticism, contemporary 2–3, 18, 128
   criticism, modern-day 2–3
   definition of 187
   design of 17
   entertainment at 43, 52, 83
   exceptional 7, 42, 70, 72, 78, 94–5, 114, 116, 119, 126, 129, 136, 149, 165, 173
   expense of running 40
   façades *see* façades
   and family connections 44
   functions 16–17, 43–6, 59–61, 187
   and identity 5, 6
   as individuals' homes 56–7
   insubstantiality 3, 18, 195, 198, 200
   literature, modern-day 5–10
   as marker of new status 57
   as market commodity 55, 70
   'meaning' of 12, 13, 16, 56, 189
   negative perceptions of 18, 138, 190, 196–200
   new versus old 82, 88
   as object of civic pride 125–6
   omission from works on architecture 7
   over-expenditure on 71, 106–7
   ownership and transmission 54–69
   people associated with 46
   prominence in legal documents 69
   as property type 17, 54–5, 69
   remodelling 3, 21, 22
   scrutinised by visitors 190–5
   scrutiny of 118–19
   as security for loans 59–61
   significance to owner or occupier 5, 25–7, 112, 189

success 200
treated as hotel 44
use of interior space 171–81
uses 5, 13, 16, 27
values attributed to 13
see also terrace houses
Townley, Charles 224n144
trust, properties held in 57, 65, 67
Tufnell, Mr 186
Turner, Charles 117

Universal Register Office 99
upholsterers, as creditors 109
Upper Brook Street 9, 33, 40, 46, 93, 95, 100, 193
Upper Grosvenor Street 62, 73
Upper Ossory, 2nd Earl of 47, 77–8

Vane, Mrs 39
Veblen, Thorstein 108
vernacular buildings 8, 12, 138
   definition 235n4
Vesey, Agmondesham 73–4, 82, 117
Vesey, Mrs 73
views (from house) 79–80, 141–2
villas 176, 237n71, 237n72
Vitruvius 130
Vitruvius Britannicus 40

Walcot, Charles 127
Waldegrave, Dowager Countess 81–2
wall treatments 174–5
Walpole, Horace 20, 22, 179, 197, 232n40
Walter, Edward 60
Warburton, Mrs 44, 48
Warburton, William 48
Ware, Isaac 43, 128, 138–51, 154, 157, 160, 161, 162, 165, 168, 187, 194
   Complete Body of Architecture 139, 140, 141, 147
Warwick, Dowager Countess of 77, 83, 96
Weddell, William 9, 33, 62, 95, 193
Welbeck Street 81
Wentworth, 2nd Viscount 41, 46
Westmorland, 7th Earl of 59
Whigs 8–9, 45
White, John 120
widows *see* women, as widows
Wilkes, John 46
Williams, David 94
wills and settlements 54, 55, 61–9, 180
Wilton House, Wilton, Wiltshire, Double Cube room 180
Wimpole Street 47